MW00439828

ROOTED
IN CHRIST

366
Scriptural Devotions
for Growing Christians

PAUL CHAPPELL

First published in 2012 by Striving Together Publications, a ministry of Lancaster Baptist Church, Lancaster, CA 93535. Striving Together Publications is committed to providing tried, trusted, and proven books that will further equip local churches to carry out the Great Commission. Your comments and suggestions are valued.

Striving Together Publications
4020 E. Lancaster Blvd.
Lancaster, CA 93535
800.201.7748

Cover design by Andrew Jones
Layout by Craig Parker
Edited by Monica Bass, Robert Byers, Lauren Goddard,
and Kimberly Harven
Special thanks to our proofreaders

The contents of this book are the result of decades of spiritual growth in life and ministry. The author and publication team have given every effort to give proper credit to quotes and thoughts that are not original with the author. It is not our intent to claim originality with any quote or thought that could not readily be tied to an original source.

ISBN 978-1-59894-201-9

Printed in the United States of America

Table of Contents

A Word from the Author

Dear Friend,

We live in a distracted and uprooted society. Ours is an age of change—and this change often moves at a pace with which we can hardly keep up. Although many factors of our lives—location, vocation, relationships, opportunities, health, finances—may change frequently (and sometimes painfully), we as Christians can be firmly rooted in our relationship with Christ Himself. He desires for our hearts to be fixed on Him and established in His grace.

Just as a tree draws nourishment through its roots, so a Christian receives spiritual nourishment for growth by being "rooted in Christ." Colossians 2:6–7 says, "As ye have therefore received Christ Jesus the Lord, so walk ye in him: Rooted and built up in him, and stablished in the faith, as ye have been taught, abounding therein with thanksgiving."

Being rooted in Christ begins by receiving our nourishment through God's Word. James 1:21 instructs us to, "receive with meekness the engrafted word, which is able to save your souls." If we are to be firmly rooted in Christ, we must be taking in God's truth and applying these truths to our daily living.

I pray that this book is a help to you as you intentionally determine to dig your roots deeper in Christ every day.

It is my prayer that each devotion in *Rooted in Christ* will help you in your spiritual growth and encourage you to draw closer to the Lord every day.

Sincerely in Christ,
Paul Chappell

PRACTICES
OF EFFECTIVE
CHRISTIANS

The Effective Christian Memorizes Scripture

The following principles for effective Scripture memory are taken from *Homiletics from the Heart,* written by Dr. John Goetsch.

1. **Choose a specific time and a quiet place.**
   What gets scheduled gets accomplished. When memorizing the Word of God, you want to free yourself from all distractions.

2. **Organize by topic.**
   Many people attempt to learn the "Golden Chapters" or whole books of the Bible. While this is a noble attempt, it is not the way the Word of God will be used while teaching or preaching. Choose a topic you would like to study and then memorize every verse that deals with it. The next time you are speaking on that particular subject, your mind will be able to tie these verses together to truly allow you to "preach the Word…"

3. **Work out loud.**
   Even though it may sound odd, your mind memorizes better and faster that which it audibly hears. This is why you should choose a specific time and a quiet place!

4. **Walk while you memorize.**
   Your body has a natural sense of rhythm. This is why we memorize the words of songs so quickly. We will memorize much more quickly (and retain it longer) if we are walking around.

5. **Review, review, review.**
   Repetition is the key to learning. The one who is serious about memorizing Scripture cannot simply keep learning new passages weekly. Rather, he must also make the time to review the previous passages already committed to memory. It becomes readily apparent that memorization will take work, but the rewards are worth it!

6. **Set goals of time.**

   If you are not careful, you may ask for disappointment by setting goals of verses per week. The reason why is that some verses are more difficult to learn than others. If you set goals of time spent in memorization, God will honor that.

On the following pages you will find many major Bible doctrines and key verses to memorize. It is time to put into practice these six principles.

The Bible

Psalm 119:160—*Thy word is true from the beginning: and every one of thy righteous judgments endureth for ever.*

Isaiah 40:8—*The grass withereth, the flower fadeth: but the word of our God shall stand for ever.*

2 Timothy 3:16–17—*All scripture is given by inspiration of God, and is profitable for doctrine, for reproof, for correction, for instruction in righteousness: That the man of God may be perfect, throughly furnished unto all good works.*

Hebrews 4:12—*For the word of God is quick, and powerful, and sharper than any twoedged sword, piercing even to the dividing asunder of soul and spirit, and of the joints and marrow, and is a discerner of the thoughts and intents of the heart.*

John 17:17—*Sanctify them through thy truth: thy word is truth.*

Matthew 24:35—*Heaven and earth shall pass away, but my words shall not pass away.*

1 Thessalonians 2:13—*For this cause also thank we God without ceasing, because, when ye received the word of God which ye heard of us, ye received it not as the word of men, but as it is in truth, the word of God, which effectually worketh also in you that believe.*

God

Psalm 111:9—*He sent redemption unto his people: he hath commanded his covenant for ever: holy and reverend is his name.*

Isaiah 57:15—*For thus saith the high and lofty One that inhabiteth eternity, whose name is Holy; I dwell in the high and holy place, with him also that is of a contrite and humble spirit, to revive the spirit of the humble, and to revive the heart of the contrite ones.*

Lamentations 3:22–23—*It is of the LORD's mercies that we are not consumed, because his compassions fail not. They are new every morning: great is thy faithfulness.*

Deuteronomy 32:4—*He is the Rock, his work is perfect: for all his ways are judgment: a God of truth and without iniquity, just and right is he.*

Psalm 138:2—*I will worship toward thy holy temple, and praise thy name for thy lovingkindness and for thy truth: for thou hast magnified thy word above all thy name.*

John 4:24—*God is a Spirit: and they that worship him must worship him in spirit and in truth.*

Psalm 90:2—*Before the mountains were brought forth, or ever thou hadst formed the earth and the world, even from everlasting to everlasting, thou art God.*

Jesus Christ

John 1:1, 14—*In the beginning was the Word, and the Word was with God, and the Word was God. And the Word was made flesh, and dwelt among us, (and we beheld his glory, the glory as of the only begotten of the Father,) full of grace and truth.*

Philippians 2:6–8—*Who, being in the form of God, thought it not robbery to be equal with God: But made himself of no reputation, and took upon him the form of a servant, and was made in the likeness of men: And being found in fashion as a man, he humbled himself, and became obedient unto death, even the death of the cross.*

Colossians 1:16–17—*For by him were all things created, that are in heaven, and that are in earth, visible and invisible, whether they be thrones, or dominions, or principalities, or powers: all things were created by him, and for him: And he is before all things, and by him all things consist.*

1 Timothy 2:5–6—*For there is one God, and one mediator between God and men, the man Christ Jesus; Who gave himself a ransom for all, to be testified in due time.*

Hebrews 1:8—*But unto the Son he saith, Thy throne, O God, is for ever and ever: a sceptre of righteousness is the sceptre of thy kingdom.*

Luke 19:10—*For the Son of man is come to seek and to save that which was lost.*

Holy Spirit

John 14:16—*And I will pray the Father, and he shall give you another Comforter, that he may abide with you for ever;*

John 14:26—*But the Comforter, which is the Holy Ghost, whom the Father will send in my name, he shall teach you all things, and bring all things to your remembrance, whatsoever I have said unto you.*

John 15:26—*But when the Comforter is come, whom I will send unto you from the Father, even the Spirit of truth, which proceedeth from the Father, he shall testify of me:*

John 16:13–14—*Howbeit when he, the Spirit of truth, is come, he will guide you into all truth: for he shall not speak of himself; but whatsoever he shall hear, that shall he speak: and he will shew you things to come. He shall glorify me: for he shall receive of mine, and shall shew it unto you.*

1 Corinthians 3:16—*Know ye not that ye are the temple of God, and that the Spirit of God dwelleth in you?*

Ephesians 4:30—*And grieve not the holy Spirit of God, whereby ye are sealed unto the day of redemption.*

Ephesians 5:18—*And be not drunk with wine, wherein is excess; but be filled with the Spirit;*

Mankind

Genesis 1:26–27—*And God said, Let us make man in our image, after our likeness: and let them have dominion over the fish of the sea, and over the fowl of the air, and over the cattle, and over all the earth, and over every creeping* thing that creepeth upon the earth. So God created man in his own image, in the image of God created he him; male and female created he them.

Job 14:1, 14—Man that is born of a woman is of few days, and full of trouble. If a man die, shall he live again? all the days of my appointed time will I wait, till my change come.

Psalm 8:4–5—What is man, that thou art mindful of him? and the son of man, that thou visitest him? For thou hast made him a little lower than the angels, and hast crowned him with glory and honour.

Isaiah 64:6—But we are all as an unclean thing, and all our righteousnesses are as filthy rags; and we all do fade as a leaf; and our iniquities, like the wind, have taken us away.

Romans 3:10–11—As it is written, There is none righteous, no, not one: There is none that understandeth, there is none that seeketh after God.

Romans 3:23—For all have sinned, and come short of the glory of God.

Sin

Numbers 32:23—But if ye will not do so, behold, ye have sinned against the LORD: and be sure your sin will find you out.

Ezekiel 18:20—The soul that sinneth, it shall die. The son shall not bear the iniquity of the father, neither shall the father bear the iniquity of the son: the righteousness of the righteous shall be upon him, and the wickedness of the wicked shall be upon him.

Romans 6:23—For the wages of sin is death; but the gift of God is eternal life through Jesus Christ our Lord.

James 1:15—Then when lust hath conceived, it bringeth forth sin: and sin, when it is finished, bringeth forth death.

1 John 1:8–10—If we say that we have no sin, we deceive ourselves, and the truth is not in us. If we confess our sins, he is faithful and just to forgive us our sins, and to cleanse us from all unrighteousness. If we say that we have not sinned, we make him a liar, and his word is not in us.

1 John 3:4—*Whosoever committeth sin transgresseth also the law: for sin is the transgression of the law.*

Jeremiah 17:9—*The heart is deceitful above all things, and desperately wicked: who can know it?*

Salvation

Isaiah 45:22—*Look unto me, and be ye saved, all the ends of the earth: for I am God, and there is none else.*

Isaiah 43:11–12—*I, even I, am the LORD; and beside me there is no saviour. I have declared, and have saved, and I have shewed, when there was no strange god among you: therefore ye are my witnesses, saith the LORD, that I am God.*

John 14:6—*Jesus saith unto him, I am the way, the truth, and the life: no man cometh unto the Father, but by me.*

Acts 4:12—*Neither is there salvation in any other: for there is none other name under heaven given among men, whereby we must be saved.*

Romans 10:9–10—*That if thou shalt confess with thy mouth the Lord Jesus, and shalt believe in thine heart that God hath raised him from the dead, thou shalt be saved. For with the heart man believeth unto righteousness; and with the mouth confession is made unto salvation.*

Ephesians 2:8–9—*For by grace are ye saved through faith; and that not of yourselves: it is the gift of God: Not of works, lest any man should boast.*

Titus 3:5—*Not by works of righteousness which we have done, but according to his mercy he saved us, by the washing of regeneration, and renewing of the Holy Ghost;*

Church

Matthew 16:18—*And I say also unto thee, That thou art Peter, and upon this rock I will build my church; and the gates of hell shall not prevail against it.*

Colossians 1:18—*And he is the head of the body, the church: who is the beginning, the firstborn from the dead; that in all things he might have the preeminence.*

Ephesians 5:25–27—*Husbands, love your wives, even as Christ also loved the church, and gave himself for it; That he might sanctify and cleanse it with the washing of water by the word, That he might present it to himself a glorious church, not having spot, or wrinkle, or any such thing; but that it should be holy and without blemish.*

Acts 2:46–47—*And they, continuing daily with one accord in the temple, and breaking bread from house to house, did eat their meat with gladness and singleness of heart, Praising God, and having favour with all the people. And the Lord added to the church daily such as should be saved.*

1 Corinthians 12:13—*For by one Spirit are we all baptized into one body, whether we be Jews or Gentiles, whether we be bond or free; and have been all made to drink into one Spirit.*

1 Timothy 3:15—*But if I tarry long, that thou mayest know how thou oughtest to behave thyself in the house of God, which is the church of the living God, the pillar and ground of the truth.*

Angels

Genesis 3:24—*So he drove out the man; and he placed at the east of the garden of Eden Cherubims, and a flaming sword which turned every way, to keep the way of the tree of life.*

Psalm 148:2, 5—*Praise ye him, all his angels: praise ye him, all his hosts. Let them praise the name of the Lord: for he commanded, and they were created.*

Isaiah 6:1–3—*In the year that king Uzziah died I saw also the Lord sitting upon a throne, high and lifted up, and his train filled the temple. Above it stood the seraphims: each one had six wings; with twain he covered his face, and with twain he covered his feet, and with twain he did fly. And one cried unto another, and said, Holy, holy, holy, is the Lord of hosts: the whole earth is full of his glory.*

Mark 13:32—*But of that day and that hour knoweth no man, no, not the angels which are in heaven, neither the Son, but the Father.*

Hebrews 1:5–6—*For unto which of the angels said he at any time, Thou art my Son, this day have I begotten thee? And again, I will be to him a Father, and he shall be to me a Son? And again, when he bringeth in the firstbegotten into the world, he saith, And let all the angels of God worship him.*

1 Thessalonians 4:16—*For the Lord himself shall descend from heaven with a shout, with the voice of the archangel, and with the trump of God: and the dead in Christ shall rise first:*

End Times

1 Thessalonians 4:13–18—*But I would not have you to be ignorant, brethren, concerning them which are asleep, that ye sorrow not, even as others which have no hope. For if we believe that Jesus died and rose again, even so them also which sleep in Jesus will God bring with him. For this we say unto you by the word of the Lord, that we which are alive and remain unto the coming of the Lord shall not prevent them which are asleep. For the Lord himself shall descend from heaven with a shout, with the voice of the archangel, and with the trump of God: and the dead in Christ shall rise first: Then we which are alive and remain shall be caught up together with them in the clouds, to meet the Lord in the air: and so shall we ever be with the Lord. Wherefore comfort one another with these words.*

John 14:1–3—*Let not your heart be troubled: ye believe in God, believe also in me. In my Father's house are many mansions: if it were not so, I would have told you. I go to prepare a place for you. And if I go and prepare a place for you, I will come again, and receive you unto myself; that where I am, there ye may be also.*

Acts 1:10–11—*And while they looked stedfastly toward heaven as he went up, behold, two men stood by them in white apparel; Which also said, Ye men of Galilee, why stand ye gazing up into heaven? this same Jesus, which is taken up from you into heaven, shall so come in like manner as ye have seen him go into heaven.*

Revelation 22:20—*He which testifieth these things saith, Surely I come quickly. Amen. Even so, come, Lord Jesus.*

How to Lead a Person to Christ

Someone once said: "The fruit of a Christian is another Christian." There is a lot of truth in that statement. The Christian leader will influence people to be more soul-conscious. Yet, sometimes a person will be very active in sharing the Gospel, but will not see much fruit. It is the responsibility of the Christian leader to "Train Every Available Member" to not only be available, but effective. Here are some truths that every soulwinner must remember as he prepares to help another soul spend an eternity with Christ.

1. **A soulwinner should start with the truth of God's love for every individual.**
    John 3:16 is perhaps the most familiar verse in all the New Testament. *"For God so loved the world...."* There are sinners living today who actually believe that God hates them and wants them to go to Hell because of their sin. A sinner will never accept a Saviour who he believes will never love him.

2. **A soulwinner must emphasize the fact that we are all sinners—there are no exceptions.**
    There have been some who understand the "love" of God and feel that He would never send anyone to Hell. These sinners must also understand that the God of "love" is also first, and foremost, holy. All men fall short of the holy standard He has set. As a result of this "falling short," we are condemned to an eternity in Hell. Romans 3:23 includes all men everywhere.

3. **A soulwinner must teach the sinner that his sin carries with it an expensive price tag.**
    According to Romans 6:23, *"the wages of sin is death...."* In Ezekiel 18:20, the Israelites learned that the soul that sinned would die. As a soulwinner, the person you are dealing with has the wrath of God already abiding on him (John 3:36).

4. **A soulwinner should demonstrate the good news that Jesus has already paid this price.**

   Not only does Romans 6:23 deal with the penalty of sin, it also deals with the promise of salvation. Romans 5:8 continues with this theme by showing the sinner that Christ died for us while we were yet sinners.

5. **A soulwinner must remember that a sinner must personally accept Christ as Saviour.**

   This promise is given in Romans 10:13—*"For whosoever shall call upon the name of the Lord shall be saved."* A sinner may believe that God loves him, may understand the fact that he is a sinner, and may further understand that Jesus died to pay his sin debt and still be lost. The soulwinner is not after a simple mental assent to a list of subscribed facts. He is looking for a sinner to repent, to confess, and to know the joy of being a Christian.

6. **Ask the sinner, "Is there anything that would hinder you from trusting Christ right now, today, as your Saviour?"**

   This question will show the soulwinner if there are still any "obstacles" that must be removed before a sinner trusts Christ. It will also serve as a good transition into drawing the Gospel net. After a sinner is saved, the Great Commission is still unfulfilled. We are commanded to go, to win, to baptize, and to teach (disciple). An effective soulwinner will determine to see each aspect of the Great Commission come to fruition with those he leads to Christ.

Verses Remembered by Effective Christians

When you lose sight of His greatness:
Jeremiah 32:17; Jeremiah 33:3; Psalm 147:5; Romans 11:33–36; and 1 Chronicles 29:11–14

When you have needs:
Matthew 6:33; Philippians 4:19; Psalm 37:3; Psalm 37:25; and Deuteronomy 2:7

When you are overwhelmed:
Psalm 55:5; Psalm 55:18; Psalm 107:6–8; and 2 Corinthians 4:16

When problems seem insurmountable:
2 Corinthians 4:15–18; Romans 8:18; Psalm 32:7; Psalm 60:12; Psalm 61:2; and Psalm 62:6–8

When you need purpose:
1 Corinthians 10:31; Ephesians 3:16–21; John 10:10; and Psalm 139:14

When you have stress:
Philippians 4:4–7; Deuteronomy 20:1–4; and Jeremiah 32:27

When you are under pressure:
Psalm 27:1–2; Psalm 27:13–14; Psalm 46:1–2; and 2 Corinthians 12:9–10

When you worry:
Philippians 4:6–7; 1 Peter 5:7; Psalm 55:22; and Psalm 46:10

When you are afraid:
Psalm 56:3; Genesis 15:1; Psalm 27:1; 2 Timothy 1:7; and John 14:27

When you have a big decision to make:
Psalm 32:8; Psalm 143:10; Psalm 40:8; Proverbs 3:5–6; and Psalm 37:3–6

When you are discouraged:
1 Samuel 30:6; Joshua 1:9; Isaiah 41:10; Isaiah 40:26–28; and 2 Corinthians 4:15–16

When you are disheartened:
Joshua 1:5–9; Psalm 73:2; Psalm 73:17; and Psalm 73:24–26

When you are facing opposition:
2 Timothy 3:12; 2 Timothy 2:3; 1 Peter 4:12–13; 1 John 4:4; and Romans 8:31–32

When friends seem to let you down:
2 Timothy 4:16–17; Hebrews 12:2–3; Matthew 28:20; and Deuteronomy 32:27

When you are lonely:
Isaiah 41:10; Hebrews 13:5–6; Acts 18:9–10; and Isaiah 43:2

When you ask if it is worth it:
Matthew 25:21; 1 Corinthians 15:58; Galatians 6:9; and 2 Corinthians 4:17

The Effective Christian's Daily Bible Reading

Christians used by God have one thing in common: a daily walk with God. A Christian's daily walk is based upon the foundation of Bible reading and prayer. It has often been said, "The Book will keep you from sin, or sin will keep you from the Book."

Printed at the bottom of the page for each day is a segmented reading calendar that will allow you to read through the Old and New Testaments during the course of a year.

When considering whether or not to spend time in the Word of God, it is advisable to listen to the words of David, a man after God's own heart, who under the inspiration of the Holy Spirit wrote:

Psalm 119:105
"Thy word is a lamp unto my feet, and a light unto my path."

Psalm 119:9
"Wherewithal shall a young man cleanse his way? by taking heed thereto according to thy word."

May God's Word draw you closer to Him, and help you be the Christian He saved you to be.

One-Year Bible Reading Schedule

January

❏	1	Gen. 1–3	Matt. 1
❏	2	Gen. 4–6	Matt. 2
❏	3	Gen. 7–9	Matt. 3
❏	4	Gen. 10–12	Matt. 4
❏	5	Gen. 13–15	Matt. 5:1–26
❏	6	Gen. 16–17	Matt. 5:27–48
❏	7	Gen. 18–19	Matt. 6:1–18
❏	8	Gen. 20–22	Matt. 6:19–34
❏	9	Gen. 23–24	Matt. 7
❏	10	Gen. 25–26	Matt. 8:1–17
❏	11	Gen. 27–28	Matt. 8:18–34
❏	12	Gen. 29–30	Matt. 9:1–17
❏	13	Gen. 31–32	Matt. 9:18–38
❏	14	Gen. 33–35	Matt. 10:1–20
❏	15	Gen. 36–38	Matt. 10:21–42
❏	16	Gen. 39–40	Matt. 11
❏	17	Gen. 41–42	Matt. 12:1–23
❏	18	Gen. 43–45	Matt. 12:24–50
❏	19	Gen. 46–48	Matt. 13:1–30
❏	20	Gen. 49–50	Matt. 13:31–58
❏	21	Ex. 1–3	Matt. 14:1–21
❏	22	Ex. 4–6	Matt. 14:22–36
❏	23	Ex. 7–8	Matt. 15:1–20
❏	24	Ex. 9–11	Matt. 15:21–39
❏	25	Ex. 12–13	Matt. 16
❏	26	Ex. 14–15	Matt. 17
❏	27	Ex. 16–18	Matt. 18:1–20
❏	28	Ex. 19–20	Matt. 18:21–35
❏	29	Ex. 21–22	Matt. 19
❏	30	Ex. 23–24	Matt. 20:1–16
❏	31	Ex. 25–26	Matt. 20:17–34

February

❏	1	Ex. 27–28	Matt. 21:1–22
❏	2	Ex. 29–30	Matt. 21:23–46
❏	3	Ex. 31–33	Matt. 22:1–22
❏	4	Ex. 34–35	Matt. 22:23–46
❏	5	Ex. 36–38	Matt. 23:1–22
❏	6	Ex. 39–40	Matt. 23:23–39
❏	7	Lev. 1–3	Matt. 24:1–28
❏	8	Lev. 4–5	Matt. 24:29–51
❏	9	Lev. 6–7	Matt. 25:1–30
❏	10	Lev. 8–10	Matt. 25:31–46
❏	11	Lev. 11–12	Matt. 26:1–25
❏	12	Lev. 13	Matt. 26:26–50
❏	13	Lev. 14	Matt. 26:51–75
❏	14	Lev. 15–16	Matt. 27:1–26
❏	15	Lev. 17–18	Matt. 27:27–50
❏	16	Lev. 19–20	Matt. 27:51–66
❏	17	Lev. 21–22	Matt. 28
❏	18	Lev. 23–24	Mark 1:1–22
❏	19	Lev. 25	Mark 1:23–45
❏	20	Lev. 26–27	Mark 2
❏	21	Num. 1–2	Mark 3:1–19
❏	22	Num. 3–4	Mark 3:20–35
❏	23	Num. 5–6	Mark 4:1–20
❏	24	Num. 7–8	Mark 4:21–41
❏	25	Num. 9–11	Mark 5:1–20
❏	26	Num. 12–14	Mark 5:21–43
❏	27	Num. 15–16	Mark 6:1–29
❏	28	Num. 17–19	Mark 6:30–56

March

❏	1	Num. 20–22	Mark 7:1–13
❏	2	Num. 23–25	Mark 7:14–37
❏	3	Num. 26–28	Mark 8
❏	4	Num. 29–31	Mark 9:1–29
❏	5	Num. 32–34	Mark 9:30–50
❏	6	Num. 35–36	Mark 10:1–31
❏	7	Deut. 1–3	Mark 10:32–52
❏	8	Deut. 4–6	Mark 11:1–18
❏	9	Deut. 7–9	Mark 11:19–33
❏	10	Deut. 10–12	Mark 12:1–27
❏	11	Deut. 13–15	Mark 12:28–44
❏	12	Deut. 16–18	Mark 13:1–20
❏	13	Deut. 19–21	Mark 13:21–37
❏	14	Deut. 22–24	Mark 14:1–26
❏	15	Deut. 25–27	Mark 14:27–53
❏	16	Deut. 28–29	Mark 14:54–72
❏	17	Deut. 30–31	Mark 15:1–25
❏	18	Deut. 32–34	Mark 15:26–47
❏	19	Josh. 1–3	Mark 16
❏	20	Josh. 4–6	Luke 1:1–20
❏	21	Josh. 7–9	Luke 1:21–38
❏	22	Josh. 10–12	Luke 1:39–56
❏	23	Josh. 13–15	Luke 1:57–80
❏	24	Josh. 16–18	Luke 2:1–24
❏	25	Josh. 19–21	Luke 2:25–52
❏	26	Josh. 22–24	Luke 3
❏	27	Judges 1–3	Luke 4:1–30
❏	28	Judges 4–6	Luke 4:31–44
❏	29	Judges 7–8	Luke 5:1–16
❏	30	Judges 9–10	Luke 5:17–39
❏	31	Judges 11–12	Luke 6:1–26

April

❏	1	Judges 13–15	Luke 6:27–49
❏	2	Judges 16–18	Luke 7:1–30
❏	3	Judges 19–21	Luke 7:31–50
❏	4	Ruth 1–4	Luke 8:1–25
❏	5	1 Sam. 1–3	Luke 8:26–56
❏	6	1 Sam. 4–6	Luke 9:1–17
❏	7	1 Sam. 7–9	Luke 9:18–36
❏	8	1 Sam. 10–12	Luke 9:37–62
❏	9	1 Sam. 13–14	Luke 10:1–24
❏	10	1 Sam. 15–16	Luke 10:25–42
❏	11	1 Sam. 17–18	Luke 11:1–28
❏	12	1 Sam. 19–21	Luke 11:29–54
❏	13	1 Sam. 22–24	Luke 12:1–31
❏	14	1 Sam. 25–26	Luke 12:32–59
❏	15	1 Sam. 27–29	Luke 13:1–22
❏	16	1 Sam. 30–31	Luke 13:23–35
❏	17	2 Sam. 1–2	Luke 14:1–24
❏	18	2 Sam. 3–5	Luke 14:25–35
❏	19	2 Sam. 6–8	Luke 15:1–10
❏	20	2 Sam. 9–11	Luke 15:11–32
❏	21	2 Sam. 12–13	Luke 16
❏	22	2 Sam. 14–15	Luke 17:1–19
❏	23	2 Sam. 16–18	Luke 17:20–37
❏	24	2 Sam. 19–20	Luke 18:1–23
❏	25	2 Sam. 21–22	Luke 18:24–43
❏	26	2 Sam. 23–24	Luke 19:1–27
❏	27	1 Kings 1–2	Luke 19:28–48
❏	28	1 Kings 3–5	Luke 20:1–26
❏	29	1 Kings 6–7	Luke 20:27–47
❏	30	1 Kings 8–9	Luke 21:1–19

May

❏	1	1 Kings 10–11	Luke 21:20–38
❏	2	1 Kings 12–13	Luke 22:1–30
❏	3	1 Kings 14–15	Luke 22:31–46
❏	4	1 Kings 16–18	Luke 22:47–71
❏	5	1 Kings 19–20	Luke 23:1–25
❏	6	1 Kings 21–22	Luke 23:26–56
❏	7	2 Kings 1–3	Luke 24:1–35
❏	8	2 Kings 4–6	Luke 24:36–53
❏	9	2 Kings 7–9	John 1:1–28
❏	10	2 Kings 10–12	John 1:29–51
❏	11	2 Kings 13–14	John 2
❏	12	2 Kings 15–16	John 3:1–18
❏	13	2 Kings 17–18	John 3:19–36
❏	14	2 Kings 19–21	John 4:1–30
❏	15	2 Kings 22–23	John 4:31–54
❏	16	2 Kings 24–25	John 5:1–24
❏	17	1 Chr. 1–3	John 5:25–47
❏	18	1 Chr. 4–6	John 6:1–21
❏	19	1 Chr. 7–9	John 6:22–44
❏	20	1 Chr. 10–12	John 6:45–71
❏	21	1 Chr. 13–15	John 7:1–27
❏	22	1 Chr. 16–18	John 7:28–53
❏	23	1 Chr. 19–21	John 8:1–27
❏	24	1 Chr. 22–24	John 8:28–59
❏	25	1 Chr. 25–27	John 9:1–23
❏	26	1 Chr. 28–29	John 9:24–41
❏	27	2 Chr. 1–3	John 10:1–23
❏	28	2 Chr. 4–6	John 10:24–42
❏	29	2 Chr. 7–9	John 11:1–29
❏	30	2 Chr. 10–12	John 11:30–57
❏	31	2 Chr. 13–14	John 12:1–26

June

❏	1	2 Chr. 15–16	John 12:27–50
❏	2	2 Chr. 17–18	John 13:1–20
❏	3	2 Chr. 19–20	John 13:21–38
❏	4	2 Chr. 21–22	John 14
❏	5	2 Chr. 23–24	John 15
❏	6	2 Chr. 25–27	John 16
❏	7	2 Chr. 28–29	John 17
❏	8	2 Chr. 30–31	John 18:1–18
❏	9	2 Chr. 32–33	John 18:19–40
❏	10	2 Chr. 34–36	John 19:1–22
❏	11	Ezra 1–2	John 19:23–42
❏	12	Ezra 3–5	John 20
❏	13	Ezra 6–8	John 21
❏	14	Ezra 9–10	Acts 1
❏	15	Neh. 1–3	Acts 2:1–21
❏	16	Neh. 4–6	Acts 2:22–47
❏	17	Neh. 7–9	Acts 3
❏	18	Neh. 10–11	Acts 4:1–22
❏	19	Neh. 12–13	Acts 4:23–37
❏	20	Esther 1–2	Acts 5:1–21
❏	21	Esther 3–5	Acts 5:22–42
❏	22	Esther 6–8	Acts 6
❏	23	Esther 9–10	Acts 7:1–21
❏	24	Job 1–2	Acts 7:22–43
❏	25	Job 3–4	Acts 7:44–60
❏	26	Job 5–7	Acts 8:1–25
❏	27	Job 8–10	Acts 8:26–40
❏	28	Job 11–13	Acts 9:1–21
❏	29	Job 14–16	Acts 9:22–43
❏	30	Job 17–19	Acts 10:1–23

July

❏	1	Job 20–21	Acts 10:24–48
❏	2	Job 22–24	Acts 11
❏	3	Job 25–27	Acts 12
❏	4	Job 28–29	Acts 13:1–25
❏	5	Job 30–31	Acts 13:26–52
❏	6	Job 32–33	Acts 14
❏	7	Job 34–35	Acts 15:1–21
❏	8	Job 36–37	Acts 15:22–41
❏	9	Job 38–40	Acts 16:1–21
❏	10	Job 41–42	Acts 16:22–40
❏	11	Ps. 1–3	Acts 17:1–15
❏	12	Ps. 4–6	Acts 17:16–34
❏	13	Ps. 7–9	Acts 18
❏	14	Ps. 10–12	Acts 19:1–20
❏	15	Ps. 13–15	Acts 19:21–41
❏	16	Ps. 16–17	Acts 20:1–16
❏	17	Ps. 18–19	Acts 20:17–38
❏	18	Ps. 20–22	Acts 21:1–17
❏	19	Ps. 23–25	Acts 21:18–40
❏	20	Ps. 26–28	Acts 22
❏	21	Ps. 29–30	Acts 23:1–15
❏	22	Ps. 31–32	Acts 23:16–35
❏	23	Ps. 33–34	Acts 24
❏	24	Ps. 35–36	Acts 25
❏	25	Ps. 37–39	Acts 26
❏	26	Ps. 40–42	Acts 27:1–26
❏	27	Ps. 43–45	Acts 27:27–44
❏	28	Ps. 46–48	Acts 28
❏	29	Ps. 49–50	Rom. 1
❏	30	Ps. 51–53	Rom. 2
❏	31	Ps. 54–56	Rom. 3

August

❏	1	Ps. 57–59	Rom. 4
❏	2	Ps. 60–62	Rom. 5
❏	3	Ps. 63–65	Rom. 6
❏	4	Ps. 66–67	Rom. 7
❏	5	Ps. 68–69	Rom. 8:1–21
❏	6	Ps. 70–71	Rom. 8:22–39
❏	7	Ps. 72–73	Rom. 9:1–15
❏	8	Ps. 74–76	Rom. 9:16–33
❏	9	Ps. 77–78	Rom. 10
❏	10	Ps. 79–80	Rom. 11:1–18
❏	11	Ps. 81–83	Rom. 11:19–36
❏	12	Ps. 84–86	Rom. 12
❏	13	Ps. 87–88	Rom. 13
❏	14	Ps. 89–90	Rom. 14
❏	15	Ps. 91–93	Rom. 15:1–13
❏	16	Ps. 94–96	Rom. 15:14–33
❏	17	Ps. 97–99	Rom. 16
❏	18	Ps. 100–102	1 Cor. 1
❏	19	Ps. 103–104	1 Cor. 2
❏	20	Ps. 105–106	1 Cor. 3
❏	21	Ps. 107–109	1 Cor. 4
❏	22	Ps. 110–112	1 Cor. 5
❏	23	Ps. 113–115	1 Cor. 6
❏	24	Ps. 116–118	1 Cor. 7:1–19
❏	25	Ps. 119:1–88	1 Cor. 7:20–40
❏	26	Ps. 119:89–176	1 Cor. 8
❏	27	Ps. 120–122	1 Cor. 9
❏	28	Ps.123–125	1 Cor. 10:1–18
❏	29	Ps. 126–128	1 Cor. 10:19–33
❏	30	Ps. 129–131	1 Cor. 11:1–16
❏	31	Ps. 132–134	1 Cor. 11:17–34

September

❏	1	Ps. 135–136	1 Cor. 12
❏	2	Ps. 137–139	1 Cor. 13
❏	3	Ps. 140–142	1 Cor. 14:1–20
❏	4	Ps. 143–145	1 Cor. 14:21–40
❏	5	Ps. 146–147	1 Cor. 15:1–28
❏	6	Ps. 148–150	1 Cor. 15:29–58
❏	7	Prov. 1–2	1 Cor. 16
❏	8	Prov. 3–5	2 Cor. 1
❏	9	Prov. 6–7	2 Cor. 2
❏	10	Prov. 8–9	2 Cor. 3
❏	11	Prov. 10–12	2 Cor. 4
❏	12	Prov. 13–15	2 Cor. 5
❏	13	Prov. 16–18	2 Cor. 6
❏	14	Prov. 19–21	2 Cor. 7
❏	15	Prov. 22–24	2 Cor. 8
❏	16	Prov. 25–26	2 Cor. 9
❏	17	Prov. 27–29	2 Cor. 10
❏	18	Prov. 30–31	2 Cor. 11:1–15
❏	19	Eccl. 1–3	2 Cor. 11:16–33
❏	20	Eccl. 4–6	2 Cor. 12
❏	21	Eccl. 7–9	2 Cor. 13
❏	22	Eccl. 10–12	Gal. 1
❏	23	Song 1–3	Gal. 2
❏	24	Song 4–5	Gal. 3
❏	25	Song 6–8	Gal. 4
❏	26	Isa. 1–2	Gal. 5
❏	27	Isa. 3–4	Gal. 6
❏	28	Isa. 5–6	Eph. 1
❏	29	Isa. 7–8	Eph. 2
❏	30	Isa. 9–10	Eph. 3

October

❏	1	Isa. 11–13	Eph. 4
❏	2	Isa. 14–16	Eph. 5:1–16
❏	3	Isa. 17–19	Eph. 5:17–33
❏	4	Isa. 20–22	Eph. 6
❏	5	Isa. 23–25	Phil. 1
❏	6	Isa. 26–27	Phil. 2
❏	7	Isa. 28–29	Phil. 3
❏	8	Isa. 30–31	Phil. 4
❏	9	Isa. 32–33	Col. 1
❏	10	Isa. 34–36	Col. 2
❏	11	Isa. 37–38	Col. 3
❏	12	Isa. 39–40	Col. 4
❏	13	Isa. 41–42	1 Thess. 1
❏	14	Isa. 43–44	1 Thess. 2
❏	15	Isa. 45–46	1 Thess. 3
❏	16	Isa. 47–49	1 Thess. 4
❏	17	Isa. 50–52	1 Thess. 5
❏	18	Isa. 53–55	2 Thess. 1
❏	19	Isa. 56–58	2 Thess. 2
❏	20	Isa. 59–61	2 Thess. 3
❏	21	Isa. 62–64	1 Tim. 1
❏	22	Isa. 65–66	1 Tim. 2
❏	23	Jer. 1–2	1 Tim. 3
❏	24	Jer. 3–5	1 Tim. 4
❏	25	Jer. 6–8	1 Tim. 5
❏	26	Jer. 9–11	1 Tim. 6
❏	27	Jer. 12–14	2 Tim. 1
❏	28	Jer. 15–17	2 Tim. 2
❏	29	Jer. 18–19	2 Tim. 3
❏	30	Jer. 20–21	2 Tim. 4
❏	31	Jer. 22–23	Titus 1

November

❏	1	Jer. 24–26	Titus 2
❏	2	Jer. 27–29	Titus 3
❏	3	Jer. 30–31	Philemon
❏	4	Jer. 32–33	Heb. 1
❏	5	Jer. 34–36	Heb. 2
❏	6	Jer. 37–39	Heb. 3
❏	7	Jer. 40–42	Heb. 4
❏	8	Jer. 43–45	Heb. 5
❏	9	Jer. 46–47	Heb. 6
❏	10	Jer. 48–49	Heb. 7
❏	11	Jer. 50	Heb. 8
❏	12	Jer. 51–52	Heb. 9
❏	13	Lam. 1–2	Heb. 10:1–18
❏	14	Lam. 3–5	Heb. 10:19–39
❏	15	Ezek. 1–2	Heb. 11:1–19
❏	16	Ezek. 3–4	Heb. 11:20–40
❏	17	Ezek. 5–7	Heb. 12
❏	18	Ezek. 8–10	Heb. 13
❏	19	Ezek. 11–13	James 1
❏	20	Ezek. 14–15	James 2
❏	21	Ezek. 16–17	James 3
❏	22	Ezek. 18–19	James 4
❏	23	Ezek. 20–21	James 5
❏	24	Ezek. 22–23	1 Peter 1
❏	25	Ezek. 24–26	1 Peter 2
❏	26	Ezek. 27–29	1 Peter 3
❏	27	Ezek. 30–32	1 Peter 4
❏	28	Ezek. 33–34	1 Peter 5
❏	29	Ezek. 35–36	2 Peter 1
❏	30	Ezek. 37–39	2 Peter 2

December

❏	1	Ezek. 40–41	2 Peter 3
❏	2	Ezek. 42–44	1 John 1
❏	3	Ezek. 45–46	1 John 2
❏	4	Ezek. 47–48	1 John 3
❏	5	Dan. 1–2	1 John 4
❏	6	Dan. 3–4	1 John 5
❏	7	Dan. 5–7	2 John
❏	8	Dan. 8–10	3 John
❏	9	Dan. 11–12	Jude
❏	10	Hos. 1–4	Rev. 1
❏	11	Hos. 5–8	Rev. 2
❏	12	Hos. 9–11	Rev. 3
❏	13	Hos. 12–14	Rev. 4
❏	14	Joel	Rev. 5
❏	15	Amos 1–3	Rev. 6
❏	16	Amos 4–6	Rev. 7
❏	17	Amos 7–9	Rev. 8
❏	18	Obad.	Rev. 9
❏	19	Jonah	Rev. 10
❏	20	Micah 1–3	Rev. 11
❏	21	Micah 4–5	Rev. 12
❏	22	Micah 6–7	Rev. 13
❏	23	Nahum	Rev. 14
❏	24	Hab.	Rev. 15
❏	25	Zeph.	Rev. 16
❏	26	Hag.	Rev. 17
❏	27	Zech. 1–4	Rev. 18
❏	28	Zech. 5–8	Rev. 19
❏	29	Zech. 9–12	Rev. 20
❏	30	Zech. 13–14	Rev. 21
❏	31	Mal.	Rev. 22

90-Day Bible
Reading Schedule

Day	Start	End	✔	Day	Start	End	✔
1	Genesis 1:1	Genesis 16:16	❑	46	Proverbs 7:1	Proverbs 20:21	❑
2	Genesis 17:1	Genesis 28:19	❑	47	Proverbs 20:22	Ecclesiastes 2:26	❑
3	Genesis 28:20	Genesis 40:11	❑	48	Ecclesiastes 3:1	Song 8:14	❑
4	Genesis 40:12	Genesis 50:26	❑	49	Isaiah 1:1	Isaiah 13:22	❑
5	Exodus 1:1	Exodus 15:18	❑	50	Isaiah 14:1	Isaiah 28:29	❑
6	Exodus 15:19	Exodus 28:43	❑	51	Isaiah 29:1	Isaiah 41:18	❑
7	Exodus 29:1	Exodus 40:38	❑	52	Isaiah 41:19	Isaiah 52:12	❑
8	Leviticus 1:1	Leviticus 14:32	❑	53	Isaiah 52:13	Isaiah 66:18	❑
9	Leviticus 14:33	Leviticus 26:26	❑	54	Isaiah 66:19	Jeremiah 10:13	❑
10	Leviticus 26:27	Numbers 8:14	❑	55	Jeremiah 10:14	Jeremiah 23:8	❑
11	Numbers 8:15	Numbers 21:7	❑	56	Jeremiah 23:9	Jeremiah 33:22	❑
12	Numbers 21:8	Numbers 32:19	❑	57	Jeremiah 33:23	Jeremiah 47:7	❑
13	Numbers 32:20	Deuteronomy 7:26	❑	58	Jeremiah 48:1	Lamentations 1:22	❑
14	Deuteronomy 8:1	Deuteronomy 23:11	❑	59	Lamentations 2:1	Ezekiel 12:20	❑
15	Deuteronomy 23:12	Deuteronomy 34:12	❑	60	Ezekiel 12:21	Ezekiel 23:39	❑
16	Joshua 1:1	Joshua 14:15	❑	61	Ezekiel 23:40	Ezekiel 35:15	❑
17	Joshua 15:1	Judges 3:27	❑	62	Ezekiel 36:1	Ezekiel 47:12	❑
18	Judges 3:28	Judges 15:12	❑	63	Ezekiel 47:13	Daniel 8:27	❑
19	Judges 15:13	1 Samuel 2:29	❑	64	Daniel 9:1	Hosea 13:6	❑
20	1 Samuel 2:30	1 Samuel 15:35	❑	65	Hosea 13:7	Amos 9:10	❑
21	1 Samuel 16:1	1 Samuel 28:19	❑	66	Amos 9:11	Nahum 3:19	❑
22	1 Samuel 28:20	2 Samuel 12:10	❑	67	Habakkuk 1:1	Zechariah 10:12	❑
23	2 Samuel 12:11	2 Samuel 22:18	❑	68	Zecharaih 11:1	Matthew 4:25	❑
24	2 Samuel 22:19	1 Kings 7:37	❑	69	Matthew 5:1	Matthew 15:39	❑
25	1 Kings 7:38	1 Kings 16:20	❑	70	Matthew 16:1	Matthew 26:56	❑
26	1 Kings 16:21	2 Kings 4:37	❑	71	Matthew 26:57	Mark 9:13	❑
27	2 Kings 4:38	2 Kings 15:26	❑	72	Mark 9:14	Luke 1:80	❑
28	2 Kings 15:27	2 Kings 25:30	❑	73	Luke 2:1	Luke 9:62	❑
29	1 Chronicles 1:1	1 Chronicles 9:44	❑	74	Luke 10:1	Luke 20:19	❑
30	1 Chronicles 10:1	1 Chronicles 23:32	❑	75	Luke 20:20	John 5:47	❑
31	1 Chronicles 24:1	2 Chronicles 7:10	❑	76	John 6:1	John 15:17	❑
32	2 Chronicles 7:11	2 Chronicles 23:15	❑	77	John 15:18	Acts 6:7	❑
33	2 Chronicles 23:16	2 Chronicles 35:15	❑	78	Acts 6:8	Acts 16:37	❑
34	2 Chronicles 35:16	Ezra 10:44	❑	79	Acts 16:38	Acts 28:16	❑
35	Nehemiah 1:1	Nehemiah 13:14	❑	80	Acts 28:17	Romans 14:23	❑
36	Nehemiah 13:15	Job 7:21	❑	81	Romans 15:1	1 Corinthians 14:40	❑
37	Job 8:1	Job 24:25	❑	82	1 Corinthians 15:1	Galatians 3:25	❑
38	Job 25:1	Job 41:34	❑	83	Galations 3:26	Colossians 4:18	❑
39	Job 42:1	Psalms 24:10	❑	84	1 Thessalonians 1:1	Philemon 25	❑
40	Psalms 25:1	Psalms 45:14	❑	85	Hebrews 1:1	James 3:12	❑
41	Psalms 45:15	Psalms 69:21	❑	86	James 3:13	3 John 14	❑
42	Psalms 69:22	Psalms 89:13	❑	87	Jude 1	Revelation 17:18	❑
43	Psalms 89:14	Psalms 108:13	❑	88	Revelation 18:1	Revelation 22:21	❑
44	Psalms 109:1	Psalms 134:3	❑	89	Grace Day	Grace Day	❑
45	Psalms 135:1	Proverbs 6:35	❑	90	Grace Day	Grace Day	❑

JANUARY

Rooted for the New Year

As ye have therefore received Christ Jesus the Lord, so walk ye in him: Rooted and built up in him, and stablished in the faith, as ye have been taught, abounding therein with thanksgiving.—**Colossians 2:6–7**

Over the course of its lifetime, an oak tree goes through many changes. If the roots of that tree are deeply grounded, it will sustain health and growth through its seasons of change.

I remember when our church first moved to what is now our current church property. Because we purchased an empty lot, some of our first steps were to plant trees along the roadside to make the campus more lifelike. Today when I pull onto our church campus and see those trees, I remember how they were only the size of little bushes when I first planted them. They have changed form and size, yet their DNA remains the same.

People don't like the word "change" for the most part, but in reality, everything that's growing is changing. As we enter a new year, we desire growth and change in different areas of our lives. We must be careful, however, to obey God's instruction in Colossians 2 to remain rooted in Christ. As we grow, we should keep a biblical foundation.

Root yourself in God's truth and determine to remain biblically grounded through any life changes in this coming year. Root yourself in Bible reading, Scripture memory, church attendance, prayer, witnessing, and other godly activities as God commands, "As ye have therefore received Christ Jesus the Lord, so walk ye in him." God desires that you would walk with Him this new year no matter what changes you face.

Changes will come. Some will be good, some may be more challenging; but as you stay rooted in Christ and His Word, you can remain faithful through any change you experience.

Today's Rooted Principle: Root yourself in God's truth so you can experience growth through whatever changes come your way in the new year.

Genesis 1–3 Matthew 1

Stability in Christ

That he would grant you, according to the riches of his glory, to be strengthened with might by his Spirit in the inner man; That Christ may dwell in your hearts by faith; that ye, being rooted and grounded in love.—**Ephesians 3:16–17**

Things are changing in our world. Every morning when you turn on the news, changes are evident...and many times volatile. The stock market swings, sometimes dropping hundreds of points at a time; governments are being overthrown; wars are being fought on nearly every continent; and economies are failing.

It's safe to say that our world is in a state of unrest. While the world's hope in its leaders and its systems is being uprooted, our hope in Jesus and His Word is still as strong as ever.

Ephesians 3 gives us a look at the root system we have through Christ: "That Christ may dwell in your hearts by faith; that ye, being rooted and grounded in love." God desires that even as this world changes and the systems of man fail, we will remain stable through faith in Him.

What governs your life? Is your life a roller coaster happy one day, down the next? Although we all have times of joy and sadness, God desires to stabilize our lives and keep us rooted in Him.

We have the promise that no matter what happens in the world, no matter how bad the news may be, God has everything in control. Don't become so wrapped up in the news of this world that you let it affect your stability. Remain confident that God's will is being done, and remain faithful to studying His Word and walking with Him.

This world will change in the year ahead. We don't know what is to come, but we can be confident that God is still Lord and that through faith in Him and faithfulness to His commands, our lives can remain stable in the new year.

Today's Rooted Principle: Stabilize your heart and mind by remembering that God is in control.

A Real Relationship

But his delight is in the law of the LORD; and in his law doth he meditate day and night. And he shall be like a tree planted by the rivers of water, that bringeth forth his fruit in his season; his leaf also shall not wither; and whatsoever he doeth shall prosper.—**Psalm 1:2–3**

Many of us have plants, flowers, and other living things decorating our homes. While some people are good at cultivating live plants, others know they're better off with fake plants that require no attention.

A fake plant has no real life. It doesn't require nourishment or feeding and doesn't take much upkeep. It looks nice on the outside, but there are no roots or depth to it. A fake plant won't survive a harsh storm, but a rooted plant will have the depth to revive after nature's fury.

As we enter another year, we've seen that changes will come. Storms are part of all of our lives. One thing that will help us stay rooted in Christ is a real, daily relationship with Him.

Just as a plant's origin is the seed that was planted, so our beginning in Christ is the seed of salvation that we accepted. From that point forward, we begin to grow. Every day we're given the opportunity to grow in Christ through cultivating our relationship with Him.

If you are going to be faithful this year, you must have a vital, personal relationship with Christ. You must walk with Him, talk with Him, listen to the preaching of His Word, and spend time in prayer. Anyone can play the part and look good on the outside, just like fake plants; but if you wish to be rooted in Christ so you can withstand whatever comes this year, you must have a real relationship with Him.

Disappointments will come, people will hurt you, and you'll face challenges this year; but when you are firmly rooted in Christ and daily growing in Him, you can weather any storm you face.

Today's Rooted Principle: The only way to remain rooted in Christ through the storms of life is to maintain a vibrant, daily relationship with the Lord.

A Purpose of Faithfulness

For who hath known the mind of the Lord? or who hath been his counsellor? Or who hath first given to him, and it shall be recompensed unto him again? For of him, and through him, and to him, are all things: to whom be glory for ever. Amen.—**Romans 11:34–36**

It's easy to look at life and judge success based on results. Do you look any more fit after going to the gym? Do you have more money after working so hard? Are you in a higher position in the company than you were last year? Our world is focused on seeing tangible results.

God's work, however, isn't measured by visible results. God doesn't judge us based on how many people we lead to Christ or how large our sphere of influence has grown. God has a different plan for every person. His purpose and measure of success is based on faithfulness.

Sometimes we become discouraged in faithful living. Things go wrong, we don't see results like we'd thought, and discouragement sets in. Yet despite how quickly or slowly things progress in life, realize that God's purpose for your life is being fulfilled as long as you're faithful to Him.

Charles Spurgeon commented on the Christian ministry by saying, "The grand object of the Christian ministry is the glory of God. Whether souls are converted or not, if Jesus Christ be faithfully preached, the minister has not laboured in vain, for he is a sweet savour unto God as well in them that perish as in them that are saved."

God's purpose for your life is to live faithfully and obey His commands. No matter what results you may or may not see, you can have joy knowing that God's will is being done.

Take heart in knowing that as you faithfully follow God, you are fulfilling His purpose for your life. He knows what's best and will accomplish His will through you as you're faithful to Him.

Today's Rooted Principle: Success in God's will is measured by faithfulness to God's commands.

Strength from God

Abide in me, and I in you. As the branch cannot bear fruit of itself, except it abide in the vine; no more can ye, except ye abide in me.—**John 15:4**

In the 1950s, while a pastor in Australia was starting a new church his home pastor back in the States sent him a letter of encouragement. Part of the letter spoke of how he could have peace amidst the devil's attacks:

> The devil always seeks to take advantage of fatigue or any physical disability and always tries to discourage! His one objective only and always is to separate us from Christ, if he can do that by making us concentrate on ourselves, our symptoms, our work, or our future, he is content. He can only be met and conquered in the Name of Christ. Do not listen to him therefore. Tell him that you are in the hands of Christ and that you are leaving all things to Him.

As we enter a new year, we must be wise to the attacks Satan will bring our way. He is ever present in our lives, seeking to steal our joy and to keep us from following Christ, but we can see victory over the devil by abiding in Christ.

As children of God, we have the hope of resistance and the promise of strength through God. In John 15:4, Jesus told His disciples, "Abide in me, and I in you. As the branch cannot bear fruit of itself, except it abide in the vine; no more can ye, except ye abide in me." A plant is nothing apart from its roots. A branch is fruitless unless it is attached to the vine. Even so, we are weak apart from Christ.

We can see victory over temptation and resist the devil's attacks as we are daily abiding in Christ through prayer, Scripture reading and memory, and faithful living. Apart from God, you are susceptible to the devil's attacks, but as you daily stay close to God, you will have His strength to resist the devil.

Today's Rooted Principle: Abide in Christ to have access to His strength.

Your Identity in Christ

*For the perfecting of the saints, for the work of the ministry, for the edifying of the body of Christ: Till we all come in the unity of the faith, and of the knowledge of the Son of God, unto a perfect man, unto the measure of the stature of the fulness of Christ:—***Ephesians 4:12–13**

The story is told of artist Paul Gustave Dore who was traveling Europe when he faced a predicament. He reached a border crossing and discovered that he had misplaced his passport. Without his papers, the officer wouldn't allow Dore to pass. Finally, Dore was given a test to prove his identity. The official gave him a piece of paper and a pencil and requested he draw a group of nearby peasants. Dore did so with such ease that the official was convinced he was indeed the famed artist.

Paul Dore's identity was affirmed through his work. Many people in our world find their identity through their work or accomplishments. For example, say the name "Kobe Bryant," and most people think "basketball player." Say the name "Albert Einstein," and most think "physicist." We tend to attach our own identities and other people's identities to what they do.

Yet, the glad truth for Christians is that our identity is not in what we do but that we belong to Christ. We are children of God, heir to His kingdom.

Apart from God, we have no identity and are but another lost soul in this world. But with God, we are a child of the King. We have hope, purpose, and meaning. No matter what fails in your life, if you have trusted Christ as your Saviour, you are a son or daughter of the Heavenly Father. Circumstances may change, but you will always be one of God's own.

Your purpose and identity is found in being God's child. Cultivate your relationship with Him, and live to glorify Him in everything you do.

Today's Rooted Principle: Your identity is not found in what you do, but in Who you belong to.

Genesis 16–17   Matthew 5:27–48

Rooted in Joy

Therefore my heart is glad, and my glory rejoiceth: my flesh also shall rest in hope. For thou wilt not leave my soul in hell; neither wilt thou suffer thine Holy One to see corruption. Thou wilt shew me the path of life: in thy presence is fulness of joy; at thy right hand there are pleasures for evermore.—**Psalm 16:9–11**

Most people know the story of Helen Keller. She was not born blind and deaf, but at the age of 19 months she contracted what doctors noted as "an acute congestion of the stomach and brain," which was likely scarlet fever. Since medical advances had not been made at that time, this illness, which is now easily treatable, had a major impact on Helen and left her without sight or hearing. Yet Helen overcame these disabilities and even became a source of hope and encouragement for many others facing difficulties and dealing with handicaps.

Helen's life was not easy because of the disabilities, yet in her adult years she made the shocking statement, "I thank God for my handicaps, for through them, I have found myself, my work, and my God."

Helen Keller faced more challenges than many of us will ever face, yet she could rejoice in her trials because she had the joy of the Lord. How often do we allow little things to steal our joy and put us in a sour mood? Helen had every right to complain, yet she persevered and even found joy in difficulty.

What trial or challenge are you facing today? Have you allowed it to leave you bitter, complaining, and hopeless? As a child of God, you have joy that no one can steal. You have the hope of eternal life.

Psalm 16 states "in thy presence is fulness of joy." You can have joy in any situation this new year as you are faithfully abiding in God's presence. Root yourself in God and in His Word, and, like Helen Keller, you can rejoice even when the darkest of trials comes your way.

Today's Rooted Principle: Joy is not found in the absence of difficulty, but in the presence of Christ.

Walking with God

As ye have therefore received Christ Jesus the Lord, so walk ye in him:
—**Colossians 2:6**

Most of us begin the new year with an emphasis on getting "in shape." We put physical exercise and healthy diets at the top of our priority list, but how are we as Christians doing with our spiritual exercise?

It is easy to become spiritually tired and sluggish, but there is a simple solution—begin walking with God.

Christianity is enjoying a relationship with God through Christ. It is interacting with God throughout the course of a day, feeling His presence and power, and receiving His strength and guidance. Your spiritual growth is directly related to your walk with God.

Walking is a step-by-step process, and, similarly, the Christian life is a day-by-day process. To walk with God you must read His Word every day. Just as you must exercise faithfully to see physical results, so you must walk with God faithfully to grow.

Walking with God also involves talking to Him. Just as walking with a friend lends itself to conversation, so God desires that we converse with Him through prayer. Bring your needs and struggles to God when you spend time with Him, and continue to pray throughout your day as you walk with Him.

If your walk with God has slowed or even stopped, it's time to get back into shape and start walking with Him again. This year determine that you're going to build spiritual muscles by maintaining a strong, steady walk with God.

Today's Rooted Principle: Spend time walking with God daily to grow in your Christian life.

Genesis 20–22   Matthew 6:19–34   31

Christ-Centered Balance

But seek ye first the kingdom of God, and his righteousness; and all these things shall be added unto you.—**Matthew 6:33**

Life places many demands on us. We struggle to balance work, school, sport's practices, church activities, family needs, and the list goes on and on. Life is just plain busy, and sometimes we become so busy with life that we forget Who we are living for.

One of the greatest needs of our lives is balance, and this can only be achieved as we keep Christ at the center of all other activity. How can you have balance in your life?

Find a place where you can daily spend time alone with God. Look at the beautiful picture of the sweetness of God's presence the hymn writer paints through this song: "I come to the garden alone while the dew is still on the roses. And the voice I hear falling on my ear, the Son of God discloses. And He walks with me, and He talks with me, and He tells me I am His own; and the joy we share as we tarry there, none other has ever known." God desires to share personal fellowship with you, but you must make the time to enjoy it.

Schedule a specific time to read God's Word and talk to Him through prayer. God's Word will encourage and strengthen you throughout the day. When your day seems too hectic to control or too hard to handle, bring your problems to the Lord.

Make a plan to keep Christ as your center. Ephesians 5:16 says "Redeeming the time, because the days are evil." Instead of getting swept away with the chaos of life, surrender every day to God. Focus on His priorities for your day, and watch Him turn wasted time into eternal treasure.

When you make Christ the center of your life, the cares of this world become less weighty, and you will discover His joy and peace.

Today's Rooted Principle: Make Christ the center of your life to experience balance and His peace.

Genesis 23–24   Matthew 7

Planning to Prosper

But his delight is in the law of the LORD; and in his law doth he meditate day and night. And he shall be like a tree planted by the rivers of water, that bringeth forth his fruit in his season; his leaf also shall not wither; and whatsoever he doeth shall prosper.—**Psalm 1:2–3**

What is success? The world tells us that success is being wealthy or popular, but God's Word shows us the true definition of success: a fruitful Christian life.

The Bible gives the formula for a prosperous, Christian life.

Delight in God's Word. Think back to the time when you first accepted Christ as your Saviour. God's Word was so fresh and new, and you couldn't wait to read it whenever you had the opportunity! It seemed like God was with you in person and speaking directly to you. Reading and hearing God's Word was a delight to you.

As we become older Christians, it is easy for our devotions to become a ritual rather than a real relationship with God. But we need to realize that when we choose to delight in God's Word, He will give us true success.

Meditate on God's Word. What's on your mind throughout the day? Is it work, family problems, or financial strains? Instead of dwelling on the negative issues of life, focus your mind on God's Word. Memorize encouraging promises from God, and think about them throughout your day. Post notes with verses that God has given you throughout your home and in your car, listen to preaching as you drive or exercise, or hang your favorite verses in your house. Meditating on God's Word will transform your mind and give you God's perspective on life.

Success is not found in money or fame; it is found in the wonderful Word of God.

Today's Rooted Principle: Delight in and meditate on God's Word to bear fruit in your Christian life.

When Jesus Gave Thanks...

And he shall be like a tree planted by the rivers of water, that bringeth forth his fruit in his season; his leaf also shall not wither; and whatsoever he doeth shall prosper.—**Psalm 1:3**

I have the privilege to pastor in the Mojave Desert of Southern California. Our arid terrain is actually similar to that of Israel, so it is easy for me to see why a lush tree serves as a fitting symbol of blessing in Scripture. A thriving tree in the desert can only mean one thing—strong roots.

There is no true or lasting growth where there are no roots. In our culture, we're often far more focused on the outward evidences of progress than on the roots that support true growth.

Even in spiritual growth, we tend to believe that if we look good on the outside, we must be okay. This makes for a shallow Christianity that will not sustain through the desert times of life. We may have external evidences of growth, but if we are not firmly rooted in Christ, we will eventually wither.

Sometimes we need to step back a moment and consider our roots. Ask yourself, do I have a growing relationship with Christ? Am I delighting more in Him and in His Word?

David knew the importance of having a real and growing relationship with God, and he prayed, "Search me, O God, and know my heart: try me, and know my thoughts: And see if there be any wicked way in me, and lead me in the way everlasting" (Psalm 139:23–24). More than looking good to others, David wanted to be sure his heart was right with God—that he had real roots.

How long has it been since you asked the Holy Spirit to take a spiritual inventory of your heart? God desires for you to prosper spiritually—not just today, but for the rest of your life. To do so requires that you firmly root yourself in Him.

Today's Rooted Principle: Ask God to search your heart and reveal to you the health of your roots.

Abounding More and More

Furthermore then we beseech you, brethren, and exhort you by the Lord Jesus, that as ye have received of us how ye ought to walk and to please God, so ye would abound more and more.—**1 Thessalonians 4:1**

D o you desire an abundant Christian life? We all want the richness of God's blessing in our lives, but how can we achieve such a goal? George Müller, a German missionary who established orphanages in Bristol, England, discovered the key to abounding more and more—daily fellowship with God.

Müller said, "The primary business I must attend to every day is to fellowship with the Lord. The first concern is not how much I might serve the Lord, but how my inner man might be nourished. I may share the truth with the unconverted; I may try to encourage believers; I may relieve the distressed; or I may in other ways seek to behave as a child of God; yet, not being happy in the Lord and not being nourished and strengthened in my inner man day by day, may result in this work being done in a wrong spirit."

Müller knew that outward service without inward fellowship was useless. The same is true for us. We could spend our entire lifetime soulwinning, serving the pastor, and doing good deeds for others, but without a daily walk with God, we would never know the abundant life that God wants to give.

God wants us to serve others and minister to their spiritual and physical needs. But He wants to first meet our need for daily fellowship with Him. He wants us to spend personal time in His Word and talk to Him in prayer. Start fellowshipping with God daily to experience the abundant life that you desire.

Today's Rooted Principle: Find spiritual abundance by spending personal time with the Lord.

The Water of Life

And the Spirit and the bride say, Come. And let him that heareth say, Come. And let him that is athirst come. And whosoever will, let him take the water of life freely.—**Revelation 22:17**

A young salesman was disappointed about losing a big sale, and as he talked with his sales manager he complained, "I guess it just proves you can lead a horse to water, but you can't make him drink." The manager replied, "Your job is not to make him drink. Your job is to make him thirsty."

There are people all around us thirsting for the water of life, but they don't know that this is what they need. They search for something to fill the emptiness inside, but nothing satisfies. They strive to quench their inner thirst with pleasure, money, or good works, but they still feel parched inside.

As Christians, we have experienced the refreshing, thirst-quenching water of life—Jesus Christ Himself. The blood of Christ has cleansed us from every sinful stain of the past and has given us the assurance of a heavenly home. But, how good are we at inviting others to the water of life? When others look at our lives do they want what we have? Do we make lost souls thirsty for the Gospel?

Too many Christians who preach the Gospel with their lips do not live with the power of the Gospel in their daily lives. Such inconsistency actually serves to repel people from the very Gospel they need.

Jesus said, "But whosoever drinketh of the water that I shall give him shall never thirst; but the water that I shall give him shall be in him a well of water springing up into everlasting life" (John 4:14). We as Christians have the amazing privilege to tell hopeless, thirsting souls about the water of life. Remember, though, as you share the water of life, to live in such a way that others will want what you have.

Today's Rooted Principle: Make others thirsty for the Gospel by living in a way that is consistent with your message.

How to Develop Faith

So then faith cometh by hearing, and hearing by the word of God.
—Romans 10:17

Christian growth and victory is the fruit of faith. Faith is what enables us to live in the victorious reality of the promises of God, rather than in our feeble efforts that sooner or later bring defeat. Faith is vital to our Christian lives. How can we develop faith?

Read and meditate on the Word of God. The primary nourisher of faith is God's Word. Romans 10:17 plainly says, "So then faith cometh by hearing, and hearing by the word of God." If we are to increase our faith, we must spend time in God's Word, meditating on His promises.

Maintain a right conscience toward God. A person who is living in private sin (or even open rebellion) will always have doubts of what God may do for him. No matter how he hides or justifies his sin, he knows he cannot claim God's promises with confidence. Psalm 66:18 says, "If I regard iniquity in my heart, the Lord will not hear me."

Do not run from your trials of faith. God sometimes allows trying circumstances into our lives that He intends to use to strengthen our faith. James 1:3–4 challenges us to not run from these but to allow God to do His work through them: "Knowing this, that the trying of your faith worketh patience. But let patience have her perfect work, that ye may be perfect and entire, wanting nothing."

Let God be your deliverer. Faith refuses to see only the surrounding circumstances and looks past them to God's mighty power. Every time we experience God's deliverance, our faith is strengthened, and our God is glorified.

Victory in the Christian life is not based on our strength. It is the product of faith, and faith comes as we choose to know and claim the promises of God.

Today's Rooted Principle: Develop your faith by reading and meditating on God's Word.

Who Do You Trust?

But without faith it is impossible to please him: for he that cometh to God must believe that he is, and that he is a rewarder of them that diligently seek him.—**Hebrews 11:6**

One unknown author wrote, "Has it ever struck you that we trust the word of our fellow-man more easily than we trust God's Word?" Too often, this is true. We take at face value the statements of our friends, co-workers, family members, doctor, news announcers…we even believe the weather forecaster! How is it then that we fail to believe the words of our God?

Hebrews 11 records many of the heroes of the Old Testament. It lists men and women such as Noah, Abraham, Sarah, Moses, Rahab, David, and others. But it reminds us that the great exploits for God by these heroes were all accomplished "by faith."

These people did not have supernatural abilities or special gifts. They were ordinary men and women who had faith in their great God. They simply took God at His Word, and they acted in obedience to His commands.

Do you find yourself paralyzed and seemingly unable to obey God because you are afraid of the outcome? Mark it down, you can count on God's promises. Trust Him.

Hudson Taylor, a missionary to China in the 1800s, once said, "God is not looking for men of great faith, only some common souls like you or me who are willing to trust in His great faithfulness."

Faith is simply trusting God. It is believing that He is who He has revealed Himself to be in His Word—faithful, unchanging, one who keeps His promises.

The Christian who walks in faith is not necessarily talented or gifted—just someone willing to trust God.

Today's Rooted Principle: Demonstrate faith in God by obeying His Word.

Resisting Wrong

There hath no temptation taken you but such as is common to man: but God is faithful, who will not suffer you to be tempted above that ye are able; but will with the temptation also make a way to escape, that ye may be able to bear it.—**1 Corinthians 10:13**

We each face temptation every day. Sometimes it even seems as if there is no escape. Yet Joseph in the Old Testament provides a sterling example for all of us. His purity, even in the face of great temptation, shows us how we can resist wrong and overcome temptation.

Joseph refused to do wrong. Over and over he said "no" to Potiphar's wife. First Peter 5:8 says, "Be sober, be vigilant; because your adversary the devil, as a roaring lion, walketh about, seeking whom he may devour." Satan will not tempt you with sin just once; he will persistently and continually entice you, hoping that you will eventually fall. To resist wrong, you must continually say, "No!"

Joseph set boundaries against wrong. Joseph knew his moral boundaries, and in Genesis 39:9 he told Potiphar's wife, "Neither hath he kept back any thing from me but thee, because thou art his wife." No one but God would have known if Joseph yielded to temptation, but he resisted because he had pre-determined his boundaries. Don't wait until Satan tempts you to establish biblical boundaries—set boundaries for your life before you are in the place of temptation.

Joseph was conscious of God's presence. He viewed sin as a direct offense toward God. This is why he said, "…how then can I do this great wickedness, and sin against God?" (Genesis 39:9). The best motivation for avoiding sin is realizing that sin is ultimately against God. Avoiding sin for your family or job is good, but avoiding sin for God is best!

Joseph may have lost his coat, but he kept his character. You and I can likewise resist temptation by following Joseph's example.

Today's Rooted Principle: Pinpoint the areas where you struggle, and purpose to resist temptation through God's strength.

The Benefits of Salvation

Blessed be the Lord, who daily loadeth us with benefits, even the God of our salvation.—**Psalm 68:19**

What a wonderful privilege to know Jesus Christ personally! Because of salvation, we will someday enjoy a home in Heaven, a sinless body, and eternity with Christ. We all look forward to our *future* with Jesus Christ, but it's easy to forget about the benefits of salvation for *today*. Let's take a moment to remember a few of the many blessings we can enjoy every day as Christians.

We have access to God's power. In Romans 1:16, the Apostle Paul wrote, "For I am not ashamed of the gospel of Christ: for it is the power of God unto salvation to every one that believeth; to the Jew first, and also to the Greek." We who have trusted in the Gospel can experience Christ's power in our lives. As we yield to His work in us, His power transforms us to the image of Christ.

We have access to God's presence. Andrew Murray once said, "My prayer receives worth from being rooted in the sacrifice of Jesus Christ." Because Christ gave His life for us, we have the privilege of going into God's presence at any time throughout our day, but so often we ignore this wonderful benefit of salvation. Remember that you don't have to wait until Heaven to talk to God, you can talk to Him right now and enjoy His presence.

We have access to God's plan. People around us are wandering aimlessly through life because they have no real purpose without Jesus. As Christians we know that God's plan is for us to bring Him glory with our lives. Take joy in knowing that God has a purpose for every day of your life, and follow Him as He leads you.

Today's Rooted Principle: Thank the Lord for the blessings of salvation you can enjoy right now.

Making Preaching a Priority

For the preaching of the cross is to them that perish foolishness; but unto us which are saved it is the power of God.—**1 Corinthians 1:18**

A faithful churchgoer wrote a letter to the editor of his newspaper complaining about going to church every Sunday. He wrote, "I've gone for thirty years now, and in that time I have heard something like three thousand sermons. But for the life of me, I can't remember a single one of them." This disgruntled church member was silenced when someone else responded, "I've been married for thirty years now. In that time my wife has cooked some thirty-two thousand meals. But for the life of me, I cannot recall the entire menu for a single one of those meals. But I do know this: they all nourished me and gave me the strength I needed to do my work."

Biblical preaching nourishes our souls and strengthens us spiritually. It gives a spiritual charge to face trials or temptations throughout our week. It focuses our hearts and minds on the Lord and renews thinking through His Word. God wants to nourish and strengthen you through His Word, and preaching is one of God's methods of giving His children the nutrients they need.

God's Word says, "If thou put the brethren in remembrance of these things, thou shalt be a good minister of Jesus Christ, nourished up in the words of faith and of good doctrine, whereunto thou hast attained" (1 Timothy 4:6). God desires to speak to us through the preaching of His Word. But we must make it a priority in our lives, listening with an open heart.

Ask yourself, do I go to church to hear from God? Or do I think of church attendance as just another weekly obligation? Preaching is a powerful tool that God uses to grow us spiritually. Make preaching a priority for you and your family.

Today's Rooted Principle: God uses preaching to nourish your soul and help you grow spiritually.

Loving Church

I was glad when they said unto me, Let us go into the house of the LORD.
—**Psalm 122:1**

At one church, coffee was always served after the sermon. One Sunday the pastor asked a child if he knew why they had coffee hour. Without hesitating, the youngster replied, "To wake people up before they have to drive home."

A truly born-again child of God delights to be with the people of God. But when we forget the value of the church, church attendance becomes more of a duty than a delight. How can you keep your love for your church strong?

Remember that Christ died for the church. Acts 20:28 says, "Take heed therefore unto yourselves, and to all the flock, over the which the Holy Ghost hath made you overseers, to feed the church of God which he hath purchased with his own blood." Jesus paid for the church with His own blood. That alone speaks volumes as to its value!

Realize that Christ loves the church. Ephesians 5:25, reminds us how much Christ loved the church: "Husbands, love your wives, even as Christ also loved the church, and gave himself for it." If we truly love the Lord, we will love what He loves, and that includes the church.

Give of yourself to your church. You will find that the more of yourself that you invest in your church, the more you will love it. Fully commit yourself to faithful attendance. Pray for your pastor and look for ways to encourage him. Give financially to the Lord through your church. Ask for an avenue of service in the church. In short, invest yourself in your church.

One of God's most precious gifts to us is the local church. Thank Christ for giving His life for the church, and ask Him to help you love it like He does.

Today's Rooted Principle: Deepen your love for Christ by loving what He loves—the local church.

Laboring in the Church

For God is not unrighteous to forget your work and labour of love, which ye have shewed toward his name, in that ye have ministered to the saints, and do minister.—**Hebrews 6:10**

Someone once said, "Every church is filled with willing people— some willing to work, and others willing to let them." Which kind of person are you? As Christians, we have the privilege of serving the Lord by laboring in our local church. And when we serve others, the Lord sees and promises to reward us for it. Here are three ways you can invest yourself in laboring for the Lord.

Labor in your ministries. Whether you teach a Sunday school class, serve on a bus route, or clean the church, do it with all your heart. The work of the Lord is an eternally enduring work, so why not give Him 100 percent?

Labor in your witness. A wise person said, "Every saved person this side of Heaven owes the Gospel to every lost person this side of Hell." By reaching others with the Gospel and discipling new believers, we accomplish the very purpose of the church. Keep Gospel tracts handy to give to those you meet throughout the day, and always be ready to share the Gospel with those you meet.

Labor in your giving. Giving to the Lord in tithes and offerings not only provides for the work of the Lord, but sacrificial giving also increases our faith. When we trust God with our finances, we will see Him bless us and meet all our needs. Whatever you give to the Lord's work is an eternal investment, so labor in your giving and watch the windows of Heaven pour out blessings on your life.

By laboring in your church you can encourage your pastor, strengthen your church, and experience the joy of the Lord in your own life. Give yourself wholeheartedly to serving the Lord.

Today's Rooted Principle: Experience the joy and blessings of the Lord by laboring in your local church.

Unchangeable God

Jesus Christ the same yesterday, and to day, and for ever.
—Hebrews 13:8

A man dialed a wrong number and got the following recording: "I am not available right now, but I thank you for caring enough to call. I am making some changes in my life. Please leave a message after the beep. If I do not return your call, you are one of the changes."

Isn't it wonderful to know that our God never changes? He's never too busy to listen, never too weak to help, and never too unloving to care.

He is the same God of yesterday. The same God who delivered Daniel from the lion's den, David from Goliath, and the children of Israel from Pharoah is our God right now. We can look back through the pages of Scripture and see that God has always been faithful.

He is the same today. Things all around us change every day. Our friends change, our jobs change, politics change, economies change, our bodies change, the weather changes. Our life is full of constant change. But what a comfort to know that God never changes! He is always faithful, always present, and always loving.

He will be the same forever. No matter what trial you face in your future, God will be there with you. We can be comforted in knowing that God will never leave us. Hebrews 13:5 says, "Let your conversation be without covetousness; and be content with such things as ye have: for he hath said, I will never leave thee, nor forsake thee." Christ will not leave us in life, and He will not leave us in death. God will be the same for all eternity, and we can rest in His faithfulness.

What a privilege it is to serve a God who never changes. Anchor your hope in Him, and claim His promises for today.

Today's Rooted Principle: Anchor your hope in God's unchanging faithfulness.

Exodus 1–3   Matthew 14:1–21

Following God's Leading

And a vision appeared to Paul in the night; There stood a man of Macedonia, and prayed him, saying, Come over into Macedonia, and help us. And after he had seen the vision, immediately we endeavoured to go into Macedonia, assuredly gathering that the Lord had called us for to preach the gospel unto them.—**Acts 16:9–10**

D r. Bob Hughes spent his life spreading God's Word as a missionary in the Philippines. Once, while home in the states, he spoke to a group of college young people. Dr. Hughes had been diagnosed with cancer, and the doctors had given him little time to live. He said to the young people, "I have gone. I have given my life, but it looks as though the Lord will call me home soon. I need someone to go and replace me in the Philippines." In that crowd was a young man named Rick Martin who was tender to the Lord's call and felt the Lord leading him to take the challenge of missions. Rick Martin committed to follow God's leading to the Philippines, where he ministers even today.

As a Christian, your life is guided by the Holy Spirit's work, but if you aren't careful, you can often tune out God's leading. God desires to speak to you through His Word and by His Spirit. If you aren't in tune with God and daily walking in His Spirit, you can miss His leading.

Acts 16 shows us how the Holy Spirit led Paul to minister in Macedonia which led to a great work in that region. Rick Martin listened to the Holy Spirit through the preaching of Dr. Hughes and has seen over three hundred churches started in the Philippines.

Are you daily listening to the Spirit's leading? Are you reading God's Word and attentively listening to it being preached? Keep a tender heart to God's work and follow whatever direction He leads you. You'll never go wrong by following the Holy Spirit.

Today's Rooted Principle: The Holy Spirit seeks to guide us to greater blessings if we will but listen to His guidance.

Sharing Your Faith

I charge thee therefore before God, and the Lord Jesus Christ, who shall judge the quick and the dead at his appearing and his kingdom; Preach the word; be instant in season, out of season; reprove, rebuke, exhort with all longsuffering and doctrine.—**2 Timothy 4:1–2**

Some years ago a pair of missionaries visited China. While they were there, they were passing out Gospel tracts. They would give each person a handful and encourage them to share the extra with others. After a while, a guard approached them. "Please don't give them more than one," he stated. One of the missionaries asked, "Is it illegal to have faith?" "No," the guard replied, "but it is illegal to influence others to join with your faith." A faith that is not shared will become extinct. Christians around the world know this and are willing to suffer even government persecution to share their faith.

Thankfully, it's not illegal to witness here in America. And yet so many of God's children never tell anyone else about how they can receive salvation through Jesus Christ. We have all kinds of reasons—or more accurately, excuses—for why it should be someone else's job. But God has given you people whom you can reach more effectively than anyone else.

When Paul wrote to Timothy not long before he died, he emphasized the importance of the preached Word. This is a message not only to pastors to be faithful as they stand in pulpits, but also to believers to be faithful as they share the message of salvation with everyone they can.

In 2 Corinthians 5:18, the Bible tells us that God has given to us the "ministry of reconciliation," which means that we have the privilege and obligation to share our faith so that others can join us in the family of God. Are you regularly sharing the Good News of salvation with others? Of all the ministries to which we should be faithful, the ministry of reconciliation is the most important!

Today's Rooted Principle: Every believer is called to share the Gospel of Jesus Christ with others.

Exodus 7–8   Matthew 15:1–20

Being a Servant

Paul, a servant of Jesus Christ, called to be an apostle, separated unto the gospel of God, (Which he had promised afore by his prophets in the holy scriptures,)—**Romans 1:1–2**

John Kenneth Galbraith was a noted economist in the mid-1900s who was called upon by many dignitaries to help sort the economic markets. He wrote the following story in his autobiography about his housekeeper:

"It had been a wearying day, and I asked Emily to hold all telephone calls while I had a nap. Shortly thereafter the phone rang. Lyndon Johnson was calling from the White House. 'Get me Ken Galbraith. This is Lyndon Johnson.' 'He is sleeping, Mr. President. He said not to disturb him.' 'Well, wake him up. I want to talk to him.' 'No, Mr. President. I work for him, not you.' When I called the President back, he could scarcely control his pleasure. 'Tell that woman I want her here in the White House.'"

Emily the housekeeper understood an important truth—she was a servant to one man and obeyed his wishes explicitly. Her loyalties were to Mr. Galbraith alone. What a great example of a true servant.

This single focus was the heart of Paul as he described himself as "a servant of Jesus Christ" in Romans 1. As a servant he had one duty—follow and obey his Master, Christ. Other dignitaries commanded Paul, other people beseeched him, but his focus was on serving God.

Are you a servant of God? A servant follows without explanation, obeys without reason, and is faithful no matter the circumstance. Many people can say they know God, they love Him, or they read His Word; but not many are truly servants of Christ.

What would it take to keep you from obeying God? A true servant obeys no matter the cost. Evaluate your commitment to Christ and seek His help in becoming a true servant of the Lord.

Today's Rooted Principle: A servant serves even when it doesn't make sense and isn't easy.

Guarding Your Words

I said, I will take heed to my ways, that I sin not with my tongue: I will keep my mouth with a bridle, while the wicked is before me. I was dumb with silence, I held my peace, even from good; and my sorrow was stirred. My heart was hot within me, while I was musing the fire burned: then spake I with my tongue.—**Psalm 39:1–3**

Never before in history has a generation been given free reign in communication like we have today. Everything from phone calls, texting, and instant messaging, to using Facebook, Twitter, email, and other lines of communication have made it easy to contact people instantly no matter where they are or what they're doing.

We truly live in a day of unprecedented technological advancement, but is that always a good thing? With this new openness comes new ways of communicating with our words. In the past, people were told to be careful what they said, but now people must be careful with what they post, tweet, or type. Employers are even looking at social media when they consider hiring a person.

While you may watch your tongue in how you speak to someone face to face, are you watching your tongue with what you type online? Too many people take social media and other electronic communications for granted and hastily type words they later regret.

The Psalmist points to bridling the tongue and keeping in words that he wished to speak when the time was not right. Keep Psalm 39 in mind when you're dealing with online communication. Take heed to your words whether they're spoken, written, or printed.

Do you guard your communication online? While we have great tools of advancement, be wise to the devil's new ways of causing you to stumble. Realize that one angry email or one hasty post can greatly hurt your testimony. Seek God's wisdom every time you communicate.

Today's Rooted Principle: Written words often last longer than spoken words.

In the World but Not of It

When thou art come into the land which the LORD thy God giveth thee, thou shalt not learn to do after the abominations of those nations. There shall not be found among you any one that maketh his son or his daughter to pass through the fire, or that useth divination, or an observer of times, or an enchanter, or a witch, Or a charmer, or a consulter with familiar spirits, or a wizard, or a necromancer.—**Deuteronomy 18:9–11**

My uncle serves as a county commissioner where he lives in Colorado. He told me recently of legislation that mandates that cities and counties must give money for retraining the local Native Americans in the spirit beliefs of their ancestors. The government is so consumed with trying to be politically correct that they are helping to put people back into the practices that spiritually enslaved them for so long. For years, Christians have worked to free people from the bondage of false religion and sin by preaching Jesus Christ, yet now the government is leading people right back into bondage.

God gave clear instructions in Deuteronomy that the children of Israel were to enter the Promised Land, but were not to take on the customs of the unsaved inhabitants. They were to follow His commands and, although they lived in a sinful land, they were to remain true to God's Words.

We have been given a task as God's children. He desires that we would serve Him here on Earth and remain faithful to His call and commands. It doesn't take much to see the sin rampant in our world, but while we are living in this world, God calls us to be separate from the practices of the world.

Just as God commanded the Israelites, He desires that you would abstain from the sinful practices of this world. Daily seek His protection from sin's attacks and remain rooted in His truth.

Today's Rooted Principle: Jesus walked this Earth without succumbing to sin's stranglehold and through His power we can do the same.

Exodus 14–15 Matthew 17

Protected Against the Devil's Attacks

For the word of God is quick, and powerful, and sharper than any twoedged sword, piercing even to the dividing asunder of soul and spirit, and of the joints and marrow, and is a discerner of the thoughts and intents of the heart.—**Hebrews 4:12**

When Terrie and I first moved to Lancaster we lived in a small apartment that smelled of the previous tenants' pets. One summer day, the temperature was about 112 degrees outside and the swamp cooler was broken. When I came home for lunch, I noticed that Terrie was pale in the face. Thinking it was the heat or the smell of the apartment, I asked her what was wrong. "I just met my first lady friend from Lancaster." Terrie then told me of how a lady had come to the door looking for the past tenants. Terrie told the lady that we were the new residents, and that is when the lady flipped out onto the floor. She started rolling around and screaming while foaming at the mouth. It could have been a medical condition or it could have just been the devil's opposition to what God was about to do in the city of Lancaster.

The devil has a very real presence in this world, and he will do whatever he can to keep God from being glorified. While he cannot keep God's children from Heaven, he still seeks to keep us from following God's will. Satan's attacks may seem daunting, but remember, you have God's power at your disposal! Hebrews 4 tells us that God's Word is powerful enough to ward off even the most powerful of Satan's attacks.

Don't overlook the importance of studying God's Word each day. It's your protection against Satan. Take time to protect your heart with Scripture, and commit to answering each of Satan's attacks with God's truth.

Today's Rooted Principle: Even the devil's strongest attacks are no match against a Christian firmly rooted in God's Word.

Exodus 16–18 Matthew 18:1–20

Joyful during Trials

Make a joyful noise unto the LORD, all ye lands. Serve the LORD with gladness: come before his presence with singing. Know ye that the LORD he is God: it is he that hath made us, and not we ourselves; we are his people, and the sheep of his pasture.—**Psalm 100:1–3**

In June of 2002, things went terribly wrong for missionaries Martin and Gracia Burnham as the couple were captured by the Abu Sayyaf terrorist group in the Philippines. The terrorists kept the Burnhams in jungle captivity for 376 days while the Philippine army pursued the terrorists and eventually surrounded the group. As the Scout Rangers opened fire, Martin and Gracia sought shelter. Both were caught in crossfire. Gracia was shot in the leg, but Martin was fatally hit in the chest. After being taken back to the States, Gracia shared how just before the shootout and while both were in captivity, Martin told her, "The Bible says to serve the Lord with gladness. Let's go out all the way. Let's serve Him all the way with gladness."

Most of us will never know the level of persecution and terror that Martin and Gracia Burnham experienced, yet we all face trials and difficult times in life.

Our trials might come in the form of a wayward child, a lost job, a health crisis, a cross-country move, a dying loved one, a financial meltdown, or another burden to carry. The unsaved person has no hope during trials and is left to face them alone, but as God's children, we have reason to rejoice in even the darkest of nights.

Whatever your trial, you can still rejoice even through the pain. Psalm 100 tells us to serve the Lord with gladness and approach God with singing. Those commands aren't based on how well life is working out for us, but based on the inherent goodness of our God.

Spend time praising God today despite whatever trials you face.

Today's Rooted Principle: God deserves praise based on who He is regardless of what is happening in your life.

Exodus 19–20   Matthew 18:21–35   51

Facing Opposition

And the multitude rose up together against them: and the magistrates rent off their clothes, and commanded to beat them. And when they had laid many stripes upon them, they cast them into prison, charging the jailor to keep them safely: Who, having received such a charge, thrust them into the inner prison, and made their feet fast in the stocks.
—**Acts 16:22–24**

When Paul started preaching God's message in Macedonia, people began to take notice. Most notably, the owners of a demon-possessed girl who trusted Christ took notice, and they didn't like what was happening. Christ had changed the girl's life and these men were left without an income.

The girl's owners made false accusations against Paul and had him thrown in jail. Roman imprisonment was preceded by being stripped and then beaten until the prisoner was bloody. Most cells were dark and damp. Unbearable cold, lack of water, cramped quarters, and sickening stench from few toilets made sleeping difficult and waking hours miserable. Because of the miserable conditions, many prisoners begged for a speedy death. Others simply committed suicide.

If anyone faced opposition, it was Paul. The irony? Paul was a Roman citizen which made his imprisonment against Roman law. Paul had reason to curse what was happening, yet he kept his faith.

When God's work abounds, the devil's work goes down. Most people don't mind if you're religious. It's when you actively live out God's commands and spread His Word that feathers get ruffled and the devil sends opposition.

You can't control what opposition you face, but you can control how you react to it. What opposition are you facing today? Commit to remaining faithful and glorifying God even during hard times.

Today's Rooted Principle: God receives greatest glory when you continue serving Him during opposition.

Praise during Persecution

Offer unto God thanksgiving; and pay thy vows unto the most High: And call upon me in the day of trouble: I will deliver thee, and thou shalt glorify me. But unto the wicked God saith, What hast thou to do to declare my statutes, or that thou shouldest take my covenant in thy mouth?—**Psalm 50:14–16**

Oswald Chambers once wrote the following about trials, "Faith for my deliverance is not faith in God. Faith means, whether I am visibly delivered or not, I will stick to my belief that God is love. There are some things only learned in a fiery furnace."

We all face trials and times of persecution. Even Paul was wrongfully imprisoned and unlawfully beaten as he preached the Gospel. But whether the persecution is unwarranted or even illegal, God shows us that we can give Him praise during difficult times.

First Peter 4:12–13 is a needful passage for those facing difficulties, "Beloved, think it not strange concerning the fiery trial which is to try you, as though some strange thing happened unto you: But rejoice, inasmuch as ye are partakers of Christ's sufferings; that, when his glory shall be revealed, ye may be glad also with exceeding joy."

How can someone sing praise during a time of sorrow? Praise often comes after prayer. During trials, your best course of action is to spend much time in God's presence. Pour your heart out to Him. Tell Him of your trials and seek His help. God alone can help you during difficulties, and He should be the first one you turn to.

God doesn't always remove trials. Sometimes His work can only be accomplished as you face the difficulty. So, more than praying for God's deliverance, pray for God to give you strength to praise Him.

Have you praised God during your trial? Bathe yourself in prayer and glorify God's goodness in your life despite the outside circumstances.

Today's Rooted Principle: Praise comes not from a feeling of happiness but from an understanding of God's goodness.

The Power of God

For by him were all things created, that are in heaven, and that are in earth, visible and invisible, whether they be thrones, or dominions, or principalities, or powers: all things were created by him, and for him.
—**Colossians 1:16**

The Tournament of Roses is a New Year's parade of floats each year in Pasadena, California. Many colorful floats are built by companies to entertain guests and promote their business. One year, the entire parade was held up as one of the floats ran out of gas in the middle of the event. Ironically, the float was built by the Standard Oil Company. A company known for powering vehicles had their own vehicle run out of power.

When you think about the power of God, you can become overwhelmed at just how great our God is. He formed the world from nothing, orders everything that happens, and takes notice of even the smallest of changes in the world. And that doesn't even begin to describe how powerful God is.

In the grand scheme of the world, we are but minute beings on the face of the earth, yet God shows that He cares about every detail of our lives. God cares if you're facing a trial. He cares if you're going through a tough time. He cares if you need wisdom to make a life-changing decision. God cares about you.

Never take for granted the fact that God is interested in every aspect of your life. God has the power to change the world, and He engages that power on your behalf if you will but ask Him for help.

No one in this world loves you as much as God does, and no one can help you like God can. He's promised to help. All you must do is seek His power. Take some time today to seek God's help in your life. He has the power to help in your difficult situation, and He delights to help you.

Today's Rooted Principle: The God who created all the world wants to use His power to help your weaknesses.

Exodus 25–26   Matthew 20:17–34

FEBRUARY

A Focus on Preaching

Labour not for the meat which perisheth, but for that meat which endureth unto everlasting life, which the Son of man shall give unto you: for him hath God the Father sealed.—**John 6:27**

A pastor of a large church was dedicated to preaching God's Word as he began his ministry. As the ministry began to grow, he realized that not everyone agreed with strong biblical preaching. Every week he'd receive letters criticizing his messages. Some said they were too strong. Some said they should be mellowed out to appeal to a wider base. Some said the pastor should take a more loving approach. As time went on, the pastor soon noticed that the letters became fewer and the criticism was less. Convicted that this was a sign he had not been challenging his congregation enough, he stated, "I'm afraid that when I'm pleasing everybody, I'm not pleasing the Lord, and pleasing the Lord is what counts."

Church is a great place to gather and fellowship with like-minded people. It's great to develop friendships with people who are saved and seeking to live holy lives. But when attending church, there should be a focus on preaching.

Sometimes we become so caught up in the *events* of church that we forget the *focus* of church—listening to God's Word. The preaching of God's Word is one of the most important weekly activities in our lives. It strengthens, cleanses, equips, and guides us.

Value the preaching of God's Word. Open your heart to God's leading before every message and make preaching a priority. God's Word is a great asset in life, but it does no good if you aren't actively listening to it and heeding its commands.

Today's Rooted Principle: God's Word can help you in every aspect of life but only if you're allowing it into your life.

Exodus 27–28   Matthew 21:1–22

The True Measure of Success

And he said unto them, Take heed, and beware of covetousness: for a man's life consisteth not in the abundance of the things which he possesseth.—**Luke 12:15**

According to a poll published in USA Today some years ago, a majority of Americans believed they could have a comfortable life if they had $8,000 to $11,000 of additional income per year. The reality is that, if most people did get an $8,000 raise, they would say at the end of the next year, "If I just had $8,000 more a year!" When our income increases, the tendency is for our spending to increase at least as much as—and sometimes even more than—our income was increased.

There is nothing wrong with having nice things. If God has blessed you, give Him thanks and glory for what He has done for you. But if your thoughts and interests are focused on getting more and more "stuff," you will never be truly happy. The popular bumper sticker says, "He who dies with the most toys wins." That worldly philosophy does not lead to true joy.

The person with a mentality of materialism will never be content. Someone who is materialistic will always want more and more and more…and will never be satisfied. But while the world promotes that attitude, God offers His children an alternative—contentment based on our relationship with Him and His presence in our lives. Hebrews 13:5 says, "…be content with such things as ye have: for he hath said, I will never leave thee, nor forsake thee."

All of the things you have today could vanish in a moment. During times of turmoil and change, those who are driven by materialism have nothing left to cling to. But Christians who are trusting in the promises of God and finding their happiness in a close relationship with Him will always have everything they need.

Today's Rooted Principle: The foundation of true happiness is built on contentment, not possessions.

Exodus 29–30　　　Matthew 21:23–46　　　57

A Matter of Focus

If ye keep my commandments, ye shall abide in my love; even as I have kept my Father's commandments, and abide in his love. These things have I spoken unto you, that my joy might remain in you, and that your joy might be full.—**John 15:10–11**

The verb *rejoice* is found ninety-six times in the New Testament (including those times when used as a greeting). Also, the noun *joy* is used another fifty-nine times. It's easy to see that God puts a priority on joy and on the believer experiencing a life of joy.

Joy isn't a feeling or emotion based on circumstances; it is a state of being, a gift from the Holy Spirit. God has given us joy through the Holy Spirit and we must look to Him for joy each day. God points to Himself in John 15 as the source of joy. Because of who He is, what He's done, and where you're going one day, you can have joy.

Schedules frustrate, meetings bore, problems anger, responsibilities overwhelm, and life is hectic. But even when you are swamped or things don't go your way, God desires for you to experience His joy. Unconditional joy is not found in yourself, your surroundings, or others; it is from God.

What situation on Earth is so terrible that it overshadows the joy of knowing one day you'll live with God forever in Heaven? What can be so bad that knowing Christ cannot bring you joy? If we were truthful, we'd have to admit that our lack of joy comes from focusing on earthly problems rather than God's goodness.

Take a few minutes to consider the goodness of God. Focus on Him today and allow His joy to fill your life.

Today's Rooted Principle: Situations can change, but they can't steal your joy if it's rooted in God.

Keeping Your Joy

*For he longed after you all, and was full of heaviness, because that ye
had heard that he had been sick. For indeed he was sick nigh unto
death: but God had mercy on him; and not on him only, but on me also,
lest I should have sorrow upon sorrow.*—**Philippians 2:26–27**

As Paul penned the epistle of Philippians, the church at Philippi was
concerned about a man from their church named Epaphroditus who
had been very sick. Epaphroditus was away from Philippi, and when the
church heard that he was battling sickness, they became so concerned
for him that they allowed it to overshadow their lives and steal their joy
in serving God. Of course, we should pray for a sick or hurting fellow
believer, but this church let it hinder their work.

The devil is actively trying to steal your joy as a Christian. He can't
change your eternal future once you're saved, but he can limit your
effectiveness on Earth and steal your joy.

Maybe your plans got changed last minute and created frustration.
Maybe a friend or family member reacted harshly toward you and hurt
you. Maybe a coworker lied about you. Whatever the circumstance, the
devil seeks to use life's ups and downs to steal your joy.

Don't allow life's problems to keep you from joyfully serving the
Lord. Things go wrong, plans change, and rough times come; but if you
are daily in God's Word, you can still have joy despite the bad times.

Have you allowed the devil to steal your joy? It may not even come
through something major or something outwardly bad, but little changes
can take away a Christian's once joyful spirit of service. Readjust your
heart and focus on having God's joy today.

Today's Rooted Principle: As long as you're rooted in God's Word,
there's always reason to be joyful.

Rejoice in His Victory

These things I have spoken unto you, that in me ye might have peace. In the world ye shall have tribulation: but be of good cheer; I have overcome the world.—**John 16:33**

The story is told of a patient who went to see his doctor for test results. The doctor entered the room and said, "I have bad news and worse news." Troubled, the patient asked, "Well, what's the bad news?" The doctor replied, "You have twenty-four hours to live." The patient replied, "What could be worse than that?" The doctor said, "I forgot to tell you yesterday."

Do you ever feel like your life just seems to go that way? Times are tough, and they just keep getting tougher. Despite your best efforts, you face one trial after another. As a Christian, God points to one main reason to remain joyful even in the midst of trials, "I have overcome the world."

There is no trial that God cannot fix, no problem He cannot solve, and no situation He cannot work through. Yet many times we can feel that if God doesn't immediately remove the trial, we are justified in letting Satan steal our joy.

Even during trials, God points to His goodness and His victory over sin as reason to rejoice. He says that through His victory, you can have peace. No matter how bad things get on Earth, He has conquered the world and offers you eternal joy in Heaven. Nothing can take that away from you!

What trial is causing you to worry? We all face tough times, and if we're not careful, we can let trials get us down. Realize that even during trials, God is in control. He has overcome the world! Rejoice in His victory today and keep joy in your heart knowing that even if the world throws its worst at you, Christ has overcome it.

Today's Rooted Principle: When the world gives you its worst, choose to be of good cheer remembering that Christ has overcome the world.

Exodus 36–38 Matthew 23:1–22

Being a Blessing to Others

And when she was baptized, and her household, she besought us, saying,
If ye have judged me to be faithful to the Lord, come into my house, and
abide there. And she constrained us.—**Acts 16:15**

Early in our years as a married couple, Terrie and I had the opportunity
to drive out to Salton Sea, California, each weekend to preach to
a small group of people who met in one of their homes. The group
expanded, and eventually we planted a church there. The first people we
saw saved in that area were Fred and Alice Riley.

One Sunday morning as I was late coming in for the prayer meeting
before the service, Fred, with a caring heart asked, "Pastor Paul, how
come you're late?" I explained how we lived many miles away and that
we had been delayed a bit that morning. After lunch, Fred approached
me, "Pastor Paul, Alice and I have a nice motorhome that we'd like to
bring down to this house. You could stay here on Saturday night, and you
won't have to drive so much." That couple will probably never know what
a blessing that was to us.

The first to receive Paul's message in Macedonia, Lydia, was
likewise willing to share of her resources. After she trusted Christ, she
immediately offered Paul and his companions her hospitality. She didn't
know everything about the Bible nor was she well versed in Christianity,
but she gave of what she had to help others.

Perhaps the most basic of God's commands is to love your neighbor.
No matter who someone is or what they have, God desires that you
would love them and show that love through giving. God desires that
His children would show His love through being a blessing to those
around them.

Who can you be an encourager to by sharing your resources? Follow
Lydia's example of hospitality and be a blessing to others.

Today's Rooted Principle: God desires that you would be a conduit of
blessings—receiving from Him and passing them on to others.

Being a Co-Laborer

But I trust in the Lord Jesus to send Timotheus shortly unto you, that I also may be of good comfort, when I know your state. For I have no man likeminded, who will naturally care for your state.
—**Philippians 2:19–20**

In studying war and the development of the armies of the United States, it's hard to overlook a man some historians have called "the first modern general"—William Tecumseh Sherman. He served as a general in the Union army during the Civil War, and through his "scorched earth" policies, really introduced Americans to complete war.

The story is told of his relationship with General U.S. Grant who headed up the Union armies. Sherman and Grant were close friends and traded letters often. Sherman demonstrated the strength of the friendship in an 1865 letter where he wrote, "I knew wherever I was that you thought of me, and if I got in a tight place you would come—if alive."

Every human being desires companionship—a friend, a mate, an acquaintance, someone to care and help in tough times. God made us to need and receive help from others.

As Christians, God brings people into our lives to lift us up and help us along our Christian journey. For Paul, Timothy was that co-laborer who helped his ministry. While it's a great blessing to *have* a friend like Timothy, it's an even greater blessing to *be* a friend like Timothy. God desires that you would actively help those around you to stay faithful in their Christian journey.

What can you do to help and encourage your friends? Perhaps it's through keeping someone accountable, lending a helping hand during a trial, or praying for strength for others. Ask God how you can be a Timothy to someone in your life today.

Today's Rooted Principle: Determine to be a friend who provides spiritual encouragement and replenishment for others.

Leviticus 1–3   Matthew 24:1–28

The Believer's Description

As obedient children, not fashioning yourselves according to the former lusts in your ignorance: But as he which hath called you is holy, so be ye holy in all manner of conversation; Because it is written, Be ye holy; for I am holy.—**1 Peter 1:14–16**

When beginning a new job, one of the first things a company provides the new employee is a list of requirements. Whether in an official document or through verbal instructions, a company tells the employee what is required, how he or she should act, and what guidelines he or she should follow.

When you became a Christian, you weren't handed a job description or a list of requirements, but God does give us a clear description of what He desires from His children in the Bible. Three of those requirements deal with the believer's interaction with the world around him or her.

To be holy. God desires that His children would be holy in all areas of life—thought, speech, actions. The carnal person has no guidance in what they say or do, but God desires that believers would show forth holy words and actions.

To be set apart. God set us in this world to be a testimony to others. While it's easy to be caught up in the day-to-day grind, God desires that we would remember we are in the world but not of it.

To fellowship with Him. What will help us speak and act holy and stay apart from the world's influence? Daily fellowshipping with God through prayer and Bible reading guard us from sin and guide us in God's will.

If someone were to describe your life as a believer, what characteristics would they mention? Take account of your life and how you interact with the world around you. Daily spend time with God and seek to be a shining light of God's holiness to others.

Today's Rooted Principle: Seek to change the world around you rather than the world changing you.

Leviticus 4–5   Matthew 24:29–51   63

Tuned to Christ

Now I beseech you, brethren, by the name of our Lord Jesus Christ, that ye all speak the same thing, and that there be no divisions among you; but that ye be perfectly joined together in the same mind and in the same judgment.—**1 Corinthians 1:10**

In his book *The Pursuit of God*, author A.W. Tozer wrote the following:

> Has it ever occurred to you that one hundred pianos all tuned to the same fork are automatically tuned to each other? They are of one accord by being tuned, not to each other, but to another standard to which each one must individually bow. So one hundred worshipers [meeting] together, each one looking away to Christ, are in heart nearer to each other than they could possibly be, were they to become "unity" conscious and turn their eyes away from God to strive for closer fellowship.

With any sort of human interaction, there's likely to be a difference of opinion or some sort of contention. We aren't all robots, so naturally we'll butt heads with other people. But as believers we should be so focused on Christ and the advancement of His kingdom that we forget the petty differences and work toward His glory.

When you're tuned to God and His will, you'll find that the little differences between you and others don't matter as much. Fighting over church responsibilities or seating preference seems trivial in light of the salvation of others.

How tuned are you to Christ's will? If you find yourself disagreeing over petty things, take some time to rethink the purpose of the church and your role in it. Ask God to keep you focused on His will rather than your own.

Today's Rooted Principle: Great things can be accomplished for God's glory when we're fully tuned to Him.

A Focus on Family

This is a true saying, if a man desire the office of a bishop, he desireth
a good work. A bishop then must be blameless, the husband of one
wife, vigilant, sober, of good behaviour, given to hospitality, apt to teach.
—1 Timothy 3:1–2

The story is told of two riverboats that were set to race down the
Mississippi River to see which was faster. Both started out and, when
one pulled ahead, the captain of the losing vessel commanded his first
mate to begin feeding the fire with all the wood they had. The vessel
began gaining ground but soon the first mate informed the captain the
ship was out of fuel. Desperate to win, he directed his crew to begin
tearing off pieces of the boat to use as fuel. The ship continued to gain
ground and even pulled ahead, but at what cost? At the end of the course,
the ship was ruined.

Many in our day strive to advance their own interests, but at the cost
of hurting their family in the process. Whether you are a pastor, Sunday
school teacher, choir member, or parent, your first ministry in life is your
family. The church can hire another pastor, but God only gives you one
husband or wife, one family.

Realize the extreme importance of family in your life. Getting ahead
at work means little if you lose time with your children. Becoming the
best in your field gains nothing if your children turn aside from God's
will. Ask yourself this—is your job, hobby, or desires worth losing
your family?

Being a parent comes with high responsibility. God desires that you
will train your child in His commands and guide them into a loving
relationship with Him. You can't do that if you aren't actively involved in
your child's life. Your family needs you. Ask the Lord to help you make
family one of your top priorities this week.

Today's Rooted Principle: What is it to gain the whole world and lose
the family God has entrusted to you?

Called to Serve

Make a joyful noise unto the LORD, all ye lands. Serve the LORD with gladness: come before his presence with singing. Know ye that the LORD he is God: it is he that hath made us, and not we ourselves; we are his people, and the sheep of his pasture.—**Psalm 100:1–3**

The story is told of a young man who had been hired by the personnel department of a large supermarket chain. The young man was excited for the opportunity as he reported to work at one of the stores. The manager greeted him with a warm handshake and a smile, handed him a broom and said, "Your first job will be to sweep out the store." Shocked, the boy replied, "But I'm a college graduate." The manager looked down and replied, "I'm sorry. I didn't know that. Here, give me the broom and I'll show you how."

Sometimes we can pridefully believe that we are better than menial jobs. Whether because of training or degree or prestige, we can look down on "lesser" jobs and refuse to do them. In God's plan, however, no job is too menial for a believer.

There are many jobs that must be done to support God's church each week. Some need to teach, others must sing, others will conduct the service, some help in the nursery, while others clean up afterward. Whatever the task, the result is helping God's work advance each week.

How are you serving the Lord in your local church? God has called everyone to serve Him in some capacity. For instance, while you may not be able to sing in the choir, you could perhaps send weekly encouraging emails or cards to people in your Sunday school class.

God wants every believer to actively be involved in serving Him. Ask God how He would have you be involved in serving Him through your church.

Today's Rooted Principle: There is no job too small that God will not be glorified in you doing it.

A Steady Focus

And it came to pass, as we went to prayer, a certain damsel possessed with a spirit of divination met us, which brought her masters much gain by soothsaying: The same followed Paul and us, and cried, saying, These men are the servants of the most high God, which shew unto us the way of salvation.—**Acts 16:16–17**

Right after Paul and those with him saw Lydia saved, they faced opposition. Acts 16 says they faced a demon-possessed girl who began mocking their ministry. This girl had the "spirit of divination," meaning she was similar to a modern day fortune teller. She followed Paul around town, mocking him and those preaching Christ's message.

It is not uncommon to face opposition in life. Even right after a victory or a joyous event, the devil can strike at your joy and seek to shift your focus. Weak Christians are thrown with every up and down in life, but the rooted Christian will recognize the devil's attack and remain focused on God's work.

Our country had much religious influence in her younger days. Even schools like Dartmouth, Yale, and Harvard had the original purpose of teaching God's Word, but have since shifted focus. If we aren't careful, we can allow people or circumstances to shift our focus from God.

Whether you're a missionary in a foreign land or a teacher in the public school system, every one of us will encounter people who have rejected Christ and who resist our message. They may not come in the form of witch doctors or demon-possessed people, but there are people who wish to mock your faith and divert your focus from serving God.

Has the devil been seeking to steal your focus off God's plan? It can come in many different ways, but be wise to the devil's tricks and determine to remain focused on God through all of life's variations.

Today's Rooted Principle: During life's highs and lows, keep a steady focus on the Lord and His ultimate plan for your life.

Eternally Secure

And I give unto them eternal life; and they shall never perish, neither shall any man pluck them out of my hand.—**John 10:28**

A German botanist, who was traveling in Turkey, saw a rare flower hanging from an inaccessible precipice. He saw a young boy nearby and offered to pay him to go down the precipice on a rope and fetch the flower. The boy was tempted but hesitant. Then, struck with a new thought, the boy said, "Wait a moment, and I will go for my father to come and hold the rope; then I will willingly go down and get it." He trusted his father to hold the rope securely.

Just like the young boy, our souls are secure in our Father's hand. The moment we accept Jesus Christ as our Saviour, God promises us eternal life. Today, let's remember some of the blessings we have because of God's promise of eternal life.

Our eternal security gives us peace in a troubled world. Jesus said in John 16:33, "These things I have spoken unto you, that in me ye might have peace. In the world ye shall have tribulation: but be of good cheer; I have overcome the world." We can be joyful in knowing that we have the source of all peace dwelling in our hearts.

Our eternal security gives us comfort during trials. No matter what hardship you face today or tomorrow, you can be comforted in knowing that God is always with you.

Our eternal security gives us hope for a bright future. What a joy to know that because of God's promise of eternal life we will enjoy a home in Heaven for all eternity.

What fear or insecurity has gripped your heart? In any circumstance, we can rejoice in remembering that we are safe in the Father's hand. No foe can pluck us from His loving grace, and no fear can remove us from His care.

Today's Rooted Principle: Our security in Christ is firmly attached to the unfailing faithfulness of God.

Let Love Shine

We know that we have passed from death unto life, because we love the brethren. He that loveth not his brother abideth in death. Whosoever hateth his brother is a murderer: and ye know that no murderer hath eternal life abiding in him.—**1 John 3:14–15**

On May 2, 1962, a dramatic advertisement appeared in the *San Francisco Examiner*: "I don't want my husband to die in the gas chamber for a crime he did not commit. I will therefore offer my services for 10 years as a cook, maid, or housekeeper to any leading attorney who will defend him and bring about his vindication." One of San Francisco's biggest lawyers saw the advertisement, felt pity, and contacted the woman. After much work, he took on the case and ended up getting the innocent man released from all charges. Afterward, the attorney refused the lady's offer of ten years of service, noting that he was satisfied to have saved an innocent man from death.

Stories of kindhearted humans helping others with no kickback or reward offsets the grimness of news and gives hope of good in the world. Yet as Christians, we know a stronger kind of love, a love that gives the ultimate sacrifice.

The very core of Christ's message is one of love. God loved so much that He gave His all. Those saved have experienced that love fully, and now God desires that they turn around to show others that love as well.

Love isn't common in our world. Hearing of someone giving of themselves stands out in a world of selfish pursuit. So when someone shows love, others notice. As Christians, our very existence should be to show love to those around us.

How can you show love to someone today? It doesn't have to be extravagant or cost much. Imagine the impact you can have on another person today just by taking time to show God's love.

Today's Rooted Principle: Our greatest testimony is through imitating Christ's love.

Reflecting God's Image

But we all, with open face beholding as in a glass the glory of the Lord, are changed into the same image from glory to glory, even as by the Spirit of the Lord.—**2 Corinthians 3:18**

A woman watched a silversmith as he heated a piece of silver over the fire. He explained that to refine silver he needed to hold it where the flames were the hottest to burn away all impurities. The silversmith said that he had to watch the silver carefully because if it was left even a moment too long in the flames, it would be destroyed.

The woman was silent for a moment. Then she asked, "But how do you know when the silver is fully refined?"

"Oh, that's easy," he answered, "when I see my image reflected in it."

Like the silversmith looking into the precious metal, Christ desires to see His image reflected in our lives. The moment God saved us, He formed a new creature, and He expects us to be constantly changing into His image and reflecting that image to others. Ephesians 4:24 explains the goal of every Christian: "And that ye put on the new man, which after God is created in righteousness and true holiness."

Do you reflect God's righteousness and holiness in your daily life? Can others see Christ's image in what you say and do? This is not only a humbling thought, but it is also a thrilling thought that we have the opportunity to reflect the image of our Saviour and Creator.

During trials and troubles, reflect Christ's joy and strength. During temptation, reflect the power and righteousness of Christ. During periods of blessing, reflect His graciousness and love.

The process of becoming more Christlike may, at times, be painful as God allows "fires" to remove the impurities from our lives. But even then, we can rejoice knowing that the end result is a clearer reflection of Christ to others.

Today's Rooted Principle: Allow God to change and mold your life so you can reflect His image more clearly.

Salvation for All

The Lord is not slack concerning his promise, as some men count slackness; but is longsuffering to us-ward, not willing that any should perish, but that all should come to repentance.—**2 Peter 3:9**

After the terrorist attacks on September 11, 2011, the former mayor of New York City, Rudy Giuliani, was asked to share a few thoughts. Although he referred to the physical salvation of rescuing people from the burning World Trade Center, his comments are insightful when applied to rescuing people from an eternity apart from God:

> When everybody was fleeing that building, and the cops and the firefighters and the EMS people were heading up into it, do you think any of them said, "I wonder how many blacks are up there for us to save? I wonder what percentage are whites up here? How many Jews are there? Let's see—are these people making $400,000 a year, or $24,000?" No, when you're saving lives, they're all precious.... I'm convinced that God wants us to...value every human life the way He does.

We are God's only representatives on the planet, and we simply cannot take time to pick and choose who needs help. Every person has an eternal soul, and they all need the love and forgiveness of Jesus Christ. They all need to be rescued from the horror of an eternity apart from God.

As Christians, we can take part in fulfilling God's will by sharing the Gospel with everyone. Instead of seeing a dirty kid on the streets, see a soul who can be washed in the blood of Christ. When you meet a wealthy businessman who seems to have it all, realize that he desperately needs Jesus.

God is not a respecter of persons; so how can we be any different? Let's catch a fresh glimpse of God's vision for souls and share the Gospel with every person we meet.

Today's Rooted Principle: Refresh your passion for souls by focusing on God's desire for all to be saved.

Stay Close to God

Blessed is the man that walketh not in the counsel of the ungodly, nor standeth in the way of sinners, nor sitteth in the seat of the scornful.
—**Psalm 1:1**

One day a farmer grabbed his shotgun to shoot at a flock of pesky crows. Unfortunately, he didn't see his sociable parrot that had joined the crows. After firing a few shots, he walked over to the fallen birds and was surprised to find his parrot badly ruffled with a broken wing. When the farmer's children saw the injured bird, they asked, "Dad, what happened?" The farmer simply replied, "Bad company."

Scripture often warns us to avoid harmful influences. Regardless of our age or spiritual strength, over time, unwise influences will negatively affect our walk with the Lord. Satan is determined to pull us into sin and wreck our lives, and he often uses wrong influences to accomplish his goal.

As Christians, we must stay near to God in order to discern between good and bad influences in our lives. As we remain sensitive to the Holy Spirit and obey God's Word, God will help us to recognize bad influences and remove them from our lives.

Perhaps you have a friend who constantly encourages you to sin, or maybe your own flesh pulls you to make sinful choices. Whatever the case, determine to avoid those people, places, or situations that bring you further from the Lord. Much temptation can be avoided if we will simply walk with the Lord and with those who love Him. Satan's fiery darts are no match for our God; so stay close to the one who protects you.

Ask God to help you remove bad influences in your life and to be sensitive to the direction of the Holy Spirit. Staying close to God is the safest and happiest place you can be.

Today's Rooted Principle: Stay close to God to recognize wrong influences in your life and to develop spiritual discernment.

Stewarding God's Time

This is the day which the LORD hath made; we will rejoice and be glad in it.—**Psalm 118:24**

In each day there are 24 hours, 1,440 minutes, and 86,400 seconds—and every one of them is a precious gift from God.

Time is something we feel we never have enough of, yet we give it away so easily. Someone once said, "Time is free, but it's priceless. You can't own it, but you can use it. You can't keep it but you can spend it. Once you've lost it you can never get it back."

God is the Creator, the possessor of time. Therefore, we are the stewards of the time that God has given us. One day, we will answer to God for what we did with the time He gave us. This can be a sobering thought because we easily waste the precious time God has given. But it can also be a motivating thought. We can have joy in knowing that God has given us today, right now, to serve Him.

Ask yourself, what am I doing for God right now? Before you go to work or school, spend time alone with God and ask Him to show you how to use your time for Him. When you use your time to accomplish the priorities God has given you, you invest your time into eternity.

All of us have regrets concerning wasted time of the past. But let's determine to give today to the Lord—to use it for His purposes and for His glory. When I stand before the Lord, I want to have wisely stewarded the time He has so graciously given me.

None of us know if we will have another year, another day, another hour to serve God; so use today for the Lord.

Today's Rooted Principle: Use the time God has given you right now to serve Him and bring Him glory.

Leviticus 23–24   Mark 1:1–22   73

Confidence in Christ

Forasmuch as ye know that ye were not redeemed with corruptible things, as silver and gold, from your vain conversation received by tradition from your fathers; But with the precious blood of Christ, as of a lamb without blemish and without spot.—**1 Peter 1:18–19**

While driving in a remote camping area, the father of a vacationing family came across a large sign that read, "Road Closed. Do Not Enter." The man proceeded around the sign because he was confident it would save them time. His wife was resistant to the adventure, but there was no turning back for this persistent road warrior. After a few miles of successful navigation, he began to boast about his gift of discernment. His proud smile was quickly replaced with humble sweat when the road led to a washed-out bridge. He turned the car around and retraced his tracks to the main road. When they arrived at the original warning sign he was greeted by large letters on the back of the sign "Welcome back, stupid!"

Sometimes we can have utmost confidence in ourselves to figure out issues or fix problems but we let ourselves down. Confidence is only as good as the object it's placed in. When going through life, the wise person places their confidence in an unchanging, all-powerful God.

When you face a problem or come upon life's challenges, what's your first course of action? God desires that you would turn to Him for strength and place your confidence in Him. As He reminds the believer in 1 Peter 1, your salvation is bought by His powerful blood and He alone has the strength to help in your daily life.

The human reaction to difficulty is self-reliance, but God wants you to be Jesus-reliant. Man can plan and scheme but only God controls the situation entirely. Take a few minutes now to lay your problems before God. Give up your control of the situation, and place your confidence in Christ's plan.

Today's Rooted Principle: The only way you'll see growth is by abandoning control and placing confidence in Christ.

Leviticus 25   Mark 1:23–45

Asking for Help

They part my garments among them, and cast lots upon my vesture. But be not thou far from me, O LORD: O my strength, haste thee to help me. Deliver my soul from the sword; my darling from the power of the dog.—**Psalm 22:18–20**

During the Spanish-American War, Clara Barton was overseeing the work of the Red Cross in Cuba. One day, Colonel Theodore Roosevelt came to her wanting to buy food for his sick and wounded Rough Riders, but she refused to sell him any. Roosevelt was perplexed. His men needed the help and he was prepared to pay out of his own funds. When he asked someone why he could not buy the supplies, he was told, "Colonel, just ask for it!" A smile broke over Roosevelt's face. All he had to do was simply ask.

Human nature has a clear self-reliant gene. From the early days of the world, people have relied on themselves for food, shelter, provision, and survival. When life is threatened, the human body naturally relies on self for preservation. But while the human body looks to itself for help, God desires that His children would look to Him for help.

One of the most common threads of the great believers of the Bible is a humble willingness to ask God for help. Moses needed help to cross the Red Sea. Noah needed help to preserve his family. David needed help to defeat Goliath. Wise men and women have always realized their inability and God's ability.

You can't survive in this world without seeking God's help every day. The devil's attacks are real. The world's problems are overwhelming. And the Christian life requires constantly asking God for guidance.

How often do you seek God's help? How reliant are you on Him for help each day? You need God's help every day, and He gladly offers you the full strength of His power for every situation if you only ask.

Today's Rooted Principle: The sooner you realize your shortcomings and rely on God's strength, the stronger you'll be.

Killing the Spider

For we are his workmanship, created in Christ Jesus unto good works, which God hath before ordained that we should walk in them.
—Ephesians 2:10

A man was praying with his pastor one morning after church. He had been dealing with temptation in his life and had been seeking counseling and accountability with the leaders of his church. On that morning, he prayed a prayer the pastor had heard many times before, asking God to remove temptation, "Lord, take the cobwebs out of my life." Just as he said this the pastor interrupted, "Kill the spider, Lord."

Sometimes it's easy to fall into the cycle of clearing the cobwebs of life. Falling into sin's trap, giving up control to the devil, repenting, then beginning the cycle again. As Christians, God has given us power to break the cycle by killing the spider—self.

The devil is bent on bringing in temptation and sin to Christian's lives to wear down their strength and joy. When you become so bogged down with repeatedly falling into sin then repenting, you cannot experience the full blessings of a life lived in God's freedom.

The surest way to break the cycle is by dying to self every day. When you're dead to self and realize that your desires don't have to control you, you can be alive to Christ.

God desires that you would purposefully die to self every day. Realize that your flesh doesn't control you and give complete control to God. As Ephesians 2 says, you are created in Christ for the purpose of fulfilling His will and living a life of holiness.

God has a life of spiritual freedom and blessing planned for you. He wants the best life possible for you every day! But first He desires that you die to self, to the old fleshly desires and wants, and live for God's desires.

Today's Rooted Principle: When you die to self, you can truly be alive to God's richest blessings.

Numbers 1–2   Mark 3:1–19

God's Repairs

Being confident of this very thing, that he which hath begun a good work in you will perform it until the day of Jesus Christ.—**Philippians 1:6**

London businessman Lindsay Clegg told the story of a warehouse property he was selling. The building had been empty for months and needed repairs. Vandals had damaged the doors, smashed the windows, and strewn trash all over the place. As he showed a prospective buyer the property, he took pains to say that he would replace the broken windows, bring in a crew to correct any structural damage, and clean out the garbage. The buyer said, "Forget about the repairs. When I buy this place, I'm going to build something completely different. I don't want the building; I want the site."

Compared with the renovation God has in mind, our efforts to improve our own lives are as trivial as sweeping a warehouse slated for the wrecking ball. When we become God's, the old life is over. He makes all things new. All God wants is the site and the permission to build.

There are still some Christians trying to renovate, but God offers complete redemption. All we have to do is give Him the property, and He will do the necessary building in our lives.

Know today that you will never be bad enough to be beyond God's grace to save and to sanctify, and you could never be good enough to be beyond the need of His grace for the same purpose. God has plans to completely transform your life but only if you give Him complete control of your life.

What do you want out of life—a renovated sinful life or a completely new life from God? God has the blueprints to a wonderful life of blessings and joy and He wants to complete that in you! As Philippians says, the good work God started in you at salvation He desires to continue until the day you reach Heaven. Will you let Him?

Today's Rooted Principle: Surrender yourself completely to God's ongoing work in your life.

Stewarding Life

Therefore, as ye abound in every thing, in faith, and utterance, and knowledge, and in all diligence, and in your love to us, see that ye abound in this grace also.—**2 Corinthians 8:7**

The following fable is told of a man's interaction with God about stewarding:

> Once a man said, "If I had some extra money, I'd give it to God, but I have just enough to support myself and my family." And the same man said, "If I had some extra time, I'd give it to God, but every minute is taken up with my job, my family, and my clubs." And the same man said, "If I had a talent I'd give it to God, but I have no lovely voice; I have no special skill; I've never been able to lead a group the way I would like to." And God was touched and gave that man money, time, and talent. And then He waited but the man never changed.

Sometimes we become like the man in this fable. We look around and see what we don't have and use that as an excuse for not spending more time, effort, and money on God's work. We complain about what we don't have so much that we fail to use what we do have.

God's plan for stewardship is basic. Often, it begins with entrusting a little to our care and building from there. He might give you a modest job, a small salary, a small role in your church, or a humble family, but He desires for you to use them for Him.

You can faithfully steward exactly what you have right now. While you may look at it as not much, God looks at it as a way for you to faithfully obey Him. Consider how you can use what you have for God's kingdom. God puts more emphasis on your faithfulness than the size of your gift.

Today's Rooted Principle: The success of stewardship is not based on the amount stewarded but on the faithfulness of the steward.

Numbers 5–6   Mark 4:1–20

Giving Thanks

*For if I by grace be a partaker, why am I evil spoken of for that for which
I give thanks?.*—**1 Corinthians 10:30**

In 1860, a ship went aground on the shore of Lake Michigan near
Evanston, Illinois. Edward Spencer, a nearby ministerial student, saw
the event and waded again and again into the frigid waters to rescue
seventeen passengers. In the process, his health was permanently damaged
and he had to live with complications for the rest of his life. Years later
at his funeral, it was noted that not one of the people he rescued ever
thanked him.

Giving thanks, even for such a monumental task as saving someone's
life, seems to go unnoticed today. And if something so large as this can
go unthanked, how many smaller acts of kindness go unnoticed on a
daily basis?

How often do you give God thanks? God desires that we would live
in a spirit of thankfulness each day, daily pointing out kindness from
others and being grateful for the goodness of others and from Him.

When was the last time you made a special note to thank God for all
He's done for you? We may say thanks for a meal or express gratitude after
an answer to prayer, but how often do we make time to thank God? God
has blessed each of us in so many countless ways and deserves constant
praise from our lips.

Take time today to thank God for His goodness. Carve out a time
in your schedule when you can be alone with God and reflect on His
blessings. Perhaps write them down. You'll soon find that God's goodness
cannot be fathomed. Make a point of constantly living in a state of
thankfulness and never go a day without giving God thanks.

Today's Rooted Principle: Taking time to give God thanks will remind
you just how blessed you truly are.

Numbers 7–8 Mark 4:21–41 79

The Source of Peace

Therefore being justified by faith, we have peace with God through our Lord Jesus Christ: By whom also we have access by faith into this grace wherein we stand, and rejoice in hope of the glory of God.
—**Romans 5:1–2**

Charles Wesley and John Wesley are well known for their preaching in the 1700s. Charles wrote many hymns and ministered through song around England. Wesley's life wasn't always easy and he faced much opposition from other religious leaders (and sometimes from his own family). Yet he felt confident in the peace he found through Christ. He once wrote the following poem about that peace:

> I rest beneath the Almighty's shade,
> My griefs expire, my troubles cease;
> Thou, Lord, on whom my soul is stayed,
> Wilt keep me still in perfect peace.

Charles understood an important principle that men and women for centuries have been seeking to discover. The only source of true peace is found in the person of Christ.

Our world is bent on finding peace and calm in the midst of life. It seems a never-ending pursuit for most. Yet the "secret" to peace has been given by God in Romans 5. God cannot give us peace apart from Himself because it is not there. There is no such thing. True peace in life can only come through an unchanging, unmovable object and that is Jesus Christ.

While the world searches for peace through religious thinkers, calming activities, or reflective lifestyles, peace is only found in God. The storms of life swell and problems come; but through God, you can know that all is well. When storms arise in your life, don't react like those who do not know Christ. Run to God and seek the peace only He can provide.

Today's Rooted Principle: True peace can only be found in Christ—our unchanging, unmovable Saviour.

Numbers 9–11   Mark 5:1–20

Finding Joy

For this cause also thank we God without ceasing, because, when ye received the word of God which ye heard of us, ye received it not as the word of men, but as it is in truth, the word of God, which effectually worketh also in you that believe..—**1 Thessalonians 2:13**

For years people have been pursuing joy. Some seek it in hobbies or pleasures; yet one thing is true—no man has found joy apart from God.

Someone once wrote the following list of places people futilely seek joy:

In Unbelief—Voltaire was an infidel of the most pronounced type, yet wrote: "I wish I had never been born."

In Pleasure—Lord Byron lived a life of pleasure if anyone did, yet wrote: "The worm, the canker, and grief are mine alone."

In Money—Jay Gould, the American millionaire, had plenty of money, yet when dying said: "I suppose I am the most miserable man on earth."

In Position and Fame—Lord Beaconsfield enjoyed more than his share of both, yet wrote: "Youth is a mistake; manhood a struggle; old age a regret."

God tells us that living a life of humble obedience to His Word can bring joy no earthly thing can provide. Joy comes from knowing and serving God.

Joy is knowing you have a home in Heaven. Joy is seeing God work through you to change lives. Joy is being a part of God's plan in life. You will never regret obeying God over giving in to the devil's temptations. Only God's joy lasts beyond what this world offers.

Today's Rooted Principle: The devil's offer pales in comparison to the eternal, life-changing joy God offers.

The Object of Our Praise

He is thy praise, and he is thy God, that hath done for thee these great and terrible things, which thine eyes have seen.—**Deuteronomy 10:21**

What comes to your mind when you think about God? Do you praise Him daily for who He is and for what He does in your life?

A.W. Tozer wrote, "The history of mankind will probably show that no people has ever risen above its religion, and man's spiritual history will positively demonstrate that no religion has ever been greater than its idea of God. Worship is pure or base as the worshiper entertains high or low thoughts of God. For this reason the gravest question before the Church is always God Himself, and the most portentous fact about any man is not what he at a given time may say or do, but what he in his deep heart conceives God to be like."

Our God is omniscient, unchangeable, righteous, just, holy, eternal, pure, and good—and these are only a few of His many attributes. When we start praising God for who He is, we will experience pure and genuine worship—the kind God desires from us.

Let's not allow the sin and superficial worship of this world to blur our spiritual eyes and injure our view of God. Take time today to praise God for who He is. Begin a list of God's attributes and thank Him for each of them.

When we make God the object of our praise, we, like the psalmist, will be able to say, "I will praise thee, O LORD, with my whole heart; I will shew forth all thy marvellous works. I will be glad and rejoice in thee: I will sing praise to thy name, O thou most High" (Psalm 9:1–2).

Today's Rooted Principle: Experience a clearer and purer view of God by making Him the object of your praise.

A Clear Identity

*Let your light so shine before men, that they may see your good works and glorify your Father which is in heaven..—***Matthew 5:16**

When a fully booked flight to Denver was canceled, an irate passenger pushed his way to the front of the line. He slammed his boarding pass on the desk and demanded immediate service. "I will be glad to help you, sir," the agent responded gently. "But I must first assist these other customers. If you will take your place in the line, I will be with you soon."

"But, do you have any idea who I am?" the angry traveler fumed. With a charm that transcended the intensity of the moment, the airline agent responded by immediately picking up her phone and broadcasting on the public address system, "Attention, all passengers. We have a passenger here at the gate who does not know who he is. If anyone can help him find his identity, please come to gate C-14." As you might guess, the angry passenger retreated to the end of the line, deciding he would rather retain his identity and miss his flight.

Unlike the inconvenienced passenger, we know who we are—we are the children of God. The moment we trusted Christ we became Christ's representatives to the world. As members of God's family, we must strive to live so that others can clearly see our Christian identity.

Every day presents us with new opportunities to represent Christ. We can share the Gospel with our coworkers, do a kind deed for a stranger, or send an encouraging note to a friend. By consistent godly living we can clearly represent Christ to the people around us.

Satan seeks to ruin our testimony and hide our godly identity. But as the children of God, we must never allow sin to conceal our Christianity. Being a Christian is the greatest privilege of our lives, so let's unashamedly represent Christ so that others can clearly see our identity.

Today's Rooted Principle: Make your identity as Christ's representative clear with consistent, godly living.

Building Your Testimony

My brethren, count it all joy when ye fall into divers temptations; Knowing this, that the trying of your faith worketh patience. But let patience have her perfect work, that ye may be perfect and entire, wanting nothing.
—**James 1:2–4**

Although none of us want to go through times of suffering, trials refine our faith and strengthen our testimony for Christ. A strong testimony that honors the Lord is built as you faithfully live out God's truth through the trials of life.

Perhaps one of the best examples from the Bible of that principle is the life of Paul. Over and over he persevered through persecution.

As Paul arrived in the city of Antioch during his first missionary journey, he was greeted with hostility. "But the Jews stirred up the devout and honourable women, and the chief men of the city, and raised persecution against Paul and Barnabas, and expelled them out of their coasts" (Acts 13:50). Although Paul was expelled from Antioch, he continued on his journey to Iconium.

As he entered Iconium, he once again faced persecution. "But the unbelieving Jews stirred up the Gentiles, and made their minds evil affected against the brethren" (Acts 14:2). The people of this city attempted to kill Paul, yet he persevered on his journey to Lystra. Once again, Paul met another trial. The people of Lystra stoned Paul and left him for dead. But Paul rose up and kept going in spite of the persecution.

As Christians, we all will face persecution. But we must not allow bitterness or anger to destroy our testimony for God. Rather, we can strengthen our testimony by trusting and praising God in spite of our trials. Never give up during hard times so that you, like Paul, can say, "I have fought a good fight, I have finished my course, I have kept the faith" (2 Timothy 4:7).

Today's Rooted Principle: A godly testimony is built as you faithfully live out God's truth through the trials of life.

MARCH

Transforming Our Thoughts

And be not conformed to this world: but be ye transformed by the renewing of your mind, that ye may prove what is that good, and acceptable, and perfect, will of God.—**Romans 12:2**

Our minds are constantly filled with thoughts, and these thoughts create many types of emotional and physical responses. A doctor once shared the following:

> The sickest people I have encountered—those who were ill not only in their bodies but also in their emotions—were those who were harboring long-term resentment, bitterness, anger and even hatred against another person, against God, or against themselves....

Studies show that changing your thinking is the best cure for stress. And the best way to change your thinking is by meditating on God's Word. The Bible will change our focus from inward to upward and will help us to avoid the kind of thinking that makes us feel stressed and overwhelmed.

When we feel burdened with the cares of life, Christ invites us to entrust our worries to Him: "Casting all your care upon him; for he careth for you" (1 Peter 5:7).

Allow God to begin transforming and renewing your mind today by spending time in His Word. Read it daily and meditate on its truths throughout the day. Allow God to transform and renew your mind, changing your thoughts from negative to positive, encouraging you with His promises, and relieving your anxieties.

Experience God's peace of mind today by focusing on the Word of God. "Thou wilt keep him in perfect peace, whose mind is stayed on thee: because he trusteth in thee" (Isaiah 26:3).

Today's Rooted Principle: Renew your mind and transform your thoughts by meditating on God's Word.

Gaining Stability Through Trials

But he knoweth the way that I take: when he hath tried me, I shall come forth as gold.—**Job 23:10**

A missionary couple once brought some African pastors to the United States for a big meeting. During their free time, these pastors wanted to go shopping. Even though they were in a small town, the missionaries knew there was a chance one might have difficulty finding his way around or get lost, so they gave them their phone number for such an emergency. In less than an hour, the phone rang, and one of the pastors said, "I am lost."

The missionary replied, "Lay the phone down, go to the street corner, find out the names of the two streets, and come back and tell me." In a few minutes the African pastor returned and reported, "I am at the corner of 'Walk' and 'Don't Walk.'" The trials of life sometimes make us feel lost and unstable. We feel directionless and don't know which way to turn. Sometimes it even seems that there are no good options. But God often allows trials in our lives so we will lean on Him and experience stability through His strength.

The worst thing that could happen to us would be not to have any difficulties—we'd never know our need of the Lord. God allows enough difficulty to bring us to Him, but then, God gives us enough grace to meet those difficulties—every day.

Are you struggling in a trial? Are you unstable? God will give sufficient grace for every difficulty you face. Each day He gives us enough difficulty to draw us to Him, and then, God gives us enough grace to live that day as we ought.

Rely on the strength of God, trust His love and goodness, and experience His marvelous grace.

Today's Rooted Principle: God can use the trials of life to give you stability if you will rely on His strength.

Numbers 23–25   Mark 7:14–37   87

The Sovereignty of God

And we know that all things work together for good to them that love God, to them who are the called according to his purpose.—**Romans 8:28**

A nervous airline passenger began pacing the terminal when bad weather delayed his flight. During his walk, he came across a life insurance machine that offered $100,000 in the event of an untimely death, and the insurance was only three dollars.

The passenger looked out the window at the threatening clouds and thought of his family at home. For that price it was foolish *not* to buy, so he took out the coverage. He then looked for a place to eat and settled on a Chinese restaurant in the airport.

It was a relaxing meal until he opened his fortune cookie. It read, "Your recent investment will pay big dividends."

We may have reason to feel unrest based on outer indicators, but what a comfort to know that we as Christians can trust our sovereign God for tomorrow and all eternity.

Hymn writer Margaret Clarkson wrote, "The sovereignty of God is the one impregnable rock to which the suffering human heart must cling. The circumstances surrounding our lives are no accident: they may be the work of evil, but that evil is held firmly within the mighty hand of our sovereign God… All evil is subject to him, and evil cannot touch His children unless He permits it. God is the Lord of human history and of the personal history of every member of his redeemed family."

We can trust the sovereignty of God because He has a perfect plan for our lives. God knows our past, has a plan for our present, and has already secured our future.

Rather than worrying about the future, trust your sovereign God. His ways are always perfect; you can rest securely in His Almighty hands.

Today's Rooted Principle: Find security by trusting in God's sovereignty.

Experiencing Ability in Trials

And he said unto me, My grace is sufficient for thee: for my strength is made perfect in weakness. Most gladly therefore will I rather glory in my infirmities, that the power of Christ may rest upon me.
—**2 Corinthians 12:9**

John Wesley once visited a sick woman who was grieving the recent loss of close family members. Over the previous six months, she had buried seven of her family members, and just that day she had heard that her sailor husband had been lost at sea.

"Do you not fret at any of those things?" Wesley asked.

She replied with a smile, "Oh, no! How can I fret at anything which is the will of God? Let Him take all besides; He has given me Himself. I love and praise Him every moment."

This woman experienced the power of God while enduring a great trial. Her trust in God was so great that she even praised the Lord in the midst of her suffering.

Paul, too, knew the comfort of God in the midst of suffering. Because he experienced God's sufficient grace and enabling strength, he actually rejoiced in his trials.

We may not think we are able to bear the death of a loved one or the loss of a job; and truthfully, we can't. But we serve a God who gives us His power and strength to go through *any* difficulty.

Take comfort in knowing that you have the ability—God's power—to endure and overcome the trials in your life. Ask God to give you strength and power for whatever difficulty you face today, and rest in His sufficient grace.

Today's Rooted Principle: During trials, God gives us His grace, strength, and power.

Nothing Is Too Hard for God

And the LORD said unto Abraham, Wherefore did Sarah laugh, saying, Shall I of a surety bear a child, which am old? Is any thing too hard for the LORD? At the time appointed I will return unto thee, according to the time of life, and Sarah shall have a son.—**Genesis 18:13–14**

For Abraham and Sarah to have a child was impossible, yet the Bible records the miraculous birth of Isaac. Our God has been working miracles for eternity, and nothing is impossible with Him.

We all face circumstances and problems when no human can help, but these seemingly impossible times are the perfect opportunity for us to watch God's miracle-working power. When we trust God with the "hard things," we will see our faith strengthened, our joy increased, and our lives bringing glory to God.

Are you facing an impossible situation that is too hard for you to handle? Take comfort in knowing that no trial, difficulty, or circumstance is too hard for our God.

Like Sarah, our sinful human nature tends to doubt God rather than trust Him. We see a circumstance through our human eyes and doubt that God could bring anything good from it. But what a joy to know that God is greater than our human reasoning. He reassures us of His supernatural power in Luke 1:37 where we read, "For with God nothing shall be impossible." That word *nothing* covers any circumstance we face—no matter how hard it may seem.

We serve the God of the impossible. The same God who performed miracles for Abraham and Sarah is our God today. Trust God with your circumstances and trials. Remember that nothing is too hard for Him and review His promises while you wait on Him.

Today's Rooted Principle: Through your most difficult and perplexing difficulties, remember that nothing is too hard for God.

Using Time Wisely

So teach us to number our days, that we may apply our hearts unto wisdom.—**Psalm 90:12**

Do you feel that you have more responsibilities than you do time? It is helpful to remember that God has a purpose for our lives, and time is His gift to us so we can accomplish His purpose. The following principles can help us wisely use the precious commodity of time:

Realize what God has given you is sustainable. God knows the number of our days here on Earth, and He knows we can accomplish His purpose in His time frame.

You can do too much of a good thing. Time spent for God is never wasted time, but we must be careful to not get "weary in well doing." God wants us to serve Him and work for Him, but we must take time to let God restore us daily. Serve God with your whole heart, but remember to make your quiet time with God your first priority so that you can serve in His strength.

Opportunity does not equal obligation. Life will present you with many great opportunities, but remember to seek God's face in every decision. We need God's wisdom to help us discern between good, better, and best.

Identify and focus on a few things. By identifying exactly what God wants you to accomplish each day, you can focus on your goal and work wholeheartedly on each task. "And whatsoever ye do, do it heartily, as to the Lord, and not unto men" (Colossians 3:23).

Tarrying times are not idle times. God gives waiting periods to all of us. During these times when life seems to be moving slower than normal, spend time getting to know God better and enjoying His presence.

Spend time each morning seeking God's face and asking Him to give you wisdom to manage your time for His purposes.

Today's Rooted Principle: We need God's wisdom to make our time count for eternity.

Answered Prayer

And all things, whatsoever ye shall ask in prayer, believing, ye shall receive.—**Matthew 21:22**

The story is told of a poor, elderly Christian widow in dire straights. She had no money, no food, and no one to whom she could turn for help. In her desperate condition, she fell to her knees and audibly cried out to God, "Oh Lord, please help me; please send me ham and collard greens."

A passerby—who happened to be an atheist—overheard her prayer. Partly in pity and partly to mock her, he went to the market and purchased ham and collard greens. He then climbed to the roof of her house and dropped the supplies down her chimney so it would seem to her that it "fell from Heaven."

Still praying for food, the woman saw the ham and collard greens as they fell to the fireplace. Immediately, she cried out in thanks, "Oh Lord, thank You for answering my prayer!"

The benefactor climbed off the roof and presented himself at the woman's front door. "Your God didn't give you that food," he said, "I dropped it down the chimney."

"Then God must have sent you to drop it. I prayed, and here it is."

How long has it been since God has answered a specific prayer request for you? God desires to meet our needs and show His power by answering our prayers, but so often we forfeit this blessing because we neglect our communication with God. Perhaps your hectic schedule has crowded out your daily prayer time. If so, it's time to make prayer a priority again. Your faith will become stronger and your walk with God closer as you see God answer your personal prayers.

Today's Rooted Principle: Daily ask God for specific requests to experience the blessings of answered prayers.

Humbled to Serve

Circumcised the eighth day, of the stock of Israel, of the tribe of Benjamin, an Hebrew of the Hebrews; as touching the law, a Pharisee; Concerning zeal, persecuting the church; touching the righteousness which is in the law, blameless. But what things were gain to me, those I counted loss for Christ.—**Philippians 3:5–7**

During the Battle of the Wilderness in the Civil War, Union General John Sedgwick was inspecting his troops. At one point he came to a parapet over which he gazed out in the direction of the enemy. His officers suggested that this was unwise and perhaps he ought to duck rather than exposing himself. "Nonsense," snapped the general. "They couldn't hit an elephant at this distance." It was at that moment that a bullet struck Sedgwick in the chest, fatally wounding him.

Pride makes us vulnerable to the devil's attacks. When we become prideful, we have no need for God and no desire to rely on His strength. If we wish to serve God and be used of Him, we must first humble ourselves.

Consider the Apostle Paul. In Philippians 3, he gives a very clear description of his earthly qualifications. He was a Roman citizen and Jewish religious leader. Yet rather than taking pride in his achievements, he counted all of that as loss for Christ's sake.

The name Saul means "to be desired," but he left that name and became Paul, meaning "small or little." Paul realized that worldly status means nothing in light of the opportunity to serve Almighty God. If we're not careful, we can value earthly rank over humbled service. Regardless of your station in life, God doesn't see you in light of your social status.

How humble are you today? Is there a task God could ask you to do that you would consider "beneath" you? Truthfully, your place in society matters little in light of God's kingdom. Humble yourself and remain obedient to even the smallest of God's commands.

Today's Rooted Principle: God values humility and service over social status.

 Deuteronomy 4–6 Mark 11:1–18 93

The Protection of Church

Take heed therefore unto yourselves, and to all the flock, over the which the Holy Ghost hath made you overseers, to feed the church of God, which he hath purchased with his own blood. For I know this, that after my departing shall grievous wolves enter in among you, not sparing the flock.—**Acts 20:28–29**

Francois Fenelon was the court preacher for King Louis XIV of France in the seventeenth century. One Sunday, when the king and his attendants arrived at the chapel for the regular service, no one else was there but the preacher. King Louis demanded, "What does this mean?" Fenelon replied, "I had published that you would not come to church today, in order that Your Majesty might see who serves God in truth and who flatters the king."

Sometimes believers go through the motions of church attendance without realizing the importance of gathering in God's house. Some Christians view the church as a non-essential piece of their lives. Yet God's command to gather at His church is, in part, to protect the believer from the world's attacks.

As Acts says, there are wolves waiting, ready to pull believers away from the Lord into complacency and dangerous doctrine. The church is a vital tool of protection for Christians. Just as the shepherd keeps his sheep in a herd to protect them from predators, so God has designed the church to be a body that provides support and protection for Christians. Making attendance and accountability to the local New Testament church a priority will help to protect you against the devil's attacks.

Church is not just another "thing to do" on the Christian agenda. Church is a vital tool for your own protection! Value the opportunity to listen to God's Word every chance you get and strengthen your armor against attack.

Today's Rooted Principle: The wise believer takes every precaution available to protect against the devil.

Deuteronomy 7–9   Mark 11:19–33

Working Together

Now he that planteth and he that watereth are one: and every man shall receive his own reward according to his own labour.
—1 Corinthians 3:8

When a six foot four inch, muscularly built man tried to light an explosive hidden in his shoe on Flight #63 on its way from Paris to Miami, several passengers and flight attendants took action. A flight attendant noticed the man bent over in his seat trying to light a match. When she saw the fuse leading to his shoe, she screamed before he attacked her. Several other flight attendants came to her aid, and several passengers jumped the man. The flight was re-routed to Boston's airport where the man was arrested before the passengers were safely taken to their destination.

As Christians, we need to utilize everything available to us to see that others can be delivered to their safe destination in Heaven since the enemy is doing everything in his power to stop people from reaching Heaven's shore.

God has set His church as a beacon in this world to guide people to safety. The church functions to spread God's Good News and rescue those trapped in sin. Yet sometimes we become so preoccupied with the minute details of our own ministry and recognition that we fail to accomplish more by working with others.

Does it matter if you get to sing the special as long as God is glorified? Does it matter if you get to sit in your favorite seat as long as a lost person gets to hear of God's hope and as long as lives are being changed?

Focus on the greater good of your work for Christ. Value production over glory. Humbly pitch in to help advance God's kingdom without worrying about receiving credit or praise.

Today's Rooted Principle: God's glory means more than earthly praise or personal recognition.

Wishing Grace on Others

If we live in the Spirit, let us also walk in the Spirit. Let us not be desirous of vain glory, provoking one another, envying one another.
—**Galatians 5:25–26**

One morning two Christian friends ran into each other. One asked the other how he was that morning, to which he received the unexpected reply, "I'm burdened this morning!" But his happy countenance contradicted his words. So the questioner exclaimed in surprise, "Are you really burdened?" "Yes, but it's a wonderful burden— it's an over-abundance of blessings for which I cannot find enough time or words to express my gratitude!"

We have all been liberally laden with God's grace! Grace is a foreign concept to many people in our world. Literally, it means a bestowing of favor on someone who does not deserve it. While people can show grace to others, the most frequent showing of grace is from God to His children.

None of us deserve the good things God has given us. Yet as Psalm 68:19 says, we have continual reason to praise the Lord! "Blessed be the Lord, who daily loadeth us with benefits, even the God of our salvation. Selah." In His love, God has given us salvation. And, on top of that, He blesses us each day through so many provisions that we don't deserve!

Why is it then that we sometimes feel envy or jealousy when another Christian receives a blessing we did not receive? When we see others blessed, it can be easy to wonder why we didn't receive that same favor or grace. As brothers and sisters in Christ, however, we should wish grace on other Christians, rejoicing when God chooses to bless them.

Have you felt some jealousy or resentment at the favor of others? Rejoice with others when they receive blessings and praise God for His grace in their lives and yours.

Today's Rooted Principle: Daily thank God for His many blessings in your life, and rejoice with others at God's grace in their lives.

Deuteronomy 13–15   Mark 12:28–44

God Is the Owner

The earth is the LORD's, and the fulness thereof; the world, and they that dwell therein.—**Psalm 24:1**

In south Florida, a film team was scouting for the perfect location for their movie. They searched the coast for an impressive house with a large front lawn where they could film an exciting car chase scene. After a few hours the film team found the perfect house, and the residents eagerly accepted the opportunity to have their home in a movie. The filming process was going great for a few days until a neighbor called the owner of the house—who lived in New York. The residents of the home were renters, not owners.

Our verse today teaches us that God owns everything. We are the stewards of the resources He has entrusted to our care. God has blessed us with so many resources—time, health, finances, family, even our lives! But we often forget that, as the owner, God holds the rights to these resources, and He has instructed us to steward them for His glory.

George Müller, the faithful evangelist and prayer warrior, said, "Let us walk as stewards and not act as owners, keeping for ourselves the means with which the Lord has entrusted us. He has not blessed us that we may gratify our own carnal mind but for the sake of using our money in His service and to His praise."

Does your use of the resources God has given you reflect wise stewardship? Do you remember that what you have belongs to the Lord? Do you seek His direction in how you use those resources?

Sometimes we simply forget that we are stewards and not owners. We forget that we are accountable to the Lord for how we steward that which He has entrusted to our care. How freeing it is to remember that everything we have belongs to God, and He will give us the wisdom to faithfully use our resources for Him!

Today's Rooted Principle: God is the Owner of everything; our responsibility is to faithfully steward His resources with wisdom.

Deuteronomy 16–18   Mark 13:1–20

Putting It in Perspective

*Yeah doubtless, and I count all things but loss for the excellency of
the knowledge of Christ Jesus my Lord: for whom I have suffered the
loss of all things, and do count them but dung, that I may win Christ.*
—**Philippians 3:8**

David Livingstone was a Scottish missionary and explorer who spent
thirty-three years in the heart of Africa. He endured much suffering
as he labored to spread the Gospel and open the continent to missionaries.
This godly missionary once remarked:

> People talk of the sacrifice I have made in spending so much of my life
> in Africa. Can that be called a sacrifice which is simply acknowledging
> a great debt we owe to our God, which we can never repay?… It is
> emphatically no sacrifice. Rather it is a privilege. Anxiety, sickness,
> suffering, danger, forgoing the common conveniences of this life—
> these may make us pause, and cause the spirit to waver and the soul to
> sink; but let this only be for a moment. All these are nothing compared
> with the glory which shall later be revealed in and through us. I never
> made a sacrifice. Of this we ought not to talk, when we remember the
> great sacrifice which He made who left His Father's throne on high to
> give Himself for us.

The testimony of David Livingstone is a humbling reminder for us
to keep our focus on the sacrifice of Christ. During times of difficulty it
is easy to focus on ourselves, but if we remember the painful death of our
Saviour on the cross, our personal trials fade in comparison.

Perhaps a trial you are facing has caused your focus to turn inward.
Spend time reading about Christ's sacrifice for you, meditate on His love,
and ask Him to help you adjust your focus to the joy in serving Him.

Today's Rooted Principle: Renew your focus by remembering Christ's
love for you and His sacrifice on the cross.

Set Free with Forgiveness

As far as the east is from the west, so far hath he removed our transgressions from us.—**Psalm 103:12**

The story is told of an elderly Christian lady who was asked by a young man if Satan ever troubled her with her past sins. The elderly woman calmly responded, "Yes, he does."

The curious inquirer then asked, "Well, how do you handle it?"

With a small smile on her face the woman replied, "I tell him to go east."

Puzzled, the young man questioned, "What happens when he comes back from the east?"

"I tell him to go west," the elderly woman said with a grin.

"Well what about when he comes from the west?"

"I just keep sending him from the east to the west."

What a comfort to know that God's forgiveness is never-ending. As Christians, we are new creatures living in the old man, therefore, we constantly struggle with our flesh's pull to sin. Although our desire is to live in a way that is pleasing to God, we still battle temptation and sin.

But thankfully, Christ's position is greater than our condition. Hebrews 7:25 reminds us of Christ's position as our Mediator: "Wherefore he is able also to save them to the uttermost that come unto God by him, seeing he ever liveth to make intercession for them." We can experience peace in knowing that no sin is greater than the forgiveness of Christ.

Satan wants to bind us with thoughts of our past sins and failures, but realize today that Jesus Christ set us free from our sin with His own blood on the cross. No past mistake, sinful habit, or wrong choice is too great for God's forgiveness. When you sin, confess your sin to God, trust in His promise to forgive, and experience the freedom in knowing that your sin is gone forever.

Today's Rooted Principle: We can live with confident joy knowing that Christ's forgiveness is greater than our sin.

A Good Friend

Wherefore putting away lying, speak every man truth with his neighbour: for we are members one of another. Be ye angry, and sin not: let not the sun go down upon your wrath:—**Ephesians 4:25–26**

A middle school teacher asked her class to write imaginative definitions of a friend. These were some of the descriptions she received:

"A friend is a pair of open arms in a society of armless people."

"A friend is a mug of hot chocolate on a damp cloudy day."

"A friend is a beautiful orchard in the middle of the desert."

Although our view of friendship may differ slightly from a middle school student's view, all of us know the value of a good friend. Friends are one of God's greatest blessings to us.

Our verses today provide two important instructions for strengthening and maintaining a good, Christian friendship.

First, be truthful. Trust is the necessary foundation for every long-term relationship. This is why dishonesty and deceit—in any form—are so damaging to friendships. Truthfulness and honesty create a solid trust.

And second, be forgiving. Anger has been the destroyer of many friendships. It often begins with a small offense. The anger develops into bitterness, and over time, the bitterness develops into hatred. When we allow bitterness to creep into our lives, it will ruin our relationships. Perhaps that is why Ephesians 4:31 commands, "Let all bitterness, and wrath, and anger, and clamour, and evil speaking, be put away from you, with all malice."

Think for a moment of your relationships. Are you investing into your friendships and seeking to *be* the kind of person you want your friends to be? Are you maintaining trust through honesty, and are you being a quick forgiver? Good Christian friends are a precious gift. Be diligent to invest into these relationships with truthfulness and forgiveness.

Today's Rooted Principle: Demonstrate the value of your friendships by quickly forgiving offenses and by maintaining trust.

The Truth Will Set Them Free

Only let your conversation be as it becometh the gospel of Christ: that whether I come and see you, or else be absent, I may hear of your affairs, that ye stand fast in one spirit, with one mind striving together for the faith of the gospel;—**Philippians 1:27**

As a pastor walked by a department store where he often did business, he felt a prompting of the Holy Spirit to share the Gospel with the owner of the store. He found the owner, a man he knew well, and said, "I've talked beds, carpets, and bookcases with you; but I've never talked my business with you. Would you give me a few minutes to do so?"

The owner led the pastor to his office, and the pastor began to show the man his need to accept Jesus Christ. Tears streamed down the owner's cheeks as he replied, "I'm seventy years of age. I was born in this city, and more than a hundred ministers have known me, as you have, to do business with, but in all these years you are the only man who ever spoke to me about my soul."

People everywhere are searching for truth. Some believe they have discovered it in a false religion that denies Jesus. Others have failed in their search and claim that real truth never existed. Blinded by sin, these people wander aimlessly through life. As Christians, we have the privilege of sharing the truth with others and seeing God work in their lives.

Sharing the truth is simply giving the Gospel to people. We all meet unsaved people every day, but often we neglect to share God's simple plan of salvation with them. Too often our busy schedule, pride, or fear hinders our witness. God will help us overcome these obstacles and give us boldness to share the truth if we will listen and obey Him.

Satan wants to keep people locked in the prison of sin, but we as Christians hold the key—the Gospel of Jesus Christ—which will set them free forever. Let's boldly proclaim the truth to everyone we meet today.

Today's Rooted Principle: You hold the truth that will set others free; look for opportunities to share it today.

Deuteronomy 28–29   Mark 14:54–72

Marks of Growth in Humility

Humble yourselves therefore under the mighty hand of God, that he may exalt you in due time:—**1 Peter 5:6**

Booker T. Washington, the renowned black educator, was an outstanding example of humility. Once, shortly after he became the president of Tuskegee Institute, he was walking through town when a wealthy woman offered him a few dollars to chop her wood. Mr. Washington smiled, rolled up his sleeves, and completed the chore. A young neighbor recognized the famous Booker T. Washington and later told the lady who he was. The following morning, the embarrassed lady found her way to Mr. Washington's office and profusely apologized. "It's perfectly all right, Madam," he replied. "Occasionally I enjoy a little manual labor. Besides, it's always a delight to do something for a friend."

Humility is a vital Christian grace, and its marks are obvious. Notice these five distinctives of a person who is growing in biblical humility:

Seeks guidance in prayer from above: "If any of you lack wisdom, let him ask of God…and it shall be given him" (James 1:5).

Seeks godly counsel: "Where no counsel is, the people fall: but in the multitude of counsellors there is safety" (Proverbs 11:14).

Admits failure: "I acknowledged my sin unto thee, and mine iniquity have I not hid. I said, I will confess my transgressions unto the LORD; and thou forgavest the iniquity of my sin. Selah" (Psalm 32:5).

Defers credit to others: "Let nothing be done through strife or vainglory; but in lowliness of mind let each esteem other better than themselves" (Philippians 2:3).

Gives glory to God: "That, according as it is written, He that glorieth, let him glory in the Lord" (1 Corinthians 1:31).

Do these five marks of humility describe your life? Ask the Lord to help you develop and display humility today.

Today's Rooted Principle: God delights to honor the person who chooses to humble himself.

Deuteronomy 30–31   Mark 15:1–25

Realms of Peace

And let the peace of God rule in your hearts, to the which also ye are called in one body; and be ye thankful.—**Colossians 3:15**

In a Peanuts cartoon, Lucy expressed her frustration to Charlie Brown: "I hate everything. I hate everybody. I hate the whole, wide world!" Surprised, Charlie Brown replied, "But I thought you had inner peace." "I do have inner peace," Lucy retorted. "But I still have outer obnoxiousness!"

We all have people or situations that threaten to upset our peace. Thankfully, a Christian who is walking in fellowship with the Lord can know God's peace on every level. Specifically, Scripture describes three realms of peace.

First, there is **peace with God**. Romans 5:1 teaches that this peace is established at the point of our salvation: "Therefore being justified by faith, we have peace with God through our Lord Jesus Christ." When we trust Christ as our Saviour, we have no need to fear the wrath of God because we are forever justified through Christ.

After our salvation, God desires to give us **inner peace.** Philippians 4:6–7 tell us how this is possible: "Be careful for nothing; but in every thing by prayer and supplication with thanksgiving let your requests be made known unto God. And the peace of God, which passeth all understanding, shall keep your hearts and minds through Christ Jesus." As we bring our needs to the Lord with trust and thankfulness, we will experience His powerful peace.

Finally, God gives us the **ability to live in peace with others.** Romans 12:18 instructs, "If it be possible, as much as lieth in you, live peaceably with all men." God desires that because of His peace in our hearts we would be peaceable—living in harmony and unity with others.

Some Christians know only a fraction of the peace God desires to give them. Are you experiencing God's peace in every realm?

Today's Rooted Principle: Having peace with God makes it possible for us to experience the peace of God and peace with others.

Seek God's Wisdom

If any of you lack wisdom, let him ask of God, that giveth to all men liberally, and upbraideth not; and it shall be given him.—**James 1:5**

When I was in eighth grade, our school visited the governor's mansion in Sacramento. Although I didn't get to meet Governor Ronald Reagan, I left a letter for him with his secretary. She kindly assured me that she would get it to the governor.

I was thrilled a few weeks later when I received a personal reply from Governor Reagan. He thanked me for my letter and said, "I could not bear the responsibility of being governor for even one day if it were not for my abiding faith in God." That statement of humble dependence upon God made such an impression on me, even as an eighth grader. Today, the framed letter sits on display in my office—a reminder to me of the value of humility in leadership.

Everybody is in some position of leadership. Whether you are a parent, a student, a teacher, a coach, an employer, or an employee, there are people who look to your example for guidance. This is a weighty responsibility, and it demands a wisdom greater than you or I possess. Are you providing an example of someone who humbly depends on God for your guidance?

We need to seek God's wisdom in each of the many details of our daily lives. Just as Governor Reagan knew he could not bear his responsibility alone, so we must recognize that we need God's help to live out our responsibilities. Thankfully, God gives us the perfect resource to help us bear our responsibilities—His wisdom. He freely invites us to ask Him for it, and He promises to liberally provide as much as we need!

One of my first prayer requests every day is for God's wisdom. If you have not already done so, take a moment now to ask God for His wisdom for your needs today.

Today's Rooted Principle: God's wisdom is the equipping resource for our responsibilities.

Joshua 1–3 Mark 16

A Manifest of Love

In this was manifested the love of God toward us, because that God sent his only begotten Son into the world, that we might live through him.... Beloved, if God so loved us, we ought also to love one another.
—1 John 4:9, 11

If you were to go on a cruise you would most likely see the crew members loading up the luggage and various things onto the ship before departure. Each of these items would be listed on a *manifest*—a document that would be checked meticulously to ensure that nothing was left behind. The *manifest* is a record—a written proof of the items on board.

God's manifest of love is Christ's death on Calvary. This visible action proves that His love is real and offered to all. Think about the magnitude of God's sacrifice for a moment. Jesus came into this world not to make God's love possible, but to make it visible. He displayed His love in such a way that no one could ever question its validity.

As Christians, we are called to love as God loves. Merely saying we love others is not enough; we must display this love in the same sacrificial manner that Christ displayed His love. Were it not for God's love within us, this would be an impossible responsibility.

Take a moment to ask yourself how you can make a conscious effort to manifest your love towards others in a sacrificial way. What personal comfort could you forgo in an effort to love someone in a Christlike manner?

Even as God manifested His love toward us, He commands us to love one another. What do your loved ones see when they look at the manifest of your love towards them? Are there visible accounts, or is the manifest empty? Ask the Lord to show you specific ways to display His love today!

Today's Rooted Principle: God manifested His love visibly, and He calls us to likewise visibly demonstrate love.

Because God Is Love

Beloved, let us love one another: for love is of God; and every one that loveth is born of God, and knoweth God. He that loveth not knoweth not God; for God is love.—**1 John 4:7–8**

A lady in Spain made the news when she chose a unique way to test her husband's love. With the help of a friend, she manipulated her own kidnapping and sent a ransom notice to her husband. When the police discovered the kidnapping was a hoax, they asked the lady why she did it. "I wanted to find out what my husband would do for me," she replied.

People in our world are desperate to know if they are truly loved, and they are often skeptical of the possibility of real love. Human love apart from God is only a cheap imitation—a selfish emotion that seeks personal gratification.

Our verses today tell us that God *is* love. His very nature is love, and His sacrifice for us on the cross defines the extent of real love. If our Creator's nature was not the very essence of love, there would be none in us. No mercy, grace, compassion, or kindness exists apart from Him.

As Christians, God commands us to love one another. Because He is love, and because He has given us His nature, He instructs us to display His love to others.

We must remember, however, that apart from God, we cannot love others with the pure love that Christ gave to us. Loving others is not something that we work hard to muster up. Love is a fruit that God produces in us. Galatians 5:22 reminds us, "But the fruit of the Spirit is love...." If we desire to consistently demonstrate God's love to others, we must abide in Christ and allow His love to freely flow through us.

Does your life reveal the true love of Christ? Can others see the attribute of God's nature in you? Take a moment now to ask the Lord how you can express His love to someone today.

Today's Rooted Principle: Because God is love, He gives us the capacity and ability to demonstrate His love to others.

What Must I Do to Be Saved?

And he took them the same hour of the night, and washed their stripes; and was baptized, he and all his, straightway. And when he had brought them into his house, he set meat before them, and rejoiced, believing in God with all his house.—**Acts 16:33–34**

P aul and Silas were faithfully following God. They hadn't strayed from God's calling like Jonah. They hadn't modified God's plans like Saul. They were preaching God's Word when they were thrown into prison. From a human standpoint, Paul and Silas had every right to be upset, to question God, and to wonder why. Yet these men spent their time in prison honoring God. In the midst of pain, confusion, uncertainty, and injustice, they praised God. As a result of their testimony, the Philippian jailer and his entire household came to know Christ.

Had Paul and Silas focused on their own problems they would not have experienced the blessing of seeing this man saved. Had they not been singing and praising God, they would have missed out on the miracle of salvation.

When we're wronged it's easy to focus on the circumstance and ask, "Why?" Human nature wants us to fight back, to figure a way out, and to seek revenge. But God calls us to trust Him with the problem and continue serving Him. We have the choice of either becoming upset and bitter during injustice or trusting God and seeing His ultimate plan.

When you experience injustice, realize that God has a greater purpose in your hurt. He wants to work through you to show His goodness to those around you. People notice when you respond to hate with kindness. God wants to use you.

How will you react to injustice? Like Paul and Silas, sing God's praises and continue serving Him.

Today's Rooted Principle: God is able to turn injustice into immense blessing; praise Him through the pain.

The Saving Blood

*Neither by the blood of goats and calves, but by his own blood he entered
in once into the holy place, having obtained eternal redemption for us.
For if the blood of bulls and of goats, and the ashes of an heifer sprinkling
the unclean, sanctifieth to the purifying of the flesh: How much more
shall the blood of Christ, who through the eternal Spirit offered himself
without spot to God, purge your conscience from dead works to serve the
living God?*—**Hebrews 9:12–14**

When evangelist D.L. Moody preached on salvation, which was
often, he focused on the power of the blood of Jesus to save. In one
sermon he said, "Look at that Roman soldier as he pushed his spear into
the very heart of the God-man. What a hellish deed! But what was the
next thing that took place? Blood covered the spear! Oh! Thank God, the
blood covers every sin."

The blood of Jesus Christ is our only hope for salvation and the
payment for all of our sins. No one can stand before a holy God unless
he is holy—and we are far from holy. None of our efforts can even come
close to achieving the perfection God demands. Apart from the grace
that sent Jesus to the cross, we have absolutely no hope. Yet God has given
us that grace, and we can rest in the salvation that has been purchased
and given to us.

God says, "Their sins and iniquities will I remember no more"
(Hebrews 10:17). Often Satan uses the sins of the past to keep us in
bondage. But while there may be consequences because of the past, the
sins are gone—taken away by the blood of Jesus. You can stand in the
very presence of God as His confident child because of this great gift of
His grace.

Today's Rooted Principle: Give thanks today to God for the great
salvation He has freely given you through the blood of Jesus Christ.

Joshua 13–15   Luke 1:57–80

Who Owns You?

What? know ye not that your body is the temple of the Holy Ghost which is in you, which ye have of God, and ye are not your own? For ye are bought with a price: therefore glorify God in your body, and in your spirit, which are God's.—**1 Corinthians 6:19–20**

Elizabeth Keckley was a slave in Missouri before the Civil War. Her greatest desire was to purchase freedom for herself and her son. Her owner agreed that if she could raise $1,200 she could gain her freedom. Keckley worked as a seamstress and came up with a plan to go to New York City and work there to raise the money, but her owner feared that she would not return.

Instead, some of her wealthy clients in St. Louis contributed the money she needed, and Elizabeth Keckley paid the price for her freedom as well as her son's. She moved to Washington, DC, where she counted Mary Lincoln among her dressmaking clients. Without the help of someone else, Keckley would never have been able to purchase her freedom.

All of us were enslaved to sin with no hope of ever gaining freedom. In mercy and compassion, Jesus gave His life for us, purchasing our salvation by shedding His blood on the cross. We are now free from sin, but that freedom does not mean that we do whatever we want. Instead, we are to live how Jesus wants us to live.

In Romans 1:1, Paul called himself "a servant of Jesus Christ." The word he used is the word for a bond slave—someone who has voluntarily committed his life to an owner. God is our owner not only because He created us, but because of the price He paid for our redemption. His sacrifice compels us to live for Him.

Today's Rooted Principle: The price Jesus paid for our freedom motivates us to a life of service for Him.

What Is It Going to Take?

And when he came to himself, he said, How many hired servants of my father's have bread enough and to spare, and I perish with hunger! I will arise and go to my father, and will say unto him, Father, I have sinned against heaven, and before thee.—**Luke 15:17–18**

The story of the Prodigal Son is one of the most well-known parables Jesus told. A selfish young man took all that he could get and wasted it on his own selfish and sinful pleasures. It was only after the money ran out and all of his so-called friends had vanished, that he began to realize how much trouble he was in. Because pigs were unclean animals for the Jews, the fact that he took the job of feeding them (and then coveted their food) was evidence that he had pretty much reached the bottom of the barrel.

Over the years, I have counseled with many people who weren't willing to come back to God until a major catastrophe happened—a spouse walked out on the marriage, the bank foreclosed on the house, a child went into deep sin. They knew they weren't doing what they should have been doing, but the allure of sin kept them from turning back to God.

Samuel Johnson said, "Depend upon it, sir, when a man knows he is to be hanged in a fortnight, it concentrates his mind wonderfully." It shouldn't take something major to get us to turn back to God. If we insist on continuing to go our own way, we may end up in a pigpen somewhere; but it is far better for us to make the decision to return to God a long time before we sink that low.

Like the father in the parable, God is waiting with open arms for your return. He will not scold or berate you; instead, He will rejoice that you have returned and welcome you back into a close relationship with Him.

Today's Rooted Principle: Don't wait for a pigpen experience; return to the Father now.

Good Intentions

*Say not ye, There are yet four months, and then cometh harvest? behold,
I say unto you, Lift up your eyes, and look on the fields; for they are
white already to harvest.*—**John 4:35**

If Christians did all the good things they think and talk about doing, the
church would be a much fuller place this Sunday. The offering plates
would be overflowing, the choir would need additional seats, and there
would be people waiting in line for an opportunity to teach or minister
in some other way. But though we talk about what we would and should
do, often we never go beyond the words to the action.

The poet John Greenleaf Whittier wrote, "For of all sad words of
tongue or pen, the saddest are these: 'It might have been!'" Many times
we know what we should do, but we never actually do it. So often we are
left with regrets for not having acted. James wrote, "Therefore to him that
knoweth to do good, and doeth it not, to him it is sin" (James 4:17).

The harvest is ready today. Speak to someone with whom you work,
a friend or a neighbor, and encourage that person to trust Christ today.
Call or write someone you know who is discouraged or struggling with a
difficulty, and give them a word of hope. Give a little extra when you have
an opportunity. These simple steps can make an enormous difference.

So often we forget that people may need only a small encouragement
to keep from quitting. We focus on what we need or want from others,
rather than on what we can do for others. Jesus calls us to look around
and see the need—and then take steps to meet that need. It is always
God's plan for us to do good to others.

Today's Rooted Principle: Do what you know is right today, and you
will not live with the regret of unfilled good intentions.

God Meets Us Where We Are

...Be not deceived: neither fornicators, nor idolaters, nor adulterers, nor effeminate, nor abusers of themselves with mankind, Nor thieves, nor covetous, nor drunkards, nor revilers, nor extortioners, shall inherit the kingdom of God. And such were some of you: but ye are washed, but ye are sanctified, but ye are justified in the name of the Lord Jesus, and by the Spirit of our God.—**1 Corinthians 6:9–11**

James Taylor loved to go wherever John Wesley was preaching—not to listen, but to throw stones and mock those who did listen. However, on the day before Taylor's wedding, Wesley preached on Joshua 24:15, "...as for me and my house, we will serve the LORD." Taylor came under intense conviction and was saved. This man who once was a chief scoffer became a believer who led his family in the paths of righteousness. His grandson, James Hudson Taylor, became one of the greatest missionaries in history.

No matter what you have done in the past, when God forgives you, your slate is wiped clean. The Lord does not wait for us to "clean up our act." Instead, He meets us right where we are and then begins the process of change. That is what His grace does. God knew all about us before He saved us. He knew all the things we had done and failed to do. But all of our past sins, no matter how vile, are covered under the blood.

Satan comes to us to remind us of the past. Revelation 12:10 calls him "the accuser of our brethren." He loves to point out sins from our past to keep us from serving God as we should. If you are bound by guilt today, remember that you have been washed in the blood; and, in the eyes of God, you stand innocent before Him. Do not allow who you were to keep you from being who you are meant to be.

Today's Rooted Principle: We may be shaped by our past, but we do not have to be bound by it.

Having More and Enjoying Less

They soon forgat his works; they waited not for his counsel: But lusted exceedingly in the wilderness, and tempted God in the desert. And he gave them their request; but sent leanness into their soul.
—Psalm 106:13–15

In his day, John D. Rockefeller was the richest man alive. He amassed his fortune in the late 1800s with the Standard Oil Company. His wealth was so vast that it is still being given away today—many, many years after his death. To have a comparable amount of money in today's economy, Bill Gates would need to multiply his net worth more than four times!

But even with all his wealth, Rockefeller never enjoyed many luxuries and conveniences that we take for granted—things like air conditioning, television and the internet. Studies consistently show that, even though we have more than any past generation, we are enjoying it less and less. Depression, disappointment, and a lack of fulfillment are reported as rising in survey after survey.

Why is that? Why do we find it so hard to be content? In part, it is because of our fallen nature; but it is also important that we recognize the multiplied billions of dollars being spent on advertising designed to create discontent. If we allow the messages that are constantly bombarding us to affect our thinking, we can easily fall into the trap of thinking that if we just had a little bit more, we would then be happy.

Though John D. Rockefeller was controversial in his business practices, he was faithful to tithe from his first paycheck as a teen all the way through the end of his life. As an old man looking back over the course of his life, he wrote, "I dropped the worry on the way, and God was good to me every day." Rockefeller was not content because of his wealth; he was content because of his heart.

Today's Rooted Principle: If you are not content with what you have today, you will not be content with more tomorrow.

Judges 4–6   Luke 4:31–44   113

Are You Really Happy?

Happy is that people, that is in such a case: yea, happy is that people, whose God is the LORD.—**Psalm 144:15**

A man walked up to me some time ago and said, "I want to ask you something. You're a Christian, aren't you?" I said, "Yes, I am." He asked, "Are you really happy? Does it really make a difference?" The truth is that being a Christian can make a difference, but it doesn't always. Some people look at Christianity almost like a magic pill—a simple solution for every problem. Yet the Bible clearly tells us that God's children will have trouble. Jesus said, "…In the world ye shall have tribulation…" (John 16:33).

If we are going to be happy and abounding with joy in a world filled with confusion and trouble, our hearts must be fixed on something that is unchanging. In John 16:33, Jesus also said, "…be of good cheer; I have overcome the world." We have a choice to make—we can believe what Jesus said, or we can doubt it. Your happiness today is determined more by your belief than by your circumstances.

Because God never changes, He can serve as a source of happiness no matter what is happening to us. He will never lack the resources to meet our needs. He will never lack the love to give us what is best for us. He will never lack the power to overcome the obstacles we face. Our circumstances may change frequently—God never does.

We live in a society where it often seems that everything is changing. Companies that were once giants of industry crumble into dust. The notion of working at one job for a lifetime seems almost quaint today. Americans move from place to place and town to town. In such a rootless world, we need something on which we can firmly rely; and there is nothing more certain than the promises of God.

Today's Rooted Principle: Lasting happiness comes as we remain fixed on the lasting promises of God.

What's Coming Next?

And Jesus answered and said unto them, Take heed that no man deceive you. For many shall come in my name, saying, I am Christ; and shall deceive many. And ye shall hear of wars and rumours of wars: see that ye be not troubled: for all these things must come to pass, but the end is not yet.—**Matthew 24:4–6**

In 1950, Fortune magazine interviewed some of the most successful businessmen in America about their expectations for the future. David Sarnoff, who was the head of Radio Corporation of America, was asked what things would be like in America in 1980. Sarnoff responded, "By 1980 trains and ships will refuel themselves. Homes will have atomic generators, and the mail will be transported by guided missiles." Sarnoff was no fool. He and his family came to America with nothing, and he rose to control one of the largest companies in the world. Yet he didn't really understand what would happen in the future.

We live in a day when there is great interest about the future. People are looking for someone who can explain what's coming next. Sadly, they are finding a lot of misleading answers. There is so much confusion and false doctrine regarding prophecy. False teachers attempt to set dates and predict Christ's Second Coming. False religions twist the events prophesied in Scripture to support their own claims.

When the disciples asked Jesus when He would return, He answered, "It is not for you to know the times or the seasons, which the Father hath put in his own power" (Acts 1:7). Instead, He instructed them to go and be witnesses to the world while they watched for His return. God's plan for you today is not for you to focus on every detail or question regarding the end times, but for you to be sharing the Gospel with others.

Today's Rooted Principle: The future does not trouble those whose eyes are focused on the return of Jesus Christ.

Does Anyone Care?

*I looked on my right hand, and beheld, but there was no man that would
know me: refuge failed me; no man cared for my soul. I cried unto thee,
O LORD: I said, Thou art my refuge and my portion in the land of the
living. Attend unto my cry; for I am brought very low: deliver me from
my persecutors; for they are stronger than I.—***Psalm 142:4–6**

D avid knew all too well the pain that we sometimes experience when
we feel all alone. Despite all that he had done for his nation, when
Saul was pursuing him in a jealous rage, David's former friends and
supporters deserted him. His was no small difficulty, for David's very life
was in danger. He was brought to the point of desperation and found no
one to help.

Charles Spurgeon wrote of this time in David's life, "He did not
miss a friend for want of looking for him, nor for want of looking in a
likely place. Surely some helper would be found in the place of honour;
someone would stand at his right hand to undertake his defense. He
looked steadily, and saw all that could be seen, for he 'beheld'; but his
anxious gaze was not met by an answering smile."

The good news is that even when others fail you, Jesus never does.
On his darkest day, David could still cry out to the Lord for strength and
encouragement. It's a blessing to have friends standing by you in a difficult
situation; but even if you don't, you are not truly alone. Hebrews 13:5 tells
us, "…he hath said, I will never leave thee, nor forsake thee."

Though we cannot see Christ physically, He is still very near when we
are in distress. Moses knew this truth. The Scriptures tell us that during
the difficulties and challenges of his life, "he endured, as seeing him who
is invisible" (Hebrews 11:27). The Lord does care about your situation
today, and He will support and encourage you in it.

Today's Rooted Principle: Even if all others forsake you, Jesus never will.

APRIL

God Hears Your Prayers

They shall not labour in vain, nor bring forth for trouble; for they are the seed of the blessed of the LORD, and their offspring with them. And it shall come to pass, that before they call, I will answer; and while they are yet speaking, I will hear.—**Isaiah 65:23–24**

As a young pastor, I was planning to attend a pastor's conference. As my wife and I sat down before I was to leave, we realized we didn't have enough money for me to go on the trip and for her to have the things she would need for the family while I was gone. I remember saying to her, "Honey, let's pray about it." We knelt down to pray, and while we were praying the phone rang.

A dear friend said, "I had been meaning to do something for you, but I had forgotten about it. God has laid it on my heart that I need to give you some money." I said, "Thank you. That's wonderful." He said, "No, you don't understand. I am supposed to come over and give it to you right now!" He came to the house and gave me some money—and he gave my wife some money, too. God wonderfully provided even while we were praying.

Prayer is not just something for famous Christians of the past and well-known pastors; it is a vital resource for every believer. Prayer is the means by which God meets your needs and empowers your life. The great hymn writer William Cowper said it well: "Satan trembles when he sees the weakest saint upon his knees."

Many times we tell everyone except God what our problems are. There is a time to seek help and counsel from others, but there is no substitute for entering the throne room of Heaven and speaking to the God who hears and answers when we cry out to Him.

Today's Rooted Principle: Before sharing your needs with others, take them to the Lord in prayer.

Judges 13–15 Luke 6:27–49

Making Your Marriage Better

Wives, submit yourselves unto your own husbands, as unto the Lord. Husbands, love your wives, even as Christ also loved the church, and gave himself for it; Nevertheless let every one of you in particular so love his wife even as himself; and the wife see that she reverence her husband.—**Ephesians 5:22, 25, 33**

I'll never forget the first time I counseled a couple about their marriage. I had all my notes from college, and I thought I was ready to help. After a little initial conversation, I asked what the problem was. She said, "I hate him!" He said, "I hate her!" That wasn't really in my notes. So I went on to the next question: how long has this problem been going on. In unison they replied, "Ten years." Ten years was also how long they had been married.

I learned that theirs had been an arranged marriage which their parents negotiated, but neither one thought it was a good idea. I prayed for wisdom and spent a lot of time talking with them. They both received Christ as Saviour that day, and today they're still married. As a pastor, I regularly counsel couples that are struggling in their relationship. The world is attacking marriage today like never before, and that means we need to work to intentionally protect and build our relationships.

The notion that when a marriage has problems it means you should just give up and look for greener pastures is a deception from Satan. Yet millions are following that advice, and it is taking a devastating toll on our culture and our young people. God intended for marriage to last for life, but He did not promise that it would do so without our efforts. If we follow the instruction of Scripture for how we are to treat our spouse— rather than hoping or expecting the other person to take the first step— we will find our marriages strengthened and happier.

Today's Rooted Principle: Take the responsibility today to invest in your marriage to make it stronger.

The Principle of Accountability

So then every one of us shall give account of himself to God. Let us not therefore judge one another any more: but judge this rather, that no man put a stumblingblock or an occasion to fall in his brother's way.
—**Romans 14:12–13**

We live in a society that has raised avoiding responsibility to an art form. It seems like everything that happens is someone else's fault. The criminal had a bad family background; the unemployed had a bad education; the addicted have a disease. The problem with this approach is that there can be no change for the better until we first allow ourselves to be held accountable for what we have done.

There is an old story about a Roman senator traveling across the Mediterranean Sea on a galley rowed by convicted criminals. He went from one man to the next asking why they were there. Each one protested his innocence, saying that he had been wrongfully accused or convicted. Finally, he came to one man who admitted that he was responsible for the wrong he had done. The senator called the captain of the ship and said, "Release this man at once. It would be unfair for all of these innocent men to have such a criminal in their midst!"

The Apostle Paul was continually aware of the fact that one day he would render an account to God for what he had done. Under the inspiration of the Holy Spirit, he frequently refers to this day of judgment in his epistles. Knowing that one day we will stand before the Lord Jesus to have our works for Him evaluated is a powerful encouragement for us to do what we should. Even if no one else in your workplace, your home, your neighborhood, or your nation is willing to be accountable, accept the responsibility that is yours; you will find blessing as a result.

Today's Rooted Principle: Remembering our accountability motivates us to a life of faithfulness.

The Basis of Acceptance

According as he hath chosen us in him before the foundation of the world, that we should be holy and without blame before him in love: Having predestinated us unto the adoption of children by Jesus Christ to himself, according to the good pleasure of his will, To the praise of the glory of his grace, wherein he hath made us accepted in the beloved.
—Ephesians 1:4–6

Much of the acceptance people receive today is based on what they do rather than who they are. If the acceptance you receive has that basis, you will never know real security in a relationship. God does not love us because of our good works or our avoidance of bad works. He loves us because of who He is, and He accepts us because of His grace and the sacrifice of His Son.

Knowing and believing that we are acceptable to God can also help us change the way we look at others. Rather than demanding that they measure up to our expectations and standards, we can grant them grace and accept them just as God accepts us.

God offers us complete acceptance. When we understand that truth and live in it, it provides great comfort and hope. In the same way, offering your spouse, your children, or your friends that kind of acceptance provides the foundation for wonderful and strong relationships. Take a moment to evaluate how you interact with others. Do you demand that people "jump through hoops" to make you happy? Do you remember every failure and bring it up over and over again? Do you hold past offenses over people's heads? If so, resolve to make a change—begin showing grace and true acceptance. It will transform your life and your relationships.

Today's Rooted Principle: Accept others the same way God accepts you, and your relationships will grow stronger.

Your "Want To"

And it came to pass, that, as they went in the way, a certain man said unto him, Lord, I will follow thee whithersoever thou goest. And Jesus said unto him, Foxes have holes, and birds of the air have nests; but the Son of man hath not where to lay his head.—**Luke 9:57–58**

I remember talking to a man who didn't like what we were doing at Lancaster Baptist Church. "You just do everything the Bible says to do," he accused. I told him, "I love the Author of the Book, and I want to do what He says." Although I don't always succeed at that effort, it is my goal to do what God wants me to do.

The reason for that "want to" is that I love Christ and desire to follow Him. It is not that the Bible is a list of rules for me to keep. There are commands of God which carry blessings for obedience and punishments for disobedience; but the Christian life is far more than just that. Walking with God in a close personal relationship through prayer and spending time in His Word creates a desire in our hearts to follow what He has said to do.

Someone once said, "Rules without relationships bring rebellion; rules with relationships bring response." The closer I am to Jesus, the more likely I am to want to do what He wants me to do. Remember, before Peter three times denied the Lord, he was first following Him "afar off" (Matthew 26:58).

The more time we spend with Jesus, the more like Him we become. Acts 4:13 says, "Now when they saw the boldness of Peter and John, and perceived that they were unlearned and ignorant men, they marvelled; and they took knowledge of them, that they had been with Jesus." The more like Jesus we become, the stronger our desire to please the Father becomes, and the more we desire do right.

Today's Rooted Principle: If your "want to" concerning following Christ's commands is weak, check the strength of your walk with Jesus Christ.

Failure Is Not Final

But the God of all grace, who hath called us unto his eternal glory by Christ Jesus, after that ye have suffered a while, make you perfect, stablish, strengthen, settle you. To him be glory and dominion for ever and ever. Amen.—**1 Peter 5:10–11**

All of us have days when it seems like nothing is working right. We may feel like complete failures at life, at church, or at home. I talked to a pastor some time ago who said, "I feel as though I am failing in the ministry." I replied, "You are not a failure. You are going through a time of testing that God means for your growth to prepare you for the future." Sometimes we feel that we have failed when we really haven't; other times we do fail. All of us fall short in some areas, but that isn't the whole story.

I remember well a saying I have heard many times: "Failure isn't final." If you are a Christian, there is always hope. Romans 8:28 says "all things" work together by God for His purpose. "All things" includes more than just our successes and victories. You may be wondering how the pieces can ever be put back together, but God has the wisdom and power to bring things back together in an amazing way.

Peter knew a lot about failure. He fished all night and caught nothing. He sank when he tried to walk on the water. He denied Christ even though he vowed he never would. He gave up and went back to fishing even after he saw the resurrected Lord. Yet Peter also knew a lot about success. He preached on the day of Pentecost and saw three thousand people saved. He healed the sick and raised the dead. He was inspired by the Spirit of God to write two powerful books of the New Testament.

If you allow God to continue working in your life, He can turn your failures into His successes.

Today's Rooted Principle: Failure is never final as long as God's grace is at work in your life.

God's Working in Hearts

And a certain woman named Lydia, a seller of purple, of the city of Thyatira, which worshipped God, heard us: whose heart the Lord opened, that she attended unto the things which were spoken of Paul.—**Acts 16:14**

Lydia worked hard as a businesswoman who ran a textile company. She was a "seller of purple," which refers to the dye extracted from the Murex sea shell and used in dying clothing and materials. She had a busy life, yet the Lord had been working in her heart. Lydia did not know the Lord, but she had an open heart and was seeking for peace and meaning in life.

As Paul preached in the region of Macedonia, Lydia listened to his preaching and her heart was opened by the Lord. The word "heard" in Acts 16:14 is a past imperfect tense verb, which indicates that Lydia had probably heard the Gospel message more than once. God had been working in her heart for a while before she heard Paul's message and responded to God's leading.

People are at different points of spiritual maturity. Some have hard hearts toward God's message while others are curious like Lydia. God calls us all to minister to other people and spread His Gospel. But it is He alone who works in hearts to affect change.

As often as we go soulwinning or as passionate as we are to see souls saved, only God can change hearts and bring people to salvation. I'm sure many people heard Paul's message in Macedonia and rejected it, yet God had worked in Lydia's heart so that she accepted His truth.

Being faithful without seeing immediate results can become discouraging, but God promises that as you follow Him, He will bless your faithfulness. Rather than becoming discouraged, pray that God will work in the hearts of those around you. Be faithful to share the Gospel, and trust God to convict hearts of His truth.

Today's Rooted Principle: God alone can save, but those faithful to His leading can share in the joy of seeing others saved.

Especially Peter

And entering into the sepulchre, they saw a young man sitting on the right side, clothed in a long white garment; and they were affrighted. And he saith unto them, Be not affrighted: Ye seek Jesus of Nazareth, which was crucified: he is risen; he is not here: behold the place where they laid him. But go your way, tell his disciples and Peter that he goeth before you into Galilee: there shall ye see him, as he said unto you.
—**Mark 16:5–7**

The last thing Peter did before Jesus died was to deny Christ. Though Peter vehemently protested when Jesus told him it would happen, when the pressure was on, Peter folded. He caved in to his fears and repeatedly lied, even cursing to add emphasis to his denial of Christ. I think if most people knew only that part of the story they would think Peter's case was hopeless—there was no chance someone who had failed like that could ever do anything for God.

Yet after the resurrection, when the angel brought the good news that Jesus was alive, he had a very special message. "Tell his disciples and Peter," the angel instructed Mary and the other women who had come to the tomb. What a wonderful blessing and encouragement those words must have been to the distressed disciple! He had wept bitterly over his denial, and now Peter heard that he was still included in Jesus' plans. Jesus especially mentioned his name.

It would be nice if we were perfect and always did what we should, but we don't. That means that each of us needs to experience the forgiveness and mercy of God—and He makes it available to us freely. Isaiah 55:7 says, "Let the wicked forsake his way, and the unrighteous man his thoughts: and let him return unto the LORD, and he will have mercy upon him; and to our God, for he will abundantly pardon."

Today's Rooted Principle: Rest in God's forgiveness and His love today. He knows your name and will never forsake you.

Keep the Faith

Beloved, when I gave all diligence to write unto you of the common salvation, it was needful for me to write unto you, and exhort you that ye should earnestly contend for the faith which was once delivered unto the saints. For there are certain men crept in unawares, who were before of old ordained to this condemnation, ungodly men, turning the grace of our God into lasciviousness, and denying the only Lord God, and our Lord Jesus Christ.—**Jude 3–4**

In 1944, a twenty-two-year-old Japanese soldier named Hiroo Onoda was sent to the island of Lubanga in the Philippines. His orders were to do as much damage as he could to prevent the Americans from retaking the island. Along with a small group of fellow soldiers, Onoda did his best to carry out his orders. When the Americans did capture the island in 1945, Onoda took to the hills.

Despite leaflets being dropped by both the Americans and the Japanese after the war ended, Onoda believed the war was still going on. In 1952, photos from his family and letters urging him to give up were sent, but Onoda refused. Finally in 1974, nearly thirty years after his commission, the Japanese government sent Major Taniguchi, Onoda's former commanding officer, to order him to lay down his weapons and come home.

God has called us to be soldiers for His Kingdom in hostile territory. The Christian life is not a pleasure cruise; it is warfare. To succeed and be good soldiers for the Lord, we must keep the faith, never laying down our weapons. We must never compromise our principles. We must never let down our guard. The enemy will use every means at his disposal to convince us to surrender—but when we resist him in the power of the Lord, he cannot overcome us. In fact, the Bible says that when we resist him, he flees (James 4:7)!

Today's Rooted Principle: Committed soldiers resist the temptation to lay down their weapons while they earnestly contend for the faith.

Purpose for Living

For I am now ready to be offered, and the time of my departure is at hand. I have fought a good fight, I have finished my course, I have kept the faith: Henceforth there is laid up for me a crown of righteousness, which the Lord, the righteous judge, shall give me at that day: and not to me only, but unto all them also that love his appearing.
—**2 Timothy 4:6–8**

The famous and very successful football coach Bear Bryant often told reporters, "I'd croak in a month if I quit coaching." After twenty-five years as the head coach at his alma mater, Bryant announced he would be stepping down at the end of the season. On December 29, 1982, he coached his Alabama football team for the last time in the Liberty Bowl against Illinois. On January 26, 1983, he died of a massive heart attack.

Every one of us needs a reason to live—a compelling cause and purpose that keeps us going when we would rather quit. The truth is that we all face obstacles that hinder us and make life difficult. Some people allow those obstacles to stop them. Others overcome. The difference is not in the obstacles, but in the determination and drive of the person who faces the obstacles.

The passion and purpose of every believer should be to glorify God and bring others to Him. If that is our purpose, then nothing will stop us from continuing on the right course. When Paul faced the threat of imprisonment or even death for preaching, he said, "…none of these things move me, neither count I my life dear unto myself…" (Acts 20:24). His purpose for life was so compelling that it drove him to overcome and finish the course which God had laid out for Him. May that be true of each of us.

Today's Rooted Principle: Overcome life's obstacles by focusing on God's purpose and calling for your Christian life.

1 Samuel 15–16   Luke 10:25–42   127

The Consequences Follow

Let no man say when he is tempted, I am tempted of God: for God cannot be tempted with evil, neither tempteth he any man: But every man is tempted, when he is drawn away of his own lust, and enticed. Then when lust hath conceived, it bringeth forth sin: and sin, when it is finished, bringeth forth death.—**James 1:13–15**

It's one of the most successful and longest running series of commercials on television. The ads promise a fun and happy experience in "Sin City" (Las Vegas) and then sell the false notion that there are no consequences. "What happens in Vegas stays in Vegas," they say. But, in reality, the consequences of sin always follow us.

Think of the story of Achan in Joshua 7. God commanded the Israelites that all the spoils from the city of Jericho were to be sacred and holy unto Him. They were to take nothing for themselves. There would be more than enough spoils of war for the Israelites from among the other cities over which God would give them victory. Yet Achan was tempted by the gold and silver and clothing he saw.

Disobeying God, Achan took those for himself and hid them in his tent. No doubt he thought that, after another battle or two, he could bring them out and no one would ever know the difference. But God knew what Achan had done, and the results of Achan's sin stretched far beyond what he had considered. In the battle at Ai, many Israelite soldiers were killed because God's protection had been withdrawn. When the sin was discovered, Achan, his wife and their children were all stoned to death.

I'm sure Achan would never have chosen those results for just a little money and some nice clothes, but we don't control the consequences of our sins. When you are tempted to sin, remember that sin always finds us out. Rather than enjoying the short pleasure of sin, choose the victory available through Christ.

Today's Rooted Principle: The only way to escape the consequences of sin is to overcome the temptation to sin.

Victory in Jesus

For I delight in the law of God after the inward man: But I see another law in my members, warring against the law of my mind, and bringing me into captivity to the law of sin which is in my members. O wretched man that I am! who shall deliver me from the body of this death? I thank God through Jesus Christ our Lord...—**Romans 7:22–25**

Eugene Bartlett was a prolific hymn writer. Of the several hundred hymns he composed, the last is his best known. Late in his life he suffered a stroke, which left him mostly paralyzed and unable to speak. Though his health was broken, his spirit was not. He laboriously scribbled out a few words at a time until he had completed the words and music for the final song of his long career. We still sing this song of triumph today—"Victory in Jesus."

Temptation comes to every Christian, but Jesus proved that we can know victory over temptation. Jesus was faced with temptation during His life. The Bible tells us in Matthew 4:1 that the Spirit of God led Him into the wilderness to be tempted. This was an intentional part of God's plan, both to demonstrate the power of His Son over Satan as well as to provide us with a pattern for overcoming temptation. Jesus responded to each temptation with the Scriptures. This is our pattern—to use the Word of God to overcome the evil one.

As children of God, we go through difficulties and struggles. We face temptation, and we sometimes give in to it and sin. Yet Scripture promises us that we are victors through Christ. We can rest in complete confidence in the power of God that has triumphed over the enemy. Like Jesus did, we can memorize and meditate on the Bible to have the strength to overcome any temptation.

Today's Rooted Principle: God has already given us the victory over sin and the world through His Son.

Questioning Truth

Now the serpent was more subtil than any beast of the field which the LORD God had made. And he said unto the woman, Yea, hath God said, Ye shall not eat of every tree of the garden?...And the serpent said unto the woman, Ye shall not surely die: For God doth know that in the day ye eat thereof, then your eyes shall be opened, and ye shall be as gods, knowing good and evil.—**Genesis 3:1, 4–5**

A man who was taking flying lessons related this story: "[My instructor] was flying the aircraft and he had it banked to the left. He then told me to close my eyes and to focus on my physical feelings….Then he said this, 'I want you concentrate on those feelings and tell me when you feel the plane is no longer turning but is now flying straight and level.'

"With my eyes still closed, I concentrated and, sure enough, I could feel the plane level out. My instructor told me to open my eyes and, to my complete surprise, we were still banked to the left but even more so! What was he trying to teach me? Always trust your instruments, not your feelings."

One of the tactics that Satan uses to lead people astray is to encourage them to question the truth of the Word of God. His plan is simple: if your faith in the Bible weakens, you are far more vulnerable to temptation. He tells us to rely on our feelings of truth rather than trusting in God's declared truth.

We may not understand everything in the Scriptures, but we can fully and completely rely on the inerrant, unfailing, eternal Word of God. It is settled forever in Heaven (Psalm 119:89), and it is a completely reliable and trustworthy guide to life. We must beware of allowing anything—be it a person or a philosophy or our own mind—to cause us to question the truth of God's Word. Our feelings will deceive us, but God's truth will never lead us astray.

Today's Rooted Principle: When we question Scripture, we increase our vulnerability; when we obey it, we increase our success.

The Devil's Broken Promises

And the servant of the Lord must not strive; but be gentle unto all men, apt to teach, patient, In meekness instructing those that oppose themselves; if God peradventure will give them repentance to the acknowledging of the truth; And that they may recover themselves out of the snare of the devil, who are taken captive by him at his will.—**2 Timothy 2:24–26**

In 1939 just before the outbreak of World War II, Germany and Russia signed the Molotov–Ribbentrop Pact. This treaty promised that neither nation would attack the other, and it laid out a plan for how they would divide the nations of Eastern Europe between them. Yet in 1941, without warning or provocation, Adolf Hitler sent his tanks across the Russian border in a sneak attack. Hitler had no interest in keeping his word; the treaty was meant only as a temporary measure until he could do what he wanted.

The devil will you tell you anything you want to hear to get you to do what he wants you to do. He is a master liar; in fact, Jesus declared Satan to be the father of lies (John 8:44). The devil breaks every promise that he makes. He never delivers what he leads us to expect. While sin may be enjoyable for a little while (Hebrews 11:25), it always leads to a bitter end.

Every temptation we face is rooted in a lie. An evangelist of yesteryear used to preach a famous sermon entitled "All Satan's Apples Have Worms." No matter how attractive or appealing sin is made to look, the "wages of sin" is still death. We face all kinds of temptations, but they all have one similarity—they never deliver. The false promises of Satan have led many astray. Choose the truth, and you will be able to resist the lie that leads only to enslavement and death.

Today's Rooted Principle: Every promise from the devil is a lie; and if you believe his lies, you will find yourself enslaved.

The Deceitfulness of Sin

Take heed, brethren, lest there be in any of you an evil heart of unbelief,
in departing from the living God. But exhort one another daily, while it
is called To day; lest any of you be hardened through the deceitfulness
of sin.—**Hebrews 3:12–13**

I counseled a man some time ago who was enslaved by pornography. He wanted to get rid of that vile habit, and sometimes he managed to stay away from it for a week or two. But after a little time passed, the craving for sin returned, and he would go to almost any lengths to find something to feed his addiction. I'll never forget what he said to me: "I just don't think normally anymore. Lust has destroyed my mind."

This man was once a loving and committed husband. He had no intention of becoming enslaved to a destructive habit. Sin is deceitful because it shows you the pleasure without showing you the pain that follows later on. To overcome temptation, you need to consider the end result of the sin. Many of us learned this saying back when we were in Sunday school: "Sin will take you further than you want to go, keep you longer than you want to stay, and cost you more than you want to pay."

It's not hard to cut down a tree when it's only three or four inches tall. But allow that tree to grow for a few years, and the task becomes much more difficult. Allow it to grow for decades, and it will take power tools and a full day's work to cut it down. Sin works the same way. It slowly grows over time until it becomes so large and powerful that it is almost impossible to remove.

Destroy your sins while they are small; don't be deceived into thinking they will remain that way.

Today's Rooted Principle: There are no harmless or little sins.

Learn to Use Your Weapon

Wherefore take unto you the whole armour of God, that ye may be able to withstand in the evil day, and having done all, to stand...Above all, taking the shield of faith, wherewith ye shall be able to quench all the fiery darts of the wicked. And take the helmet of salvation, and the sword of the Spirit, which is the word of God:—**Ephesians 6:13, 16–17**

One of the best-known military units of World War II was Easy Company of the 101st Airborne. Their story was told in the book *Band of Brothers* which was later turned into a film. One of the most interesting things about this unit is that, even though the war was raging in Europe, they spent over a year in training in the United States and then an additional nine months of training in England prior to being part of the D-Day invasion in 1944.

In nearly two years of intense training and drill, this unit became a well-oiled machine. They knew exactly what to do and how to best fight against their enemy. As a result, they played an important part in fighting and winning some of the most critical battles in the European theater of the war. They had become military experts by training and practicing over and over again. A number of the soldiers said their basic training experience was more challenging than actual combat.

Jesus overcame the temptation of Satan by using the Word of God. Three times He was tempted, and all three times He responded, "It is written." There is power found in the Bible to overcome every temptation. It is a living book (Hebrews 4:12), and it is no accident that God chose the analogy of a sword to compare to the power and impact of the Scriptures. It is critically important that you take the time to study and learn the Word so that you can overcome the enemy.

Today's Rooted Principle: Every believer should be a careful and thorough student of the Word of God.

There Is an Exit

There hath no temptation taken you but such as is common to man: but God is faithful, who will not suffer you to be tempted above that ye are able; but will with the temptation also make a way to escape, that ye may be able to bear it. Wherefore, my dearly beloved, flee from idolatry.—**1 Corinthians 10:13–14**

In 1994, a fire broke out at a club in Elizabeth, New Jersey. In the stampede to get away from the fire, four young people were trampled to death. The investigation revealed that the lighted sign over one of the two exits was not working at the time of the fire. Even worse, it was discovered that the exit door had been nailed shut—apparently to keep people from slipping in without paying. For those young people, there was no way of escape.

When we are tempted and give in to sin, we sometimes look for someone else to blame. But every sin is our responsibility. James 1:14 says that each of us is led to temptation "of his own lust." There is always a way for us to escape; the door is never nailed shut. But sometimes we don't really want to take that escape. Someone said, "The hard part of resisting temptation is that we don't want to discourage it completely."

Playing with sin is one of the most dangerous things we can ever do. Instead of seeing how close we can get to the fire without being burned, the Bible instructs us, "flee also youthful lusts" (2 Timothy 2:22). God places the responsibility for escape on us because He provides the way to escape.

Next time you find yourself in a moment of temptation, remember that God provides the way for escape, and quickly flee before you find yourself trapped in sin.

Today's Rooted Principle: God provides a way of escape, but we must choose to walk through the exit door.

2 Samuel 1–2   Luke 14:1–24

Why God Chastens His Children

And ye have forgotten the exhortation which speaketh unto you as unto children, My son, despise not thou the chastening of the Lord, nor faint when thou art rebuked of him: For whom the Lord loveth he chasteneth, and scourgeth every son whom he receiveth. If ye endure chastening, God dealeth with you as with sons; for what son is he whom the father chasteneth not?—**Hebrews 12:5–7**

When our son Matthew was two years old, he loved to run the other direction when we called him. He thought that was great fun. One day he was playing on the front part of the lawn when I called him. He turned around and ran right into the middle of the road. Thankfully, there weren't any cars coming, and he didn't get hurt. Concerned for Matthew's future safety, however, I took him into the house where I gave him a correction to his behavior.

Why did I do that? Was I upset at Matthew? Not at all; I just wanted to protect him from doing something that could hurt or even kill him. In the same way, God chastens us—His children—for our own good. In fact Hebrews 12:8 tells us that if we are not being chastised when we are doing wrong, we are not really part of His family.

When hard times come, we are sometimes tempted to think that perhaps God is being unfair or hard on us. Of course, not every difficulty that comes into our lives is the result of some sin or a failure, but there are times when the pressures and trials we face are God's way of trying to get our attention and bring us back to doing right and to Him. When we refuse to listen to what Proverbs 15:31 calls the "reproof of life," we place ourselves into a very dangerous position. Don't reject or despise God's chastening in your life. If you sense that God may be correcting you, submit to Him and thank Him for His love.

Today's Rooted Principle: If you are being chastened by the Lord, recognize that it is done in love and return to Him.

2 Samuel 3–5   Luke 14:25–35

The World Is Not Your Friend

If the world hate you, ye know that it hated me before it hated you. If ye were of the world, the world would love his own: but because ye are not of the world, but I have chosen you out of the world, therefore the world hateth you. Remember the word that I said unto you, The servant is not greater than his lord. If they have persecuted me, they will also persecute you; if they have kept my saying, they will keep yours also.
—**John 15:18–20**

Years ago, a man came to me at the close of a church service and said, "I was saved at a young age, but I've been away from the Lord." We knelt together and prayed, and he rededicated his life to the Lord. The following evening, I visited his home and shared the Gospel with his wife. She was saved that night, and this couple's lives were transformed.

The following Sunday he walked into church with a black eye. "What happened to you?" I asked. Then he explained: "When I got to work and started reading my Bible at lunch time and turned down the drugs my co-workers offered me, they didn't like me anymore. They took me out behind the building and beat me up!"

Sometimes we expect praise and appreciation for doing right. But we should not expect the enemies of God to be pleased when we do what He wants. This vile world is no friend to grace, so hatred and persecution should be no surprise to us.

Today, the man who took a stand for Christ is the pastor of a church. Although his co-workers were upset by his loyalty to the Lord, he is experiencing the joy of serving Christ. Jesus warned us that persecution would come, but He also gives us the strength to remain faithful to Him through it.

Today's Rooted Principle: If you are finding the world against you today, be encouraged—God loves you and He will give you the victory.

Don't Waste Your Trials

Beloved, think it not strange concerning the fiery trial which is to try you, as though some strange thing happened unto you: But rejoice, inasmuch as ye are partakers of Christ's sufferings; that, when his glory shall be revealed, ye may be glad also with exceeding joy.—**1 Peter 4:12–13**

Dr. Lee Roberson, a great pastor for many years in Chattanooga, Tennessee, experienced great tragedy in his life. His baby daughter, Joy, died not long after she was born. He was serving the Lord, leading a church, and faithfully preaching the Word. Yet that did not mean he was exempt from suffering trials. Through this tragedy, Dr. Roberson led his church to establish a camp in memory of his daughter. At this camp, thousands of underprivileged children attended free of charge each year. They heard the Gospel and learned that they were loved and important to God, and thousands were saved.

If Dr. Roberson had become bitter against God because of the loss of his daughter, he would have missed his opportunity to be a blessing to so many people. It is not easy to go through a time of trials. The temptation is to feel that we are being treated unfairly in some way when things don't go as we think they should. But God's plans are far higher than ours (Isaiah 55:8–9). When we respond to pain with faith in Him, He uses even trials and tragedies to provide us great opportunities for service to others.

Trials are a test of whether or not we truly trust God. We may say that we believe He knows all things and has all power when things are going well, but when things go wrong do we still believe? Job said it this way: "shall we receive good at the hand of God, and shall we not receive evil?" (Job 2:10). God always brings us what we need and what He knows is best. Trust Him in all circumstances.

Today's Rooted Principle: God can transform your trials into great blessings.

A Law Against Prayer

All the presidents of the kingdom, the governors, and the princes, the counsellors, and the captains, have consulted together to establish a royal statute, and to make a firm decree, that whosoever shall ask a petition of any God or man for thirty days, save of thee, O king, he shall be cast into the den of lions. Now, O king, establish the decree, and sign the writing, that it be not changed, according to the law of the Medes and Persians, which altereth not. Wherefore king Darius signed the writing and the decree.—**Daniel 6:7–9**

There are some pretty interesting laws in the California books. For example, it is illegal to shoot any game from a moving vehicle—unless that game is a whale! Women are not allowed to drive while wearing housecoats. Peacocks have the right of way when crossing any street. And it is against the law for any car to go more than sixty miles an hour if it does not have a driver.

But strange as our laws may be, there is no law against prayer in our country such as the one that Daniel faced. He was threatened with death in a den of lions if he prayed to anyone except King Darius. Yet even this law did not stop the faithful servant of God. He opened his windows as he always had toward Jerusalem and prayed to the God of Heaven. Daniel continued in his established practice of prayer, and God delivered him from the lions.

While it is true that our society is becoming more hostile to true Christianity, we can freely pray. The tragedy is that even though we are allowed to pray, too often we do not. Prayer is a means for us to communicate with God, and we must be people of prayer if we are to be rooted in our Christian walk.

Today's Rooted Principle: If prayer is not part of your daily routine, determine not to miss out on this vital communication with God.

Prepared by Purpose

*And the king appointed them a daily provision of the king's meat, and of the wine which he drank: so nourishing them three years, that at the end thereof they might stand before the king... But Daniel purposed in his heart that he would not defile himself with the portion of the king's meat, nor with the wine which he drank: therefore he requested of the prince of the eunuchs that he might not defile himself.—***Daniel 1:5, 8**

When the Empire State Building in New York City officially opened in 1931, it was the tallest building in the world. The architectural firm of Shreve, Lamb and Harmon designed the building from the top down. The quality of their work was tested in 1945 when a B-25 bomber flying in thick fog struck the side of the building. Although, tragically, fourteen people were killed in the accident, the building itself reopened the following Monday.

Strength and stability do not come accidentally. If you see a person who has been a consistent and faithful Christian for many years, it is not a coincidence; it is the result of purposeful decisions they have made and followed over time. No one accomplishes great things for God by drifting.

When your purpose is certain and settled, you do not allow obstacles to keep you from achieving your goal. The strength of Daniel's character was rooted in his commitment to his God. Before he declined the meat and wine which would have violated the Old Testament dietary laws, he had already "purposed in his heart" to live for God.

Paul, too, lived with purpose. In Philippians 3:14, he wrote, "I press toward the mark...." The Greek word he used is such a strong word that it is sometimes translated "persecute." That represents the level of commitment and purpose that prepares us to do great things for God.

Today's Rooted Principle: Make it your purpose to honor and obey God, and then follow through on that commitment no matter what happens.

Not My Will

And he came out, and went, as he was wont, to the mount of Olives; and his disciples also followed him. And when he was at the place, he said unto them, Pray that ye enter not into temptation. And he was withdrawn from them about a stone's cast, and kneeled down, and prayed, Saying, Father, if thou be willing, remove this cup from me: nevertheless not my will, but thine, be done.—**Luke 22:39–42**

One of the most powerful books revealing the horrors of the prison system in the former Soviet Union is Alexander Solzhenitsyn's *A Day in the Life of Ivan Denisovitch.* The main character, Ivan, undergoes unspeakable hardship and horror. One day, another inmate notices Ivan in silent prayer. In mockery the inmate says, "Prayers won't help you get out of here any faster." Opening his eyes, Ivan replies, "I do not pray to get out of prison but to do the will of God."

God has given us the privilege to come to Him in prayer, but sometimes we fall into the trap of praying according to our own will and purposes. While we certainly may ask God for what we desire, our prayers must always be in submission to His will. We do not pray to tell God our needs—He already knows them even before we ask. And we should not pray to tell God the solution to our problems. That is His sovereign choice.

Instead we should pray that our lives will bring honor and glory to Him and that our needs will be met according to His plan. When Jesus prayed in the Garden of Gethsemane, He was facing greater suffering than any of us can imagine, yet He was still willing to endure the pain and death of the cross to accomplish God's will and our salvation. Our prayers should be offered in the same spirit of submission.

Today's Rooted Principle: Pray for God's will rather than your own, and you will pray powerful and effective prayers.

Get Up Again

We are troubled on every side, yet not distressed; we are perplexed, but not in despair; Persecuted, but not forsaken; cast down, but not destroyed; Always bearing about in the body the dying of the Lord Jesus, that the life also of Jesus might be made manifest in our body.
—2 Corinthians 4:8–10

The story is told that Andrew Jackson's boyhood friends just couldn't understand how he became a famous general and then the President of the United States. They knew of other men who had greater talent but who never succeeded. One of Jackson's friends said, "Why, Jim Brown, who lived right down the pike from Jackson, was not only smarter but he could throw Andy three times out of four in a wrestling match. But look where Andy is now."

Another friend responded, "How did there happen to be a fourth time? Didn't they usually say three times and out?" "Sure, they were supposed to, but not Andy. He would never admit he was beat—he would never stay 'throwed.' Jim Brown would get tired, and on the fourth try Andrew Jackson would throw him and be the winner." Picking up on that idea, someone has said, "The thing that counts is not how many times you are 'throwed,' but whether you are willing to stay 'throwed.'"

The Christian life is a battle. Scripture often speaks of God's children as soldiers, and we should not expect to have things always be calm and peaceful. The question is not whether we ever fail, but whether we get back up when we do. Proverbs 24:16 says, "For a just man falleth seven times, and riseth up again: but the wicked shall fall into mischief."

You cannot be defeated by the enemy; you can only lose by giving up. Don't let defeats or setbacks discourage you. Instead, commit yourself to standing firm and not giving up no matter how tough things get.

Today's Rooted Principle: Get up one more time than you fall, and in the end you will be victorious.

You Have a Faithful Friend

Seeing then that we have a great high priest, that is passed into the heavens, Jesus the Son of God, let us hold fast our profession. For we have not an high priest which cannot be touched with the feeling of our infirmities; but was in all points tempted like as we are, yet without sin. Let us therefore come boldly unto the throne of grace, that we may obtain mercy, and find grace to help in time of need.—**Hebrews 4:14–16**

From a young age, Anne Steele experienced deep pain. Her mother died when Anne was just three years old. At nineteen, she suffered a hip injury that left her an invalid. At twenty-one, her fiancé drowned the day before they were to be married.

Although Anne was deeply grieved, she did not sink into despair. Through what she learned by these tragedies, she wrote the following hymn:

> Father, whate'er of earthly bliss
> Thy sovereign will denies,
> Accepted at Thy throne of grace,
> Let this petition rise:
> Give me a calm, a thankful heart,
> From every murmur free!
> The blessings of Thy grace impart,
> And make me live to Thee.

When we are going through hard times, we sometimes feel abandoned and alone. But we never are. Hebrews 13:5 says, "…he hath said, I will never leave thee, nor forsake thee." Even if there is no one who seems to care, you will always have one faithful and steadfast friend in Jesus Christ. He has already endured every suffering and hardship we face, and He knows how it feels to be forsaken. No matter how many other people let you down, He will lift you up.

Today's Rooted Principle: When you are tired or discouraged, run to the Friend who sticks closer than any brother.

Personal Responsibility

And he said, Behold now, I have taken upon me to speak unto the Lord: Peradventure there shall be twenty found there. And he said, I will not destroy it for twenty's sake. And he said, Oh let not the Lord be angry, and I will speak yet but this once: Peradventure ten shall be found there. And he said, I will not destroy it for ten's sake. And the LORD went his way, as soon as he had left communing with Abraham: and Abraham returned unto his place.—**Genesis 18:31–33**

When Dr. Richard Halverson was the U.S. Senate chaplain, he spoke before a group of Christians who were irritated that Congress had not acted with a strong initiative to restore prayer in schools. To this audience who were seeking greater initiative from the government, Dr. Halverson asked, "How many of you have prayed with your children this month, outside of church?" Not one member of the assembly raised his hand. The problem is not only in Washington or in our state capitals, but in our own hearts.

If Lot had been a faithful witness, the cities of Sodom and Gomorrah would not have been destroyed. Abraham begged God for mercy, and God declared that if there were just ten righteous people in Sodom, He would spare the city. But Lot had failed to win even his own family, and as a result, judgment fell. While there is much wrong with our society, we must remember to personally choose to live for God and to accept the responsibility to lead our families in seeking God as well.

After John Quincy Adams was defeated for re-election as president, he became a member of the House of Representatives. There he worked for many years to end slavery in America. As he neared the end of his life, a friend asked if Adams was discouraged because he had not succeeded. Adams replied, "Duties are ours; results are God's." If you do what you should and can do, you can leave everything else in God's hands.

Today's Rooted Principle: Pray for change in your nation, but accept personal responsibility for yourself and your family.

2 Samuel 23–24   Luke 19:1–27   143

Which Direction Are You Facing?

And Lot lifted up his eyes, and beheld all the plain of Jordan, that it was well watered every where, before the LORD destroyed Sodom and Gomorrah, even as the garden of the LORD, like the land of Egypt, as thou comest unto Zoar. Then Lot chose him all the plain of Jordan; and Lot journeyed east: and they separated themselves the one from the other. Abram dwelled in the land of Canaan, and Lot dwelled in the cities of the plain, and pitched his tent toward Sodom.—**Genesis 13:10–12**

In the 1929 Rose Bowl, the California Golden Bears squared off against the Georgia Tech Yellow Jackets and provided one of the most famous plays in college football history. In the second quarter, California player Roy Riegels recovered a fumble, but instead of advancing it, he got confused and began running toward his own end zone. A teammate finally stopped him at the goal line, but the two points Georgia Tech scored following "Wrong Way" Riegels' mistake proved the winning margin in the game.

Many times believers make the mistake of thinking they can face the world and even move toward it without adverse consequences. They think that since they are not yet too close, they are fine. But in truth, the direction in which we are pointed tells the story of where we will end up.

Lot made the same tragic mistake. When Abraham offered him a choice of land for his flocks, Lot chose based on short-term rather than long-term benefit. Then when he reached the well-watered grasslands, he set up camp so that he was facing Sodom. It wasn't long before he ended up in that wicked city, which eventually led to the destruction of his family.

If you fall into the trap of thinking your direction doesn't matter, you are headed for trouble. It is far better to turn your back on the things of the world and to fix your eyes on Jesus.

Today's Rooted Principle: Are you facing toward the Lord or toward the world? The direction you face determines the destination you will reach.

Get Your Feet Wet

And it came to pass, when the people removed from their tents, to pass over Jordan, and the priests bearing the ark of the covenant before the people; And as they that bare the ark were come unto Jordan, and the feet of the priests that bare the ark were dipped in the brim of the water, (for Jordan overfloweth all his banks all the time of harvest,) That the waters which came down from above stood and rose up upon an heap very far from the city Adam, that is beside Zaretan: and those that came down toward the sea of the plain, even the salt sea, failed, and were cut off: and the people passed over right against Jericho.
—**Joshua 3:14–16**

I once read a simple but profound saying: "There are no correspondence courses for swimming." In truth, the only way to learn to swim is to get in the water. Similarly, the only way to learn to walk by faith is to start moving.

It is tempting for us to sit back and wait until we see the way ahead of us to be clear, but often the only way to truly go forward is to march ahead in obedience to God even when we cannot see the way.

When the Children of Israel were preparing to enter the Promised Land, they had to cross the flooded Jordan River. God promised Joshua to make a way for the people, but He did not part the river until the priests who were carrying the Ark of the Covenant were standing in the water. Every time we see faith in the Bible, we see it expressed in action. There is no such thing as passive faith.

There are still great things that need to be done in our day, and God's power has not changed. What we need are believers who will act in faith. As the missionary William Carey said, "Expect great things from God. Attempt great things for God."

Today's Rooted Principle: Stretch your faith today by doing something for God even if you don't see how you can.

Make the Most of Today

See then that ye walk circumspectly, not as fools, but as wise, Redeeming the time, because the days are evil. Wherefore be ye not unwise, but understanding what the will of the Lord is.—**Ephesians 5:15–17**

The great military leader Napoleon, who conquered much of Europe at the height of the French Empire, once said: "There is in the midst of every great battle a ten- to fifteen-minute period that is the crucial point. Take that period, and you win the battle. Lose it, and you will be defeated." The idea of "redeeming the time" is to make the most of every moment and every opportunity. None of us know which ten- or fifteen-minute period may be crucial to our job, our family, our Lord…so we must make the most of every minute we have.

There are more than six hundred references to time in the Bible. Obviously, how we use our time is important to God. In Psalm 90:12 Moses prayed, "So teach us to number our days, that we may apply our hearts unto wisdom." When we carefully count our days according to the teachings of the Word of God, we realize that this day is the only one we know that we have. We cannot go back to yesterday; we have no certainty of tomorrow. If we are going to accomplish anything for God, it must be done now rather than later.

We will always be able to come up with reasons why we could put off what needs to be done, but we'll later wish we had overcome them. Many people look back at the end of their lives with regret for what they failed to accomplish. The only way to avoid that is to take action today. There is enough time to do everything God has planned for us to do, provided that we use that time wisely. Just as with our money, investing time well brings great results.

Today's Rooted Principle: Make the most of every minute you have today; we are not promised tomorrow.

Stay Committed to Your Marriage

And the LORD God caused a deep sleep to fall upon Adam, and he slept: and he took one of his ribs, and closed up the flesh instead thereof; And the rib, which the LORD God had taken from man, made he a woman, and brought her unto the man. And Adam said, This is now bone of my bones, and flesh of my flesh: she shall be called Woman, because she was taken out of Man. Therefore shall a man leave his father and his mother, and shall cleave unto his wife: and they shall be one flesh.
—**Genesis 2:21–24**

At the Harry Truman Presidential Library in Missouri, there are more than 1,300 letters that President Truman wrote to his wife Bess during their marriage. He made a commitment to write his wife a letter every day they were apart. Such consistent dedication to expressing love goes a long way to building a marriage that can stand the tests of time.

Even though our society has fallen prey to an epidemic of divorce, we do not have to allow our relationships to be measured or influenced by that standard. God created marriage to be a picture of His faithfulness, and He desires that we would express consistent, faithful love in our marriages.

No marriage is perfect, because every marriage is composed of two imperfect people. But that is no reason to give up on the most important human relationship you will ever have. So many people think the grass will be greener with a different husband or wife, only to find the same problems when they find someone new.

Focus on building and strengthening your marriage by focusing on what you can and should do for your spouse rather than on what you want your spouse to do for you. The strongest marriages are those where each person is dedicated to building up and encouraging the other. A marriage built on the Word and joined in faith will not fail.

Today's Rooted Principle: Don't allow anything to draw you away from commitment to your marriage.

MAY

Grace Abounded More

For as by one man's disobedience many were made sinners, so by the obedience of one shall many be made righteous. Moreover the law entered, that the offence might abound. But where sin abounded, grace did much more abound: That as sin hath reigned unto death, even so might grace reign through righteousness unto eternal life by Jesus Christ our Lord.—**Romans 5:19–21**

Charles Spurgeon wrote: "Here, my brethren and sisters in Christ, is a force that is fully equal to the requirements of the duel with sin; for this grace, of which I am going to speak, is divine grace, and hence it is omnipotent, immortal, and immutable. The gracious purpose of God's free favor to an undeserving man is more than a match for that man's sin, for it brings to bear, upon his sin, the blood of the incarnate Son of God, and the majestic and mysterious fire of the eternal Spirit, who burns up evil and utterly consumes it. With God the Father, God the Son, and God the Holy Ghost united against sin, the everlasting purposes of grace are bound to be accomplished, sin must be overcome."

It is a blessing to understand that we are not fighting against sin and temptation in our own strength. In fact, all such efforts are doomed to failure. "Trying harder" will not make us right and holy before God. Only His grace has the power to overcome sin in our lives. This is not just true regarding our salvation, but of our daily walk with Him as well.

When we face a heightened level of testing and temptation, we find there is more grace available to help us meet the challenge and pass the test. Our responsibility is to access that grace and tap in to its power so that we overcome. It is at His throne that we "find grace to help in time of need" (Hebrews 4:16).

Today's Rooted Principle: Walk today with the awareness of the presence of God's grace as a reality in your life.

Who Can You Trust?

Every good gift and every perfect gift is from above, and cometh down from the Father of lights, with whom is no variableness, neither shadow of turning. Of his own will begat he us with the word of truth, that we should be a kind of firstfruits of his creatures.—**James 1:17–18**

In 1999, John F. Kennedy, Jr. attempted to fly his small airplane from New York City to his family home in Massachusetts for a wedding. On board were his wife Carolyn and her sister. Though Kennedy was a licensed pilot, he had not yet been approved for instrument flight (using only instruments to navigate). When their takeoff was delayed until after dark, Kennedy should have waited for daylight or sought a more experienced pilot to help. Yet Kennedy took off into the darkness. The plane never reached its destination, and all three passengers were killed in the crash.

Investigators determined that the crash was likely caused by disorientation from flying over open water at night without any landmarks or visible horizon. Kennedy's lack of experience may well have led him to trust what he thought he was seeing more than what his instrument panel was telling him.

Our human nature is such that we frequently are not sure who or what we can trust. All of us face the temptation to walk according to sight instead of faith. Faith—if it is based on the right thing—will keep us from crashing. The reason faith in God and His Word keeps us on the right path is because God never fails. There is not even the slightest hint that He will ever change His nature, His character, or His promises.

No promise is better than the one who makes it. We have seen many examples of people who trusted investments, companies and governments only to find that their confidence was misplaced. Those who put their faith in God never suffer the disappointment of broken promises.

Today's Rooted Principle: Instead of relying on your own wisdom, trust the Word of the God who never changes.

1 Kings 12–13   Luke 22:1–30   151

The End Result Is Settled

Because sentence against an evil work is not executed speedily, therefore the heart of the sons of men is fully set in them to do evil. Though a sinner do evil an hundred times, and his days be prolonged, yet surely I know that it shall be well with them that fear God, which fear before him: But it shall not be well with the wicked, neither shall he prolong his days, which are as a shadow; because he feareth not before God.
—**Ecclesiastes 8:11–13**

One of the best-loved hymns of the faith, "It Is Well with My Soul," was written by Horatio Spafford. Mr. Spafford, a wealthy businessman in Chicago, lost much of his real estate holdings in the Great Chicago Fire. After the fire, he sent his wife and four daughters on a ship to Europe, intending to join them later. But the voyage was also struck by disaster, and Spafford received a cable from his wife with the painful message, "Saved alone."

Spafford quickly made arrangements to join his wife. When they reached the spot where his daughters had drowned, Spafford marked that sad event with words of hope: "When peace like a river attendeth my way; when sorrows like sea billows roll; whatever my lot, Thou hast taught me to say, 'It is well, it is well with my soul.'"

These powerful words written in the midst of such pain are a reminder to us today that, even though we may be enduring great suffering and hardship, it is not the end of God's plan for us. Sometimes God's children get discouraged because it appears that life is going better for those who are doing wrong. Yet the end result of both paths is already settled. Those who fear God will be able to say, "It is well." Those who oppose God will quickly find that the end of their path is death and destruction. Keeping the end result in mind helps us keep doing right.

Today's Rooted Principle: God's good results are already settled for those who love and fear Him.

The Sign Doesn't Change

For what if some did not believe? shall their unbelief make the faith of God without effect? God forbid: yea, let God be true, but every man a liar; as it is written, That thou mightest be justified in thy sayings, and mightest overcome when thou art judged.—**Romans 3:3–4**

Suppose you were driving on a mountain road one day and saw a sign that said, "Slow—Dangerous Curves Ahead." There are three basic responses to such a sign. You could heed the warning and slow down. You could choose to ignore it and continue driving as you were. Or you could choose to defy it and accelerate. No matter which response you choose, the sign will not change. The only thing that changes by your heeding, ignoring, or defying the sign is the amount of the repair and medical bills you will incur.

The Word of God is the same. It never changes. The warnings it gives that spell out the dangers of wrong behavior are not in the least affected by whether or not we believe them. So many people today are convinced that truth is relative—that truth is determined by what they believe to be true. That lie has been destroying lives ever since Satan first presented it in the Garden of Eden. Rather than trying to decide for ourselves what is right and true, we need to be willing to take God's absolute standard and adopt it as our own.

When we choose to ignore the warning signs posted along the road of life, we are placing our wisdom and judgment above that of God. That approach always leads to destruction. Faith in God requires that we trust Him to know what is best, even if it does not seem right to us.

Has God been bringing warning signs into your life lately? Heed the commands of Scripture and the biblical counsel and concerns of godly people. You will be thankful you did!

Today's Rooted Principle: The difference between safety and tragedy is found in heeding and following the warnings and commands of Scripture.

God's Face Is Toward You

Hear my prayer, O LORD, and let my cry come unto thee. Hide not thy face from me in the day when I am in trouble; incline thine ear unto me: in the day when I call answer me speedily. For my days are consumed like smoke, and my bones are burned as an hearth. My heart is smitten, and withered like grass; so that I forget to eat my bread.—**Psalm 102:1–4**

Dr. Lee Roberson once told the story of a young family who went through the tragic death of the young mother. The first night after the funeral service, the little daughter couldn't sleep. She went to her father's bedroom and asked if she could sleep with him. He agreed, and she climbed into bed. She still couldn't sleep, and through the darkness her voice came, "Daddy, is your face turned toward me?"

All of us go through times when we wonder if there is anyone who cares about us. David knew that feeling when he was fleeing for his life to get away from Saul. He lamented: "…no man cared for my soul…" (Psalm 142:4). Yet no matter how alone we feel, even if those closest to us abandon us, God never turns away from us. There is nothing you can do that will change His love and compassion for you. The sacrifice of Jesus on the cross for our salvation is the ultimate testimony to the depth of God's love for us.

Spend some time today rejoicing and giving thanks for your salvation. When you do, you will find that the burdens of life are lighter, and your hope for the future is greater. Jesus cried out on the cross, "My God, my God, why hast thou forsaken me?" (Matthew 27:46). His sacrifice to make atonement for your sins is all the guarantee that you will ever need that God's face is toward you.

Today's Rooted Principle: The face of God is toward you today—you are not and never will be alone or forsaken.

God Always Does Right

Assemble yourselves and come; draw near together, ye that are escaped of the nations: they have no knowledge that set up the wood of their graven image, and pray unto a god that cannot save. Tell ye, and bring them near; yea, let them take counsel together: who hath declared this from ancient time? who hath told it from that time? have not I the LORD? and there is no God else beside me; a just God and a Saviour; there is none beside me.—**Isaiah 45:20–21**

Jack Benny was one of the most successful comedians of the last century. He was known for his wry sense of humor and his stage persona as a tightwad. In real life, he was actually a very generous man. Benny once received an award and said, "I really don't deserve this award. But then I have arthritis, and I really don't deserve that either!"

Most of us have experienced situations where we don't think the outcome worked out right or we got what we think we deserve. We ask questions like: "Why was that Christian family killed while the drunk driver walked away?" "Why does that couple who never goes to church seem to have a better marriage than I do?" "Why is my company going under despite my working so hard?" In order to have a proper perspective on life, we must never forget that God always does what is right.

Joseph did not understand why his brothers sold him into slavery, why he was falsely accused by Potiphar's wife, or why he was forgotten by those he helped in prison. Yet through all of those circumstances God was at work, and in the end He placed Joseph exactly where He intended for Joseph to be. It is God's nature to do what is right, and every part of your life will work according to His purpose and plan.

Today's Rooted Principle: Even if you do not understand why and how God is working, you can always count on Him to be just and do right.

More Than a Promise

And Jesus came and spake unto them, saying, All power is given unto me
in heaven and in earth. Go ye therefore, and teach all nations, baptizing
them in the name of the Father, and of the Son, and of the Holy Ghost:
Teaching them to observe all things whatsoever I have commanded you:
and, lo, I am with you alway, even unto the end of the world. Amen.
—**Matthew 28:18–20**

One of the great preachers and Bible expositors of the past,
G. Campbell Morgan, was often asked to speak to groups in special
settings—prisons, nursing homes, and orphanages—when he was
holding evangelistic campaigns. Once he spoke in a nursing home from
Matthew 28:18–20. Reading the words of Christ "I am with you always,"
Morgan paused and asked, "Isn't that a wonderful promise?" "No," one of
the ladies replied aloud. "It is a wonderful reality!"

All of the promises of the Word of God are true, but perhaps none
is so precious and so important as the promise of Jesus to be present
with us throughout our lives until we see Him face to face. This presence
of the Son of God is a reality—every moment of every day. When we
recognize that He is always with us, it influences everything about our
behavior, our attitudes, our speech, and our relationships.

The Jewish leaders who opposed the early church brought Peter and
John before them to try to stop their preaching about Jesus. As they looked
upon these two ordinary fishermen, "they took knowledge of them, that
they had been with Jesus" (Acts 4:13). The presence of Jesus in your life
day by day transforms everything so that you begin to live as He lived.
This is the purpose of God for our lives according to Romans 8:29—that
we be "conformed to the image of his Son." Meditate on the presence of
God today, realizing that He is with you wherever you go.

Today's Rooted Principle: God's presence in your life is more than just
a promise—it is a life-changing reality.

Make Your Choice

*Now therefore fear the LORD, and serve him in sincerity and in truth:
and put away the gods which your fathers served on the other side of the
flood, and in Egypt; and serve ye the LORD. And if it seem evil unto you
to serve the LORD, choose you this day whom ye will serve; whether the
gods which your fathers served that were on the other side of the flood,
or the gods of the Amorites, in whose land ye dwell: but as for me and
my house, we will serve the LORD.*—**Joshua 24:14–15**

When A.C. Green was a professional basketball player for the Los
Angeles Lakers, he was almost as well known for the commitment
he had made to remain morally pure as he was known for his skill as an
athlete. He had the same temptations that have drawn so many others
astray, yet he did what was right. An interviewer once asked him about
the stand he had taken, and Green said, "I have been given the power of
choice. I have the power to make a choice. Once I make a choice, it has
power over me."

As you go through this day, you will face a series of choices between
right and wrong. These decisions, both large and small, will determine
the course of your life and your future. Though an individual choice may
not seem to be that important, each choice takes you closer to God or
further away from Him. For example, I've never yet had someone tell me
they set out intending to destroy their marriage, but I've counseled many
people who have destroyed their marriages.

It has been said, "You control your choices, but you don't control the
consequences." When you are tempted to do wrong, to cut corners, to let
down your guard, to tell a "little white lie," resist, and instead choose to
do right. You will find when you do resist, your character is strengthened
and your purity is protected.

Today's Rooted Principle: Each choice you make today will shape your
future, so make each one with godly wisdom as your guide.

Truth in Advertising

And there was war in heaven: Michael and his angels fought against the dragon; and the dragon fought and his angels, And prevailed not; neither was their place found any more in heaven. And the great dragon was cast out, that old serpent, called the Devil, and Satan, which deceiveth the whole world: he was cast out into the earth, and his angels were cast out with him.—**Revelation 12:7–9**

In response to the rapid growth in radio advertising, the Federal Trade Commission was tasked in 1938 with regulating the advertising industry to protect customers from false advertising. They passed a series of laws and regulations designed to ensure that any claims made about a product be based on facts. Each year they bring a number of cases against companies that violate their restrictions.

The devil certainly is a master at false advertising. The book of Revelation calls him a dragon and a serpent. Yet when he appears to us, he comes in a different guise. Warning about the deceptiveness of the devil, Paul wrote, "…Satan himself is transformed into an angel of light" (2 Corinthians 11:14). Satan is not only deceitful about his person and in his appearance, but he is deceitful in his promises as well. The temptations that he offers always lead to disappointment and bitter ends.

If the true cost of sin were displayed in the beginning, most of us would have no problem fleeing temptation. But instead, we get the pretty picture painted by a master deceiver. The dragon appears as an angel to better convince us to turn away from what is right. When you face temptation today, look behind the mask. If you are allured by the promises he makes, look back at the history of the lies he has successfully convinced you of in the past, and turn your back on him. Resist temptation through the power of Scripture, and you will never be sorry.

Today's Rooted Principle: Every enticement of the devil is based on a lie; every promise of God is based on His eternal truth.

2 Kings 7–9   John 1:1–28

Love and Sacrifice

As the Father hath loved me, so have I loved you: continue ye in my love.
If ye keep my commandments, ye shall abide in my love; even as I have
kept my Father's commandments, and abide in his love. These things
have I spoken unto you, that my joy might remain in you, and that your
joy might be full. This is my commandment, That ye love one another,
as I have loved you. Greater love hath no man than this, that a man lay
down his life for his friends.—**John 15:9–13**

On February 2, 1943, a ship named The Dorchester was carrying more than nine hundred soldiers and military personnel across the North Atlantic. A German U-boat spotted the convoy and fired three torpedoes at the ship. Only one struck the target, but the blast below the waterline fatally damaged the ship. In the cold darkness, the crew was ordered to abandon ship. There were not enough lifeboats for all the men, nor were there enough life jackets.

Four chaplains onboard the ship that night helped comfort those injured in the explosion and those who feared the coming of death. When the ship was ready to sink, the chaplains took off their life jackets and handed them to four young soldiers who had none. They gave up their own lives in order to save others. The heroic gesture inspired a nation, and Congress voted a special posthumous medal in their honor.

Most of us are not called upon to physically lay down our lives, but there are many people who need our help. People all around us who don't know the Lord need us to give them the Gospel. Others need perhaps a kind word or an investment of our time or a gift of our finances. Whatever sacrifice is required, if we are to truly live as children of the King, we must be willing to make sacrifices to demonstrate Christ's love.

Today's Rooted Principle: Love is best demonstrated through personal sacrifice.

God Is in Charge

Why do the heathen rage, and the people imagine a vain thing? The kings of the earth set themselves, and the rulers take counsel together, against the LORD, and against his anointed, saying, Let us break their bands asunder, and cast away their cords from us. He that sitteth in the heavens shall laugh: the Lord shall have them in derision.
—**Psalm 2:1–4**

Someone once observed, "Man proposes; God disposes." This simple expression sums up a vital Bible truth: God is sovereign over everything on Earth and over every part of our lives. No plan that we make will ever surprise Him; no opposition can overcome His purposes. He is God, and we are not.

Scripture tells us that God laughs at those who think they can exalt themselves against His will. Every plot of man against His design is doomed to failure. But the sovereignty of God is more than just a shield against our enemies; it is an assurance to us as His children. There is no attribute of God that is more comforting than the attribute of His sovereignty. Under the most adverse circumstances, in the most severe trials, we can know and be certain that God has not forsaken us.

God's sovereignty overrules our afflictions so that through these circumstances He can sanctify us and make us more like His Son. God's loving exercise of His sovereignty assures us that we can always trust Him, even if we do not understand the trials that He has allowed in our lives. There are no accidents with God. Although we are often tempted to question our circumstances, we can trust that everything that comes to us has gone through the filter of His love. When we trust His faithful sovereignty, we can be confident of two things: God knows what is best for us; and, because He is in control, He will see to it that we receive what is best.

Today's Rooted Principle: The circumstances of life that you face today are no challenge to the power and purpose of God.

It All Belongs to God

Wherefore David blessed the LORD before all the congregation: and David said, Blessed be thou, LORD God of Israel our father, for ever and ever. Thine, O LORD, is the greatness, and the power, and the glory, and the victory, and the majesty: for all that is in the heaven and in the earth is thine; thine is the kingdom, O LORD, and thou art exalted as head above all.—**1 Chronicles 29:10–11**

The great missionary David Livingstone was inspired to go to Africa by the testimony of Robert Moffat who reported seeing the smoke rise from a thousand villages where the name of Christ had never been heard. Livingstone determined that he would take the Gospel where it had never been preached. Leaving England behind, he spent most of the rest of his life penetrating the interior of Africa—exploring unreached territory for future missionaries and preaching the Gospel everywhere he went.

A strong sense of purpose drove Livingstone to face hardship and danger and give up much of what the world holds dear. He said, "I place no value on anything I have or may possess, except in relation to the kingdom of God. If anything will advance the interests of the kingdom, it shall be given away or kept, only as by giving or keeping it I shall most promote the glory of Him to whom I owe all my hopes in time or eternity."

Since everything that we have already belongs to God, we are not making great sacrifices when we give back to Him part of what is already His. The priority of our lives is not meant to be our comfort and safety, but our priority should be to advance God's kingdom and to bring Him glory. The good gifts we have are from God, that we might steward them for Him. If we lose sight of that fact, we are in danger of becoming selfish rather than using our possessions in ways that lay up treasure for us in Heaven.

Today's Rooted Principle: Remembering that everything you have belongs to God keeps your priorities in proper order.

2 Kings 15–16 John 3:1–18

The Only Way

And whither I go ye know, and the way ye know. Thomas saith unto him, Lord, we know not whither thou goest; and how can we know the way? Jesus saith unto him, I am the way, the truth, and the life: no man cometh unto the Father, but by me.—**John 14:4–6**

In our culture today the idea that all religions or belief systems (or none at all) are equally valid and true is becoming more widely accepted. A popular American entertainer was interviewed on a television program a few years ago. She has dabbled in a number of religions, but she is known for the blatant anti-religious elements of much of her music.

In the interview, this woman explained, "I can disagree with doctrines and still celebrate them. I go to the synagogue; I study Hinduism…in the end all paths lead to God." Her statements are an expression of what many believe today.

No matter how many people adopt this view, the Bible is clear that Jesus is the only way to Heaven. There are no alternatives and no options to salvation—it must come through Jesus Christ. Sincerity, misplaced faith, obedience to laws, and moral living will never atone for sin. Only a sinless sacrifice can substitute in our place.

The exclusivity of Jesus places a great responsibility on those of us who are believers and who know the Lord to share this truth with others. Each of our family members, co-workers, neighbors and friends need to be saved—and we are the ones who must tell them.

God's plan is for every follower of Jesus Christ to be a witness of faith. It is not enough for us to just have taken the only path to Heaven for ourselves; we have a privileged obligation to invite others to join us on the journey. There is nothing more important you can do today than to be a witness of the Gospel.

Today's Rooted Principle: Tell someone today that Jesus is the only way to Heaven, and share with them how they can know Him and be saved.

The World Hates the Word

For the word of God is quick, and powerful, and sharper than any twoedged sword, piercing even to the dividing asunder of soul and spirit, and of the joints and marrow, and is a discerner of the thoughts and intents of the heart. Neither is there any creature that is not manifest in his sight: but all things are naked and opened unto the eyes of him with whom we have to do.—**Hebrews 4:12–13**

When I travel, I often take out my Bible to read or study. Over the years I have found that the Bible provokes strong reactions. Some people love the Word of God and are happy to see it, but many are anything but happy. Some even react very strongly against the very presence of Scripture. The reason for that is that the Bible forces people to confront the truth.

There is a widespread acceptance today of the notion that there are no absolute truths. Yet the unchanging and eternal Word of God directly contradicts that notion. It does not merely suggest good ideas; it declares the very Word of the Lord and sets the standard for everyone in every age. Jesus said, "…thy word is truth" (John 17:17). The intense negative reaction of the world to the Word is but one more evidence that the Bible is from God rather than from man.

It is no accident that when Jesus was tempted by Satan, He responded to every challenge by quoting Scripture. There is enormous power in the Word of God. The author of Hebrews compared the Bible to the swords carried by the Roman soldiers of the day; those swords could be used in battle in both directions because both edges were sharp. The Bible has the answers to every challenge, and the more you know about its truths, the better prepared you will be to face the world.

Today's Rooted Principle: The Bible is your sword. Learn to use it, and you will be prepared for the spiritual battles of life.

Be Real

Now the end of the commandment is charity out of a pure heart, and of a good conscience, and of faith unfeigned: From which some having swerved have turned aside unto vain jangling; Desiring to be teachers of the law; understanding neither what they say, nor whereof they affirm.—**1 Timothy 1:5–7**

The story is told of a zoo that was noted for their great collection of different animals. One day the gorilla died, and to keep up the appearance of a full range of animals, the zookeeper hired a man to wear a gorilla suit and fill in for the dead animal. It was his first day on the job, and the man didn't know how to act like a gorilla very well. As he tried to move convincingly, he got too close to the wall of the enclosure and tripped and fell into the lion exhibit. He began to scream, convinced his life was over…until the lion spoke to him: "Be quiet, or you're going to get us both fired!"

Not everyone is who they appear to be. One of the common excuses people give for not trusting Christ is that there are so many hypocrites in the church. While that excuse does not justify not being saved, it is all too often a valid complaint. Our faith and our love are supposed to be genuine and unfeigned.

It is a great testimony for us to be known as someone who is real—that our Christianity is more than just a cultural affiliation or a belief system in name only, but that it actually changes the way in which we live. One of the things that distinguished the members of the early church was that their lives had been transformed by their faith. No longer were they focused on themselves, but on the things of God. May it truly be said of us that our religion is more than just skin deep—that we are real disciples of Jesus Christ.

Today's Rooted Principle: Ask God to search your heart and reveal any inconsistencies between who you are on the inside and who you appear to be on the outside.

A Generous Heart

*But godliness with contentment is great gain. For we brought nothing
into this world, and it is certain we can carry nothing out. And having
food and raiment let us be therewith content. But they that will be rich
fall into temptation and a snare, and into many foolish and hurtful
lusts, which drown men in destruction and perdition. For the love of
money is the root of all evil: which while some coveted after, they have
erred from the faith, and pierced themselves through with many sorrows.*
—1 Timothy 6:6–10

R obert Arthington lived in a single room in England in the 1800s.
Known as a bit eccentric by some, he cooked for himself, lived by
only the barest of necessities, and wore the same coat for seventeen years.
Although he lived a simple life, he was actually a millionaire. When he
died, his estate was worth about five million dollars. Why then did he live
so simply? Arthington lived frugally so he could give generously. He gave
large amounts of money to Christian missions during his lifetime, and
he willed his entire state to the cause of missions upon his death.

After his death, a letter from a missionary was found in his belongings.
It read, "Were I in England again, I would gladly live in one room, make
the floor my bed, a box my chair, another my table, rather than the
heathen should perish for the lack of knowledge of Jesus Christ."

Our society values how much a person has; God values how much
a person gives. When Jesus watched the people giving in the Temple, He
praised the widow who cast in just two mites—a fraction of a penny—
because it represented such a sacrifice.

Though money itself is not evil, loving money leads to all kinds of
evil. The best protection we have against the sorrows that come from
loving money is to cultivate generous hearts. Look for opportunities to
use the resources God has given to you for the benefit of others.

Today's Rooted Principle: Measure your financial success by how much
you do for others and you will never fall into the snare of covetousness.

2 Kings 24–25 John 5:1–24

No Condemnation

There is therefore now no condemnation to them which are in Christ Jesus, who walk not after the flesh, but after the Spirit. For the law of the Spirit of life in Christ Jesus hath made me free from the law of sin and death. For what the law could not do, in that it was weak through the flesh, God sending his own Son in the likeness of sinful flesh, and for sin, condemned sin in the flesh: That the righteousness of the law might be fulfilled in us, who walk not after the flesh, but after the Spirit.
—**Romans 8:1–4**

I read about a young boy who accidentally killed a goose on the family farm. His sister saw what happened and leveraged the incident to her advantage. "If you will wash the dishes every day and do all of my chores, I won't tell Mom," she promised. Soon, the boy tired of being his sister's slave and decided to take matters into his own hands. When he told his sister that he was quitting on her agreement, she reminded him that she would tell their mother. "It doesn't matter anymore," he said cheerfully. "I already told Mom myself, and she forgave me."

God has given us complete forgiveness through the blood of Jesus Christ that was shed on the cross. The price of sin has already been paid in full. There is no remaining condemnation. Yet many Christians struggle with guilt for things they have done or failed to do. The devil is a master at using these things against us. Revelation 12:10 calls him "the accuser of our brethren." Satan not only accuses us before the Father, but He accuses us to our own conscience.

Like the girl in our story, the devil taunts us with our past sins. He knows that if he can keep us consumed by guilt, he can limit our effectiveness for God. We must remember that God has fully forgiven us for every sin because of Jesus. When God sees us, He sees only the righteousness of His Son.

Today's Rooted Principle: Do not allow Satan to condemn you with the sins of the past—you are completely forgiven!

God Has Plans for Your Life

For I know the thoughts that I think toward you, saith the LORD, thoughts of peace, and not of evil, to give you an expected end. Then shall ye call upon me, and ye shall go and pray unto me, and I will hearken unto you. And ye shall seek me, and find me, when ye shall search for me with all your heart.—**Jeremiah 29:11–13**

Some time ago I came across this "message from God" that shows His love and concern for you and me so beautifully:

My Precious Child,

I am in control. I am sovereign. Yes, I allow you to make your own choices. And I know you don't fully understand how these ideas can operate side by side. But I'm able to work within and around the choices you make to cause My ultimate purposes to succeed. For this, you must trust Me. Ask Me about your choices and plans. My wisdom is yours if you'll ask.

I want you to cooperate with My plans. When the people around you don't do that, be assured, I am still in control. I will fulfill My plan. Their choices are their own, but I'm still in control. Trust me. I'll use it for your good.

Lovingly,
Your Heavenly Father, the King

Sometimes we forget that God is in control of our lives. Even when others hurt us by acting against God's will, God is able to turn their choices into our good. With God in control, there are no accidents or coincidences. God told the people of Israel through Jeremiah that even though their current circumstances were bad and showed no hope, the future was bright indeed. With God planning for your life, the future is bright for you as well!

Today's Rooted Principle: Nothing touches your life without first passing through the hands of your loving Father in Heaven.

Understanding Who God Is

In the year that king Uzziah died I saw also the Lord sitting upon a throne, high and lifted up, and his train filled the temple. Above it stood the seraphims: each one had six wings; with twain he covered his face, and with twain he covered his feet, and with twain he did fly. And one cried unto another, and said, Holy, holy, holy, is the LORD of hosts: the whole earth is full of his glory. And the posts of the door moved at the voice of him that cried, and the house was filled with smoke.
—**Isaiah 6:1–4**

We live in a society that has a distorted view of God. When the prophet Isaiah saw his vision of God in Heaven, he saw a God who was transcendent in holiness. Around His throne, seraphims cry out with unceasing worship, "Holy, holy, holy, is the LORD of hosts: the whole earth is full of his glory."

God could have chosen any attribute of His character and nature to highlight. He could have commanded the seraphims to cry out "Love, love, love" or "Just, just, just." But He has especially created angels to declare His holiness.

To understand that God is holy means that we understand how far His standards for righteousness are above our own. No one who truly grasps how exalted God is can do anything except fall on his face and beg for mercy.

When angels appeared to men and women in the Bible as angels (sometimes they appeared as men) the immediate response was terror. In fact, the angels almost always had to calm the person they visited with the words, "Fear not." And that is just the angels—God is far above them in His glory and grandeur. An appreciation for God's holiness will give us a holy reverence and fear of Him that will cause us to examine our ways and make sure we are walking according to His will.

Today's Rooted Principle: Keep the vision of God's holiness in the forefront of your mind, and your life will be holy and pleasing to Him.

Character Counts

Put on the whole armour of God, that ye may be able to stand against the wiles of the devil. For we wrestle not against flesh and blood, but against principalities, against powers, against the rulers of the darkness of this world, against spiritual wickedness in high places. Wherefore take unto you the whole armour of God, that ye may be able to withstand in the evil day, and having done all, to stand.—**Ephesians 6:11–13**

We are in a battle in the Christian life. As someone said, "We travel to Heaven on a battleship, not a cruise ship." In the battle, it is vital that we stand firm and maintain our character. The devil knows that if he can get us to let down our guard in even a small area, it will not be long until he has free reign to go to work in our lives. There are no small character failures.

Oscar Wilde was a brilliant and much-praised writer, but also a greatly immoral man. Late in life as he suffered the consequences of his lifestyle, he wrote: "I grew careless of the lives of others. I took pleasure where it pleased me, and passed on. I forgot that every little action of the common day makes or unmakes character, and that therefore what one has done in the secret chamber, one has some day to cry aloud from the house-top. I ceased to be lord over myself. I allowed pleasure to dominate me. I ended in horrible disgrace."

The devil is perfectly content to take small pieces of ground. If you do not stand firm, you will find yourself continually moving backward until you are completely defeated. When the temptation comes, remember the warning of Scripture, "Neither give place to the devil" (Ephesians 4:27). Guard your character so that he has no room to work in your life, and you will be on the road to victory.

Today's Rooted Principle: Stand fast and maintain your character against temptation—both public and private, both large and small.

Swim Upstream

When I call to remembrance the unfeigned faith that is in thee, which dwelt first in thy grandmother Lois, and thy mother Eunice; and I am persuaded that in thee also. Wherefore I put thee in remembrance that thou stir up the gift of God, which is in thee by the putting on of my hands. For God hath not given us the spirit of fear; but of power, and of love, and of a sound mind.—**2 Timothy 1:5–7**

I heard about a dad who took his son on a fishing trip to a nearby river. They caught a couple of fish early in the morning, but the fish stopped biting. When they were done they didn't have enough fish for a meal, so they released the ones they had caught back into the water. "Will they be okay?" the boy asked his dad. "They'll be fine," the father replied. "Any dead fish can go downriver, but when we put those fish in the water they swam upstream."

We live in a culture that is filled with negative influences, but ours is hardly the first generation with that experience. I think of a young man who grew up in a home without a Christian father, but with a godly mother and a godly grandmother; and this young man became a major influence for the cause of Jesus Christ in the first century. His name was Timothy. How did a little boy from the city of Lystra, a mystical place given over to idol worship, develop into such a great leader for the cause of Jesus Christ?

Paul tells us that Timothy had a real, living faith in his heart. He had more than just a profession of faith; he had an active faith. This faith equipped a young man to rise up and go against the tide of the world around him. God has given us the Spirit of power that allows us to overcome the world through faith.

Today's Rooted Principle: Stand strong in your faith today, and swim against the current of the world.

The Purpose of Trouble

My brethren, count it all joy when ye fall into divers temptations; Knowing this, that the trying of your faith worketh patience. But let patience have her perfect work, that ye may be perfect and entire, wanting nothing.
—**James 1:2–4**

I have never forgotten a saying I heard some years ago, "Every adversity carries with it the seed of an equivalent or greater benefit." We will all go through hard times, but if we respond properly, those troubles can be the tool God uses to make us more effective for His kingdom. For example, some of the greatest preachers I have ever heard had to grow up without a father in the home. Some of the sweetest Christian kids in our school are dealing with huge family troubles.

The difference between people who benefit from their troubles and those who do not is found in their response, not in their troubles. One ancient philosopher said that if everyone in the world could see all the problems of all the people in the world and could choose which ones to have, everyone would go home with their own. The difference is not that some people have trouble while others don't; the difference is that some people respond properly while others don't.

If we realize the purpose and meaning of our troubles—God's plan is that they will make us mature believers—then we can truly rejoice even during hard times. Of course, we're not happy about having trouble, but by keeping our eyes focused on the end result of our trials, we find the patience and strength to endure them and reach the other side. The greatest tragedy is not when things go wrong in our lives. It is when we don't let God work through the things that go wrong to make us what He wants us to be.

Today's Rooted Principle: Resolve today to take advantage of the opportunities for growth presented by your troubles.

A God Who Is Faithful

This I recall to my mind, therefore have I hope. It is of the LORD'S mercies that we are not consumed, because his compassions fail not. They are new every morning: great is thy faithfulness. The LORD is my portion, saith my soul; therefore will I hope in him.—**Lamentations 3:21–24**

One of my favorite hymns is "Great Is Thy Faithfulness." I love the way it describes God's goodness to us no matter what happens. This hymn was written by a man named Thomas Chisholm. He was born in Kentucky just after the Civil War, and following his salvation, he became a pastor. But his broken health did not allow him to continue in the ministry, and he served the Lord for the rest of his life as a layman. He wrote well over one thousand poems, but this one celebrating God's constant love is the best known.

Late in his life, Chisholm wrote a friend: "My income has not been large at any time due to impaired health in the earlier years which has followed me on until now. Although, I must not fail to record here the unfailing faithfulness of a covenant-keeping God and that He has given me many wonderful displays of His providing care, for which I am filled with astonishing gratefulness."

Often we struggle to believe that God is faithful because we live in a world filled with people who are untrustworthy. But no matter how others may fail us and no matter how we may fail Him, God is always there with new mercy to meet the needs of a new day. I love the image of our "mercy account" being refilled as the sun rises each morning. There is wonderful peace and hope in knowing that God's compassion and love for His children will never falter or fail. Great is His faithfulness indeed.

Today's Rooted Principle: Rejoice in God's new mercies for this day and praise Him for being your faithful God.

Every Promise Stands

Having therefore these promises, dearly beloved, let us cleanse ourselves
from all filthiness of the flesh and spirit, perfecting holiness in the fear
of God.—**2 Corinthians 7:1**

I read about a starving man who wandered into a colonial town to beg for food. A young man brought him bread and soup. As he watched the man eat it, he noticed a pouch that was hanging around his neck.

"What's inside the pouch?" the teenager asked.

"It's a paper I've had since we won the war," the man proudly replied. "But I can't read, so I don't know what it says."

The teenager opened the pouch and found an aged official discharge from the Federal Army. It was signed by General Washington himself, and it entitled the old man to a pension for life.

He had a promise, but he had never claimed it!

The promises found in Scripture are not simply platitudes or kind expressions—they are guarantees, backed by the power of Almighty God and His unfailing nature. Solomon said, "...there hath not failed one word of all his good promise..." (1 Kings 8:56). It was true in the days of the wise king, and it is still true today. There are always circumstances that could cause us to doubt and lose heart, but God's promises never fail.

The only thing that hinders us from experiencing what God has promised is when we fail to do what He has commanded—to claim those promises. We must come to Him in faith, believing that we will receive His reward (Hebrews 11:6), and we must fulfill the duties which allow us to reap the rewards of obedience.

Today's Rooted Principle: Claim God's promises today—He will do everything His Word offers you as His child.

You Are Being Followed

Yea, though I walk through the valley of the shadow of death, I will fear no evil: for thou art with me; thy rod and thy staff they comfort me. Thou preparest a table before me in the presence of mine enemies: thou anointest my head with oil; my cup runneth over. Surely goodness and mercy shall follow me all the days of my life: and I will dwell in the house of the LORD for ever.—**Psalm 23:4–6**

Early American Indians had a tough initiation for young braves. On the night of a boy's thirteenth birthday, he was blindfolded and led deep into unfamiliar woods where he was left to spend the night alone. The boy was told that if he lasted through the night and didn't return to the village before morning, he would be a man. No one who had passed this initiation ritual was allowed to speak of it to any boy under thirteen years of age.

After he was left, the young boy would remove his blindfold and discover the danger he was in. A night alone in the forest could be deadly. Yet he would bravely wait all night long, often with a tortured imagination that ran wild with every rustle of leaves or snap of a twig.

However, when the first rays of dawn would appear, what should he see just several feet from him, but the figure of his father with a bow and arrow in hand. All night long, his father had watched the ordeal and stood nearby to protect him.

There may be times when we feel like we are alone, but in truth we are always surrounded by the love and goodness of God. There is never a time when we are truly on our own. Even when we do not believe Him as we should, "he abideth faithful" (2 Timothy 2:13). The struggles and battles you face today do not have to be fought and won in your own strength. The Creator of Heaven and Earth is your "very present help in trouble" (Psalm 46:1).

Today's Rooted Principle: God has sent His goodness and mercy to follow you every step you take this day.

A Testimony of Fruitfulness

*Henceforth I call you not servants; for the servant knoweth not what his lord doeth: but I have called you friends; for all things that I have heard of my Father I have made known unto you. Ye have not chosen me, but I have chosen you, and ordained you, that ye should go and bring forth fruit, and that your fruit should remain: that whatsoever ye shall ask of the Father in my name, he may give it you.—***John 15:15–16**

At my grandmother's 90th birthday celebration a few years ago, our family gathered to honor her lifetime of service to the Lord and love for us. It was a wonderful time of celebration and reminiscing as we talked about the years she has been a powerful influence on our lives.

One of the things that made the biggest impression on me was hearing from adults whose lives she had touched back when they were children. One man stood and said, "I just want to give thanks that as a teenager back in 1957, I came into the Chappell home and had a wonderful meal there with the family. Afterwards Edith [my grandmother] said, 'Alex, can I speak to you over here in the living room?' And I sat down with her and she asked me, 'Alex, if you die today do you know you'd spend eternity in Heaven?' And she opened the Bible and showed me what it meant to be a Christian. In 1957, I made the most important decision I've ever made in my life to trust Christ as my Saviour."

There is nothing we can do in this life that is more important than sharing the Gospel with others and teaching them to be disciples of Jesus Christ. Jesus said that it was for this purpose that we were chosen and called. What a joy it will be to spend eternity with those we have led to Christ!

Today's Rooted Principle: Invite someone today to join you on the road to Heaven.

Keep Looking Up

By faith Abraham, when he was called to go out into a place which he should after receive for an inheritance, obeyed; and he went out, not knowing whither he went. By faith he sojourned in the land of promise, as in a strange country, dwelling in tabernacles with Isaac and Jacob, the heirs with him of the same promise: For he looked for a city which hath foundations, whose builder and maker is God.—**Hebrews 11:8–10**

For her birthday celebration, one of the things my grandmother wanted was for us to sing some of her favorite songs. Her requests revealed a lot about the things that mattered to her. Why did she want to hear "I've Got a Mansion Just Over the Hilltop"? Because her heart was fixed on Heaven. The interests and affections that filled her heart governed the things that she loved.

The story of Abraham is a story of great faith. This Old Testament saint did not have the Scriptures to guide him, but he believed the promises of God and radically altered his entire life to obey what God told him to do. Our faith is not found in our declaration of allegiance to God, but in our obedience to Him. Abraham was willing to leave behind everything to obey God because he was seeking an eternal reward.

Too often the busyness of life can get our eyes off of the goal. Once we are distracted from our calling and purpose, it is easy for us to be turned aside from the right path and to stop obeying God. Hebrews 12:2 urges us to run the race of life with focus: "Looking unto Jesus the author and finisher of our faith." The concerns and cares of the world around us are temporary; the city of gold that God has prepared for those who love Him is eternal.

Today's Rooted Principle: We have not yet seen the great things God has in store for us, but through faith we can persevere until we do.

God's Transforming Power

And he said unto me, My grace is sufficient for thee: for my strength is made perfect in weakness. Most gladly therefore will I rather glory in my infirmities, that the power of Christ may rest upon me. Therefore I take pleasure in infirmities, in reproaches, in necessities, in persecutions, in distresses for Christ's sake: for when I am weak, then am I strong.
—2 Corinthians 12:9–10

Sir Edwin Landseer was one of the most famous painters of the Victorian era. His talent developed early, and he had the first showing of his work at the Royal Academy when he was just thirteen years old. He was commissioned to do a number of official portraits of the royal family and even gave private drawing lessons to Queen Victoria and Prince Albert. But he was best known for his depictions of the natural settings and life in the Scottish highlands.

One day as he was visiting a family in an old mansion in Scotland, one of the servants spilled a pitcher of soda water, leaving a large stain on the wall. While the family was out for the day, Landseer remained behind. Using charcoal, he incorporated the stain into a beautiful drawing. When the family returned they found a picture of a waterfall surrounded by trees and animals. He used his skill to make something beautiful out of what had been an unsightly mess.

God works in much the same way in our lives. The things that we think of as weaknesses and handicaps can, through His grace, become our greatest strengths—and the very things He uses the most to bring glory to Himself. Rather than wishing that the "stains" in our lives would go away, we should give thanks to God for our infirmities and seek His grace so that even those things can be used for His purposes. God's grace provides the strength to meet every challenge and overcome every weakness.

Today's Rooted Principle: When you allow God's grace to transform your weaknesses, beautiful things result.

2 Chronicles 4–6   John 10:24–42   177

Understanding Grace

But not as the offence, so also is the free gift. For if through the offence of one many be dead, much more the grace of God, and the gift by grace, which is by one man, Jesus Christ, hath abounded unto many. And not as it was by one that sinned, so is the gift: for the judgment was by one to condemnation, but the free gift is of many offences unto justification.—**Romans 5:15–16**

John Newton wrote what is probably the most famous hymn in the world, "Amazing Grace." Before his conversion he was a wicked man, making his living as a slave trader—taking people from Africa and selling them into a lifetime of bondage. When Newton was saved, he was completely transformed by God's grace. But through his later years of serving God as a changed man, he never forgot the kind of man he once had been. Newton wrote, "By nature I was too blind to know Him, too proud to trust Him, too obstinate to serve Him, too base-minded to love Him."

There is a danger that faces those who have been saved for a number of years. Sometimes we forget how desperately we need God's grace. Even those of us who grew up in Christian homes and were saved early in life still had no hope of salvation apart from God's grace. We should never forget the incredible debt that was paid for our salvation and the free gift that was offered us through no merit or work of our own.

But we also need God's grace for our daily lives as believers. Just as we could not save ourselves, we cannot live a consecrated Christian life in our own power. The world, the flesh, and the devil work against us constantly. Only the grace of God gives us the strength to be overcomers. The power of grace is something we must never forget.

Today's Rooted Principle: Never forget that just as you needed God's grace for your salvation, you need His grace for each day of your life.

2 Chronicles 7–9   John 11:1–29

One Way

Verily, verily, I say unto you, He that entereth not by the door into the sheepfold, but climbeth up some other way, the same is a thief and a robber. But he that entereth in by the door is the shepherd of the sheep. To him the porter openeth; and the sheep hear his voice: and he calleth his own sheep by name, and leadeth them out.—**John 10:1–3**

Sometime ago I was at the airport getting ready for a flight when I saw an actor. I remembered having seen him on television reruns in Korea when I was a boy, so I introduced myself and began to talk to him. As he was very friendly and open to talking, I asked about some of his acting work and then took the opportunity to witness to him. As I shared the Gospel with him, he told me he had played a big role in a Christian film back in the 1970s and that he "knew about that stuff."

I hope that he truly is converted, but it is certain that being in a Christian film, going to church, getting baptized, being confirmed, or anything else that we do or don't do will not save us. Salvation through faith in Jesus Christ is the only way to Heaven. Our world pushes the idea of all religions being different yet viable paths to the truth; the premise is that any kind of faith will be pleasing to God.

Those of us who know the truth have a great responsibility to stand against that false idea and explain clearly that Jesus is God's only plan of salvation. Jesus said that in the day of judgment, "Many will say to me" that they are His children only to hear the awful words, "I never knew you: depart from me" (Matthew 7:22–23). I don't want that to happen to anyone, so I never assume that anyone knows that he must trust Christ in order to enjoy salvation.

Today's Rooted Principles: Today, find someone you can talk to about Jesus being the only way to salvation.

God's Grace Is Enough

And lest I should be exalted above measure through the abundance of the revelations, there was given to me a thorn in the flesh, the messenger of Satan to buffet me, lest I should be exalted above measure. For this thing I besought the Lord thrice, that it might depart from me. And he said unto me, My grace is sufficient for thee: for my strength is made perfect in weakness. Most gladly therefore will I rather glory in my infirmities, that the power of Christ may rest upon me.—**2 Corinthians 12:7–9**

Charles Spurgeon once told of a time when he had just finished a heavy day's work. He was riding home and was very tired and weary in his spirit, when he suddenly thought of 2 Corinthians 12:9, "My grace is sufficient for thee." He smiled and said, "I should think it is, Lord!" Then he started laughing as the thought made him think of how foolish our unbelief is to God. It would be like if a small fish that was very thirsty was afraid it might drink the river dry, and the river said, "Drink away, little fish, my stream is sufficient for thee." Or, it would be as though after the seven years of plenty, a mouse was afraid it might die of a famine, and Joseph might say, "Cheer up, little mouse, my granaries are sufficient for thee." Or, if a man on top of a mountain feared that he would exhaust the oxygen in the atmosphere, and the earth might say, "Breathe away, oh man, and fill thy lungs ever; my atmosphere is sufficient for thee."

We all have trials in life. Like the Apostle Paul, we may find ourselves begging God to deliver us from a severe test. Sometimes God does grant us deliverance, but other times He grants us a measure of grace that is sufficient to allow us to endure the hardship.

Regardless of which answer God gives for our individual situation, it is vital that we allow His grace to play its role in our hearts and lives. His grace never runs out, and it is always sufficient.

Today's Rooted Principle: God's grace is more than enough to meet any challenge you face today.

JUNE

If We Faint Not

And let us not be weary in well doing: for in due season we shall reap, if we faint not. As we have therefore opportunity, let us do good unto all men, especially unto them who are of the household of faith.
—**Galatians 6:9–10**

Frances Chadwick was one of the great open water swimmers of all time. She was the first woman to swim across the English Channel in both directions, and she also broke the time records for making the long and difficult swim. In 1952, she set out to cover the twenty-six miles from Catalina Island to the coast of California.

After Chadwick had been swimming for about fifteen hours, she was surrounded by a thick fog and began to struggle. She told her mother, who was in one of the boats accompanying her on the trip, that she didn't think she could make it. After struggling a little longer, she gave up. It wasn't until after she got in the boat that she learned she had only been one mile from shore. The next day she told an interviewer: "I'm not excusing myself. But if I could have seen the land, I think I might have made it."

So many times we fall short of reaching our goals and doing what we should for God because we get discouraged and lose heart just before we would have seen the victory. We must not be impatient when we do not see results immediately. The fact that we have not yet received the promises of God does not mean that we will not—every promise of God is certain from the moment He made it, whether it has yet come to pass or not.

Two months after her failed attempt, Frances Chadwick was back in the water to again attempt the swim from Catalina to California. Again the fog set in after she had been swimming for hours, but this time instead of quitting, she pushed on and reached the shore.

Today's Rooted Principle: No matter how much fog surrounds you today, stay in the water and keep swimming.

Faithful Promises

My covenant will I not break, nor alter the thing that is gone out of my lips. Once have I sworn by my holiness that I will not lie unto David. His seed shall endure for ever, and his throne as the sun before me. It shall be established for ever as the moon, and as a faithful witness in heaven. Selah.—**Psalm 89:34–37**

When Saul turned away from obeying God, God instructed Samuel to anoint a new king who would be "a man after his own heart" (1 Samuel 13:14). That man was David, and during his reign, God made many promises to him about the future. The kingdom grew and prospered during David's life and during the reign of his son, Solomon. Yet later in his life, Solomon turned away from God, and after his death the kingdom was divided. The divided nations were later conquered, and the Jewish people were scattered across the Assyrian and Babylonian empires.

What had happened to God's promises? Were they nullified and broken? No! Every promise of God is sure. As the prophet Isaiah tells us, these promises of the eternal kingdom through David's throne were and are fulfilled in Jesus Christ. Isaiah 9:7 says, "Of the increase of his government and peace there shall be no end, upon the throne of David, and upon his kingdom, to order it, and to establish it with judgment and with justice from henceforth even for ever. The zeal of the LORD of hosts will perform this." The throne from which Jesus will rule the world is the throne of David, just as God promised.

Even when it appears that things are not going according to God's plan, He is in control. You do not need to doubt or fear or wonder how things can possibly be fixed. The God of the universe, whose promises are as certain as the sun and the moon, will work to do exactly what He has promised in His Word.

Today's Rooted Principle: You can rely with complete confidence and certainty on every promise God has made to you.

Sacrifice

And Araunah said unto David, Let my lord the king take and offer up what seemeth good unto him: behold, here be oxen for burnt sacrifice, and threshing instruments and other instruments of the oxen for wood. All these things did Araunah, as a king, give unto the king. And Araunah said unto the king, The LORD thy God accept thee. And the king said unto Araunah, Nay; but I will surely buy it of thee at a price: neither will I offer burnt offerings unto the LORD my God of that which doth cost me nothing. So David bought the threshingfloor and the oxen for fifty shekels of silver.—**2 Samuel 24:22–24**

During World War II a young soldier named David Webster of Easy Company of the 101st Airborne wrote his mother: "Stop worrying about me. I joined the parachutists to fight. I intend to fight. If necessary, I shall die fighting, but don't worry about this because no war can be won without young men dying. Those things which are precious are saved only by sacrifice."

Scripture often refers to the Christian life as a war—a spiritual battlefield. To answer the question of hymn writer Isaac Watts, we will not be carried to the skies on flowery beds of ease. And there is no victory apart from sacrifice. Just as our salvation was purchased at great cost, overcoming the enemy and walking in the Spirit require that we be willing to give up some things in order to triumph.

Whether it is large or small, there should be nothing we hold onto so tightly that it becomes more important to us than pleasing God. Paul said that if he knew eating meat would create an offense to others, then, "I will eat no flesh while the world standeth" (1 Corinthians 8:13). Willingness to submit our desires and dreams to God places us in a position to receive His blessings.

Today's Rooted Principle: There should not be anything in your life that you are not willing to give up in order to better serve the Lord.

The Crowns Are Yet to Come

For I am now ready to be offered, and the time of my departure is at hand. I have fought a good fight, I have finished my course, I have kept the faith: Henceforth there is laid up for me a crown of righteousness, which the Lord, the righteous judge, shall give me at that day: and not to me only, but unto all them also that love his appearing.
—2 Timothy 4:6–8

O f all the memorials and monuments that have great meaning to our nation, perhaps the most solemn is the Tomb of the Unknown Soldier at Arlington National Cemetery. There lie the remains of one unknown soldier in a place of respect that is dedicated to all soldiers who have given their lives in our past wars but could not be identified. An honor guard keeps watch day and night as a symbol of our gratitude for their sacrifice. Inscribed on the tomb are these words: "Here rests in honored glory an American Soldier known but to God."

Sometimes we may wonder if anyone notices, appreciates or even realizes what we are doing. Elijah felt that way when he was standing for right against Ahab and Jezebel. He told God, "I, even I only, am left; and they seek my life, to take it away" (1 Kings 19:10). Of course Elijah was wrong—God had thousands of other faithful servants. But even if he had been right and there had been no one else following God, Elijah still could and should have done so.

There will be a day in the future when all of our efforts, all of our labors, and all of our sacrifices made in service for God will be remembered and rewarded. Whether anyone on this Earth ever knows your name or not, you can be sure that God sees all that you have done and will greet you with the words, "Well done" (Matthew 25:21).

Today's Rooted Principle: Don't be discouraged if it seems that no one notices your labors. One day God will give crowns of glory to those who love and serve Him.

Through the Fire

Beloved, think it not strange concerning the fiery trial which is to try you, as though some strange thing happened unto you: But rejoice, inasmuch as ye are partakers of Christ's sufferings; that, when his glory shall be revealed, ye may be glad also with exceeding joy.—**1 Peter 4:12–13**

Gold is one of the most valuable materials on Earth. It has been used for centuries as money, but it also has many uses in industry, manufacturing, and even space flight. One of the traits that makes gold so useful is that it can be shaped and formed so easily. In fact, a single ounce of gold can be flattened out to cover three hundred square feet.

But gold ore dug out of the ground contains many other elements that must be removed prior to the gold being useful. The refining process for gold involves intense heat. Gold melts at a temperature of almost two thousand degrees Fahrenheit. That incredibly high temperature is required for gold to be ready for use. The Christian life involves the same process. Sometimes we are surprised when "bad things happen to good people." But Scripture tells us that fiery trials are part of God's refining process for our lives. Rather than complaining or doubting God's goodness when trials come, we should rejoice as we think of the end result they will produce.

It is impossible for us to be like Jesus without taking part in His sufferings. The notion that believers never get sick, never have financial difficulties, never have problems at work, or never have relationship struggles is popular in our culture; but it is contrary to the Word of God. Jesus promised, "In the world ye shall have tribulation" (John 16:33a). However, though the trials are real, so is the victory. For Jesus went on to say, "but be of good cheer; I have overcome the world" (John 16:33b). Every trial is part of His plan.

Today's Rooted Principle: When you view your trials as part of God's refining process, you can endure them with patience.

The Process of Bearing Fruit

I am the vine, ye are the branches: He that abideth in me, and I in him, the same bringeth forth much fruit: for without me ye can do nothing. If a man abide not in me, he is cast forth as a branch, and is withered; and men gather them, and cast them into the fire, and they are burned. If ye abide in me, and my words abide in you, ye shall ask what ye will, and it shall be done unto you. Herein is my Father glorified, that ye bear much fruit; so shall ye be my disciples.—**John 15:5–8**

Here in California we have wonderful oranges. As you drive through agricultural regions, you can see grove after grove of orange trees. Over the years I've seen a lot of work go into those orchards. I've seen watering and pruning and, of course, harvesting. But I have never yet seen a planter out in the field talking to the orange trees and telling them that they need to get busy having oranges.

Why? Because oranges are a natural result of healthy orange trees. In the same way, spiritual fruit is the natural result of a healthy Christian. If your life is not producing fruit, it is a sign that something is wrong. Jesus tells us that if we abide in Him—if our hearts are fixed on Him and we are filling our minds and heart with His Word—we will bear fruit. A fruitless Christian is a contradiction, an indication that something abnormal is going on.

Rather than command us to bear fruit, Jesus tells us that we must abide in Him. If we do that, fruitfulness is assured. Then He lays out the purpose of our fruitfulness—to bring glory to God. Everything we do is meant to honor our Father in Heaven, and fixing our hearts and minds on Jesus assures that we will be fruitful.

Today's Rooted Principle: If your life is not fruitful, abide in Christ. You will find that fruit naturally follows that close relationship.

God Wants People to Be Saved

Therefore if any man be in Christ, he is a new creature: old things are passed away; behold, all things are become new. And all things are of God, who hath reconciled us to himself by Jesus Christ, and hath given to us the ministry of reconciliation; To wit, that God was in Christ, reconciling the world unto himself, not imputing their trespasses unto them; and hath committed unto us the word of reconciliation.
—2 Corinthians 5:17–19

I heard about a pastor who preached a strong salvation sermon. When he gave the invitation, a five-year-old boy came forward. Not knowing whether the boy understood what it meant to be saved, the pastor began to ask him questions. The more questions he asked, the more confused the boy became. Finally the boy interrupted and asked, "Pastor, in your message this morning you said that if I would come and trust Jesus to save me, He would! Did you really mean that?" The pastor said, "I did not ask him any more questions after that!"

God has called every believer to be a witness of the Good News. This call is not restricted to pastors, evangelists, and missionaries. The reason that God wants each of us to be sharing the Gospel is that He wants people to be saved. God could have made salvation difficult; instead He made it as simple as possible—so simple even a child can understand and obey. Salvation is not cheap. Jesus paid an unspeakable price so that our sins could be forgiven and we could be reconciled to God. But salvation is simple.

Paul said that God has given us "the word of reconciliation" (2 Corinthians 5:19). We can't keep the wonderful message of reconciliation with God to ourselves. Knowing that God wants people to be saved should motivate and encourage us to faithfully give the plain and simple truth of the Gospel to everyone we can.

Today's Rooted Principle: Find someone today with whom you can share the wonderful news of salvation in Jesus Christ.

How God Treats Those Who Repent

What shall we then say to these things? If God be for us, who can be against us? He that spared not his own Son, but delivered him up for us all, how shall he not with him also freely give us all things? Who shall lay any thing to the charge of God's elect? It is God that justifieth. Who is he that condemneth? It is Christ that died, yea rather, that is risen again, who is even at the right hand of God, who also maketh intercession for us.—**Romans 8:31–34**

Years ago, a well-known evangelist was pulled over for speeding in a small southern town and taken to traffic court. The preacher pleaded guilty because he had been speeding. Recognizing him, the judge said, "You are guilty and the fine must be paid—but I am going to pay it for you." The preacher said that not only did the judge pay the fine, but after court the judge took him out for a steak dinner. The preacher said, "That is how God treats repentant sinners!"

All of us are sinners. But when we trusted Christ as our Saviour, God in mercy and grace replaced our debt with the perfect righteousness of Jesus Christ. Nothing will ever be laid to our charge. We were guilty, but Jesus paid the price of our sins on the cross, and through faith we have received justification through His blood. No sin will ever be held against us.

But there is even more. Not only has God freely given us salvation and removed the penalty and guilt of sin, but He also promises to freely give us all of the things that we need to live for Him. Do not let anything in your past keep you from experiencing His great love and provision.

Today's Rooted Principle: God has fully and freely forgiven your sins; do not live with the guilt of the past when God has blotted it out.

The Precious Name of Jesus

Be it known unto you all, and to all the people of Israel, that by the name of Jesus Christ of Nazareth, whom ye crucified, whom God raised from the dead, even by him doth this man stand here before you whole. This is the stone which was set at nought of you builders, which is become the head of the corner. Neither is there salvation in any other: for there is none other name under heaven given among men, whereby we must be saved.—**Acts 4:10–12**

John Dyer, a Welsh poet and pastor from the 1700s once wrote, "A man may go to Heaven without health, without riches, without honors, without learning, without friends; but he can never go there without Christ." Today our world is filled with people who are seeking some other way to God than the one found in the blood of Jesus and His precious name, but all such efforts are doomed to failure. Jesus is the only way to Heaven.

Our salvation, however, is more than just a ticket to Heaven; it is a daily provision for our lives here on Earth as well. Jesus has also given us the access to come to the Father in the power and authority of His name to present our requests. Jesus said, "And whatsoever ye shall ask in my name, that will I do" (John 14:13). Being able to act and pray in His name is a powerful delegation of authority.

In His Great Commission Jesus said, "All power is given unto me in heaven and in earth" (Matthew 28:18). It is this power that He has offered to us that enables us to be faithful witnesses for Him and to see our daily needs met. There is no power that can stand against the name of Jesus as we work, worship, walk, and witness in that precious name.

Today's Rooted Principle: The same Jesus who saved you has offered you the ability to ask the Father for your needs in His precious name.

Citizenship in Heaven

For our conversation is in heaven; from whence also we look for the Saviour, the Lord Jesus Christ: Who shall change our vile body, that it may be fashioned like unto his glorious body, according to the working whereby he is able even to subdue all things unto himself.
—**Philippians 3:20–21**

There was a time in America when our government acknowledged that we were a nation under God. Carved into the stone walls of the Capitol, the Supreme Court, and our national monuments are reminders from Scripture of the role of faith in the founding of our country. Today those truths are under attack. But even if these attacks succeed and every vestige of our heritage is taken away, this nation that we love is not our home. We are ultimately citizens of Heaven.

The fact that our home is in another land should produce a difference in the way that we live. The great preacher Charles Spurgeon said it this way: "Christians ought so to live that it were idle to speak of a comparison between them and the men of the world. It would not be a comparison but a contrast. No scale of degrees should be possible; the believer should be a direct and manifest contradiction to the unregenerate. The life of a saint should be altogether above and out of the same list as the life of a sinner. Wide as the poles asunder are life and death, light and darkness, health and disease, purity and sin, spiritual and carnal."

The problem in our country is not that the sinners are rebelling against God; that has been true throughout history. The problem is that God's children have adopted the manners and morals of the world around us. We should live each day with the knowledge that we are representatives of the King and behave in a way that brings honor and glory to His name.

Today's Rooted Principle: Focus your affections on things in Heaven today, and you will find the problems of Earth growing smaller.

Pray, Then Pray Again

Confess your faults one to another, and pray one for another, that ye may be healed. The effectual fervent prayer of a righteous man availeth much. Elias was a man subject to like passions as we are, and he prayed earnestly that it might not rain: and it rained not on the earth by the space of three years and six months. And he prayed again, and the heaven gave rain, and the earth brought forth her fruit.
—**James 5:16–18**

George Müller was a man of incredible faith and prayer. He supported, educated, and led to Christ thousands of children in his orphanages in Bristol, England. Yet despite the vast scope of his ministry, Müller never asked anyone for money. He told those who wanted to know how they could help to ask God, as he had already taken his needs before the Lord. Over his life the equivalent of what would today be millions of dollars came in to provide all that the work needed.

Müller prayed for more than fifty years for the salvation of two of his friends from his wicked youth. One friend was saved just before Müller's death, the other shortly after. Müller wrote, "The great fault of the children of God is, they do not continue in prayer; they do not go on praying; they do not persevere. If they desire anything for God's glory, they should pray until they get it."

There are times when God answers our prayers immediately, sometimes sending the answer even before we ask. But there are other times when we must learn the discipline of patience and perseverance in continued prayer. Unless God has definitely closed the door as He did with Paul and the thorn in the flesh, we should continue to be faithful in prayer. Many times we do not receive the answer to prayer simply because we give up on praying before it comes.

Today's Rooted Principle: If the answer to your prayer is delayed, pray again. Never give up until your answer comes.

The Hinges of Opposition

But I will tarry at Ephesus until Pentecost. For a great door and effectual is opened unto me, and there are many adversaries.
—**1 Corinthians 16:8–9**

Dr. Bob Jones, Sr. said, "The door to the room of success swings on the hinges of opposition." Sometimes we mistakenly believe that because we are having difficulty we are on the wrong track. We think that if we were doing the right thing it would be easy. However, the presence of obstacles and opposition does not mean that we are doing wrong; in fact, that can even be a sign that we are close to seeing wonderful things happen.

Russell Conwell, a Baptist pastor in Philadelphia, was the author of one of the best-selling books of the 1800s called *Acres of Diamonds*. In it Conwell told the story of a man obsessed with finding diamonds. He sold his home and travelled the world for years in a futile search. Meanwhile, the buyer of the man's property discovered one of the richest diamond mines in the world on that land. Too often we dream of greener pastures or easier paths when what we need to do is just persist in doing right where we are.

It is said that the great missionary David Livingstone received a letter from a young man who wanted to come and join his work. "Please tell me the easiest way to get to Africa to join," he wrote. Livingstone replied, "I am not interested in someone who is looking for the easiest way." The Christian life is described in Scripture as both a war and a long distance race. Success at what God has called us to do requires struggle, intensity, and the commitment to overcome obstacles. If you are facing opposition today, rejoice—that may be the best sign yet that victory is close at hand.

Today's Rooted Principle: Do not allow any opposition to deter you from doing what is right.

You Don't Have to Stand Alone

There shall not any man be able to stand before thee all the days of thy life: as I was with Moses, so I will be with thee: I will not fail thee, nor forsake thee. Be strong and of a good courage: for unto this people shalt thou divide for an inheritance the land, which I sware unto their fathers to give them.—**Joshua 1:5–6**

There is nothing of lasting and eternal value that a Christian can accomplish in his own strength. We cannot stand alone. The good news is that we don't have to. The same God who stood with and empowered Moses, Joshua, Esther, Daniel, and other heroes of the faith throughout the centuries is alive and active in your life today. The same power that worked miracles in the past can still work miracles today.

Hudson Taylor said, "Many missionaries estimate difficulty in light of their own resources, and thus they attempt very little, and they always fail. All who have done great things for God first reckon on His presence and power to guide them." The work that Hudson Taylor did in opening China to the Gospel and seeing multiplied thousands brought to Christ was a miracle work that can be explained only by God's power.

Our culture values the rugged individual who stands alone. But while there are times when we may have no human help, we are never truly alone. God will never forsake or abandon us. The promises of God are just as true today as when they were first given. One of the names of Jesus is Emmanuel—God with us. We do not serve an absent or distant God; we serve the God who is "a very present help in trouble" (Psalm 46:1). When you face your battles and struggles today, rely on His strength, and you will find that the victory is assured.

Today's Rooted Principle: Allow the presence of Christ to strengthen your resolve today—you are not alone.

Saved for a Purpose

And I heard a loud voice saying in heaven, Now is come salvation, and strength, and the kingdom of our God, and the power of his Christ: for the accuser of our brethren is cast down, which accused them before our God day and night. And they overcame him by the blood of the Lamb, and by the word of their testimony; and they loved not their lives unto the death.—**Revelation 12:10–11**

Bible teacher Warren Wiersbe said, "In the Christian life you're either an overcomer or you're overcome, a victor or a victim. After all, God didn't save us to make statues out of us and put us on exhibition. He saved us to make soldiers out of us and move us forward by faith to claim our rich inheritance in Jesus Christ."

Every believer has a place in God's plan for warfare against the enemy. The world has no power to resist the devil. The Bible tells us that they "are taken captive by him at his will" (2 Timothy 2:26). But that is not true for the child of God. We are no longer helpless against Satan, but that is true not because of our strength, but through the blood of Jesus.

The power of the blood pays the price for our salvation, but it does far more than just that. The same blood that saves us makes us victors—overcomers—by empowering us to win the victory over the temptations and trials that we face. The truth is that our battles are not just for our own benefit. Each of us has a powerful influence on others. Our family members, neighbors, co-workers, and friends at church need us to help them in the battle as well. If we forget the purpose for which God has saved us, we are likely to fall victim to the wiles of Satan. Remain focused today on the calling of God, and rest in His power as you walk with Him.

Today's Rooted Principle: Find your place in God's purpose today, and you will be an overcomer.

Follow

Then said Jesus unto his disciples, If any man will come after me, let him deny himself, and take up his cross, and follow me. For whosoever will save his life shall lose it: and whosoever will lose his life for my sake shall find it. For what is a man profited, if he shall gain the whole world, and lose his own soul? or what shall a man give in exchange for his soul?—**Matthew 16:24–26**

I once read the story of a young woman who wanted to go to college, but her heart sank when she read the question on the application that asked, "Are you a leader?" Being both honest and conscientious, she wrote, "No," and returned the application, expecting the worst. To her surprise, she received this letter from the college: "Dear Applicant: A study of the application forms reveals that this year our college will have 1,452 new leaders. We are accepting you because we feel it is imperative that they have at least one follower."

There are times for all of us to lead in various roles and ways in our lives, but sometimes we become so focused on leadership, that we forget our first responsibility is to be followers of Jesus Christ. The first command that He gave to His disciples was to follow Him, and the same is true for us. There is no way to be a successful, victorious Christian without first walking in the footsteps of Jesus.

Often we hear people ask the question, "What would Jesus do?" While that is a good question to help us order our actions, His life was not the only example for us—we also find a pattern of behavior in His death. "Christ also suffered for us, leaving us an example, that ye should follow his steps" (1 Peter 2:21). Jesus died for others, and as we follow Him, what we do should also be for others.

Today's Rooted Principle: Above all else, resolve today to follow Jesus and do His will.

Wasted Correction

*And ye have forgotten the exhortation which speaketh unto you as unto
children, My son, despise not thou the chastening of the Lord, nor faint
when thou art rebuked of him: For whom the Lord loveth he chasteneth,
and scourgeth every son whom he receiveth. If ye endure chastening,
God dealeth with you as with sons; for what son is he whom the father
chasteneth not?—***Hebrews 12:5–7***

We know that God corrects every one of His children, but it is also
true that not every believer benefits from that correction. Andrew
Murray said it this way: "A believer may pass through much affliction,
and yet secure very little blessing from it all. Abiding in Christ is the
secret of securing all that the Father meant the chastisement to bring us."

God never chastens us arbitrarily. There is always a purpose behind
His correction, but the author of Hebrews warns us that there are two
reactions that will cause us to miss the benefit of that correction.

First, we can despise it—holding God's rebuke in contempt and
refusing to agree with Him that we need to change our ways. This
attitude of rebellion makes it impossible for us to receive the blessing of
a restored relationship with the Father.

The second wrong response is to faint—to give up because of the
severity of the correction. The important thing to remember during
chastening is that it is meant to help us. We can fall into the trap of
thinking that God is judging us to "get even" or "settle the score." But
the price for our sin has already been paid in full by Jesus. We are not
punished for our sins; we are chastened as a means of bringing us back
to right and godly living. If you have done something for which you are
being chastened, quickly repent. You will find that God awaits you with
open arms.

Today's Rooted Principle: If God chastens you, quickly respond to His
correction and trust in His love.

Invest in Your Children

And Joshua said unto them, Pass over before the ark of the LORD your God into the midst of Jordan, and take ye up every man of you a stone upon his shoulder, according unto the number of the tribes of the children of Israel: That this may be a sign among you, that when your children ask their fathers in time to come, saying, What mean ye by these stones? Then ye shall answer them, That the waters of Jordan were cut off before the ark of the covenant of the LORD; when it passed over Jordan, the waters of Jordan were cut off: and these stones shall be for a memorial unto the children of Israel for ever.—**Joshua 4:5–7**

Charles Francis Adams, son of President John Quincy Adams and grandson of President John Adams, kept a diary. One day this busy political leader entered this description: "Went fishing with my son today—a day wasted." His son, Brooks Adams, also kept a diary, which is still in existence. On that same day, Brooks Adams made this entry: "Went fishing with my father—the most wonderful day of my life!"

God has given fathers a special responsibility to make a meaningful investment of time in the lives of their children. This is His pattern for continuing faith through the generations of a family. There need to be memorials in our lives—signposts that we can point out to our children to show them that the God they read about in the Bible is still active in our world today. This does not happen accidentally or without the investment of serious time.

Many believe it to be wise and proper to make financial preparation for our children's future, and it is. But far more important are the spiritual investments we make through spending time with them talking about the things God has done in our own lives.

Today's Rooted Principle: Take time today to invest in things that matter for eternity, and your day will not be wasted.

Courage

Then said David to the Philistine, Thou comest to me with a sword, and with a spear, and with a shield: but I come to thee in the name of the LORD of hosts, the God of the armies of Israel, whom thou hast defied. This day will the LORD deliver thee into mine hand; and I will smite thee, and take thine head from thee; and I will give the carcases of the host of the Philistines this day unto the fowls of the air, and to the wild beasts of the earth; that all the earth may know that there is a God in Israel. And all this assembly shall know that the LORD saveth not with sword and spear: for the battle is the LORD'S, and he will give you into our hands.—**1 Samuel 17:45–47**

When you are confronted with what seems to be an overwhelming problem, how do you react? Do you cower in fear and look for a different way to reach your goal, or do you charge ahead, confident in what God has called you to do? It is impossible for us to win the victory apart from courage.

Famed World War II tank commander General George Patton said, "Courage is fear holding on a minute longer." If you give in to your fears, you are on the path to defeat. However, if you stand strong in spite of your fears, you are on the path to victory. And we must never forget that we are not in the battle alone. With the power of God on our side, we cannot be defeated.

When David went out to fight Goliath, the Bible says he "hasted, and ran…to meet the Philistine" (1 Samuel 17:48). Even though Goliath was huge and heavily armed and David had only a sling, David's faith gave him the courage to face and defeat his foe—and faith will do the same for you.

Today's Rooted Principle: Be strong and courageous today. God is with you, and He will never leave or forsake you.

Nehemiah 10–11　　Acts 4:1–22　　199

Waiting on God

My soul, wait thou only upon God; for my expectation is from him. He only is my rock and my salvation: he is my defence; I shall not be moved. In God is my salvation and my glory: the rock of my strength, and my refuge, is in God. Trust in him at all times; ye people, pour out your heart before him: God is a refuge for us. Selah.—**Psalm 62:5–8**

Amy Carmichael, missionary to India, wrote, "Blessed are the single-hearted, for they shall enjoy much peace…If you refuse to be hurried and pressed, if you stay your soul on God, nothing can keep you from that clearness of spirit which is life and peace. In that stillness you know what His will is."

We live in an impatient society. We want what we want, and we want it right now. There is even a pot roast now that you can cook in a microwave in less than ten minutes—but it's not as good as the real thing. When we refuse to wait on God and allow Him to work according to His schedule, when we take matters into our own hands, the result is always disaster.

We see this illustrated so clearly in the life of Abraham. Because he had not yet received the son of promise, he listened to Sarah's plan and had a son with Hagar. Some four thousand years later our world is still dealing with the fallout from that impatient decision as the descendants of Isaac and the descendants of Ishmael struggle for control of the land of Israel.

Take advantage of every opportunity and open door that God places before you. But if you do not see the doors opening according to your schedule, take heart. God knows exactly where you are. If you wait on His timing, you will find Him to be a refuge and defense in every test that you face.

Today's Rooted Principle: Rest in God today. He is never late, and in His time, He will work His purpose in your life.

Grow Up

For when for the time ye ought to be teachers, ye have need that one teach you again which be the first principles of the oracles of God; and are become such as have need of milk, and not of strong meat. For every one that useth milk is unskilful in the word of righteousness: for he is a babe. But strong meat belongeth to them that are of full age, even those who by reason of use have their senses exercised to discern both good and evil.—**Hebrews 5:12–14**

Every person who is a born-again believer starts life as a baby in Christ. Whether the new convert is six or sixty, that person is still a new Christian. Leonard Ravenhill tells about a group of tourists visiting a picturesque village who walked by an old man sitting beside a fence. In a rather patronizing way, one tourist asked him, "Were any great men born in this village?" The old man replied, "Nope, only babies."

It's a good thing to be a baby, but it's not a good thing to remain a baby. This is just as true in the spiritual realm as it is in the physical realm. A baby Christian who has been saved for forty years is a tragedy. God intends for us to grow and mature so that we can be a positive influence in the lives of others. Until we learn to dig into the meat of the Word for ourselves, we will never grow.

I have the privilege of pastoring a local New Testament church. I take the Word of God to the pulpit and preach His Word. Attending a good Bible-preaching church is vital to your spiritual growth, but it is not enough. In addition to hearing the teaching and preaching of the Word, you need to be a student of Scripture yourself.

Today's Rooted Principle: Go beyond the milk of the Word today; be a serious and thoughtful student of Scriptures so that you can grow and mature as a Christian.

Don't Lose Your Freedom

Stand fast therefore in the liberty wherewith Christ hath made us free, and be not entangled again with the yoke of bondage.—**Galatians 5:1**

Charles Spurgeon used this parable to illustrate the bondage of sin. He said, "There was once a tyrant who summoned one of his subjects into his presence and ordered him to make a chain. The poor blacksmith—that was his occupation—had to go to work and forge the chain. When it was done, he brought it into the presence of the tyrant and was ordered to take it away and make it twice the length. He brought it again to the tyrant, and again he was ordered to double it. Back he came when he had obeyed the order, and the tyrant looked at it, then commanded the servants to bind the man hand and foot with the chain he had made and cast him into prison."

Spurgeon continued with an application. "That is what the devil does with men. He makes them forge their own chain, and then binds them hand and foot with it and casts them into outer darkness."

Every sin places us in bondage to the enemy. We hear in religious circles today about freedom, but too often those who use the word use it wrongly because they do not understand the danger of sin. In many cases, they speak of being free to sin, rather than being made free from sin.

We who know the Lord have been made free from sin. But Christian liberty does not entitle us to do wrong. That is the path back into bondage. Think about the Israelites as they wandered in the wilderness. Again and again they complained against Moses and against God. They often said, "We wish we were back in Egypt." In Egypt they were slaves and their male children were killed at birth. Why would they want to go back to such awful circumstances? Yet, when we choose to sin, we are placing similar chains of bondage on ourselves.

Today's Rooted Principle: Do not allow the devil to enslave you through sin and steal away the freedom Christ purchased for you.

Esther 3–5   Acts 5:22–42

When We Sin

My little children, these things write I unto you, that ye sin not. And if any man sin, we have an advocate with the Father, Jesus Christ the righteous: And he is the propitiation for our sins: and not for ours only, but also for the sins of the whole world. And hereby we do know that we know him, if we keep his commandments.—**1 John 2:1–3**

A pastor finished his message early one Sunday, then he decided to see if his congregation understood what he had preached. So he asked, "Can anyone tell me what you must do before you can obtain forgiveness of sin?" There was a short pause and then, from the back of the room, a small boy spoke up, "You have to sin."

There are some people who teach that it is possible for a Christian never to sin. I've often thought that it would be nice if they were right! But Scripture makes it plain that although we should always obey God and His Word, we will not. Paul wrote, "For the good that I would I do not: but the evil which I would not, that I do" (Romans 7:19). The question is not whether we will sin, but whether we will respond properly when we do sin.

There is an old saying in the legal community that a lawyer who represents himself in court has a fool for a client. I am so grateful that when we sin we do not have to stand on our own before God. Jesus acts as our attorney—placing His blood and His righteousness on our account in place of our sin.

This truth is critical for us to grasp. I have counseled many people who were struggling with guilt over a past sin. They are being held captive by the enemy rather than living in the freedom that is available to every child of God.

Today's Rooted Principle: God is always faithful to forgive when we repent and seek His mercy.

Good Forgetters

For this is the covenant that I will make with the house of Israel after those days, saith the Lord; I will put my laws into their mind, and write them in their hearts: and I will be to them a God, and they shall be to me a people: And they shall not teach every man his neighbour, and every man his brother, saying, Know the Lord: for all shall know me, from the least to the greatest. For I will be merciful to their unrighteousness, and their sins and their iniquities will I remember no more.
—**Hebrews 8:10–12**

Two little neighbor boys had quarreled bitterly one night. But the next morning Johnny took his cap and headed for Bobby's house. Surprised, an older member of the family said teasingly, "What! Going to play with him again? I thought you quarreled only last evening and were never going to have anything more to do with each other. Funny memory you have." Johnny looked a little sheepish, dug his toe into the carpet for a moment, then flashed a satisfied smile as he hurried away. "Oh! Bobby and me are good forgetters!"

It is a virtual certainty that someone is going to disappoint you today in some manner. A friend may not stand up for you when you need him to. A family member may say something unkind. A spiritual leader may not respond properly. Whatever the case, you are faced with a question: How will you respond? The key to a proper response is found in the way God deals with our sins.

When we fall short, as all of us do, and ask for His forgiveness, God does not demand that we go through a long process to prove we have learned our lesson; He forgives. Then He forgets—never bringing up our sin again. While we cannot forget as God does, we can refuse to ever bring up the sins of the past.

Today's Rooted Principle: Forgive those who have wronged you in the same gracious way God has forgiven you.

Esther 9–10   Acts 7:1–21

Open Your Mail

Grace and peace be multiplied unto you through the knowledge of God, and of Jesus our Lord, According as his divine power hath given unto us all things that pertain unto life and godliness, through the knowledge of him that hath called us to glory and virtue: Whereby are given unto us exceeding great and precious promises: that by these ye might be partakers of the divine nature, having escaped the corruption that is in the world through lust.—**2 Peter 1:2–4**

I read about a Christian attorney who, after meditating on several Scriptures, decided to cancel the debts of all his clients who had owed him money for more than six months. He drafted a letter explaining his decision and its biblical basis and sent the letters via certified mail to seventeen past due accounts. One by one, the letters began to return to his office. Eventually sixteen of the seventeen letters came back unopened. A few people had moved, but the most common reason was that his clients refused to sign for and open the envelopes fearing that he was suing them for their debts!

Sometimes people approach the Word of God as a long list of rules rather than a message of love and forgiveness. The Bible is not trying to ruin your life by telling you all the things you can't do; it is telling you how to experience freedom and the joy of the Lord. God has given us everything we need to live a happy and godly life in the promises of Scripture, yet too many of His children never "open their mail" from Him.

Set aside time to read, study, and meditate on the Bible. You will find that God's promises of forgiveness and hope lighten your load and set you free.

Today's Rooted Principle: Spend time today in the Word of God—don't miss His message of love and forgiveness for you.

Job 1–2   Acts 7:22–43

Under Pressure

Behold, I go forward, but he is not there; and backward, but I cannot perceive him: On the left hand, where he doth work, but I cannot behold him: he hideth himself on the right hand, that I cannot see him: But he knoweth the way that I take: when he hath tried me, I shall come forth as gold.—**Job 23:8–10**

The largest piano in the world is the Challen Grand Concert Piano. It is more than two feet longer than a standard grand piano and weighs over a ton. When the 230 strings are connected, the frame tension is more than 60,000 pounds—thirty tons of pressure! That's a lot of pressure, but without that pressure, the piano cannot make beautiful music.

Life works in much the same way. All of us have times when we experience extreme pressure. Whether it is sickness, financial difficulty, a strained relationship, a besetting sin, or something else, these times of trial and testing can produce something beautiful. Job certainly experienced far worse trials than most of us will ever endure. He lost his wealth, his health, and his children; and his wife suggested he curse God so he could die. At the lowest point in his life, even when he could not see or understand what God was doing, he had faith that he was being refined and made better by the pressures he was enduring.

The attitude we take toward the pressures of life goes a long way toward determining whether those pressures will produce improvement or bitterness. If we react with anger or complain about our circumstances, our lives will not be made better by what we experience. If, like Job, we respond in faith, God can use those trials to refine us and make us more useful to His work and to others. The pressures of your life hold the key to your productivity for Him.

Today's Rooted Principle: View your struggles as a tool God can use for your improvement, and you will find the pressure easier to endure.

Someone Cares

When my spirit was overwhelmed within me, then thou knewest my path. In the way wherein I walked have they privily laid a snare for me. I looked on my right hand, and beheld, but there was no man that would know me: refuge failed me; no man cared for my soul. I cried unto thee, O LORD: I said, Thou art my refuge and my portion in the land of the living.—**Psalm 142:3–5**

I read a tragic story about a young lady in England who told the world on her Facebook page that she was about to end her life. She wrote, "Took all my pills be dead soon bye bye everyone." She had 1,048 "friends" on Facebook. Most did not respond, and there is some indication that some of her friends posted mocking statements on her wall and did not take her seriously. While there are reports that some out-of-town "friends" tried to obtain her contact information, no one local came to her physical rescue.

We live in a world that is constantly "in touch" online and yet also increasingly disconnected at the same time. There are people all around us with hidden hurts and heartbreaks that they may never reveal in public, but they are in desperate need of someone to care for them—and someone to remind them that God loves them as well. The comfort of a friend and a kind word can make all the difference to someone in need.

In our fast-paced society it is easy for these people to be overlooked and ignored, sometimes until it is too late. Many people have perfected the art of looking fine on the outside while covering a broken heart. Take the time to look beneath the surface and find out what is happening. Express your love, and remind people of God's unfailing love. No one should ever leave our presence feeling that there is no one who cares for and loves him.

Today's Rooted Principle: Someone who will cross your path today desperately needs the help and encouragement you can provide.

The God Who Does the Impossible

And he asked his father, How long is it ago since this came unto him? And he said, Of a child. And ofttimes it hath cast him into the fire, and into the waters, to destroy him: but if thou canst do any thing, have compassion on us, and help us. Jesus said unto him, If thou canst believe, all things are possible to him that believeth. And straightway the father of the child cried out, and said with tears, Lord, I believe; help thou mine unbelief.—**Mark 9:21–24**

A young boy, who was traveling by airplane to visit his grandparents, sat beside a man who happened to be a seminary professor. The boy was reading a Sunday school take-home paper, and the professor thought he would have some fun with the lad. "Young man," said the professor, "if you can tell me something God can do, I will give you a big, shiny apple." The boy thought for a moment and then replied, "Mister, if you can tell me something God can't do, I'll give you a whole barrel of apples!"

Each of us face difficult circumstances at times in our lives. There may even be days when we see no way out of the problems we face. But when God is involved, nothing is impossible. No obstacle you face challenges His strength and resources; no decision you must make challenges His wisdom and knowledge. If there is a problem, it is not with God's ability but with our faith.

After Jesus began His public ministry and became well known for the miraculous works He had done, He returned to His home region. Yet there in his home region, the same power that had awed so many others was not widely displayed. Matthew 13:58 explains, "He did not many mighty works there because of their unbelief." Believe God today—not only that He can do what you need, but also that He will.

Today's Rooted Principle: Trust God with the difficult situations you face today, for they pose no challenge to Him.

Standing in the Face of Hardship

But thou hast fully known my doctrine, manner of life, purpose, faith, longsuffering, charity, patience, Persecutions, afflictions, which came unto me at Antioch, at Iconium, at Lystra; what persecutions I endured: but out of them all the Lord delivered me. Yea, and all that will live godly in Christ Jesus shall suffer persecution.—**2 Timothy 3:10–12**

Paul sent his young associate Titus to the island of Crete to set elders over the churches there and establish strong churches. Though the Bible doesn't continue the story, church history tells us the story of a job well done. Titus led the church in Crete until 105 AD, when he died at age 94. Nearly one hundred and fifty years later, in January 250 AD, the Roman Emperor Decius issued an edict for the suppression of Christianity. He demanded that the bishops and officers of the church make sacrifices to the Emperor as a sign that their allegiance was to him rather than to God.

Leaders from the churches of Crete who became known as the "ten surmountable martyrs" refused and died for their faith. Their stories were told for centuries to encourage others to stand firm in their faith.

There are many places in the world today where Christians face grave persecution, but most of us in America have enjoyed religious liberty and do not face the choice between being faithful to God and saving our lives.

However, the day may come when we are faced with such a decision. Scripture tells us that persecution should not come as a surprise to us, because of the hatred of the world for the things of God. Every committed, consistent Christian is a rebuke to those who are doing wrong, without ever saying a word. And if we do reach a point where it is no longer acceptable or even legal to be a witness for Christ, we should remain firm in our faith.

Today's Rooted Principle: Make your commitment to stand for Christ before the day of persecution comes.

Spend Time on What Matters

Hear, O Israel: The LORD our God is one LORD: And thou shalt love the LORD thy God with all thine heart, and with all thy soul, and with all thy might. And these words, which I command thee this day, shall be in thine heart: And thou shalt teach them diligently unto thy children, and shalt talk of them when thou sittest in thine house, and when thou walkest by the way, and when thou liest down, and when thou risest up.—**Deuteronomy 6:4–7**

The Annenberg Center for the Digital Future at USC released a study on how American families are impacted by technology. Their report shows that more and more families are spending less and less time together. The number of Americans who acknowledged they are spending less time with those in their household has nearly tripled since 2006, from 11 percent to 28 percent. With the proliferation of social networking, time spent with family members has dropped from 28 hours per month just 6 years ago to 18 hours per month. Facebook, Twitter, and a whole list of social networks are capturing the time and attention of American families.

Each day we have opportunities to have an impact on others, particularly on our families. But that requires a decision to take advantage of those opportunities and spend our time on things that really matter. It is easy to fritter away an entire day without doing anything of lasting importance—easier today than at any time in the past. But as someone once observed, "A wasted life is nothing more than a bunch of wasted days put together."

Determine to focus your energy and attention on what is eternal. As you go through the day, talk about the principles and precepts of the Word of God. Encourage others to see Bible truth illustrated in the events of daily life. Taking this approach, you will find that you are a strength and help to those you influence.

Today's Rooted Principle: Do not allow anything to take away from investing time in your family.

Job 14–16   Acts 9:22–43

What You Can Count On

For we are labourers together with God: ye are God's husbandry, ye are God's building. According to the grace of God which is given unto me, as a wise masterbuilder, I have laid the foundation, and another buildeth thereon. But let every man take heed how he buildeth thereupon. For other foundation can no man lay than that is laid, which is Jesus Christ.—**1 Corinthians 3:9–11**

Edward Mote was born in England in 1794. His father ran a pub, and Edward received little care as a child. After working as a cabinet maker, he was saved and eventually became a Baptist pastor. He also wrote a number of hymns.

The hymn by Edward Mote that we best remember is "The Solid Rock." Mote was working on the hymn when he learned about the dying wife of a church member. Mote went to visit the woman and shared his words of comfort: "On Christ the solid Rock I stand, All other ground is sinking sand." These words brought the woman hope, and Mote finished his hymn which we still sing today.

You have been given a solid and unshakable foundation as a child of God. The faithfulness of every one of His promises has been proven again and again by centuries of believers. You have that place to stand today on the promises of God.

Knowing the certainty of God's truth and the surety of His promises gives us a responsibility to build something of strong and lasting value on that foundation. Our lives are not our own; they are meant for His purpose. The Christian life is not an unstable or uncertain life; rather it is a life of meaning built upon a firm and solid Rock.

Today's Rooted Principle: Even if all others fail you, the faithfulness of God is a foundation on which you can build.

JULY

Focusing on What Matters Most

When they therefore were come together, they asked of him, saying, Lord, wilt thou at this time restore again the kingdom to Israel? And he said unto them, It is not for you to know the times or the seasons, which the Father hath put in his own power. But ye shall receive power, after that the Holy Ghost is come upon you: and ye shall be witnesses unto me both in Jerusalem, and in all Judaea, and in Samaria, and unto the uttermost part of the earth.—**Acts 1:6–8**

Over recent decades, nationally-known preachers and authors have specifically and publicly predicted the date for the Lord's return. In almost every case, they state that their declarations are the result of careful study of Scripture, and that there is no chance they may be mistaken. When one preacher's date proved to be incorrect, he recalculated and declared a second date later in the year. The mistaken declarations provided great humor for the world and great embarrassment to those who believed them.

As children of God we should all be looking forward to the day when the Lord will return. We know that His coming could be at any moment, but the Scripture is also clear that no one is able to set a date or a time for "that blessed hope, and the glorious appearing" (Titus 2:13).

It is possible for us to become so focused on future prophetic events that we miss the tasks that God has assigned for us today. In fact, the disciples found themselves in just that position. Just before the Lord returned to Heaven, their focus was on figuring out God's timetable. Jesus told them that instead of worrying about "the times or the seasons" they should instead be witnesses for Him. There is no more important mission that we have been given than bringing lost men and women to salvation in His name. When we win the lost, we are focused on what matters most.

Today's Rooted Principle: While we eagerly anticipate Christ's return, we should be busy fulfilling His Great Commission.

Wrong Praying

From whence come wars and fightings among you? come they not hence, even of your lusts that war in your members? Ye lust, and have not: ye kill, and desire to have, and cannot obtain: ye fight and war, yet ye have not, because ye ask not. Ye ask, and receive not, because ye ask amiss, that ye may consume it upon your lusts.—**James 4:1–3**

The Bible tells us that there are things we do not have simply because we do not ask God for them. That is a tragedy, because prayer is the means which God has ordained for our needs to be met. One preacher of the past told of a dream in which he was taken by an angel to a large warehouse in Heaven. Shelves were piled high with packages. He asked the angel what he was seeing, and the angel replied, "These are things God had for you for which you never asked."

But a second tragedy is when we pray for the wrong things or with the wrong motives. It is not wrong for us to ask for what we want or what we need, but we must be careful not to put ourselves in the place of God, asking Him to fulfill our will. That is not the purpose of prayer, and there is no basis for expecting answers to selfish prayers. Our desires will lead us astray unless we submit them to God's will.

As in everything, Jesus is our pattern for proper motivation in prayer. In the Garden of Gethsemane, He prayed for the cup to pass, but then said, "nevertheless not my will, but thine, be done" (Luke 22:42). God's wisdom so far exceeds ours that we must trust Him to give us what is best. The many wonderful promises of Scripture concerning answered prayer are true, but they are conditioned on proper attitudes and asking in our praying.

Today's Rooted Principle: When your prayers are in keeping with the will of God, you will be amazed at the answers you see.

Stick Together

Let us hold fast the profession of our faith without wavering; (for he is faithful that promised;) And let us consider one another to provoke unto love and to good works: Not forsaking the assembling of ourselves together, as the manner of some is; but exhorting one another: and so much the more, as ye see the day approaching.—**Hebrews 10:23–25**

If you have ever seen a video of lions hunting their prey in the wild, you have seen that, while they may chase a herd of animals, they focus their attention on stragglers and strays—those who have gotten separated from the herd. These are the ones who are taken in the hunt. Any individual animal in the group is no match for a lion, but it finds that there is safety in numbers.

God never intended for His children to be isolated and alone. When Jesus sent the disciples out to begin preaching on their own, He sent them in pairs. When Elijah was depressed and discouraged, God gave him Elisha to join him in the ministry. When God commanded the early church to send out missionaries, they sent Paul and Barnabas together. There is enormous safety and encouragement in knowing that we are not alone.

We live in a culture that glorifies individualism. One of the most popular songs of the last century is called "I Did it My Way." Satan is delighted when he can convince us to strike out on our own, leaving behind our spiritual family in the church. He knows that an isolated Christian is an easy target. There is truly safety in numbers. The giant redwood trees of California soar hundreds of feet into the air, but their roots are strong. The strength of a redwood's roots is found in other redwoods. Instead of going deep underground, they spread sideways and entwine with the roots of other redwood trees so that they hold each other up. That is God's pattern for us.

Today's Rooted Principle: Be regular in your attendance in church and in fellowship with God's people—it guards you from all kinds of trouble.

Pray for Our Leaders

I exhort therefore, that, first of all, supplications, prayers, intercessions, and giving of thanks, be made for all men; For kings, and for all that are in authority; that we may lead a quiet and peaceable life in all godliness and honesty. For this is good and acceptable in the sight of God our Saviour;—**1 Timothy 2:1–3**

In 1776, a group of fifty-six men met in Philadelphia to set the thirteen colonies on the path to independence. Though they were not all Christians, many of them were and they set a pattern for our nation, that from the beginning of our history, declared our reliance upon God Almighty. The Declaration concludes with these words:

> We, therefore, the Representatives of the United States of America, in General Congress, Assembled, appealing to the Supreme Judge of the world for the rectitude of our intentions, do, in the Name, and by Authority of the good People of these Colonies, solemnly publish and declare, That these United Colonies are, and of Right ought to be Free and Independent States… And for the support of this Declaration, with a firm reliance on the protection of divine Providence, we mutually pledge to each other our Lives, our Fortunes and our sacred Honor.

Though many today would deny the godly heritage of America, the testament to our historical reliance on God is written into our founding documents and carved in stone on the walls of our national buildings and monuments. Those of us who are believers have a responsibility to both God and our country to pray for our leaders, regardless of who they may be. The Roman emperors during Paul's day were certainly not friends of the Christians, but that did not change the command to faithfully pray for them. Just as our Founding Fathers once did, today we must again turn to God and seek His grace and favor for our land.

Today's Rooted Principle: Pray for our country and our leaders today. It is pleasing to God, and it is good for any nation.

Living on Purpose

And the king appointed them a daily provision of the king's meat, and of the wine which he drank: so nourishing them three years, that at the end thereof they might stand before the king. Now among these were of the children of Judah, Daniel, Hananiah, Mishael, and Azariah: But Daniel purposed in his heart that he would not defile himself with the portion of the king's meat, nor with the wine which he drank: therefore he requested of the prince of the eunuchs that he might not defile himself.—**Daniel 1:5–6, 8**

In 1992, we took some time apart as a family to establish a written "Chappell Family Purpose Statement." It was our desire to have a focus that would guide our activities and interactions, so we sat down and talked about how we wanted to live our lives as a Christian family. Here is what we wrote and each of us signed: "The purpose of our family is to glorify the Lord Jesus Christ through obedience to His Word, and by edifying and exhorting one another."

Have each of us lived up to that goal every single day since then? No. We are imperfect people. But by having an established goal, we have done more to reach it than we would have if we had just drifted through the days without a purpose. As the old saying goes, "If you aim at nothing, you will hit it every time."

When Daniel was just a young man, he was ripped away from his home and family and taken to the center of the heathen world. There he was enrolled in a training program designed to break down his allegiance to his own country and his own God in order to make him a useful servant of the Babylonian Empire. Yet that well-refined program did not work on this young man because of the purpose he established and kept throughout his life.

Today's Rooted Principle: Plan what you want yourself and your family to accomplish for God, and then follow that plan.

Don't Give an Inch

Wherefore putting away lying, speak every man truth with his neighbour: for we are members one of another. Be ye angry, and sin not: let not the sun go down upon your wrath: Neither give place to the devil.—**Ephesians 4:25–27**

A hunter raised his rifle and took careful aim at a large bear. When he was about to pull the trigger, the bear spoke in a soft, soothing voice, "Isn't it better to talk than to shoot? What do you want? Let's negotiate the matter." Lowering his rifle, the hunter replied, "I want a fur coat."

"Good," said the bear, "that is a negotiable request. I only want a full stomach, so let us negotiate a compromise." They sat down to negotiate, and after a time the bear walked away alone. The negotiations had been successful. The bear had a full stomach, and the hunter had his fur coat!

If you give the devil even one inch, he will take a mile or more. The pages of Scripture and of history are filled with the sad stories of people who thought they could let down their guard just a little without suffering any negative consequences. Each of them was wrong. Lot, Noah, David, and Peter are just a few of the examples of those who made small first steps toward wrong, thinking they were still in control, only to find themselves mired in sin.

You may remember the saying many of us learned in Sunday school: "Sin will take you further than you want to go, keep you longer than you want to stay, and cost you more than you want to pay." There is no negotiating with Satan. Anything that you give up he will take, but because he is a liar, he will never keep a promise that he makes to you. Stand your ground firmly and never retreat on a single principle or conviction.

Today's Rooted Principle: Never compromise your principles—once you start down that road, you will find it hard to ever stop.

What Are You Looking For?

If ye then be risen with Christ, seek those things which are above, where Christ sitteth on the right hand of God. Set your affection on things above, not on things on the earth. For ye are dead, and your life is hid with Christ in God. When Christ, who is our life, shall appear, then shall ye also appear with him in glory.—**Colossians 3:1–4**

Both the hummingbird and the vulture fly over our nation's deserts. All that vultures see is rotting meat, because that is what they look for. But hummingbirds ignore the smelly flesh of dead animals. Instead, they look for the colorful blossoms of desert plants. The vultures live on what was. They fill themselves with what is dead and gone. But hummingbirds live on what is. They seek new life. They fill themselves with freshness and life. Each bird finds what it is looking for.

Our affections—the things that we love—determine the things we focus on. The world is filled with trouble and heartbreak, yet the same world is filled with blessings and benefits from God. Which one we choose to focus on, to a large measure, determines whether we will be content and happy or not. Believers who are joyful Christians are not somehow spared from the hardships of life. But they are focused on the things of God.

This world is just temporary. The trials that we endure and the hardships we experience do not force us into bitterness or depression. Paul certainly endured much more than his share in the way of trouble, yet he viewed it as being for his own benefit. Paul wrote that his afflictions created "a far more exceeding and eternal weight of glory" (2 Corinthians 4:17). He could say that because his heart was settled in Heaven.

Today's Rooted Principle: Check your focus today: are you looking at the things of Heaven, or are you fixated on the things of Earth?

God Will Take Care of You

Likewise, ye younger, submit yourselves unto the elder. Yea, all of you be subject one to another, and be clothed with humility: for God resisteth the proud, and giveth grace to the humble. Humble yourselves therefore under the mighty hand of God, that he may exalt you in due time: Casting all your care upon him; for he careth for you.—**1 Peter 5:5–7**

James Cash Penney had a godly heritage as a child, and he carried those convictions into adulthood. A hard worker, Penney was scrupulously honest and maintained a godly lifestyle as he became successful in business. But when the Great Depression struck, he was overextended, and it appeared he would lose everything he had worked for. His health broke, and he was hospitalized. In such severe pain that he thought he was about to die, he wrote farewell letters to his family.

Penney later wrote, "I was broken nervously and physically, filled with despair, unable to see even a ray of hope. I had nothing to live for. I felt I hadn't a friend left in the world, that even my family turned against me." But the next morning, he heard singing from the hospital chapel. "Be not dismayed, whate'er betide, God will take care of you." Those words rekindled his faith and he said, "I can't explain it. I can only call it a miracle. I felt as if I had been instantly lifted out of the darkness of a dungeon into warm, brilliant sunlight."

No matter what circumstance you are in today, God is there. He has never abandoned or forsaken a single one of His children, and He is not going to begin now. You can take your burden to the Lord and leave it with Him because of His compassion and care for you. Your needs do not take Him by surprise—He is simply waiting for you to come to Him for help.

Today's Rooted Principle: You can rest with complete confidence in God's love and care for you today.

Job 36–37   Acts 15:22–41   221

Put God First

And as she was going to fetch it, he called to her, and said, Bring me, I pray thee, a morsel of bread in thine hand. And she said, As the LORD thy God liveth, I have not a cake, but an handful of meal in a barrel, and a little oil in a cruse: and, behold, I am gathering two sticks, that I may go in and dress it for me and my son, that we may eat it, and die. And Elijah said unto her, Fear not; go and do as thou hast said: but make me thereof a little cake first, and bring it unto me, and after make for thee and for thy son.—**1 Kings 17:11–13**

I once heard a story of a missionary in Africa who received a knock on the door of his hut one afternoon. Answering, the missionary found a native boy holding a large fish in his hands. The boy said, "Missionary, you taught us what tithing is, so here. I've brought you my tithe." As the missionary gratefully took the fish, he questioned the boy. "If this is your tithe, where are the other nine fish?" At this, the boy beamed and said, "Oh, they're still in the river. I'm going back to catch them now." This boy evidenced the joy of faith in his giving.

God does not need our money. He has all the resources of Heaven and Earth at His disposal. But He does command us to give tithes and offerings. Though this teaching is clear throughout Scripture, it sometimes meets with resistance from God's people. Yet those with a heart for God have no issue with giving back to Him part of what He has given to them. When we give to God first rather than handing Him the leftovers, we show that our heart is fixed on Him rather than on the material blessings we receive.

Today's Rooted Principle: How you handle your financial resources reveals where your heart is.

How to Have a Blessed Family

*Praise ye the LORD. Blessed is the man that feareth the LORD, that delighteth greatly in his commandments. His seed shall be mighty upon earth: the generation of the upright shall be blessed. Wealth and riches shall be in his house: and his righteousness endureth for ever. Unto the upright there ariseth light in the darkness: he is gracious, and full of compassion, and righteous.—***Psalm 112:1–4**

It's no secret that families are in trouble today. The divorce rate continues to rise, with devastating consequences. A Michigan State University study of adolescent murderers found that 75 percent came from broken homes. The increasing drug use and immorality among young people is made much worse by the plague of divorce, as children struggle without the guidance two godly parents are meant to provide. This is yet another illustration of the truth that God's commands are given to us for our own good.

Ever since the Garden of Eden, man has been tempted to follow his own path. Isaiah said, "we have turned every one to his own way" (Isaiah 53:6). Yet the God who knows everything has told us what will work and what won't. If you want your family to be successful and blessed for generations to come, the first step is for you personally to be a Christian who fears and obeys God. This produces benefits that reach far into the future.

The great missionary Hudson Taylor is well known as a man of faith who was greatly used by God. But he was actually the fourth generation in his family to follow God. His great grandfather James Taylor was saved under the preaching of John Wesley when he heard a sermon called "As for Me and My House, We Will Serve the Lord." If you follow Christ faithfully, you are setting an example and securing a blessing that can reach beyond your own children for generations.

Today's Rooted Principle: Your commitment to fear and obey God will bless your family for generations to come.

Unlimited Resources

For every beast of the forest is mine, and the cattle upon a thousand hills. I know all the fowls of the mountains: and the wild beasts of the field are mine. If I were hungry, I would not tell thee: for the world is mine, and the fulness thereof.—**Psalm 50:10–12**

The renowned teacher Harry Ironside was in a prayer meeting for a seminary at which he often lectured. The school was in critical need of $10,000 to keep the work going, and a group of men were praying together for this need. Ironside prayed, "Lord, you own the cattle on a thousand hills. Please sell some of those cattle to help us meet this need." Shortly after the prayer meeting, a check for $10,000 arrived at the school, sent days earlier by a friend who had no idea of the urgent need or of Ironside's prayer. The man simply said the money came from the sale of some of his cattle!

The popular teaching in our day of the "prosperity Gospel" is completely false. It is not God's will and plan for every Christian to be rich. However, it is also true that when we pray, we are making our request to Someone who has unlimited resources. None of our needs pose any challenge to His ability to meet them. You will never offer a prayer that will require God to dig into His reserves to answer. He has more than enough for every need.

Andrew Murray wrote: "Beware in your prayer, above everything, of limiting God, not only by unbelief, but by fancying that you know what He can do." The things that are impossible for us are fully possible for Him. Yet too often we pray small prayers, not expecting God to do great and mighty things. His loving nature and almighty power have not changed. God is still in the business of hearing and answering big prayers.

Today's Rooted Principle: When you pray, make sure that your requests are made in view of all that God can do—don't settle for less than He has for you.

The Priority of Prayer

And in those days, when the number of the disciples was multiplied, there arose a murmuring of the Grecians against the Hebrews, because their widows were neglected in the daily ministration. Then the twelve called the multitude of the disciples unto them, and said, It is not reason that we should leave the word of God, and serve tables. Wherefore, brethren, look ye out among you seven men of honest report, full of the Holy Ghost and wisdom, whom we may appoint over this business. But we will give ourselves continually to prayer, and to the ministry of the word.
—**Acts 6:1–4**

There are many things that are important in life, but only a few that are essential. One of the most important—but often neglected—essentials is time spent in prayer. The great evangelist R.A. Torrey said, "We are too busy to pray, and so we are too busy to have power. We have a great deal of activity but accomplish little. We have many services but few conversions. We have much machinery but few results."

Continued prayer should characterize the life of every believer. Yet often we have so much going on that we "don't have time" to pray. That is a tragedy because it cuts us off from a vital time of fellowship and communion with God and robs us of the resources that prayer is meant to provide. It is easy to set aside our time of prayer in the hurry and pressure of life, but it is a grave mistake to do so.

The disciples in the early church understood the priority of prayer. Rather than surrender their prayer time to the good and important function of caring for the needs of widows, they called the church to select the first deacons to meet that need. Nothing can substitute for the benefit of the time you spend before the throne of God in prayer.

Today's Rooted Principle: Regardless of what is on your schedule today, you have nothing more pressing than prayer.

And All the Promises of God

Grace and peace be multiplied unto you through the knowledge of God, and of Jesus our Lord, According as his divine power hath given unto us all things that pertain unto life and godliness, through the knowledge of him that hath called us to glory and virtue: Whereby are given unto us exceeding great and precious promises: that by these ye might be partakers of the divine nature, having escaped the corruption that is in the world through lust.—**2 Peter 1:2–4**

The great missionary Hudson Taylor personally baptized more than 35,000 converts during decades of service in China. He brought hundreds of missionaries to what had previously been a closed mission field and established hundreds of churches. Over those many years, God worked miraculously to supply his needs, but there were many times when the money did not arrive until the very last moment.

Though those times could have shaken Taylor's faith, he retained his confidence in God. At one point he wrote to a friend, "We have left eighty-seven cents and all the promises of God." If we have the promises of God—and we do—then there is nothing to fear. Even if we cannot see how the answer could possibly come, He is not limited by our resources or lack of them. The most overwhelming problem you will ever face does not tax His abilities or power in any way.

We see this truth beautifully expressed in the story of Jonathan and his armor bearer going out alone to attack a garrison of Philistine soldiers. Jonathan was not the least bit worried about being outnumbered. He said, "there is no restraint to the LORD to save by many or by few" (1 Samuel 14:6). When God is on your side, nothing else matters. Simply claim His promises in faith, knowing that not one has ever failed, and you will not be overtaken with fear.

Today's Rooted Principle: Trust God in faith even if you cannot see the answer. All of His promises are faithful and true.

The Cost of Love

These things have I spoken unto you, that my joy might remain in you,
and that your joy might be full. This is my commandment, That ye love
one another, as I have loved you. Greater love hath no man than this,
that a man lay down his life for his friends. Ye are my friends, if ye do
whatsoever I command you.—**John 15:11–14**

Former Congressman J.C. Watts from Oklahoma once said, "Compassion can't be measured in dollars and cents. It does come with a price tag, but the price tag isn't the amount of money spent. The price tag is love." Love is anything but free. The nature of godly love is that it is willing to make sacrifices for the good of the other, rather than being focused on protecting itself or getting its own way.

Of course, the ultimate example of this love is found in the life, death and resurrection of Jesus. He willingly came "to give his life a ransom for many" (Matthew 20:28). This is a different kind of love from the kind our world knows today. Most of what is called love would more properly be called attraction and, in many cases, simply lust. This kind of self-focused behavior is far short of what God has in mind.

It is no surprise that the world falls short when it comes to love, but that should never be true for us. Each of our relationships—with family members, friends, fellow church members and the lost—should be characterized by this divine love that "seeketh not her own" (1 Corinthians 13:5). As we evaluate our love for others, we should not measure our feelings or our words, but our actions. Are we loving as Christ did, willing to give up that which we have every right to claim in order that someone else may benefit? Truly loving another is never an inexpensive proposition.

Today's Rooted Principle: It is impossible to truly love people without being willing to sacrificially give to them.

Psalms 10–12   Acts 19:1–20   227

Gold Rush

The statutes of the LORD are right, rejoicing the heart: the commandment of the LORD is pure, enlightening the eyes. The fear of the LORD is clean, enduring for ever: the judgments of the LORD are true and righteous altogether. More to be desired are they than gold, yea, than much fine gold: sweeter also than honey and the honeycomb. Moreover by them is thy servant warned: and in keeping of them there is great reward.
—Psalm 19:8–11

In 1848, James Marshall's discovery of gold at Sutter's Mill in northern California sparked one of the greatest migrations in human history. News travelled slowly at first, but by 1849 tens of thousands of people were on their way to California. During the gold rush, some 300,000 people flocked to the area hoping for riches. The journey itself posed significant dangers. A trip across America required facing hostile Indians, wild animals, mountain snows, and desert heat. Sailing around the tip of South America took months and was quite dangerous as well. Yet people willingly took on the challenges and threats in hope of what might lie in store for them.

There are many things that people desire and are willing to sacrifice to attain. However, there is no treasure that can be compared to that found in the pages of the Bible. God's eternal truth is readily available to us, and yet we allow other interests and pursuits to fill our time. The wisdom and strength and power that we need for successful and blessed living is there, like the gold nuggets that were found resting on the surface in the creeks of California. But so often, we allow those truths to remain undiscovered and unsought while we settle for the trinkets of the world. Many, and in fact most, of the "forty-niners" went home emptyhanded, never having found treasure. Yet those who seek the unsearchable riches of Scripture are never disappointed.

Today's Rooted Principle: When you treasure and desire the Word of God rightly, you will seek to learn and apply its truths to your life.

What God Can Do with a Surrendered Life

I beseech you therefore, brethren, by the mercies of God, that ye present your bodies a living sacrifice, holy, acceptable unto God, which is your reasonable service. And be not conformed to this world: but be ye transformed by the renewing of your mind, that ye may prove what is that good, and acceptable, and perfect, will of God.—**Romans 12:1–2**

When D.L. Moody was just starting in the ministry he heard a preacher say, "The world has yet to see what God can do with a man fully surrendered to Him." Moody that night said, "By God's grace I'll be that man!" It is said that Moody shook two continents for God and over a million souls came to Christ under his preaching and ministry. Moody had little formal education, and he was not a polished speaker. But God greatly used his life.

At a memorial service some years after Moody's death, Evangelist R.A. Torrey, who had been one of his closest friends, said, "The first thing that accounts for God's using D.L. Moody so mightily was that he was a fully surrendered man. Every ounce of that two-hundred-and-eighty-pound body of his belonged to God; everything he was and everything he had, belonged wholly to God."

When we surrender our purpose and will to God and allow Him to use us as He sees fit, amazing things happen. The world is shaken not by the wise, the mighty, the intelligent, or the skilled, but by those who have yielded to God. Paul said it was "reasonable" for us to surrender our lives, but many today seem to think that it is too much to ask. Instead of surrendering, they cling tightly to their own desires and interests. How much better it is both for us and for a world in need if we surrender and let God choose our path!

Today's Rooted Principle: A surrendered and empowered life can shake the world. Are you willing to be that fully surrendered person for God?

The Source of Comfort

Blessed be God, even the Father of our Lord Jesus Christ, the Father of mercies, and the God of all comfort; Who comforteth us in all our tribulation, that we may be able to comfort them which are in any trouble, by the comfort wherewith we ourselves are comforted of God. For as the sufferings of Christ abound in us, so our consolation also aboundeth by Christ.—**2 Corinthians 1:3–5**

I remember attending the funeral of a greatly used pastor who had died suddenly at a young age. His death was so unexpected, and it was obvious that his family and the church family had been staggered by the news. Yet despite the sorrow and sadness that were very real, there was also a spirit of hope at this funeral. The people sang "Great Is Thy Faithfulness." Several of the speakers, including the pastor's family, talked about the importance of trusting God. As I spoke to the pastor's wife, she told me how she was trusting God in the storm.

Being a child of God is no guarantee that we will not endure suffering and times of grief. But as children of God, we have a resource of comfort and strength that the world does not know. We have a God who gives us comfort in the midst of our grief. Because Jesus endured suffering, He knows well the pain that we feel. In fact, the Bible calls Him "a man of sorrows, and acquainted with grief" (Isaiah 53:3).

It should always be true that our Christian friends and church family will gather around us during difficult times. But even if that does not happen and there are dark days when we feel like we are all alone, we are never abandoned or forsaken. The God who gives comfort and peace is always there for His children to help them through the darkest days they face.

Today's Rooted Principle: If you are burdened or grieving today, turn to the God of all comfort; you will find strength and help.

How the Walls Came Down

And ye shall compass the city, all ye men of war, and go round about the city once. Thus shalt thou do six days. And seven priests shall bear before the ark seven trumpets of rams' horns: and the seventh day ye shall compass the city seven times, and the priests shall blow with the trumpets. And it shall come to pass, that when they make a long blast with the ram's horn, and when ye hear the sound of the trumpet, all the people shall shout with a great shout; and the wall of the city shall fall down flat, and the people shall ascend up every man straight before him.—**Joshua 6:3–5**

The city of Jericho was the first city the Israelites had to face when they entered the Promised Land. Because the city was built on the site of an oasis and had high interlocking walls, it was considered impossible to conquer. The military technology of the day had no weapons capable of mounting an effective attack against Jericho. To the children of Israel, Jericho represented an insurmountable obstacle.

But to the God of the children of Israel the walls of Jericho did not present any challenge. Notice, however, that He did not just immediately level the enemy city. First, the Israelites had to obey His command to march around the city day after day for a week. Then, on the last day, they circled the city seven times. Only after they had followed His instructions did God miraculously deliver the city into their hands.

Often when we face a difficult challenge, we are tempted to sit back and ask God to take care of it for us. While He is certainly able and sometimes does work in that way, often He expects us to take steps of faith even before He has worked. When we obey, He acts.

Today's Rooted Principle: No obstacle you face today is greater than God. Trust Him and obey, and you can see the walls come down.

Powerful Christians

And the brethren immediately sent away Paul and Silas by night unto Berea: who coming thither went into the synagogue of the Jews. These were more noble than those in Thessalonica, in that they received the word with all readiness of mind, and searched the scriptures daily, whether those things were so.—**Acts 17:10–11**

Evangelist R. A. Torrey said this about the importance of the Word of God:

> You may talk about power; but, if you neglect the one Book that God has given you as the one instrument through which He imparts and exercises His power, you will not have it. You may read many books and go to many conventions and you may have your all-night prayer meetings to pray for the power of the Holy Ghost; but unless you keep in constant and close association with the one Book, the Bible, you will not have power.

Imagine someone training for an athletic competition by never eating. Picture a soldier preparing for battle by skipping all his meals. That would be ridiculous, yet while the Bible tells us that we are in a race and a battle, many Christians ignore their need for the spiritual food found in the pages of the Word of God. It should not come as any surprise that such people find themselves struggling to win their battles— they have cut themselves off from their power supply. It is vital to be part of a good Bible preaching and teaching church, but that is not enough. You must be a student of the Word yourself to become a powerful and victorious Christian.

Today's Rooted Principle: Nothing can substitute for time spent reading and studying the Word of God.

Contentment

And one of the company said unto him, Master, speak to my brother, that he divide the inheritance with me. And he said unto him, Man, who made me a judge or a divider over you? And he said unto them, Take heed, and beware of covetousness: for a man's life consisteth not in the abundance of the things which he possesseth.—**Luke 12:13–15**

I read about a pilot who always looked down intently on a certain valley in the Appalachians when the plane passed overhead. One day his co-pilot asked, "What's so interesting about that spot?" The pilot replied, "See that stream? Well, when I was a kid I used to sit down there on a log and fish. Every time an airplane flew over, I would look up and wish I were flying... Now I look down and wish I were fishing."

An ancient philosopher said that if all of the troubles in the world were placed in one pile so that everyone could see what burdens others bore, each person, given the choice, would take home the same problems with which he arrived.

It is always tempting to think that others have it better than we do, and that if we just had "a little more" everything would be fine. But contentment cannot be achieved by increasing possessions. Nothing will ever be enough.

Covetousness—a driving desire for more and more and more—is a snare that leads many people away from the truth. In fact, Paul wrote that covetousness "is idolatry" (Colossians 3:5). When we are not content with what God has given us, we are placing something else on the throne of our heart. While we are too sophisticated to carve idols of wood or stone and bow to them, many in our society worship cars, homes, bank accounts, and clothing. This false worship leads inevitably to disappointment and often to ruin.

Today's Rooted Principle: Rather than wishing for what you don't have, give thanks for what you do have, and covetousness will not take root in your heart.

Generosity

And if any man will sue thee at the law, and take away thy coat, let him have thy cloke also. And whosoever shall compel thee to go a mile, go with him twain. Give to him that asketh thee, and from him that would borrow of thee turn not thou away.—**Matthew 5:40–42**

One of the heroes of the American Revolution was Marquis de Lafayette. This French officer provided invaluable assistance to George Washington and the struggling American army. After the war was over, he returned to France and resumed his life as a farmer of many estates. In 1783, the harvest was a terrible one, and there were many who suffered as a result. Lafayette's farms were unaffected by the devastating crop failures. One of his workers offered what seemed to be good advice to Lafayette, "The bad harvest has raised the price of wheat. This is the time to sell." After thinking about the hungry peasants in the surrounding villages, Lafayette disagreed and said, "No, this is the time to give."

God blesses us not just for our own benefit, but also so that we can be a blessing to others in need. The tendency to hoard and try to build up more and more is a dangerous one, and the best antidote to greed is to be a generous giver. There is certainly no shortage of people in need today, and while we cannot meet every need, if we do what we can, God will multiply resources so that it is enough.

A pastor friend told me that when his father was presented with a need, he always gave immediately. He had learned that if he waited, he would be able to talk himself out of giving. So once he found someone who needed help, he reached into his pocket and gave them what he could on the spot. That's a great example for all of us to follow.

Today's Rooted Principle: When you cross paths with someone in need, give what you have to help.

Do Not Be Troubled

And Jesus answered and said unto them, Take heed that no man deceive you. For many shall come in my name, saying, I am Christ; and shall deceive many. And ye shall hear of wars and rumours of wars: see that ye be not troubled: for all these things must come to pass, but the end is not yet. For nation shall rise against nation, and kingdom against kingdom: and there shall be famines, and pestilences, and earthquakes, in divers places.—**Matthew 24:4–7**

Not long ago I read about a cult leader in the Philippines named Apollo Quiboloy who calls himself the "Appointed Son of God." Quiboloy claims to have six million followers around the world who are part of his Kingdom of Jesus Christ church. It is no surprise to any student of the Scriptures to see false messiahs arise, for Jesus told us this would happen.

Many people are very interested in the prophetic teaching of the Bible, but some approach the events we see unfolding with fear rather than with confidence. Jesus instructed us that when we see such things, we not allow them to trouble our hearts. Nothing should shake our faith and confidence in Him. Nothing takes God by surprise. Nothing happens that can hinder His plans. He is God of everything, and He is in control.

If we keep this truth in mind, then the news holds no terrors for us. The economy may improve or get worse. Our enemies may attack or be defeated. The world may see an increase in wars and natural disasters. Yet though we may face times of difficulty and even persecution, we still have the promise of the presence of Christ. He said, "I will never leave thee nor forsake thee" (Hebrews 13:5), and we do not face our trials on our own. God is always there no matter what circumstances arise.

Today's Rooted Principle: God is in control of everything that happens today, and you can fully trust His love and goodness toward you.

Put Down Roots

*That we henceforth be no more children, tossed to and fro, and carried about with every wind of doctrine, by the sleight of men, and cunning craftiness, whereby they lie in wait to deceive; But speaking the truth in love, may grow up into him in all things, which is the head, even Christ: From whom the whole body fitly joined together and compacted by that which every joint supplieth, according to the effectual working in the measure of every part, maketh increase of the body unto the edifying of itself in love.—***Ephesians 4:14–16**

Author David F. Wells wrote, "Today, we are neither rooted nor do we have much sense of belonging. We are in fact the uprooted generations, the disconnected, the drifters, the alone. We are being blown around by the windstorms of modernity. Our roots in families, place, and work have all withered or been cut off." That may be true of our culture, but it does not have to be true of us.

There may be times when we need to relocate for family or work reasons, and sometimes it is God's will for people to move. However, people frequently drift from one place to the next for less compelling reasons. We need to put down deep roots wherever we are. There needs to be a depth of commitment—to family, to God, to church—that is unable to be shaken by anything that occurs.

Psalm 1:3 promises that a believer who loves and meditates in the Scriptures "shall be like a tree planted by the rivers of water." This is the key to a stable and productive life. A fruit tree that is moved every year is not going to be a healthy and productive tree because it has no time to take root. Rather than constantly being driven from place to place by changing ideas and circumstances, we need to make the commitment to stand firm.

Today's Rooted Principle: Keep your commitments today. Do what you can to be part of building what will last.

Patience and Fruitfulness

And that which fell among thorns are they, which, when they have heard, go forth, and are choked with cares and riches and pleasures of this life, and bring no fruit to perfection. But that on the good ground are they, which in an honest and good heart, having heard the word, keep it, and bring forth fruit with patience.—**Luke 8:14–15**

I read about a lady who called American Airlines and asked the reservation clerk, "How long does it take to get from Dallas-Fort Worth to Frankfurt, Germany?" The clerk had to wait a moment for the information to come up on her computer screen, so she said, "Just a minute." The caller responded, "Thanks very much," and hung up! Most of the things that really matter in life do not happen in "just a minute."

It is easy for us to become impatient when God does not work on our timetable. Most of us want to see immediate results, but things don't usually work that way in our lives. Instead, we must go through the process of working and building and developing before we reach the goal. The great pioneer missionary Adoniram Judson labored in Burma for seven years before seeing his first convert. But rather than giving up and looking for an easier place to minister, he remained faithful, and eventually established many churches and saw thousands saved. Judson's translation of the Bible into the Burmese language is still in use today, touching lives more than 150 years after his death.

Henry Wadsworth Longfellow wrote: "The heights by great men reached and kept, were not obtained by sudden flight. But they, while their companions slept, were toiling upward in the night." If we are patient and continue steadfast in the work regardless of whether we see immediate results, we will reap the harvest "in due season" (Galatians 6:9). It is impossible to be fruitful unless we first remain patiently faithful.

Today's Rooted Principle: Do not be discouraged if you don't see immediate results. Remain faithful, and the harvest will come.

Ebenezer

And as Samuel was offering up the burnt offering, the Philistines drew near to battle against Israel: but the LORD thundered with a great thunder on that day upon the Philistines, and discomfited them; and they were smitten before Israel. And the men of Israel went out of Mizpeh, and pursued the Philistines, and smote them, until they came under Beth-car. Then Samuel took a stone, and set it between Mizpeh and Shen, and called the name of it Eben-ezer, saying, Hitherto hath the LORD helped us.—**1 Samuel 7:10–12**

When most people hear the word "Ebenezer" they think of the character of Scrooge in *A Christmas Carol* by Charles Dickens. But like many names, it is taken from Scripture and holds an important meaning. The Hebrew word means "stone of help." The prophet Samuel set up a stone as a reminder for the children of Israel after God gave them a great victory over their enemies. It is vitally important both for our own lives and for our children and grandchildren that we have reminders of God's goodness.

In their book *Disciplines of a Godly Family*, Kent and Barbara Hughes wrote that because of our rootless culture, "Every Christian family [should] take conscious and disciplined measures to cultivate tradition and memory. But there is an even more compelling reason. Namely, God's Word dramatically recommends that all believing families cultivate both spiritual memory and spiritual traditions to commemorate and celebrate God's goodness."

Because of our fallen nature, it is easy for us to take credit for the good things that happen rather than thanking and glorifying God. By reminding ourselves of the great things He has done for us, we keep our gratitude and faith strong. This is a vital spiritual discipline not only for our own lives, but for the sake of our children as well. The remembrance of what God has done should be a testimony from generation to generation.

Today's Rooted Principle: Make sure you have a lasting way to remind yourself and your family of the ways God has helped you.

Standing on Truth

As he spake these words, many believed on him. Then said Jesus to those Jews which believed on him, If ye continue in my word, then are ye my disciples indeed; And ye shall know the truth, and the truth shall make you free.—**John 8:30–32**

We live in a society that seems to be dedicated to tearing down the very concept of truth. Yet because truth is part of God's fundamental nature and is one of the defining characteristics of the Word of God, it cannot be destroyed. We serve a God who "cannot lie" (Titus 1:2). No matter what man does or chooses to believe, truth never changes. Beliefs may come and go, but truth abides.

Winston Churchill said, "Men occasionally stumble over the truth, but most of them pick themselves up and hurry off as if nothing had happened." That may be a common response to truth, but it places those who follow it on the road to tragedy and destruction. There is no way to love and follow God without loving and following truth. The two cannot be separated.

The concept that all ideas are equal and "there are no absolutes" is doing as much or more to destroy our culture than anything else. Christians who are committed to the unchanging truth of Scripture are viewed as narrowminded and bigots. However, those who reject the truth have no foundation. They may spin elaborate philosophical webs to justify their positions, but without a foundation of truth, there really is no way to determine what is acceptable and what is not.

A writer of the past said, "When men stop believing in God they don't believe in nothing—they will believe in anything." It is true that ideas are gaining acceptance today that fail every basic test of logic and truth. Ground your heart and mind in the Scriptures, and your life will be built on a firm foundation of truth.

Today's Rooted Principle: Stand on the truth today. It will bring freedom and blessing to your life.

Psalms 40–42 Acts 27:1–26 239

Desiring the Word

As newborn babes, desire the sincere milk of the word, that ye may grow thereby: If so be ye have tasted that the Lord is gracious. To whom coming, as unto a living stone, disallowed indeed of men, but chosen of God, and precious, Ye also, as lively stones, are built up a spiritual house, an holy priesthood, to offer up spiritual sacrifices, acceptable to God by Jesus Christ.—**1 Peter 2:2–5**

I've noticed something about babies—they don't need to be persuaded to eat. When a child gets to be two or three years of age, that can change. But little babies are very eager for their food. In many ways it is the same with believers. I've seen so many new Christians who couldn't wait to read and study and hear the preaching and teaching of the Word. They desired it with all their hearts. Yet as time passed, rather than wanting to learn more and more, they became "picky eaters" who only wanted the parts of Scripture that tasted good to them. It is a tragedy for any child of God not to love and desire the Word of God.

Robert Chapman wrote, "The great cause of neglecting the Scriptures is not want of time, but want of heart, some idol taking the place of Christ." All of us have more than enough to do to fill our time day after day. How then do we prioritize? What is truly most important to us (not what we *say* is most important) is what gets done.

If in our heart we truly desire the Word, we will make the time to read and study it. How many Christians have fallen into sin and gone away from God because they allowed their desire for the Word to grow cold? Renew your love for the Book, and you will stay close to the Author.

Today's Rooted Principle: Read the Bible with fresh eyes and ears today, desiring to hear what God has to say to you.

Beware of the Lion

*Be sober, be vigilant; because your adversary the devil, as a roaring lion, walketh about, seeking whom he may devour: Whom resist stedfast in the faith, knowing that the same afflictions are accomplished in your brethren that are in the world. But the God of all grace, who hath called us unto his eternal glory by Christ Jesus, after that ye have suffered a while, make you perfect, stablish, strengthen, settle you. To him be glory and dominion for ever and ever. Amen.—***1 Peter 5:8–11**

Bernard "Kip" Lagat is a world-class runner from Kenya. During the Sydney Olympics, an interviewer asked him how his country was able to produce so many great distance runners. With clever wit, Lagat told of the Kenyan strategy for motivating success in running. He said, "It's the road signs: 'Beware of Lions.'"

There is a lion stalking every believer every day. It is vitally important that we remain on guard because of the patience and persistence of our enemy. If we win a spiritual battle today, that does not offer us safety for tomorrow. The devil will return with new temptations and challenges. This was true for Jesus even after He decisively defeated Satan when He was tempted in the wilderness. The Bible says that Satan "departed from him for a season" (Luke 4:13). There are no permanent victories in spiritual warfare. As long as life continues, so do the battles.

Victory in this continuing battle requires continuing vigilance. There are no days when you can let down your guard. The devil is looking for those who have grown careless and incautious because he knows they will be easy prey. We must daily remain vigilant and walk closely with the Lord.

Today's Rooted Principle: Stay on guard today. Your enemy is looking for an opportunity to devour and destroy your life.

Memorizing Scripture

Only be thou strong and very courageous, that thou mayest observe to do according to all the law, which Moses my servant commanded thee: turn not from it to the right hand or to the left, that thou mayest prosper whithersoever thou goest. This book of the law shall not depart out of thy mouth; but thou shalt meditate therein day and night, that thou mayest observe to do according to all that is written therein: for then thou shalt make thy way prosperous, and then thou shalt have good success.—**Joshua 1:7–8**

One college professor put it this way: "Bible memorization is absolutely fundamental to spiritual formation. If I had to choose between all the disciplines of the spiritual life, I would choose Bible memorization, because it is a fundamental way of filling our mind with what it needs. This book of the law shall not depart out of your mouth. That's where you need it! How does it get in your mouth? Memorization."

Many of our churches have good programs to promote Bible memory for our children and young people, but very few encourage adults to continue to memorize the Scriptures. But the Word of God is not just necessary for children and teens. Adults need to continue to add to the store of Scriptures they have in their hearts and minds. Beyond just reading the Bible, it is important for us to continue to commit it to memory.

We know how important meditation on the Word of God is, but memorizing Scripture is a vital prerequisite for meditation. We cannot "think on these things" (Philippians 4:8) unless we first have them in our minds. It is certainly easier to memorize when we are young, and it is a blessing to have verses we have known for decades in our hearts. But even as we grow older, we need to regularly practice this vital spiritual discipline.

Today's Rooted Principle: Bible memorization is not just for children. Set out to commit the Word to your memory today.

Lonely People

Do thy diligence to come shortly unto me: For Demas hath forsaken me, having loved this present world, and is departed unto Thessalonica; Crescens to Galatia, Titus unto Dalmatia. Only Luke is with me. Take Mark, and bring him with thee: for he is profitable to me for the ministry.—**2 Timothy 4:9–11**

One writer noted an interesting reality about human nature: "People today will admit any problem—drugs, divorce, alcoholism—but there's one admission that people loathe to make, whether they're a star on television or someone who fixes televisions in a repair shop. It's just too embarrassing. It penetrates too deeply to the core of who they are. People don't want to admit that they are (sometimes) lonely. Loneliness is an affliction of losers and misfits. But—to be honest—it also affects respectable people like you and me."

There are so many people who go through life feeling alone. They may be surrounded by family, neighbors, co-workers, and others, but they do not feel that anyone really understands the situation they are in. David knew this feeling. When he was running for his life to escape from Saul he wrote, "…no man cared for my soul" (Psalm 142:4). God created us with a need for companionship and encouragement.

All around you today there are people who are desperately hoping someone will look past the façade they have established and realize that they have a hurting heart. When we take the time to see that need and meet it, lives change. Think of the overwhelming loneliness of the woman at the well whom Jesus met. Because of her past, she was cut off from the normal fellowship of her community. She was drawing water from the well at an odd time because she was not welcome. Yet Jesus reached out to her in love, describing and then meeting her needs and providing her living water.

Today's Rooted Principle: Look for someone you can encourage today with a kind word, a smile, or the Gospel itself.

Carrying Your Cross

Then said Jesus unto his disciples, If any man will come after me, let him deny himself, and take up his cross, and follow me. For whosoever will save his life shall lose it: and whosoever will lose his life for my sake shall find it. For what is a man profited, if he shall gain the whole world, and lose his own soul? or what shall a man give in exchange for his soul?—**Matthew 16:24–26**

For nearly four hundred years, the people of Oberammergau in Bavaria have been putting on a "Passion Play" depicting the events of the last week of the life of Christ. They began the performances after the village was spared from the bubonic plague in the early 1600s. The story is told that an American visitor watching the drama unfold sprang into action when the actor portraying Jesus fell while carrying the cross toward the crucifixion scene.

The tourist was caught up in the emotion of the moment and wanted to lift the cross from the back of "Jesus." Expecting it to be a prop, he reached down with one hand but found that he could not move the heavy wooden cross. After the play was over, he met with the actor who told him, "I found that I cannot look like Christ without carrying a real cross."

In another sense, this is true for every one of us. There are no light crosses for the Christian who wishes to truly follow Jesus Christ. The cross is more than just a symbol of Christianity. It is what Jesus demands from those who would follow in His steps. There is no successful model for selfish Christianity. Though there are many selfish Christians, their refusal to take up the cross limits their ability to follow Jesus. Obedience is costly, but so is the prize of hearing the words "well done" when we stand before the Father.

Today's Rooted Principle: Lay aside self today and take up the cross so that you can truly walk in His steps.

AUGUST

Faithful unto Death

And unto the angel of the church in Smyrna write; These things saith the first and the last, which was dead, and is alive; I know thy works, and tribulation, and poverty, (but thou art rich) and I know the blasphemy of them which say they are Jews, and are not, but are the synagogue of Satan. Fear none of those things which thou shalt suffer: behold, the devil shall cast some of you into prison, that ye may be tried; and ye shall have tribulation ten days: be thou faithful unto death, and I will give thee a crown of life.—**Revelation 2:8–10**

In the last year of the reign of Henry VIII in England, a new wave of persecution was launched against believers. One of those caught in the nets of the established church was a young lady named Anne Askew. Just twenty-six years old, she was taken to the Tower of London and tortured in hopes that she would name others who stood for the truth of Scripture. She refused to do so, and she refused the offer of a pardon if she would recant her faith.

Askew was sentenced to death. She had to be carried to the stake to be burned because the torture she had endured left her unable to walk. This courageous young lady was truly faithful unto death. Most of us do not face the threat of death for our beliefs today, although there are believers in many countries who literally take their lives in their hands by making a public stand for Jesus Christ.

Yet in the face of far less severe threats, many times we fail to take the stand we should for Christ. Some never witness for fear they will be rejected. Some go along with friends in doing wrong to avoid taking a stand for right. Be firm today, and you will be prepared for whatever comes tomorrow.

Today's Rooted Principle: The way to be faithful unto death is to be faithful in your Christian life each day.

The Main Thing

For Christ sent me not to baptize, but to preach the gospel: not with wisdom of words, lest the cross of Christ should be made of none effect. For the preaching of the cross is to them that perish foolishness; but unto us which are saved it is the power of God.—**1 Corinthians 1:17–18**

There are many things that are important, but there is one thing that is essential. The heartbeat of the mission of Christ, the driving purpose behind His life, death, and resurrection was "to seek and to save that which was lost" (Luke 19:10). Oswald Smith put it this way, "Oh, my friends, we are loaded down with countless church activities, while the real work of the church, that of evangelizing the world and winning the lost, is almost entirely neglected."

Our church is a busy place, and I like it that way. I love that we have programs for fellowship and encouragement and instruction and fun. But I never want us to lose sight of the fact that the primary focus—the most important thing we can do—must be winning the lost to Jesus Christ. There is no greater or more important priority for us. This is the final command that Jesus left before He returned to Heaven, and we must obey it.

Many times we lose our focus in the busyness of life. There are a thousand things—good things—that can keep us from doing the main thing. And though those things are not bad in and of themselves, they can be used to keep us from doing what matters most. The Bible said of Christ just before He met the woman at the well that He "must needs go through Samaria" (John 4:4). Jews in that day usually travelled around Samaria to avoid the people they looked down on, but Jesus needed to go there—He knew there was a hungry heart who needed a Saviour, and He went where others would not go to reach her.

Today's Rooted Principle: Take time today to tell someone the Good News. Nothing you can do will matter more.

Get Busy

I must work the works of him that sent me, while it is day: the night cometh, when no man can work. As long as I am in the world, I am the light of the world.—**John 9:4–5**

One day a lady criticized D.L. Moody for his methods of evangelism in attempting to win people to the Lord. Moody's reply was "I agree with you. I don't like the way I do it either. Tell me, how do you do it?" The lady replied, "I don't do it." Moody responded, "Then I like my way of doing it better than your way of not doing it."

Sometimes we fall into the trap of waiting for a perfect opportunity or a perfect plan before we begin doing something for the Lord. It is far better for us to be active than to sit back and critique those who are not doing things exactly as we think they should be done. It's easy to be a critic, but that does not produce anything for the kingdom of God. I would much rather see someone working hard and trying to do what he can than someone doing nothing. If a person has flaws in his methods or needs instruction to be more effective, that can be provided. As someone said, "It's easier to steer a ship that's moving than one that is sitting still."

The Apostle Paul encouraged the church at Ephesus to be busy for the Lord, "Redeeming the time, because the days are evil" (Ephesians 5:16). The idea is that we should make the most of every opportunity we have—even more because of the evil that pervades our culture. There are people today that you will have an opportunity to reach. In many cases you are the person best equipped to reach them, despite the fact that you may feel inadequate. Do your best for God, and work while there is still time.

Today's Rooted Principle: Take full advantage of every opportunity for service, ministry, and witnessing that you have today.

Be an Ambassador

And all things are of God, who hath reconciled us to himself by Jesus Christ, and hath given to us the ministry of reconciliation; To wit, that God was in Christ, reconciling the world unto himself, not imputing their trespasses unto them; and hath committed unto us the word of reconciliation. Now then we are ambassadors for Christ, as though God did beseech you by us: we pray you in Christ's stead, be ye reconciled to God.—**2 Corinthians 5:18–20**

I read about a barber who had just been gloriously saved in an old-fashioned revival meeting. The next morning at work he wanted to share his new faith and witness to the lost. A customer came in, and the barber began to shave him. He was trying to muster up the right words to say. Finally as he stood with his razor poised over the man's throat he asked, "Are you prepared to meet God?"

You may not always find exactly the right words, but God has given to you and every Christian the task of representing Him to a lost and dying world. For thousands of people, today is their last day before they enter eternity. Of course, we don't know who those people are. But we do know that God loves the people whose paths we cross and that He has entrusted to us the most important message they can ever hear. The question is whether we will be faithful to share that message with them.

It is said that D. L. Moody made a commitment to God that he would not go to bed without having witnessed to at least one person. On several occasions he went out late at night to find someone with whom he could share the Gospel. There should be a sense of urgency and passion for the lost that drives and motivates us to be effective ambassadors for Jesus Christ.

Today's Rooted Principle: Share the Gospel with someone today. You never know who may be getting a last chance to hear it.

A Settled Word

For ever, O LORD, thy word is settled in heaven. Thy faithfulness is unto all generations: thou hast established the earth, and it abideth. They continue this day according to thine ordinances: for all are thy servants. Unless thy law had been my delights, I should then have perished in mine affliction.—**Psalm 119:89–92**

Not everyone accepts that the Word of God is settled. Many religions teach that rather than being complete, Scripture is still being added in our day. For example, the official position of the Mormon church says, "To the Mormons, God is still a God of continuing revelation. Hence, the LDS canon is open; the Doctrine and Covenants becomes an official, open-ended locus for revelations that affect the whole Church; and revelations continue to come to the living prophets, seers, and revelators of the Church, to be communicated to the members."

The problem with that approach (in addition to being a rejection of what the Bible teaches) is that if the Word is not settled, our faith can never be settled. Those who are looking for additional revelation and a new word from God have no basis to be certain in what they have. Since faith comes from the Bible (Romans 10:17), we must have a Bible that we can trust and that is exactly what God has given to us.

The Scriptures give us many wonderful promises that allow us to be confident that we have the finished Word of God. Psalm 12:6–7 says, "The words of the LORD are pure words: as silver tried in a furnace of earth, purified seven times. Thou shalt keep them, O LORD, thou shalt preserve them from this generation for ever." Rather than looking for new revelation and new words from God, we should be reading and studying and obeying the settled Word of God that has been kept for us by His power and promises.

Today's Rooted Principle: Everything the Bible says is fully settled; you can have complete confidence in God's Word.

Be a Teacher

For when for the time ye ought to be teachers, ye have need that one teach you again which be the first principles of the oracles of God; and are become such as have need of milk, and not of strong meat. For every one that useth milk is unskilful in the word of righteousness: for he is a babe. But strong meat belongeth to them that are of full age, even those who by reason of use have their senses exercised to discern both good and evil.—**Hebrews 5:12–14**

While there is a spiritual gift of teaching that God gives to some individuals, there is also a very real sense in which all of us are to be teachers. What we have learned from our walk with God and our own study of the Bible is not just for our benefit. As we have opportunity, we should be sharing that with others to strengthen and encourage them. All of us have people whom we can influence for better, and we have a responsibility to do so. The main requirement for this kind of teaching is not talent but heart.

We received this wonderful testimony from a former student at West Coast Baptist College. "My teachers were interested in more than my grades. They were interested in me. Their investment in teaching me spiritual applications, life lessons, leadership skills, and knowledge allowed me to step into life with a proper confidence in who God made me to be. I went into ministry having seen the example of dedicated, godly teachers who exemplified who I wanted to be. To this day I still call them for advice and help!"

A heart filled with compassion and love for others is ready to share truth and encouragement with them. This spirit, which the Bible calls being "apt to teach" (2 Timothy 2:24), is a vital element of a healthy family and a healthy church.

Today's Rooted Principle: Share what you have learned from God with someone today—it will help both of you.

A Certain Hope

For the grace of God that bringeth salvation hath appeared to all men, Teaching us that, denying ungodliness and worldly lusts, we should live soberly, righteously, and godly, in this present world; Looking for that blessed hope, and the glorious appearing of the great God and our Saviour Jesus Christ;—**Titus 2:11–13**

B ecause sin is part of our world, we have to deal with the reality of death. But for a believer, death is not the end. We have the promise of eternal life if we die before the Lord returns—and the promise of being transformed in a moment if we are alive on that blessed day. This is a hope that we can be sure of, because the promises of God never fail. Others may not keep their promises to us, but He always does—and thus we can be certain of the future.

On a trip to the East Coast, I was able to visit Mt. Vernon. While I was there, I saw the tomb in which George and Martha Washington are buried. On the back wall of the open vault, there is a plaque with Jesus' words inscribed: "I am the resurrection, and the life: he that believeth in me, though he were dead, yet shall he live: And whosoever liveth and believeth in me shall never die" (John 11:25–26). The "Father of our Nation" found confidence in the hope of eternal life in Jesus Christ.

There is no more powerful comfort than the knowledge that we who know Christ have a hope for the future, even after death. When Jesus went to the grave of His friend Lazarus, He declared His power over death in an unmistakable way. This great enemy has already been defeated. We need no longer fear what will come—for our Lord has already faced death and conquered it. And because of His victory, we can have full certainty in our hope for the future.

Today's Rooted Principle: If you have trusted Christ as your Saviour, rejoice in the certain truth that God's love has prepared a place in eternity for you.

Incorruptible Seed

Being born again, not of corruptible seed, but of incorruptible, by the word of God, which liveth and abideth for ever. For all flesh is as grass, and all the glory of man as the flower of grass. The grass withereth, and the flower thereof falleth away: But the word of the Lord endureth for ever. And this is the word which by the gospel is preached unto you.
—1 Peter 1:23–25

At our family farm in Colorado, my uncle and cousins have acres and acres of pinto beans. Once while I was visiting, my uncle explained to me that the crucial element of growing beans is the seed itself. The beans my uncle grows come from especially cultivated and bred seeds that are designed to be fruitful in his particular growing conditions. The agronomists who produced this new variety were incredibly careful to avoid it being contaminated with any other kind of bean. They had dedicated warehouses for the seeds and plants, and would not grow the first plants in a field with any other varieties. All of this was done to ensure the purity of the final product.

God's Word is completely perfect. As He promised, God has preserved it so that we can have complete confidence in what we hold in our hands—it is His Word. Though it has been challenged and attacked through the centuries, still it stands. It cannot be corrupted by demons or men because it is kept perfect and pure by the power of God Himself.

The seeds my uncle plants have been designed and created to increase production, but despite their purity and potential, left in the barn, the seeds will never produce a harvest. The same is true of the Scripture. We must study and read and hear and memorize the incorruptible seed of the Word of God for it to produce righteousness and fruit in our lives.

Today's Rooted Principle: God has given us a perfectly inspired and preserved Word; it is a tragedy not to plant it in our hearts and minds.

Stay in the Field

I have planted, Apollos watered; but God gave the increase. So then neither is he that planteth any thing, neither he that watereth; but God that giveth the increase. Now he that planteth and he that watereth are one: and every man shall receive his own reward according to his own labour. For we are labourers together with God: ye are God's husbandry, ye are God's building.—**1 Corinthians 3:6–9**

William Carey, often called the "father of modern missions," arrived in India in 1793 with a burden to preach the Gospel of Jesus Christ to those who had never heard His name. For seven years he proclaimed the Gospel message faithfully week after week, month after month, with not a single native of India converted to Christ. Carey could have returned home defeated and empty-handed.

However, he had faith that God would bring the harvest. To his sisters back home in England Carey wrote, "I feel as a farmer does about his crop: sometimes I think the seed is springing, and thus I hope; a little blasts all, and my hopes are gone like a cloud. They were only weeds which appeared; or if a little corn sprung up, it quickly dies, being either choked with weeds, or parched up by the sun of persecution. Yet I still hope in God, and will go forth in His strength, and make mention of His righteousness, even of His only."

Carey established one of the greatest missionary works in all of history, in great measure because he stayed in the field rather than allowing discouragement to drive him to quit. When we work for the Lord, we will not always see quick results. But just as a farmer remains diligent throughout the spring and summer in hopes of the harvest in the fall, "we shall reap, if we faint not" (Galatians 6:9).

Today's Rooted Principle: Do not be discouraged if your work and witnessing do not yield immediate results, God will bring the harvest in His time.

Taking Sides

Then Moses stood in the gate of the camp, and said, Who is on the LORD'S side? let him come unto me. And all the sons of Levi gathered themselves together unto him.—**Exodus 32:26**

During the Civil War, someone asked President Abraham Lincoln whether he thought God was on the Union side in the conflict. Lincoln is said to have replied, "Sir, my concern is not whether God is on our side; my greatest concern is to be on God's side, for God is always right." There is only one standard of absolute right and truth, and that is the one set by God in His Word. Many people claim that God is for their efforts, but those claims are only valid when they are in agreement with Scripture.

Each day we are faced with decisions as to whether we will take our stand for what is right. In our world there are many competing visions of truth, and in fact a large number of people today reject the notion that there is any such thing as settled, absolute truth. When we face such an environment, we must be aware of the temptations that attempt to lure us to make "small" compromises in order to fit in better and be accepted. But each time we yield to that impulse, we move further away from being on God's side.

When the question is raised, "Who is on the Lord's side?" our answer should be swift and sure. We should be willing to stand up and be counted among those who have chosen His Word and His way. Even if our society completely rejects the standards and truth of God, we do not have to join them. When most of the Israelites were worshiping the golden calf, the sons of Levi were still willing to stand up and publicly declare allegiance to God. We should do the same.

Today's Rooted Principle: Even if no one else stands with you, you will always be on the right side while you stand on God's side.

Sound the Alarm

For if God spared not the angels that sinned, but cast them down to hell, and delivered them into chains of darkness, to be reserved unto judgment; And spared not the old world, but saved Noah the eighth person, a preacher of righteousness, bringing in the flood upon the world of the ungodly; And turning the cities of Sodom and Gomorrha into ashes condemned them with an overthrow, making them an ensample unto those that after should live ungodly;—**2 Peter 2:4–6**

Rick Rescorla was born in England, but moved to the United States as a young man. He served with distinction in the Army during the Vietnam War and received awards for his courage. After his military career ended, he became head of security for Morgan Stanley. He feared the World Trade Center would be the target of a terrorist attack, so he insisted on frequent evacuation drills to teach people how to quickly and safely exit the building.

Many of the people who worked there resented the constant drills and thought it was a waste of time. On the morning of September 11, 2001, when the first World Trade Tower was hit by a terrorist plane, Rescorla ordered the evacuation that had been practiced for so long. Despite the urging of authorities for people to remain in the building, he got virtually every Morgan Stanley employee out, and many others as well, before the second tower was hit. Rescorla was last seen going back into the building attempting to rescue more people just before it collapsed.

You and I have a message from God to sound to the world. There is a coming judgment that must be faced. Many people prefer not to hear that message, wanting to live as they please rather than dealing with a Holy God. But we have a responsibility to tell them the truth whether they listen or not.

Today's Rooted Principle: Even those who do not want to hear the truth need to hear it, tell them in love, but tell them plainly.

Engraved Sins

The sin of Judah is written with a pen of iron, and with the point of a diamond: it is graven upon the table of their heart, and upon the horns of your altars; Whilst their children remember their altars and their groves by the green trees upon the high hills. O my mountain in the field, I will give thy substance and all thy treasures to the spoil, and thy high places for sin, throughout all thy borders. And thou, even thyself, shalt discontinue from thine heritage that I gave thee; and I will cause thee to serve thine enemies in the land which thou knowest not: for ye have kindled a fire in mine anger, which shall burn for ever.
–Jeremiah 17:1–4

Diamonds are the hardest natural material known to man. In fact, our word for diamond comes from the Greek word meaning "unbreakable." Though we often associate them with jewelry, diamonds are commonly used for industrial purposes. Their hardness makes them valuable for cutting, etching, and grinding a number of surfaces.

When the Bible speaks of sins being written with diamonds, it is describing the lasting marks that sin leaves on our lives. Though God is merciful and forgiving, His forgiveness does not erase all of the consequences of sin that we experience. The scars of sin are deeply cut, like an engraving made with a diamond.

When Satan tempts us to sin, he never shows us the full picture. We see the "pleasures of sin for a season" (Hebrews 11:25), but he attempts to hide the final and awful consequences that come from turning away from God. It is impossible for us to choose or limit the consequences of sin. Once we have chosen the wrong path, "the end thereof are the ways of death" (Proverbs 16:25). Resisting temptation protects you and those you love from the ravages of sin.

Today's Rooted Principle: Utterly reject any sin that tempts you today so that it will not carve pain and tragedy into your life.

You Are Ordained by God

Ye are my friends, if ye do whatsoever I command you. Henceforth I call you not servants; for the servant knoweth not what his lord doeth: but I have called you friends; for all things that I have heard of my Father I have made known unto you. Ye have not chosen me, but I have chosen you, and ordained you, that ye should go and bring forth fruit, and that your fruit should remain: that whatsoever ye shall ask of the Father in my name, he may give it you.—**John 15:14–16**

One of the most important and meaningful days of my life occurred in 1983 when I was ordained as a preacher of the Gospel of Jesus Christ. During that service, men of God came and prayed over me as I was appointed to fill the office of ministry to which God had called me. I cherish the memory of that day.

While we have special services to ordain men as pastors and deacons for those offices of the church, there is also a very real sense in which each believer is ordained, especially appointed by God, not for a church office, but to be a fruitful Christian. Many today have fallen into the trap of thinking that "church work" is only the responsibility of full-time Christian workers. In reality, every believer is meant to be a fruitful, productive, active worker in God's kingdom.

Bearing fruit is God's calling and purpose for your life according to the words of Jesus. The Lord has appointed each one of us to "bring forth fruit." God has no backup plan for reaching the world, He has entrusted that task to each of us as His children. We must be telling the Good News and helping others come to faith in Christ. No matter what spiritual gifts and abilities you have, they are meant to be used to produce fruit.

Today's Rooted Principle: Do everything you can today to fulfill God's appointed purpose for your life by bearing fruit.

God Meant it for Good

And Joseph said unto them, Fear not: for am I in the place of God? But as for you, ye thought evil against me; but God meant it unto good, to bring to pass, as it is this day, to save much people alive. Now therefore fear ye not: I will nourish you, and your little ones. And he comforted them, and spake kindly unto them.—**Genesis 50:19–21**

Samuel Bringle was a worker with the Salvation Army in Boston many years ago. As he passed by a saloon, some men threw a brick at his head. Their aim was good, and Bringle nearly died. As it was, he spent eighteen months in recovery. During that time he wrote a little book entitled "Helps to Holiness." Thousands of copies were published. After he was able to begin preaching again, people would often thank him for the book. He would respond by saying, "If there had been no little brick, there had been no little book." His wife saved the brick and had Genesis 50:20 engraved on it.

During difficult times and trials, the difference between those who trust God and those who do not is found in the way they view those trials. Godly Christians have the same problems, heartbreaks and even tragedies as everyone else. They are not somehow exempt from suffering. But they view their difficult circumstances through the lens of an understanding of God's love and purpose for their lives.

One preacher said it well, "The only thing an enemy can do to you is to be the unwitting instrument of God's plan for your life." Of course, many things happen that are painful and hard for us to endure. Yet those circumstances do not mean God has forgotten or forsaken us. He makes "all things work together for good" (Romans 8:28). This helps us understand that even the most difficult things we experience are a necessary part of His plan.

Today's Rooted Principle: View your problems and difficulties as something God can and will use to make you a better servant for Him.

Psalms 89–90   Romans 14   259

Power in Prayer

I am the vine, ye are the branches: He that abideth in me, and I in him, the same bringeth forth much fruit: for without me ye can do nothing. If a man abide not in me, he is cast forth as a branch, and is withered; and men gather them, and cast them into the fire, and they are burned. If ye abide in me, and my words abide in you, ye shall ask what ye will, and it shall be done unto you.—**John 15:5–7**

The promises of prayer in the Bible are many, yet if we are honest, we would have to admit that most Christians do not see their prayers answered in a great and powerful way. We know that God never changes from age to age—His power is as great as it was in the days of Moses, David, Daniel, John, and Paul. The reason we do not see great answers is not found in God but in our own lives.

Charles Spurgeon said, "If you want that splendid power in prayer, you must remain in loving, living, lasting, conscious, practical, abiding union with the Lord Jesus Christ." Sometimes we treat prayer like a fire escape. It remains available but unused, until we have an emergency! Using prayer that way forfeits the close communion and fellowship that our time with God presenting our requests to Him is meant to provide for us.

God certainly does not need us to pray to inform Him of what we need. He already knows not only what we will ask, but whether what we ask is best for us. However, like a loving parent, He still encourages us to come to Him and create a meaningful relationship that includes, in part, prayer. The time that we spend in the Word and in prayer is about far more than just getting our needs met. It is the resulting fellowship that brings abundant joy.

Today's Rooted Principle: Your power in prayer is directly proportional to your abiding in Christ.

Hard Hearts

But exhort one another daily, while it is called To day; lest any of you be hardened through the deceitfulness of sin. For we are made partakers of Christ, if we hold the beginning of our confidence stedfast unto the end; While it is said, To day if ye will hear his voice, harden not your hearts, as in the provocation.—**Hebrews 3:13–15**

Not far from our church is Edwards Air Force Base. This storied flight facility has been home to some of the most famous airplanes and pilots in United States history. It was from Edwards that Chuck Yeager broke the sound barrier in the Bell X-1 test aircraft in 1947. The geological feature that originally drew the military to Edwards was the presence of the Rogers Dry Lake bed—a flat, hard surface that stretches for miles across the high desert.

While a hard surface makes an ideal location for airplane runways, it makes for a spiritual barrenness when it characterizes our hearts. When our hearts are hard, we are not ready to hear the Word of God or to allow it to produce fruit in our lives. There is simply no place for it to take root.

How do our hearts become hard? The Bible tells us that the deceitfulness of sin produces a hard heart. The word "deceitfulness" indicates that it is the result of a process we may not be fully aware of ourselves. Over time, as we allow the allure of sin to tempt us, our hearts grow hard toward the things of God. To become fruitful again, we must do what a farmer does before planting seeds in the field—break up and prepare the ground. As we confess our sins and seek the face of God, we will find our hearts softening and becoming ready once again to hear His Word.

Today's Rooted Principle: Plow the ground of your heart today so that you are ready to receive the Word of God and be fruitful.

Psalms 94–96   Romans 15:14–33   261

Dig Deep

That he would grant you, according to the riches of his glory, to be strengthened with might by his Spirit in the inner man; That Christ may dwell in your hearts by faith; that ye, being rooted and grounded in love, May be able to comprehend with all saints what is the breadth, and length, and depth, and height; And to know the love of Christ, which passeth knowledge, that ye might be filled with all the fulness of God.
—**Ephesians 3:16–19**

I heard about a farmer who had received abundant rain on his soybean and corn crops. A friend congratulated him on the green state of his fields after the rain and was surprised when the farmer replied, "My crops are especially vulnerable right now. Even a short drought could have a devastating effect." "Why?" the friend asked. The farmer explained that while we see the frequent rains as a benefit, during that time the plants are not required to push roots deeper in search of water. The roots remain near the surface. A drought would find the plants unprepared and quickly kill them.

While we should rejoice in the times where we see an extra measure of the goodness and blessings of God, it is usually in times of struggle and testing of our faith that we develop strength as believers. We need to be putting down our roots, reaching into the Word and spending time with God in prayer so that we have the strength to stand the test.

It is popular today to teach that God's children receive only good things and will live in abundance, but that is not what the Bible says. We find in actuality that we are in a battle—a war that will last as long as we live. Prepare to fight and to win the battle today by digging deep roots in faith.

Today's Rooted Principle: Dig your roots deeply into the Word so you will be prepared to stand the test when it comes.

Pull Out the Thorns

And these are they which are sown among thorns; such as hear the word,
And the cares of this world, and the deceitfulness of riches, and the lusts
of other things entering in, choke the word, and it becometh unfruitful.
—Mark 4:18–19

One of the most destructive weeds that crop farmers must deal with is the Canadian thistle. It has an extensive root system that makes it extremely difficult to eradicate once it is established. The root structure can reach a depth of fifteen feet, and the roots can also spread out the same distance horizontally. These prolific roots crowd out the plants. Just twenty thistles in one square mile of field can reduce barley yield by a third or alfalfa yield by one half! Canadian thistle is also very damaging to feed crops, as livestock will not graze near it.

In the parable of the sower and the seeds, Jesus described people who are not fruitful because the Word of God that is planted in their heart is choked out by thorns. He gave us specific thorns we must guard against, such as the cares of the world; when we succumb to this particular thorn, anxiety and fear fill our hearts and minds. We live in an uncertain world, and unless we maintain our faith, it will be easy for anxious care to choke out the Word.

Jesus also explained how money and the desire for things can ruin the fruitful ground of our hearts. While we should be grateful for the good things with which God blesses us, it is vitally important that we not allow our lives to be consumed by the pursuit of possessions. We must remember the caution of Jesus that "a man's life consisteth not in the abundance of the things which he possesseth" (Luke 12:15). Removing these thorns prepares us to be fruitful and productive in our Christian walk.

Today's Rooted Principle: Pull the weeds out of your heart today so the Word has room to grow and produce fruit.

The Vital Importance of Love

Little children, yet a little while I am with you. Ye shall seek me: and as I said unto the Jews, Whither I go, ye cannot come; so now I say to you. A new commandment I give unto you, That ye love one another; as I have loved you, that ye also love one another. By this shall all men know that ye are my disciples, if ye have love one to another.—**John 13:33–35**

There are many elements of our Christian testimony that are important. It is important that we speak right, look right, and act right. But the most important thing is that we love right. Jesus said this was to be the distinguishing mark of His followers that would convince the world that their belief in Him was genuine. We must not compromise what is true in the name of love, but we must always be characterized by a sincere compassion and concern for others.

Jesus was not accepting of sin, but He was known as a friend of sinners. In fact, He was frequently criticized for being willing to talk to those that the Pharisees deemed to be off limits. Jesus had the balance of grace and truth that allowed Him to touch the broken with kindness and love and lead them to salvation.

Such love is not the product of our own efforts or determination, but rather a product of the indwelling Holy Spirit working in our lives. The early American preacher and theologian Jonathan Edwards said, "All the fruits of the Spirit which we are to lay weight upon as evidential of grace, are summed up in charity, or Christian love; because this is the sum of all grace." As we walk in the Spirit, we will exhibit the same love toward others that Jesus did, and they will know that we are truly His disciples.

Today's Rooted Principle: Stand firm for what is right, but make sure that your life is most distinguished by love.

Doing God's Business

And as Jesus passed by, he saw a man which was blind from his birth. And his disciples asked him, saying, Master, who did sin, this man, or his parents, that he was born blind? Jesus answered, Neither hath this man sinned, nor his parents: but that the works of God should be made manifest in him. I must work the works of him that sent me, while it is day: the night cometh, when no man can work. —**John 9:1–4**

As D. L. Moody walked down a Chicago street one day, he saw a man leaning against a lamppost. The evangelist gently put his hand on the man's shoulder and asked him if he was a Christian. The fellow raised his fists and angrily exclaimed, "Mind your own business!" "I'm sorry if I've offended you," said Moody, "but to be very frank, that is my business!"

Ephesians 2:10 says we are "created in Christ Jesus unto good works, which God hath before ordained that we should walk in them." There are works that God has planned for you to accomplish today—witnessing, giving, encouraging, loving—and it is vitally important that you are busy doing God's work while there is still time.

Some weeks after he spoke to the man on the street, Mr. Moody was in bed when he heard a tremendous pounding at his front door. He jumped out of bed and rushed to the door. He thought the house was on fire. He opened the door, and there stood that same man. He said, "Mr. Moody, I have not had a good night's sleep since that night you spoke to me under the lamppost, and I have come around at this unearthly hour of the night for you to tell me what I have to do to be saved." If you are faithful to share the Gospel with those you meet, God will use you to bring in the harvest.

Today's Rooted Principle: Do not allow anything to deter you from doing God's business today.

Comfort

Now our Lord Jesus Christ himself, and God, even our Father, which hath loved us, and hath given us everlasting consolation and good hope through grace, Comfort your hearts, and stablish you in every good word and work.—**2 Thessalonians 2:16–17**

D r. Charles Fuller, the well-known radio preacher, knew what it was like to go through difficult days. He suffered great financial reverses during the Great Depression, and his only child was at the point of death twice. Through that time, Charles Fuller and his wife struggled with their faith, not understanding why so many things were going wrong. But they found that God was always faithful.

One day on his radio program, Dr. Fuller said, "I pass on to you a little of the comfort wherewith Mrs. Fuller and I have been comforted. We have come to know God in a new way because of the trials we have been going through these past three years. We have known what it is to have much sickness, financial losses, those turn against us and seek to hurt us who we thought were true friends, our only child brought down to death's door on two occasions. I want to tell you that after going through all this and much more, Mrs. Fuller and I know that God is able— that His promises are true. We never could have known the sweetness of trusting God had we not come to the place where we ourselves could do nothing."

God brings trials and testing into our lives for a variety of reasons. One of His purposes is so that we can experience His comfort in a powerful and meaningful way. Rather than allowing our difficulties to draw us away from Him, they should encourage us to run to Him, just as a child rushes to a parent for love and reassurance. God is with you today no matter what difficulties you may experience.

Today's Rooted Principle: You are not alone today—rest in the comfort and strength of God Almighty.

Rising from the Ashes

To appoint unto them that mourn in Zion, to give unto them beauty for ashes, the oil of joy for mourning, the garment of praise for the spirit of heaviness; that they might be called trees of righteousness, the planting of the LORD, that he might be glorified.—**Isaiah 61:3**

Following a massive wildfire that ravaged thousands of acres of land in Utah, a volunteer returned to the site of an eagle's nest that had been burned in the fire. He was expecting to retrieve the band he had earlier placed on a baby golden eagle, fearing that it had been killed in the fire. To his amazement, the two-month-old baby, though badly burned, was still alive, although its beak and talons and feathers were all damaged by the blaze. The baby eagle was taken to a wildlife rescue center where it was named Phoenix. The staff believed that after a year of therapy and the natural regrowth of feathers through molting, it would be able to be released into the wild.

When we experience difficult or even devastating events, we may be tempted to wonder if things will ever be right—if we will ever be happy again. But we serve a God who transforms the past, replacing mourning with joy, and sadness with praise. There are no circumstances which dictate that we are doomed to a life of regret and emptiness. Instead God promises that as we come to Him, He will replace pain with hope.

In His first sermon preached in Nazareth, Jesus said that He was the fulfillment of the Messianic promise in Isaiah 61. Jesus Himself suffered greatly, enduring the pain of the cross "…for the joy that was set before him" (Hebrews 12:2). Because of His death and resurrection, we can find freedom from the pain of the past and hope for a beautiful and glorious future.

Today's Rooted Principle: God can replace the ashes of painful events in your past with His beauty as you trust Him with your circumstances.

Psalms 110–112   1 Corinthians 5

You Are Not Alone

And it was so, when Elijah heard it, that he wrapped his face in his mantle, and went out, and stood in the entering in of the cave. And, behold, there came a voice unto him, and said, What doest thou here, Elijah? And he said, I have been very jealous for the LORD God of hosts: because the children of Israel have forsaken thy covenant, thrown down thine altars, and slain thy prophets with the sword; and I, even I only, am left; and they seek my life, to take it away.—**1 Kings 19:13–14**

The oldest of twelve children, Elizabeth Barrett received a classical education, learning Greek and Latin, and studying writers and poets. A well-received poet in her own right, she is best-remembered for her courtship by and love for another poet, Robert Browning. Barrett's father did not want any of his children to marry, threatening to disinherit any who did. So Browning and Barrett, who had met only once, carried on their courtship via letters and poems.

Barrett had suffered for a number of years from a lung disease and was generally in poor health. Yet knowing someone loved her strengthened her, and she was well enough to get married the year after their first meeting and to move to Italy where she lived for the rest of her life.

There is enormous strength and comfort in the knowledge that we are not alone—that there is someone who loves and cares for us. Isolation, on the other hand, can easily lead to discouragement and even despair.

When Elijah was running from Jezebel, he left his servant behind and went on alone. This contributed to his feelings of defeat, and he complained to God that he was the only one left who was doing right. God told him, "I have left me seven thousand in Israel" (1 Kings 19:18).

If you are feeling discouraged and lonely in your work for God, remember God's words to Elijah. Not only is God Himself with you, but you are part of an army of dedicated Christians laboring for the Lord.

Today's Rooted Principle: God has many faithful servants, and you are not alone in laboring for Him.

Compassion

But when he saw the multitudes, he was moved with compassion on them, because they fainted, and were scattered abroad, as sheep having no shepherd. Then saith he unto his disciples, The harvest truly is plenteous, but the labourers are few; Pray ye therefore the Lord of the harvest, that he will send forth labourers into his harvest.—**Matthew 9:36–38**

George Truett was a tremendously effective pastor for decades in Texas. His heart was broken when he accidentally killed his best friend while they were on a hunting trip. His daughter said that she never heard him laugh after that day. Truett had a radio program, and each day when it came to a close he would say, "Be good to everybody, because everybody is having a tough time." Because he knew personally what a heavy burden people could be carrying, he encouraged compassion toward them.

Sometimes we cross paths with people who seem to be brusque and not very easy to like. Yet there is usually a reason for their behavior, and often it is because they are hiding a heavy heart. If we take the time to understand what has happened, we may find that while they have a tough outer exterior, inwardly they are desperately wishing for someone to care about them.

When Jesus looked on people, He had compassion on them and wanted to meet their needs. There is no shortage of people we can help if we simply will open our eyes toward them in compassion. In the parable of the Good Samaritan, Jesus talked about the priest and the Levite who passed by the injured man without stopping to help. It is a tragedy when we allow the busyness of life to prevent us from taking time to reach out in compassion to those in need. Instead, we should stop and do everything we can to help them.

Today's Rooted Principle: All around you today there are people with heavy hearts. When you show them compassion, you are truly being like Jesus.

The Habit of Church

And Jesus returned in the power of the Spirit into Galilee: and there went out a fame of him through all the region round about. And he taught in their synagogues, being glorified of all. And he came to Nazareth, where he had been brought up: and, as his custom was, he went into the synagogue on the sabbath day, and stood up for to read.
—**Luke 4:14–16**

It is right and should be normal for every child of God to be a regular church attender. The Bible describes going to the synagogue as Jesus' "custom"—it was His habitual practice. We can always find excuses for not going to church. Though there are times when sickness or an emergency may require us to be absent from the assembling of God's people, it should be our normal, routine, habitual practice to go to church.

The great Christian businessman of the past, J. C. Penny, said, "If a man's business requires so much of his time that he cannot attend the services of his church, then that man has more business than God intended him to have." Church is important. A church that provides sound Bible preaching and teaching is a vital resource for your family and for your own walk with God.

The Bible frequently uses the metaphor of sheep to describe believers. Sheep are herd animals that can usually be found close together. When they do stray from the flock, they often get disoriented and lost, and find it hard to make their way back. It is much the same with people. We need to guard our church attendance and beware the many strategies the enemy uses to distract us from regular worship and fellowship with God's people. No job, no promotion, no salary increase is worth losing the vibrant and vital connection with other believers that comes only from regular church attendance.

Today's Rooted Principle: Do not allow anything to deter you from regular attendance at your church.

Where to Start

Paul, and Silvanus, and Timotheus, unto the church of the Thessalonians which is in God the Father and in the Lord Jesus Christ: Grace be unto you, and peace, from God our Father, and the Lord Jesus Christ. We give thanks to God always for you all, making mention of you in our prayers; Remembering without ceasing your work of faith, and labour of love, and patience of hope in our Lord Jesus Christ, in the sight of God and our Father; Knowing, brethren beloved, your election of God.
—**1 Thessalonians 1:1–4**

When I first came to pastor the Lancaster Baptist Church, I wanted our church to get started right. The first book of the Bible from which I preached was 1 Thessalonians. I challenged our people to have a faith that worked. The church wasn't very big back then—just a handful of families. But the starting point for every church is the same as the starting point for every individual Christian—an active, working faith.

If a person decides to run a marathon, he doesn't just wake up one morning and run twenty-six miles. Instead he begins training, running shorter distances at first and then extending until he is ready to go the distance. The Christian life works the same way. God knows that when we start out we are not ready for the big tests and challenges. So He allows circumstances that cause our faith to grow. As we see His faithfulness to us through each situation, we prepare ourselves for greater service to Him.

The challenge for all of us is to have a working faith—to attempt to do more for God than we think we can do in our own strength. Strive to develop your faith through reading, studying, and hearing the Word. And prepare for God to do great things in and through your life.

Today's Rooted Principle: Just like our muscles, our faith grows stronger as we exercise and use it.

Ancient Landmarks

Remove not the ancient landmark, which thy fathers have set.
—Proverbs 22:28

O f all the things that we have lost in our country, one of the most serious is the appreciation for the overtly Christian nature of our heritage. For example, Yale was founded as an institution dedicated to training preachers for the colonies as a conservative alternative to Harvard, which had begun as a sound institution but had become more liberal. Timothy Dwight, the grandson of Jonathan Edwards, graduated from Yale at just seventeen years of age and entered the ministry.

After a number of years as a pastor, Dwight returned as the president of Yale from 1795–1817. In an address to the graduating class of 1814, Dwight said, "Christ is the only, the true, the living way of access to God. Give up yourselves therefore to him, with a cordial confidence, and the great work of life is done." Today Yale would laugh at someone making such a claim as it goes against their belief in diversity.

How does such a massive change take place? It begins with small compromises, usually made to be more acceptable to those around us. Of course this wicked transformation is not limited to institutions; individuals must guard against it as well. Think of Lot choosing to live in well-watered lands for his cattle and placing his tent so that it faced toward Sodom. On the day Lot first made that choice, he would have been horrified by his future actions. But little by little he moved closer and closer to Sodom until he was firmly entrenched in that wicked place and lost his family as a result.

The protection we have against ending up in the wrong place is to remain firmly planted in the right one. We do not need new theology or new beliefs. The Word of God never changes, and what was true yesterday is still true today.

Today's Rooted Principle: Commit yourself to remaining faithful to the great truths of the Word no matter who else may change.

Hard Work

Remember the sabbath day, to keep it holy. Six days shalt thou labour, and do all thy work: But the seventh day is the sabbath of the LORD thy God: in it thou shalt not do any work, thou, nor thy son, nor thy daughter, thy manservant, nor thy maidservant, nor thy cattle, nor thy stranger that is within thy gates: For in six days the LORD made heaven and earth, the sea, and all that in them is, and rested the seventh day: wherefore the LORD blessed the sabbath day, and hallowed it.
—**Exodus 20:8–11**

President Ronald Reagan was the oldest man elected to the highest office in the land. He would sometimes take naps during the day, for which he was criticized. Once, when a reporter asked about his practice, Reagan replied, "They say hard work never killed anybody, but I figure, why take chances?" Of course in reality he did work hard, and so should we.

The Fourth Commandment is about more than the day of rest. It is also about our work. God created man for a purpose. Even before the Fall when sin entered the world, Adam was given tasks and responsibilities. Work is harder since the curse, but it existed before then. Beyond that, work has a purpose. We should not fear or resent work because it helps build character so that we can resist temptation.

Paul wrote that we are to view our work not just as employees, but "as the servants of Christ, doing the will of God from the heart" (Ephesians 6:6). When that is our attitude toward our work, we will not find it difficult to be diligent about our tasks. Not every assignment will be pleasant or enjoyable, but each assignment is still important. Give it your whole heart, and you will find that God will reward you even if no one else notices.

Today's Rooted Principle: Be diligent in everything you do, remembering that you are working for the Lord.

Bringing in the Sheaves

They that sow in tears shall reap in joy. He that goeth forth and weepeth, bearing precious seed, shall doubtless come again with rejoicing, bringing his sheaves with him.—**Psalm 126:5–6**

Every Christian has been given the assignment to take the Gospel to the lost. When we have a real burden and passion for that mission, it is certain that we will see results. The great evangelist D.L. Moody was led to Christ by his Sunday school teacher when he was a teenager. The teacher was burdened for his lost pupil and went to visit him where he worked in a shoe store.

Moody later told the story of his conversion this way: "When I was in Boston I used to attend a Sunday school class, and one day I recollect my teacher came around behind the counter of the shop I was at work in, and put his hand upon my shoulder, and talked to me about Christ and my soul. I had not felt that I had a soul till then. I said to myself, 'This is a very strange thing. Here is a man who never saw me till lately, and he is weeping over my sins, and I never shed a tear about them.' But I understand it now, and know what it is to have a passion for men's souls and weep over their sins. I don't remember what he said, but I can still feel the power of that man's hand on my shoulder tonight."

The concern and tears of a godly teacher resulted in the conversion of a man who saw a million souls saved in his evangelistic campaigns. What a wonderful result! We never know when we witness to someone how God can use that life to build His Kingdom. It is our responsibility to take the precious seed with a burdened and compassionate heart, then trust in God's promise that we will see an abundant harvest.

Today's Rooted Principle: Ask God to give you a genuine burden for reaching the lost.

The Snare of Acceptance

Love not the world, neither the things that are in the world. If any man love the world, the love of the Father is not in him. For all that is in the world, the lust of the flesh, and the lust of the eyes, and the pride of life, is not of the Father, but is of the world. And the world passeth away, and the lust thereof: but he that doeth the will of God abideth for ever.—**1 John 2:15–17**

Looking at the religious landscape of our country, we see that many denominations that once preached and taught truth have traded in their old beliefs in order to be better accepted by society. If what the Bible says rubs people the wrong way, they stop proclaiming what the Bible says and replace it with new interpretations—or simply ignore the Scriptures all together and teach the doctrines of men. Such acceptance comes at a very high cost.

A.W. Tozer said, "Religion today is not transforming the people—it is being transformed by the people. It is not raising the moral level of society—it is descending to society's own level and congratulating itself that it has scored a victory because society is smiling accepting its surrender."

Every church and every Christian must make a choice. Will we love the approval and the applause of the world, or will we love God and His Word? If we make the right choice, we can expect to be criticized and condemned. This should not come as any surprise to us. Jesus said, "If they have persecuted me, they will also persecute you" (John 15:20). When we take a clear stand for what is right, the world will not respond well. But such a stand is never taken alone. Like the three Hebrew children in the fiery furnace, we will find God walking in our midst.

Today's Rooted Principle: The world will not love you if you take a stand for what is right, but the world isn't supposed to love you.

The Debt of Gratitude

*But we are bound to give thanks alway to God for you, brethren
beloved of the Lord, because God hath from the beginning chosen you
to salvation through sanctification of the Spirit and belief of the truth:
Whereunto he called you by our gospel, to the obtaining of the glory
of our Lord Jesus Christ. Therefore, brethren, stand fast, and hold the
traditions which ye have been taught, whether by word, or our epistle.*
—2 Thessalonians 2:13–15

In 2006, the United States government received a payment of
$83,250,000 from the British government. It was the final installment
to pay off the loan for the military equipment and supplies furnished
by America to our allies through the Lend Lease program to help them
in the war against the Germans. England's Treasury Secretary expressed
his appreciation for the help so many years before and said, "It was vital
support which helped Britain defeat Nazi Germany and secure peace and
prosperity in the post-war period. We honor our commitments to them
now as they honored their commitments to us all those years ago."

The Apostle Paul said he was "bound to give thanks"—that he owed
an obligation to be grateful—and this is true of us as well. God has done so
many wonderful things for us, and none of them are deserved. Gratitude
guards our hearts against pride and selfishness, for if we remember that
the good things we enjoy are blessings from God rather than something
we are owed, we will remain humble before Him.

It is also important for us to express our gratitude to those who have
made investments in our lives. There is an old saying that applies here: "If
you see a turtle sitting on a fence post, it's pretty safe to assume he didn't
get there by himself." Recognizing that others have helped us get to where
we are, it is only right to thank them.

Today's Rooted Principle: Express your gratitude today, both to God
and to those who have helped you in your life.

SEPTEMBER

Get Out of the Middle

And unto the angel of the church of the Laodiceans write; These things saith the Amen, the faithful and true witness, the beginning of the creation of God; I know thy works, that thou art neither cold nor hot: I would thou wert cold or hot. So then because thou art lukewarm, and neither cold nor hot, I will spue thee out of my mouth.
—**Revelation 3:14–16**

There was a political commentator some years ago who said, "The only thing you find in the middle of the road are yellow stripes and dead opossums." While there are some who have elevated compromise to the highest level, in the end this false path leads to disaster. That was certainly true of the church at Laodicea. When God sent them a message through John in the book of Revelation, it was a stern rebuke of their accommodating ways.

Church history tells us that the Laodicean church was an accommodating church, more interested in fitting in with their culture than standing for the truth. We see that trend being repeated today as many churches take up causes that are either not in Scripture or are directly in opposition to Scripture. In far too many cases these "middle of the road" religious bodies cloak their betrayal of truth in flowery language that makes them sound very kind. But in truth it is no kindness to coddle sin. Love rebukes and exhorts a change in behavior.

Taking a firm and principled stand is not a recipe for popularity. If we refuse to compromise, we may be called haters and unloving. Yet in remaining steadfast for the truth, we win the most important approval of all—that of our Father in Heaven. It is a shocking statement that God would prefer our being cold than our being lukewarm, and it should remind us of the importance of maintaining our stand for the truth.

Today's Rooted Principle: Take your stand for what is right, and do not allow anything to sway you from the truth.

Take Your Stand

Wherefore take unto you the whole armour of God, that ye may be able to withstand in the evil day, and having done all, to stand. Stand therefore, having your loins girt about with truth, and having on the breastplate of righteousness; And your feet shod with the preparation of the gospel of peace; Above all, taking the shield of faith, wherewith ye shall be able to quench all the fiery darts of the wicked.
—**Ephesians 6:13–16**

Some years ago I received a letter from Dr. Curtis Hutson as he was nearing the end of his life. He had served God faithfully and effectively, and knew he would soon be going to Heaven. He wrote: "I challenge you to take your place in the long line of independent Baptists who have stood for separation (I speak here of ecclesiastical separation) and soulwinning, and hold that banner high until Jesus comes or God calls you home."

It is an honor for a soldier to be tasked with holding a challenging position. Union General Joshua Chamberlain became one of the most noted heroes of the Civil War for leading his men to hold the Union line at Little Round Top during the decisive battle of Gettysburg. There will always be opportunities for us to make concessions to the enemy and give in to temptation. But when faced with those, we must stand firm. Those who have gone before us have set an example that should encourage us to hold our ground.

I recognize that one day I too will reach the end of my ministry when either the Lord returns or my life ends. When that day comes, I want to be known as someone who stood firmly for the truth. May all of us choose today to take our place in the line of those who have stood. Our Lord expects and deserves nothing less than our full devotion.

Today's Rooted Principle: The armor of God equips us to withstand all the attacks of the enemy and to hold fast to the truth.

I Must Work

Jesus answered, Neither hath this man sinned, nor his parents: but that the works of God should be made manifest in him. I must work the works of him that sent me, while it is day: the night cometh, when no man can work. As long as I am in the world, I am the light of the world.
—**John 9:3–5**

God places great value on work. Even before the Fall in the Garden of Eden, Adam was given assignments and responsibilities. It is not a curse to have to work, but a blessing to be able to work. Rather than groaning and complaining when it is time to work, we should approach our jobs with a joyful heart and a determination to bring credit and honor to the Lord by the way we do our work. Jesus approached life with the attitude that work was a necessity, and we should as well.

One preacher said, "The maid who sweeps her kitchen is doing the will of God just as much as the clergy who prays—not because she may sing a Christian hymn as she sweeps but because God loves clean floors. The Christian shoemaker does his Christian duty not by putting little crosses on the shoes, but by making good shoes, because God is interested in good craftsmanship."

Work is a holy calling, no matter what field it is in, and it is worthy of our very best effort. A pastor friend of mine observed, "I work for God and get paid by the church. Many of our members work for God and get paid by General Motors." We should never lose sight of the fact that our ultimate accountability is not to a time clock or a supervisor, but to God. When we work as if He is watching, which of course He always is, we will not find it difficult to be diligent.

Today's Rooted Principle: Strive to be the best employee where you work and to bring honor to Christ by your example of diligence.

Be an Overcomer

Ye are of God, little children, and have overcome them: because greater is he that is in you, than he that is in the world. They are of the world: therefore speak they of the world, and the world heareth them. We are of God: he that knoweth God heareth us; he that is not of God heareth not us. Hereby know we the spirit of truth, and the spirit of error.
—1 John 4:4–6

The Bible often speaks of the Christian life as a war—a conflict between opposing forces. Yet though there is surely a battle going on, we must never forget that this is a battle which has already been fought and won. The Son of God already triumphed over sin and death, and His Holy Spirit who is in us is greater than any power or opponent that we may face. The victory is not won through our great strength. Instead, it is won through reliance on God's strength at work in our lives.

In the great hymn "A Mighty Fortress Is Our God," Martin Luther wrote: "Did we in our own strength confide, our striving would be losing; Were not the right Man on our side, the Man of God's own choosing." Yes, we must fight, but we are not fighting alone, nor are we fighting a battle which cannot be won. While we should never make the mistake of underestimating Satan's cunning and guile, we do not need to cower before him.

Rather we are told, "Resist the devil, and he will flee from you" (James 4:7). The losses we experience in the battles of life come from our failure to, "be strong in the Lord, and in the power of his might" (Ephesians 6:10). To be an overcomer, we must utilize the strength and power that are made available to us as children of God. Then victory is assured.

Today's Rooted Principle: Go into battle today confident in the victory that has already been won for you through Jesus Christ.

Finishing Kick

And let us consider one another to provoke unto love and to good works: Not forsaking the assembling of ourselves together, as the manner of some is; but exhorting one another: and so much the more, as ye see the day approaching.—**Hebrews 10:24–25**

In 1954, Roger Bannister became the first person in history to run a mile in under four minutes, breaking a barrier that had withstood challenges for years. Other runners soon began to match his feat, and an Australian runner named John Landry actually broke Bannister's new world record time later that summer. In August, the two met at the British Empire and Commonwealth Games in Vancouver. Though Landry led for most of the race, Bannister surged ahead on the final turn and passed him with a strong finishing kick to win the race.

Just as on the track, there is enormous value to finishing well in life. The temptation is to let up and coast as we near the end. Society promotes this concept with the view of retirement as a time to sit back and take it easy. Yet the Bible instructs us to do more. Of course there may be physical limitations as we age that will restrict what we can do, but there is no reason for a believer not to continue to grow and mature in spiritual matters throughout life.

It is a tragedy when people make the decision to cut back on their involvement with church, with witnessing, with giving, or with being a help and encouragement to others so they can "enjoy more leisure time." This robs the church of what is meant to be a great source of wisdom and godly leadership. Those who have walked with God for many years have learned things which they can and should pass on to others. Rather than looking forward to the day when we can sit back and do nothing, we should be doing all we can to finish well.

Today's Rooted Principle: Don't let up—continue running hard until you reach the finish line of your life.

Perfect Peace

*Thou wilt keep him in perfect peace, whose mind is stayed on thee: because he trusteth in thee. Trust ye in the LORD for ever: for in the LORD JEHOVAH is everlasting strength: For he bringeth down them that dwell on high; the lofty city, he layeth it low; he layeth it low, even to the ground; he bringeth it even to the dust.—***Isaiah 26:3–5**

Missionary Jack Benson to China was conducting a service in a city where a bandit army descended and took many prisoners to hold for ransom. Among the prisoners was Benson. As the bandits attempted to escape the town, they found that Benson could not run because of a recent operation. Forcing him to kneel on the road, one held a gun to his head. "I am going to kill you; aren't you afraid?"

"Afraid of what?" Benson replied. "I'm just going to meet my God."

The bandit shot and then beheaded Benson. But at Benson's funeral, the story of his calm peace was shared, and many unsaved Chinese people put their trust in Christ.

Most of us will never be faced with this type of situation, yet all of us go through difficult times. During those times, we have the opportunity to fix our minds on God and receive His peace, or we can do as Peter did when he was walking on the water. It was when he stopped looking to Jesus and began to focus on the winds and waves that Peter began to sink. One of the lovely things about that story is that even when his lack of faith got him in trouble, Peter still believed enough to cry out for help— and Jesus rescued Peter from the water.

We do not need perfect circumstances to have perfect peace. Peace is the promise of Almighty God to His children when we trust in Him. He has the power and ability to cause everything that happens to us to work for good. Peace comes from believing that truth.

Today's Rooted Principle: When we lack peace, we should view that as a reminder to focus on God rather than on our circumstances.

Try the Spirits

For such are false apostles, deceitful workers, transforming themselves into the apostles of Christ. And no marvel; for Satan himself is transformed into an angel of light. Therefore it is no great thing if his ministers also be transformed as the ministers of righteousness; whose end shall be according to their works.—**2 Corinthians 11:13–15**

During the administration of President Ronald Reagan, one of the main international issues facing the United States was a new arms control agreement with the former Soviet Union. As part of his negotiations with Russian leader Mikhail Gorbachev, Reagan refused to agree to a new treaty unless there were significant measures put in place to ensure that both sides complied with its terms. Reagan used an old Russian proverb *doveryai, no proveryai*—trust, but verify—to drive home his point. When the two men finally did sign the treaty, Reagan used that proverb again, and Gorbachev said, "You say that all the time!"

In our day, there are many who claim to be Christians who are teaching false doctrines and leading people astray. Just because someone uses Bible terms does not mean that their teaching can be accepted without comparing it to Scripture. We need to heed the warning of John when he wrote under the inspiration of God, "Beloved, believe not every spirit, but try the spirits whether they are of God" (1 John 4:1).

God has given us His Word as an accurate gauge of truth. He warns us to beware of false prophets (Matthew 7:15) and to be intentionally rooted in His truth. We must diligently study God's Word so we will recognize counterfeits when they appear.

Today's Rooted Principle: Be sure to compare the teaching you hear with the Word of God to determine whether it is true.

Getting Ready for the Wedding

Let us be glad and rejoice, and give honour to him: for the marriage of the Lamb is come, and his wife hath made herself ready. And to her was granted that she should be arrayed in fine linen, clean and white: for the fine linen is the righteousness of saints. And he saith unto me, Write, Blessed are they which are called unto the marriage supper of the Lamb. And he saith unto me, These are the true sayings of God.
—Revelation 19:7–9

Weddings are a big business in our society. In a typical year there are some 2.5 million weddings held, at a cost of more than $70 billion. It is believed that the royal wedding of Charles and Diana in 1981 is the most expensive wedding in history with a total price tag of more than $110 million in today's money. But whether the wedding is large or small, frugal or expensive, there is an air of excitement and anticipation surrounding the preparation for the wedding.

As believers, we have a wedding to look forward to. The Bible uses the illustration of a bridegroom coming to claim his bride to help us understand the relationship between Christ and the church. It is a beautiful picture of the love of God and something wonderful for us to anticipate. Paul wrote, "Christ also loved the church, and gave himself for it" (Ephesians 5:25).

Jesus paid the price for our salvation in full, and once we have trusted Him as our Saviour, we become part of the bride. There is nothing that can take away our salvation, but we are expected to prepare for the day when we see the Lord. This preparation, which is seen in our personal commitment to holiness and our witness to a lost world, is evidence that we are eagerly anticipating His return.

Today's Rooted Principle: Live today in such a way that you will be prepared for the wedding of Christ and His church when the Lord returns.

Proverbs 3–5   2 Corinthians 1   285

Spiritual Warfare

For we wrestle not against flesh and blood, but against principalities, against powers, against the rulers of the darkness of this world, against spiritual wickedness in high places. Wherefore take unto you the whole armour of God, that ye may be able to withstand in the evil day, and having done all, to stand. —**Ephesians 6:12–13**

When we drove a Ryder truck with our belongings into Lancaster on a hot July day more than twenty-five years ago, we had two children under five and another on the way. We didn't have a whole lot of stuff, so it didn't take us long to get moved in. We started going soulwinning with zeal in our hearts to do God's work. You might think that no one would oppose such a good purpose, but one of the lessons we learned very early on was that anything we do for God involves spiritual warfare.

Anything good that you try to accomplish will result in opposition. Dr. Bob Jones, Sr. said, "The door to the room of success swings on the hinges of opposition." The devil is not interested in seeing you succeed as a Christian, and he is especially unhappy if you are having a positive influence on others. Just as a soldier would not go onto the battlefield without his weapons and equipment, we should never start a day without taking time to equip ourselves for the battles that lie ahead.

There is an old story about a boxer who was losing badly during a match. In an attempt to encourage him, his manager said, "He hasn't laid a glove on you." The battered boxer replied, "Then watch the referee this round because somebody is beating the daylights out of me!" We have a very real enemy, and he will use any and every means possible to try to get us to quit doing what God has called us to do.

Today's Rooted Principle: Though our enemy is powerful, we have been given the armor to protect ourselves and the weapons to defeat him.

God Standing with Us

At my first answer no man stood with me, but all men forsook me: I pray God that it may not be laid to their charge. Notwithstanding the Lord stood with me, and strengthened me; that by me the preaching might be fully known, and that all the Gentiles might hear: and I was delivered out of the mouth of the lion.—**2 Timothy 4:16–17**

In the 1840s, John Geddie left the pastorate of a church in Canada to take his wife and two small children to the South Sea Islands to begin a mission work there. After a voyage of more than 20,000 miles, they arrived in the New Hebrides Islands at Aneityum. The island chain was filled with cannibals, and more than twenty crew members of a British ship had been killed and eaten just months before the Geddies arrived on the mission field.

They faced the difficulty of learning a language that had no written form and the constant threat of being killed. Slowly at first, a few converts came, and then soon many more received the Gospel. Geddie continued his ministry faithfully, including translating the entire Bible into the native language and planting twenty-five churches. For many of those years, Geddie labored with little help and little word from home, but God was faithful to His servant. In the pulpit of the church Geddie pastored for so many years stands a plaque in his honor which says: "When he landed in 1848, there were no Christians here, and when he left in 1872 there were no heathen."

You may find yourself needing to take a stand for God without anyone else to help you, but as you stand, you will find that God is there standing with you. You are never truly alone as a child of God. Whatever He has called you to do can be accomplished through His Spirit and His power.

Today's Rooted Principle: God is always faithful to you, and you will see a harvest from your life if you are faithful to Him.

A Time to Mourn

Saul and Jonathan were lovely and pleasant in their lives, and in their death they were not divided: they were swifter than eagles, they were stronger than lions. Ye daughters of Israel, weep over Saul, who clothed you in scarlet, with other delights, who put on ornaments of gold upon your apparel. How are the mighty fallen in the midst of the battle! O Jonathan, thou wast slain in thine high places.—**2 Samuel 1:23–25**

On September 11, 2001, we received a reminder of the brevity of life and the presence of sin and evil in our world. For a brief period after this tragedy many people showed a renewed interest in spiritual things. That did not last long, however. Soon, most returned to the same careless approach to life despite the reminder that should have focused their attention. That does not have to be true of us.

It is proper that we pause today to remember those who were killed on that day, and the thousands who have died during other wars. While we grieve for those who perished, this reminder of the brevity of life and the certainty of death should also cause us to examine our hearts. Are we living in such a way that we are prepared to meet God? Are we living in such a way that our death would be a cause for genuine sadness rather than fleeting regret? Are we living in such a way that we are honoring and glorifying God?

Those who were killed in that terrorist attack were not planning on their lives ending that day. They had plans for the future and hopes not yet fulfilled. Today we should commit ourselves again to living each day with the realization that it could be our last—and so that if it is, we will not be filled with regret.

Today's Rooted Principle: We must never forget the sacrifices that have been made for our freedom, and we must never forget that God is our only sure defense.

Loving God from Prison

For I am now ready to be offered, and the time of my departure is at hand. I have fought a good fight, I have finished my course, I have kept the faith: Henceforth there is laid up for me a crown of righteousness, which the Lord, the righteous judge, shall give me at that day: and not to me only, but unto all them also that love his appearing.
—**2 Timothy 4:6–8**

Near the end of his life, Paul wrote to his young protégé Timothy one final letter to encourage him to continue in the ministry and in service to God. The aged missionary knew that his life would soon end. He was being held in the Mamertine Prison in Rome, an underground dungeon where prisoners who had been condemned were held before they were executed.

Despite his circumstances, Paul did not complain. He was focused on what was to come—the crown that he would receive from the hand of the Lord for his love of Christ's appearing. Most of us have never endured anything like the physical suffering and abuse that Paul experienced for preaching. He was beaten and stoned and persecuted. But the love in his heart kept him going. "The love of Christ constraineth us" he wrote to the church at Corinth (2 Corinthians 5:14).

I am sure that Paul did not enjoy being chained in a damp, dark underground cell. Yet he regarded his surroundings as an opportunity to witness. Every six hours a new shift of soldiers would arrive to guard him. Clearly that witness bore fruit, because Paul told the church at Philippi about the saints, "that are of Caesar's household" (Philippians 4:22). Rather than focusing on your struggles, focus on your love for the Lord. One day we will see His face, and if we have been faithful to love and serve Him, we will hear Him say, "Well done."

Today's Rooted Principle: When we love God as we should, nothing in our circumstances will keep us from continuing to serve Him.

Faithful unto Death

I know thy works, and tribulation, and poverty, (but thou art rich) and I know the blasphemy of them which say they are Jews, and are not, but are the synagogue of Satan. Fear none of those things which thou shalt suffer: behold, the devil shall cast some of you into prison, that ye may be tried; and ye shall have tribulation ten days: be thou faithful unto death, and I will give thee a crown of life. He that hath an ear, let him hear what the Spirit saith unto the churches; He that overcometh shall not be hurt of the second death.—**Revelation 2:9–11**

George Atley was killed while serving with the Central African Mission. There were no witnesses to his death, but the evidence indicates that Atley was confronted by a band of hostile tribesmen. He was carrying a fully loaded Winchester rifle and had to choose either to shoot his attackers and run the risk of negating the work of the mission in that area, or not to defend himself and be killed. When his body was later found in a stream, it was evident that he had chosen the latter. Nearby lay his rifle still fully loaded. He had made the supreme sacrifice, motivated by his burden for lost souls and his unswerving devotion to his Saviour. With the apostle Paul, he wanted Christ to be magnified, "whether it be by life, or by death" (Philippians 1:20).

When we are faced with difficult choices, the decisions we make reveal what matters to us the most. Those who are faithful, in matters both large and small, are those whose heart's desires are fixed on the eternal. Nothing in this world, not even our lives, is more important than what waits for us in eternity. We should live with an eye on the things that matter most—those that will last.

Today's Rooted Principle: If you are focused on what is eternal, your choices today will reflect a desire for the things that matter to God.

Proverbs 16–18 2 Corinthians 6

Faithful to Christ

Servants, obey in all things your masters according to the flesh; not with eyeservice, as menpleasers; but in singleness of heart, fearing God: And whatsoever ye do, do it heartily, as to the Lord, and not unto men; Knowing that of the Lord ye shall receive the reward of the inheritance: for ye serve the Lord Christ.—**Colossians 3:22–24**

In the sixteenth century, there was a Protestant reformer in England by the name of Hugh Latimer. He was known as a great preacher of his day and as a result he had many opportunities to speak. Once he found that he was to preach before King Henry VIII of England. As he thought about his great responsibility to bring a message before the king, he realized that the message that God laid on his heart was not the message that the king would want to hear.

As he contemplated this, he said that he heard a voice saying, "Latimer, remember you are preaching before King Henry VIII who, if he wills, can take away your life." Then he heard another voice saying, "Latimer, remember you are preaching before the King of Kings, do not displease Him." Latimer faced the choice: would he preach what man wanted to hear or would he preach what Christ would have him preach. Latimer did take his stand for truth and preached boldly. Eventually, he was martyred by Henry's daughter, Queen Mary.

The work that you do today is not just done to be acceptable to a boss or supervisor, it should also be done in such a way as to be faithful to our testimony and commitment to Christ. In every sphere of life, the ultimate accountability we have is to Him. He evaluates not only what we do but the motives with which we do it. And if we are faithful to Him, the final result is secure.

Today's Rooted Principle: No matter what jobs you face today, remember that ultimately you must answer to Christ for your work and your faithfulness.

A Choice of Enemies

But thou hast fully known my doctrine, manner of life, purpose, faith, longsuffering, charity, patience, Persecutions, afflictions, which came unto me at Antioch, at Iconium, at Lystra; what persecutions I endured: but out of them all the Lord delivered me. Yea, and all that will live godly in Christ Jesus shall suffer persecution.—**2 Timothy 3:10–12**

Charles Spurgeon said, "The good man has his enemies. He would not be like his Lord if he had not. If we were without enemies we might fear that we were not the friends of God, for the friendship of the world is enmity to God." The choice that we face is not whether we will have enemies—anyone who takes sides will have enemies from the other. The choice that we face is whether we will stand with God or with His enemies.

It is a fallacy to think that we can somehow trim our message and soften our stance enough to avoid facing opposition. The devil is not content with small victories. He keeps pushing and pushing until everything has been lost. Many churches and denominations that once were faithful to the Word and to God stand as sad evidence of this truth. Little by little they gave up their convictions and commitments in search of acceptance and approval until nothing of value was left. They may still use religious symbols and language, but they are anything but Christian.

Of course, we should not be making enemies because of our temperament or disposition. It is possible to stand for the truth without wavering while being courteous and polite. But we should never allow the natural tendency to want to avoid conflict and enemies to lead us down the path of compromise and decay. It should not come as a surprise that standing for the truth leads to opposition, and we must not let that opposition deter us from our stand.

Today's Rooted Principle: It is far better to have God for a friend and the world for an enemy than the reverse.

A Motive for Reaching the Lost

Wherefore we labour, that, whether present or absent, we may be accepted of him. For we must all appear before the judgment seat of Christ; that every one may receive the things done in his body, according to that he hath done, whether it be good or bad. Knowing therefore the terror of the Lord, we persuade men; but we are made manifest unto God; and I trust also are made manifest in your consciences.
—2 Corinthians 5:9–11

We have the certain knowledge that one day we will give an account of our lives to the Lord. That should motivate us to be faithful in obeying His commands, including the final instruction He left: "Go ye into all the world, and preach the gospel to every creature" (Mark 16:15). But in addition to obedience, there is another motive for sharing the Gospel—the knowledge that each person must stand before God either saved or lost.

Charles Spurgeon described that day this way: "If you haven't looked at Christ on the cross, you'll have to look at Him on the throne—with great trembling. The sacrificial death of Christ will be brought before the eyes of all who refuse to accept His free gift of forgiveness and eternal life. In Bethlehem He came in mercy to forgive sin. In the future He will come on the clouds in glory to establish justice. What will we do without a Saviour? On the day of judgment there is nothing we can do if we have not trusted Christ."

The only hope of salvation is found through faith in Jesus Christ. There is no other way to Heaven. God's plan for people to hear the Good News and be saved is for His children to tell them. This is a wonderful privilege, but it is also a heavy responsibility. Remembering that judgment is coming, we should do all we can to reach the lost.

Today's Rooted Principle: Each person you meet today will one day stand before God. Have you warned them of the judgment to come?

A Place to Stand

Now to him that is of power to stablish you according to my gospel, and the preaching of Jesus Christ, according to the revelation of the mystery, which was kept secret since the world began, But now is made manifest, and by the scriptures of the prophets, according to the commandment of the everlasting God, made known to all nations for the obedience of faith: To God only wise, be glory through Jesus Christ for ever. Amen.
—**Romans 16:25–27**

The ancient inventor and mathematician Archimedes once said, "If you give me a lever long enough and a place on which to stand, I can move the world." The importance of a stable foundation cannot be overstated. God has given us the means through His power to firmly and securely settle us and ground our lives on the principles and truths of His Word. This is crucial to our ability to glorify Him through our lives.

God wants us to be established and settled in every area of our lives. We should be on a firm footing in our family relationships, with our church, and with Him. Paul equated the presence of stability in our lives with spiritual maturity when he wrote, "That we henceforth be no more children, tossed to and fro, and carried about with every wind of doctrine" (Ephesians 4:14). This growth comes from reading and hearing and studying the Bible.

Here in California, because of the many fault lines that run under the surface of the ground, all the buildings have to be built to a very strict code. If the foundations are not firmly settled, the building, no matter how impressive it may be, is not going to last. Instead, great care is taken to ensure that even when the earth shakes, the building will stand. As we grow in our faith, building upon a foundation which cannot be shaken, we can move the world.

Today's Rooted Principle: If you build your life on the firm foundation of God's Word, you have a foundation that will stand any test that comes.

The Son of the Comforter

*And Joses, who by the apostles was surnamed Barnabas, (which is,
being interpreted, The son of consolation,) a Levite, and of the country of
Cyprus, Having land, sold it, and brought the money, and laid it at the
apostles' feet.—***Acts 4:36–37**

Things were very hard for the early church in Jerusalem. The believers
faced intense persecution, and many who had come to Jerusalem from
other cities and countries for the Feast of Pentecost found themselves
stranded far from home. Those who had the resources made sacrifices,
in some cases major sacrifices, so that the daily living needs of the others
could be met. One of these generous people was a man named Joses,
better known to us as Barnabas.

This nickname that he was given is very revealing. The disciples
called him "the son of consolation" using the same word—*paraclete*—
that Jesus used for the Holy Spirit in John 14. They were saying that Joses
was like the Holy Spirit in the way that he interacted with other Christians
to bring them hope and comfort. We see this illustrated again in the
way Barnabas interacted with Saul after his conversion on the road to
Damascus. When the other believers were afraid to allow Saul into their
company, Barnabas championed and encouraged the new Christian and
helped place him on the road to an amazing life of ministry and service.

So many people simply need an encouraging word or a small gesture
of kindness to keep them going. They feel isolated and alone and wonder
if anyone cares about what they are going through. We can make a real
difference for them. Mark Twain once said, "I can live for two months
on a good compliment." The impact that we make on the lives of others,
sometimes without even realizing how much what we do or say means to
them, can be the difference between despair and triumph.

Today's Rooted Principle: God wants you to bring His comfort and
hope to someone in need today.

Unmoveable

But thanks be to God, which giveth us the victory through our Lord Jesus Christ. Therefore, my beloved brethren, be ye stedfast, unmoveable, always abounding in the work of the Lord, forasmuch as ye know that your labour is not in vain in the Lord.—**1 Corinthians 15:57–58**

Someone once said, "The men and women who have moved the world have been the men and women the world could not move." There is something wonderful about a person who takes a stand for God and does not allow anything to shake or change his position. In 1521, the reformer Martin Luther was summoned to appear before Charles V at the Diet of Worms because of his opposition to the false teaching of the Catholic church. Luther was told that he must recant, but he remained committed to the truth even though he was threatened with excommunication and even death.

Luther said, "Unless I am convinced by the testimony of the Holy Scriptures or by evident reason—for I can believe neither pope nor councils alone, as it is clear that they have erred repeatedly and contradicted themselves—I consider myself convicted by the testimony of Holy Scripture, which is my basis; my conscience is captive to the Word of God. Thus I cannot and will not recant."

May God give us men and women today who share that passionate commitment to God's Word. The Bible is under attack on so many fronts, and even the idea that there is such a thing as absolute truth is mocked and scorned by many. Despite what man may say or do, the truth abides. And as children of God, when we are committed to standing firm for what is right, we can know that our efforts will be rewarded. Nothing done for God is ever wasted—our work and our sacrifices and our stands are not unseen. The God who gives the victory will bless and reward our efforts.

Today's Rooted Principle: Take your stand for God, and do not allow anything to move you away from the truth.

Rejoicing in Trouble

Blessed are they which are persecuted for righteousness' sake: for theirs is the kingdom of heaven. Blessed are ye, when men shall revile you, and persecute you, and shall say all manner of evil against you falsely, for my sake. Rejoice, and be exceeding glad: for great is your reward in heaven: for so persecuted they the prophets which were before you.
—**Matthew 5:10–12**

John Bunyan, the author of Pilgrim's Progress, was repeatedly jailed for refusing to take a license to preach from the Church of England. He insisted on the truth that his authority came from God and not from man. From jail, Bunyan began his famous book as a way to convey truth to his children while he was separated from them by his stand for what was right. He was falsely accused of many things, but it did not shake his resolve.

Bunyan said, "Therefore, I bind these lies and slanderous accusations to my person as an ornament; it belongs to my Christian profession to be vilified, slandered, reproached and reviled, and since all this is nothing but that, as God and my conscience testify, I rejoice in being reproached for Christ's sake."

It is normal for us to want to be liked and accepted, but our commitment to Christ should supersede all other desires. If and when we are persecuted or criticized for doing right, we should count it an honor, rather than assuming it is a sign that we should change our position or our stand. In fact, we should celebrate the opposition we receive for doing right.

John Bunyan's jailers left a license to preach by the door of his cell, telling him he had only to take it to be free. Bunyan refused and left the license there until the rats ate it. May we be that faithful. Suffering places us in the long line of heroes of the faith who have endured abuse, ridicule, and persecution for the sake of Christ and the Gospel.

Today's Rooted Principle: If you are suffering for doing right, rejoice and give thanks.

Ecclesiastes 4–6   2 Corinthians 12   297

A Suffering Church

And when he had opened the fifth seal, I saw under the altar the souls of them that were slain for the word of God, and for the testimony which they held: And they cried with a loud voice, saying, How long, O Lord, holy and true, dost thou not judge and avenge our blood on them that dwell on the earth? And white robes were given unto every one of them; and it was said unto them, that they should rest yet for a little season, until their fellowservants also and their brethren, that should be killed as they were, should be fulfilled.—**Revelation 6:9–11**

Tertullian, one of the leaders of the early church in Africa, wrote, "The blood of martyrs is the seed of the church." From New Testament days until now that has been true. According to the World Evangelical Encyclopedia, since the death of Jesus Christ forty-three million Christians have become martyrs. More than half of those deaths occurred in the last century. More than two hundred million believers—over half of them children—face persecution on a daily basis. Each day more than three hundred people are martyred for their faith.

Because of the religious liberty that believers in America enjoy, it is important that we stop to remember those who are literally risking their lives to publicly take a stand as Christians. We should pray for and support these courageous men and women and young people, and we should also resolve to stand firm for our faith.

Even in places where the law guarantees religious freedom, there is a growing effort to silence Christians from speaking out on social issues from a biblical viewpoint. It is regarded as bigoted, hateful, and mean-spirited to speak God's uncompromising truth. And the day may come when we, too, are called on to make the choice whether to be silent or risk our lives for the truth.

Today's Rooted Principle: Pray for persecuted and suffering Christians today—and commit to take your stand in the same way.

Jesus Is Coming Again

For the grace of God that bringeth salvation hath appeared to all men, Teaching us that, denying ungodliness and worldly lusts, we should live soberly, righteously, and godly, in this present world; Looking for that blessed hope, and the glorious appearing of the great God and our Saviour Jesus Christ.—**Titus 2:11–13**

Alexander MacLaren wrote, "The apostolic church thought more about the Second Coming of Jesus Christ than about death and Heaven." Paul believed he would be alive when the Lord returned, as he declared, "We which are alive and remain shall be caught up together with them in the clouds" (1 Thessalonians 4:17).

In our day when there is so much false teaching on prophecy and so many inaccurate predictions by people who think they have figured out the date for Christ's return, it is easy to lose sight of the glorious truth—Jesus could come today. There are no events that must take place or prophecies that must be fulfilled before His return. This truth should inspire us to be busy about the Father's work, knowing that time is short.

This truth should bring us comfort and hope as well. Rather than dreading the Lord's return, we should be eager and watchful for it. The key to greeting Him with joy rather than regret is found in doing His work and His will as we wait for His return. Picture a child given a task to complete before Mom and Dad get home. If the job is done, the parents' return holds no terror. But if the child has been busy with things other than his task, the sound of a car in the driveway is not a happy one. Knowing that Christ could return at any moment, we should be busy so that we can rejoice at His appearing.

Today's Rooted Principle: Jesus could come back to Earth today. Are you eagerly anticipating His return?

Spirit Fullness

And Moses said unto the children of Israel, See, the LORD hath called by name Bezaleel the son of Uri, the son of Hur, of the tribe of Judah; And he hath filled him with the spirit of God, in wisdom, in understanding, and in knowledge, and in all manner of workmanship; And to devise curious works, to work in gold, and in silver, and in brass, And in the cutting of stones, to set them, and in carving of wood, to make any manner of cunning work.—**Exodus 35:30–33**

The Bible commands us to be filled with the Holy Spirit. This is a command for every believer, not just those who are in full time ministry. We need God's power for every aspect of life. Bezaleel, who made much of the furniture and decoration for the Tabernacle in the Old Testament, needed the filling of the Spirit for his work just as Moses needed God's power for his position of leadership.

Dr. Curtis Hutson said, "Every Christian is as full of the Holy Spirit as he or she has decided to be." We are filled with the Spirit as we are emptied of ourselves. It is said that when a group of churches met to consider inviting the evangelist D. L. Moody to come to England for a crusade, a young, prideful pastor protested, "Why do we need this 'Mr. Moody'? He's uneducated, inexperienced, etc. Who does he think he is anyway? Does he have a monopoly on the Holy Spirit?" An older, wiser pastor rose and responded, "No, but the Holy Spirit has a monopoly on Mr. Moody."

God does not want control of our lives only for a while on Sundays or when we are with others from the church—His plan is for His Spirit to control our steps every day in every area of life. Surrender your will to His, and you will find yourself walking in the Spirit.

Today's Rooted Principle: Allowing the Holy Spirit to control your life today prepares you to display His power in whatever you do.

To Be Like Jesus

For even hereunto were ye called: because Christ also suffered for us, leaving us an example, that ye should follow his steps: Who did no sin, neither was guile found in his mouth: Who, when he was reviled, reviled not again; when he suffered, he threatened not; but committed himself to him that judgeth righteously: Who his own self bare our sins in his own body on the tree, that we, being dead to sins, should live unto righteousness: by whose stripes ye were healed.—**1 Peter 2:21–24**

When the wife of the great pioneer missionary Adoniram Judson told him that a newspaper article likened him to some of the apostles, Judson replied, "I do not want to be like a Paul...or any mere man. I want to be like Christ...I want to follow Him only, copy His teachings, drink in His Spirit, and place my feet in His footprints...Oh, to be more like Christ!"

Even before the world was created, God's plan was for us to be "conformed to the image of his Son" (Romans 8:29). God did not save us solely to allow us to go to Heaven, though of course that is a wonderful and undeserved blessing. God also saved us so that we could go into the world just as Jesus did and point men and women to Him. God intends for us to be walking in the footsteps of Jesus Christ as we go through this world.

Though Jesus left us many important examples, perhaps the greatest is His sacrificial death for the sins of others. While we are not called on to do what only He could do, we are called to give up our rights and privileges for the sake of following Him and for the benefit of others. The more we are willing to give and invest in those in need, the more we are being like Jesus.

Today's Rooted Principle: God's purpose and plan for your life today is for you to be a reflection of His Son.

An Example for Your Family

Now therefore fear the LORD, and serve him in sincerity and in truth: and put away the gods which your fathers served on the other side of the flood, and in Egypt; and serve ye the LORD. And if it seem evil unto you to serve the LORD, choose you this day whom ye will serve; whether the gods which your fathers served that were on the other side of the flood, or the gods of the Amorites, in whose land ye dwell: but as for me and my house, we will serve the LORD.—**Joshua 24:14–15**

We can make no greater investment than to be a godly example of faith in action for our children. Speaking of Abraham, God said, "For I know him, that he will command his children and his household after him, and they shall keep the way of the LORD" (Genesis 18:19). This requires both spending time in positive instruction and providing a positive example in daily life—teaching our children the truth "when thou walkest by the way" (Deuteronomy 6:7).

Charles Spurgeon said, "Brethren, I wish it were more common, I wish it were universal, with all [Christians] to have family prayer. We sometimes hear of children of Christian parents who do not grow up in the fear of God, and we are asked how it is that they turn out so badly. In many, very many cases, I fear there is such a neglect of family worship that it's not probable that the children are at all impressed by any piety supposed to be possessed by their parents."

While it is possible to present a front to the outside world for a while, those who live with us know best whether our faith is real. Live your faith outside the walls of the church, and you will have a powerful impact on your entire family.

Today's Rooted Principle: Live today in such a way that you leave to the generations to come an example of faith in action.

If Today Were Your Last

But to do good and to communicate forget not: for with such sacrifices
God is well pleased. Obey them that have the rule over you, and submit
yourselves: for they watch for your souls, as they that must give account,
that they may do it with joy, and not with grief: for that is unprofitable
for you.—**Hebrews 13:16–17**

On February 1, 2003, the space shuttle Columbia exploded while
re-entering the atmosphere after completing its mission. Some of
the heat shielding tiles had been damaged during takeoff, leading to the
destruction of the ship and the death of all on board. The commander of
the mission, Col. Rick Husband, had an outstanding Christian testimony.
At a memorial service, a video that Husband had recorded before the
flight was played.

He said, "If I ended up at the end of my life having been an astronaut,
but having sacrificed my family along the way or living my life in a way
that didn't glorify God, then I would look back on it with great regret.
Having become an astronaut would not really have mattered all that
much. And I finally came to realize that what really meant the most to
me was to try and live my life the way God wanted me to and to try and
be a good husband to Evelyn and to be a good father to my children."

One day each of us will reach our last day on Earth. More than
likely we will not know in advance when that day will be. That fact
should remind us to live each day with a commitment to fulfilling our
responsibilities so that, when we do reach the end of our lives, we do not
look back with regret. Focus on what matters and what is eternal, and
you will complete your mission with success.

Today's Rooted Principle: Live today in such a way that if you knew it
would be your last day, you wouldn't change anything.

Isaiah 1–2   Galatians 5   303

September
27

Heeding Wise Counsel

And thou mourn at the last, when thy flesh and thy body are consumed,
And say, How have I hated instruction, and my heart despised reproof;
And have not obeyed the voice of my teachers, nor inclined mine ear to
them that instructed me!—**Proverbs 5:11–13**

George Washington's father died when George was just eleven, and
for a time the young Washington had his heart set on joining the
British navy. However, his mother had some serious reservations about
that path and eventually strongly urged him to reconsider. He listened to
his mother, and, rather than becoming the captain of a ship, he became
Commander in Chief of the entire military forces of the United States
of America.

Much of the course of our lives is determined by the input we get
when making decisions and whether we heed wise counsel when we
receive it. By admitting we don't know everything and by seeking counsel,
we are protecting ourselves from great damage. What the Bible says in
regard to counsel is often misquoted. It is common to hear people say, "In
the multitude of counselors there is wisdom." While there is truth in that
statement, the Scripture actually says, "In the multitude of counsellors
there is *safety*" (Proverbs 11:14).

Refusing to heed godly counsel places us on a pathway to destruction.
Each of us has a heart that is deceitful and subject to being deceived.
That is why counsel is so important—so that someone can objectively
evaluate the situation and respond from a biblical perspective. Though
the Scriptures do not directly address every area of life, the principles in
the Word of God can and should guide us in all that we do. Rather than
being a sign of weakness, seeking counsel—and following it—is a sign of
wisdom. Surround yourself with people whose thinking is influenced by
Bible principles, and you will be protected.

Today's Rooted Principle: God has placed wise people in your life for a
reason—listen to their counsel and heed it.

Isaiah 3–4   Galatians 6

The Importance of Honesty

That ye put off concerning the former conversation the old man, which is corrupt according to the deceitful lusts; And be renewed in the spirit of your mind; And that ye put on the new man, which after God is created in righteousness and true holiness. Wherefore putting away lying, speak every man truth with his neighbour: for we are members one of another.
—**Ephesians 4:22–25**

In 1987, the Rockdale County Bulldogs won the Georgia state high school basketball championship for the first time in the school's history. The celebration was short-lived, however, because the school discovered that one of the back-ups who played just one minute of one game during their entire playoff run was academically ineligible. Though they had not known it or broken the rule intentionally, the discovery meant that they had to inform the state athletic association and forfeit their championship.

"Some people have said we should have just kept quiet about it, that it was just forty-five seconds and the player wasn't an impact player," the team's coach said. "But you've got to do what's honest and right and what the rules say. I told my team that people forget the scores of basketball games; they don't ever forget what you're made of."

Our integrity is far more valuable than anything we can gain by giving it up. Any temporary and fleeting victories that may be achieved through dishonesty will never bring satisfaction. Even if we manage to deceive the rest of the world, we ourselves will always know the truth. Worse, dishonesty quickly grows into a habit that spreads into every part of our lives.

The nature of lies is that they multiply. One lie necessitates the next, and then the next. This negative process begins with one moment of dishonesty or falsehood, often one designed to protect us from the consequences of something we have done or failed to do. Doing right in those moments offers great protection.

Today's Rooted Principle: Guard your integrity today, and be honest in every area of your life.

Isaiah 5–6   Ephesians 1

Be an Encourager

The Lord give mercy unto the house of Onesiphorus; for he oft refreshed me, and was not ashamed of my chain: But, when he was in Rome, he sought me out very diligently, and found me. The Lord grant unto him that he may find mercy of the Lord in that day: and in how many things he ministered unto me at Ephesus, thou knowest very well.
—2 Timothy 1:16–18

One of the overlooked needs that people have is to be encouraged. It is often easier for us to see and identify physical needs than emotional ones. Yet, in truth, many people are discouraged as they face the challenges and pressures of life. Hearing a kind word of hope from someone else can make all the difference. William Arthur Ward said, "Flatter me, and I may not believe you. Criticize me, and I may not like you. Ignore me, and I may not forgive you. Encourage me, and I will not forget you."

In the book of Ecclesiastes, King Solomon described the importance of having an encourager this way: "For if they fall, the one will lift up his fellow: but woe to him that is alone when he falleth; for he hath not another to help him up" (Ecclesiastes 4:10). From creation we were designed with a need for fellowship and companionship. Our world may worship the myth of the rugged individual who needs help from no one, but that is not God's plan. He means for His children to use their words to build and strengthen each other.

The person who sets out to be an encourager will never find a shortage of people to help. Even simple words spoken sincerely may make all the difference and give someone who is struggling the strength to go on. We call it encouragement, which literally means to give courage to someone who needs it. Such words are beyond value to the hurting heart that receives them.

Today's Rooted Principle: Take advantage of each opportunity today to encourage someone who may be hurting.

Forget and Remember

*And unto Joseph were born two sons before the years of famine came,
which Asenath the daughter of Poti-pherah priest of On bare unto him.
And Joseph called the name of the firstborn Manasseh: For God, said
he, hath made me forget all my toil, and all my father's house. And the
name of the second called he Ephraim: For God hath caused me to be
fruitful in the land of my affliction.—***Genesis 41:50–52**

An old saying admonishes that we should learn to write our hurts in
the sand and carve our blessings in stone. Much of our happiness
and contentment is found not in what we have or don't have, but rather
in where we choose to place our focus. There are things that we should
forget and things we should remember, yet our tendency all too often is
to reverse the two.

Every person who has ever lived has had trouble and struggles with
which to deal. "Man is born unto trouble" Job 5:7 tells us. But we do
not have to remember and replay our troubles over and over in our
minds. Instead we can focus on our blessings—which is the key to living
productive and happy lives. People who are trapped in the pain of the
past will never be fruitful. The point is not that the pains are not real, but
rather that our minds should not be focused on that pain.

As an antidote to allowing the troubles of the past to overwhelm us,
the Bible commands us to be grateful. Over and over the Scriptures tell us
to remember what God has done. "Forget not all his benefits" the Psalmist
instructs in Psalm 103:2. By fixing our thoughts and our attention on
the many good things God has done for us, we can begin the process of
moving away from the painful past into a fruitful future.

Today's Rooted Principle: Focus on remembering the many blessings
you have received, and you will find it easier to forget the pains of the past.

OCTOBER

Edify and Encourage

But let us, who are of the day, be sober, putting on the breastplate of faith and love; and for an helmet, the hope of salvation. For God hath not appointed us to wrath, but to obtain salvation by our Lord Jesus Christ, Who died for us, that, whether we wake or sleep, we should live together with him. Wherefore comfort yourselves together, and edify one another, even as also ye do.—**1 Thessalonians 5:8–11**

Known for his powerful preaching, R. A. Torrey was a brilliant and educated man who was greatly used by God. His evangelistic meetings all around the world saw thousands trust Christ as Saviour. Yet within his own home, Torrey was more known for his gentle compassion than his fervent preaching. When his daughter Edith mentioned a flaw of a friend, he told her, "What looks like a flaw may be the scar of a great battle."

If we extend that spirit of compassion to those we meet, we will find that we are not harsh and judgmental toward them. In return, we will find them willing to listen to the truth. One of the interesting characteristics of Christ is that so many people felt free to come to Him despite the troubles and sins in their lives. He was always gentle, accepting those who were heavy laden and offering them rest.

The story of the woman taken in adultery found in John 8:11 beautifully illustrates this truth. Jesus said to her both "Neither do I condemn thee" and also "go and sin no more." He never accepted or expressed approval of sin, but He was and is a friend of sinners. If we view people with compassion as Jesus did, we will find it easy to reach out in love rather than condemning them because of their conduct. God has called us to be encouraging and strengthening and building up each other.

Today's Rooted Principle: Be patient with people today. Recognize they are dealing with hurts and pains, and extend grace to them.

Isaiah 11–13   Ephesians 4

Resting in Him

And this is the record, that God hath given to us eternal life, and this life is in his Son. He that hath the Son hath life; and he that hath not the Son of God hath not life.—**1 John 5:11–12**

As I witness to people, one of the most common misconceptions I hear them express is that our eternal destiny will be settled after we die. Many think that their deeds will be measured, and if they have done "enough" good things, they will be allowed into Heaven. Of course we know the truth that each person's destiny is determined by whether they accept Christ as Saviour. Yet salvation is so much more than just us getting to go to Heaven—it is also peace, comfort and security while we are here on Earth.

Charles Spurgeon once said, "Faith has a saving connection with Christ. Christ is on the shore, so to speak, holding the rope, and as we lay hold of it with the hand of our confidence, He pulls us to shore; but all good works having no connection with Christ are drifted along down the gulf of fell despair." Though there is work God has for us to do as His children, there is no work which we can or must do in order to become His children. That which we could never do for ourselves has already been done for us by our loving Saviour.

This knowledge should give us confidence. Rather than being tormented by doubt and uncertainty, we can place complete trust in the promise of eternal life through faith in Jesus Christ as our substitute. We do not need to fear the future. This knowledge should also give us a sense of urgency to share the Gospel with others. When we take the Good News to the lost, we are offering them God's gift of eternal life, as well as the blessings for this life that come from being a child of God.

Today's Rooted Principle: Rejoice today in the fact that because of Christ, your eternal future is settled and secure.

Christ Above All

For by him were all things created, that are in heaven, and that are in earth, visible and invisible, whether they be thrones, or dominions, or principalities, or powers: all things were created by him, and for him: And he is before all things, and by him all things consist. And he is the head of the body, the church: who is the beginning, the firstborn from the dead; that in all things he might have the preeminence.
—**Colossians 1:16–18**

As Christianity began to spread through the Roman Empire, the authorities often didn't know quite what to make of this new religion. As they had done with other nations they had conquered, offers were made to place a statue of Jesus in the Pantheon, which held all of the various deities worshipped in the empire so that He could be honored along with all of the other gods and goddesses.

The Christians rejected that approach. Jesus is not another god to be added to a list. He is God, and He is the only true God. Isaiah 44:8 says, "Is there a God beside me? yea, there is no God; I know not any." The person and position of Christ demand that nothing else be placed in comparison or competition with Him. He will not share His rightful place on the throne of our hearts—it belongs to Him alone. Nothing and no one else is worthy of our devotion.

Though of course we are too sophisticated to worship graven images, we can easily fall into the worship of things which takes the place in our heart meant only for Christ. Paul wrote of the danger of "covetousness, which is idolatry" (Colossians 3:5). We need to guard the desires of our heart in such a way that nothing takes the place of Christ or even assumes a position alongside Him. Only when our love is properly ordered can we truly worship and glorify Him.

Today's Rooted Principle: Let your life today reflect the truth that nothing compares to Jesus Christ.

It All Belongs to God

Beware that thou forget not the LORD thy God, in not keeping his commandments, and his judgments, and his statutes, which I command thee this day: And thou say in thine heart, My power and the might of mine hand hath gotten me this wealth. But thou shalt remember the LORD thy God: for it is he that giveth thee power to get wealth, that he may establish his covenant which he sware unto thy fathers, as it is this day.—**Deuteronomy 8:11, 17–18**

Recently, I came across an excellent quote that says much about how we view the things we have. "The law of rightful ownership says: When we are blessed with money and material things, we are not getting what we deserve but what God in His grace lovingly allows us to enjoy and care for." Everything we have belongs to God. The things we have are entrusted to us as stewards to care for on behalf of the rightful Owner.

We like to take credit for our successes and our possessions. You've maybe seen the bumper sticker that says, "He who dies with the most toys wins." That mindset fits well with our world, but it does not fit well with God's Word. The Bible teaches us that "Every good gift and every perfect gift is from above, and cometh down from the Father of lights" (James 1:17). While it is true that God expects us to work hard and be diligent, it is also true that the very strength and energy that allow us to do that are from Him.

Remembering this truth is especially important when we receive blessings. Though God should receive all of the credit, too often we boast of what we have done. Far better it is for us to give Him all the glory and cultivate a heart of gratitude for His goodness.

Today's Rooted Principle: Remember today that every benefit in your life is the good gift of a gracious God.

Before We Can Give

Now the LORD had said unto Abram, Get thee out of thy country, and from thy kindred, and from thy father's house, unto a land that I will shew thee: And I will make of thee a great nation, and I will bless thee, and make thy name great; and thou shalt be a blessing: And I will bless them that bless thee, and curse him that curseth thee: and in thee shall all families of the earth be blessed.—**Genesis 12:1–3**

God gives His children blessings for many reasons. One of the most important is so that we can in turn be a blessing to others in need. When God announced His blessing upon the life of Abraham, He said once He would bless Abraham, while twice declaring that Abraham would be a blessing to others. We cannot be what God means for us to be while at the same time being self-focused.

Murray J. Harris put it this way: "All too often we regard stewardship simply as a matter of our giving to God, but this aspect is secondary. Before we can give, we must possess, and before we possess we must receive. Therefore, stewardship is, in the first place, receiving God's good and bounteous gifts. And once received, those gifts are not to be used solely for our own good. They must also be used for the benefit of others, and ultimately for the glory of God the giver. The steward needs an open hand to receive from God and then an active hand to give to God and to others."

Knowing how freely God gives to us, we should be generous and compassionate in providing help to others. As good stewards we must carefully use the resources with which we have been entrusted to achieve the best results for the one who gives them to us. Use what you have to build His kingdom today.

Today's Rooted Principle: Look consciously today for people who are in need and do everything you can to be a blessing to them.

Justice and Mercy

Being justified freely by his grace through the redemption that is in Christ Jesus: Whom God hath set forth to be a propitiation through faith in his blood, to declare his righteousness for the remission of sins that are past, through the forbearance of God; To declare, I say, at this time his righteousness: that he might be just, and the justifier of him which believeth in Jesus.—**Romans 3:24–26**

Judge Horace Gray of Boston, who would later go on to serve as a Justice on the Supreme Court, once said to the man who escaped conviction on a technicality: "I know that you are guilty and you know it, and I wish you to remember that one day you will stand before a better and wiser Judge, and that there you will be dealt with according to justice and not according to law."

Man's justice is always subject to errors, but God's justice is perfect. No sin escapes his gaze, and though punishment is sometimes delayed as God grants room to repent, it is certain. No one gets off on a technicality from His justice. Longfellow wrote, "Though the mills of God grind slowly, yet they grind exceeding small."

And yet, though God is just, He is also merciful and loving toward us. The love of God for us is so great that He sent His Son Jesus to die so that the payment for our sins could be provided. As Romans 3:26 says, Jesus is both "just, and the justifier." His blood shed on the cross paid the penalty for our sins in full so that when through our faith His righteousness is applied to our account, we are fully justified in God's sight. When God looks at my record and your record, all He finds is the perfection of Jesus. Knowing that we have been justified should inspire us to share the Gospel with others.

Today's Rooted Principle: Rejoice in the wonderful salvation God's mercy has provided that makes you justified in His sight.

A Giving Heart

And Jesus said, Let her alone; why trouble ye her? she hath wrought a good work on me. For ye have the poor with you always, and whensoever ye will ye may do them good: but me ye have not always. She hath done what she could: she is come aforehand to anoint my body to the burying.—**Mark 14:6–8**

Giving is largely a matter of the heart, not the checkbook or bank balance. When a person has a heart to give, they cannot be stopped. The woman who came and anointed Jesus' feet with very precious oil just before His crucifixion was not giving out of great wealth but out of great love. This truth is borne out by some recent statistics on giving that I saw. Mississippi is the forty-ninth state in per capita income, yet the people there averaged $4,070.00 in charitable giving which was second highest in the nation. Conversely, Massachusetts had the fourth highest average income, yet people there only averaged $2,645 in charitable giving, which was forty-ninth in the nation.

The Lord's plan is for His work to be financed by His people. Because everything belongs to Him, He could easily have chosen another way. Yet in His wisdom He knows that it is important for us to give. It reminds us of His ownership of everything when we give part of what He has given us back to Him.

Having a giving heart does not mean that we are giving great amounts. Instead, it means that we are giving what we are able to give. The great English statesman Edmund Burke said, "No one ever made a greater mistake than he who, because he could only do a little, did nothing." We see the principle repeatedly in Scripture that when God's children give what they have to Him, He multiplies it to meet the needs of His work.

Today's Rooted Principle: If you have a giving heart God will increase your resources so that you can do more for His work.

A Matter of Life and Death

Son of man, I have made thee a watchman unto the house of Israel:
therefore hear the word at my mouth, and give them warning from me.
When I say unto the wicked, Thou shalt surely die; and thou givest him
not warning, nor speakest to warn the wicked from his wicked way, to
save his life; the same wicked man shall die in his iniquity; but his blood
will I require at thine hand. Yet if thou warn the wicked, and he turn
not from his wickedness, nor from his wicked way, he shall die in his
iniquity; but thou hast delivered thy soul.—**Ezekiel 3:17–19**

When I had the opportunity visit the NASA Mission Control Center near Houston, I saw posted on the wall their mission statement: "To always be aware that suddenly and unrepentantly, we may find ourselves in a role where our performance has ultimate consequences." Over the years the men and women working in that control center have had to make life and death decisions, often without warning. The realization of the vital importance of their task lends a sense of urgency and passion to their work.

The calling and command of God for us to declare the Gospel to a lost and dying world is not optional. The work of telling people that there is a way of salvation in Jesus Christ is the most important mission any of us will ever perform. It is truly a job with "ultimate consequences." There is no other aspect of life in which failure has such damaging eternal results.

As God commissioned the prophet Ezekiel to preach a warning, He reminded Ezekiel that to neglect the message was to assume liability for the lives he ignored. Although we cannot force people to respond to the message of salvation through Christ, we are responsible to warn them of the penalty of sin and urge them to receive the gracious gift of God.

Today's Rooted Principle: Be diligent today to tell those God brings across your path that Jesus is the only way of salvation.

Certain Return

He that hath pity upon the poor lendeth unto the LORD; and that which he hath given will he pay him again.—**Proverbs 19:17**

James L. Kraft, head of the Kraft Cheese Corporation, made his fortune on the basis of a unique process for pasteurizing cheese so that it would not spoil. Along with his brothers, he created a massive industrial enterprise. A committed Christian, Kraft gave approximately 25 percent of his enormous income to Christian causes for many years. He once said, "The only investment I ever made which has paid consistently increasing dividends is the money I have given to the Lord."

There are many things we can and should do with the resources God entrusts to us, but none of them are more important than using them to further His work. We have seen over and over in recent years that investments thought to be safe proved to be based on nothing but empty promises—sometimes even outright fraud and deception. Some of the biggest names on Wall Street have vanished. Well-known economist Irving Fisher famously said, "stock prices have reached what looks like a permanently high plateau" just three days before the stock market crashed in 1929.

In such an uncertain world, there is great comfort in having the rock of God's promise that when we give He will guarantee the return. While many today promote a false view of God's blessing that teaches every child of God should be rich, we must not let their erroneous doctrine make us forget what God actually says. There is a very certain return on our "deposits" into God's kingdom both in this world and the next.

And while seeking riches is not meant to be the purpose of our lives and our money management, God does expect us to be wise with what He gives to us. There is nothing more wise than lending money to One who always repays.

Today's Rooted Principle: Invest your resources today in things that will produce a certain and eternal return.

Construction Ahead

Behold, I go forward, but he is not there; and backward, but I cannot perceive him: On the left hand, where he doth work, but I cannot behold him: he hideth himself on the right hand, that I cannot see him: But he knoweth the way that I take: when he hath tried me, I shall come forth as gold.—**Job 23:8–10**

I am not a fan of road construction projects. When you see those big orange signs warning that there is construction ahead, the natural tendency is to groan a little. Someone said the official state flower of California is the orange traffic cone! And you may have seen the picture of the construction sign that says, "Prepare to be annoyed." However, despite the frustration that comes with the process, the end result is wonderful when we get to drive on a smooth, rebuilt road.

Life is filled with things that bring us frustration and annoyance. Often, like Job, we may not be able to see or understand what God is doing in our lives. Yet even when we cannot discern the purpose behind what is happening to us, we can be certain and confident that God knows exactly where we are and that He knows exactly what He is doing. The process may be filled with things that are painful and difficult and sometimes frustrating, but the end result is something beautifully made according to His design.

God's purpose is for us to be "conformed to the image of his Son" (Romans 8:29). That requires that the things in our life that do not match that image be removed. Many times the things God must take away for us to be like Jesus are things that we would rather cling to. In faith we must be willing to release them to His purpose, trusting that He knows what the best end result will be.

Today's Rooted Principle: God is working all things together in your life today to accomplish His purpose of making you more like His Son.

Isaiah 34–36 Colossians 2

Committed Faith

They were stoned, they were sawn asunder, were tempted, were slain with the sword: they wandered about in sheepskins and goatskins; being destitute, afflicted, tormented; (Of whom the world was not worthy:) they wandered in deserts, and in mountains, and in dens and caves of the earth. And these all, having obtained a good report through faith, received not the promise:—**Hebrews 11:37–39**

Faith is easy to maintain when things are going well—when we're in good health and the bills are paid and we are seeing results from our work. When things are going wrong (according to our perspective) it is much more difficult to continue to trust in God. He has called on us to have a committed faith that is just as certain when we are suffering as it is when we are rejoicing.

Charles Spurgeon said, "I would recommend you either believe God up to the hilt, or else not to believe at all. Believe this book of God, every letter of it, or else reject it. There is no logical standing place between the two. Be satisfied with nothing less than a faith that swims in the deeps of divine revelation; a faith that paddles about the edge of the water is poor faith at best. It is little better than a dry-land faith, and is not good for much."

James 1:6 tells us that when we pray we are to "ask in faith, nothing wavering." So many times we miss what God could and would have done for us simply because we allow our faith to be shaken. Like Peter when he walked on the water, we take our eyes off Jesus and begin to focus on the wind and the waves. And, like Peter, we sink. God will not fail you today. He never has, and you are not going to be the first of His children to be abandoned. Trust Him fully.

Today's Rooted Principle: Do not allow anything to shake your faith in God today—He knows exactly what is best for you.

The Grace of Giving

*But this I say, He which soweth sparingly shall reap also sparingly; and he which soweth bountifully shall reap also bountifully. Every man according as he purposeth in his heart, so let him give; not grudgingly, or of necessity: for God loveth a cheerful giver. And God is able to make all grace abound toward you; that ye, always having all sufficiency in all things, may abound to every good work:—***2 Corinthians 9:6–8**

We often think of giving only in financial terms, and that is certainly an important part of it. Yet there is so much more than money involved in having a giving spirit. Giving begins with our attitude, not our checkbook or wallet. When we grasp our possessions and talents tightly, wanting to keep everything we have for ourselves, we are not following the plan of God for our lives.

His grace is meant to turn us into givers, and not just givers but cheerful and generous givers. Appreciating grace means that we understand that all of the things we have are given to us by God. It also means that we understand the difference between the temporal and the eternal. The great missionary Jim Elliot who was killed in Ecuador in 1956 said, "He is no fool who gives what he cannot keep to gain what he cannot lose."

God does not need our money or our talent or anything else that we have. He owns everything and is all-sufficient. He said, "If I were hungry, I would not tell thee: for the world is mine, and the fulness thereof" (Psalm 50:12). He has designated His work to be supported and carried out by His people because we need to give and work for Him. If we allow His grace to work in our hearts, we will not find it hard to be generous and do what we can to minister to others in need.

Today's Rooted Principle: Be a giver today—of your time, your talent and your money—to things that are eternal.

After Prayer

And when they had prayed, the place was shaken where they were assembled together; and they were all filled with the Holy Ghost, and they spake the word of God with boldness. And the multitude of them that believed were of one heart and of one soul: neither said any of them that ought of the things which he possessed was his own; but they had all things common. And with great power gave the apostles witness of the resurrection of the Lord Jesus: and great grace was upon them all.
—**Acts 4:31–33**

Someone said that prayer is much more talked of than practiced. One evangelist of the past used to say that on average Christians pray about five minutes a day, and, sadly, he may have been a little optimistic in that low assessment. In truth, we need prayer to be a daily, sustained and regular part of our lives. The power of the early church as recorded in Acts was repeatedly seen following their times of prayer.

In our day we often fail to pray because we feel self-sufficient. We think that we are able to figure things out and make things happen on our own. We have lost the spirit of dependence that led President Abraham Lincoln to say, "I have been driven many times to my knees by the overwhelming conviction that I had nowhere else to go. My own wisdom, and that of all about me seemed insufficient for the day."

Dr. Curtis Hutson often said, "There is more that you can do after you pray, but there is nothing you can do until you pray." Like the early disciples, we need to be diligent about our praying. We should not allow anything to distract or deter us from seeking God's face. It is only after we have spent time in His presence asking Him for His wisdom and power and blessing that we are prepared to work for Him.

Today's Rooted Principle: If you want to shake the world today, pray first.

Patient Waiting

I waited patiently for the LORD; and he inclined unto me, and heard my cry. He brought me up also out of an horrible pit, out of the miry clay, and set my feet upon a rock, and established my goings. And he hath put a new song in my mouth, even praise unto our God: many shall see it, and fear, and shall trust in the LORD.—**Psalm 40:1–3**

As a young man preparing to go to China as a missionary, Hudson Taylor determined to learn how to wait on God in prayer. He knew that in China he wouldn't be able to immediately share needs with others, so he wrote to his family, "I want to learn before leaving England to move man through God by prayer alone." While Taylor was receiving his medical training, he worked for a doctor who paid him quarterly. A forgetful man, the doctor often neglected to give him his wages, but Taylor was determined to only ask the Lord to remind his employer to pay.

One time, when Taylor had just one coin left, he feared that his employer would not remember to pay. That Sunday, while visiting a poverty-stricken family, Taylor felt that he needed to give them his last coin. He returned to his home and prayed fervently.

In the mail the next day he received an anonymous gift with four times the amount he had given. A few days later, the doctor stopped by Taylor's house and paid him the overdue wages.

When we ask God for His help, it is important that our faith remains firm. Whether the answer comes quickly or after some time passes, we must trust that God not only knows what we need but that He knows when we need it. He is never late according to His timetable. Since He is God and we are not, we must remain patient if He does not work quickly. And even before the wind begins to blow, you can be confident in His answer.

Today's Rooted Principle: As you pray, remember to trust God both for the answer and for His timing for the answer.

In One Accord

And they, continuing daily with one accord in the temple, and breaking bread from house to house, did eat their meat with gladness and singleness of heart, Praising God, and having favour with all the people. And the Lord added to the church daily such as should be saved.
—**Acts 2:46–47**

In 1996, the pastor of a small church in Arkansas who was distressed because the members of the congregation were divided came up with a plan to unite them. When he went to the church on a Saturday evening to turn on the air conditioner for the next day's services, he lit a small fire by one of the walls. In his confession to the police, the pastor said he only meant to scorch a wall in hopes that having a repair project to work on would bring the people together. Instead the entire building burned down, and the pastor was convicted of arson.

The phrase "in one accord" appears often in the book of Acts. The early church had great power from God in large part because of their unity. When the church is divided, it should come as no surprise that very little of lasting good gets accomplished. Yet all too often we allow small matters to divide us and discord grows among the people of God.

While there certainly are things worth fighting over, most of the conflicts that divide churches are not over major doctrinal points, but rather over minor issues and preferences. We lament the church's lack of power to make an impact on our communities and culture, yet we do not copy the early church's unity of spirit and purpose. They had a common heartbeat—they were united around their love for Christ and their desire to take His Gospel to everyone they could. Like pianos tuned with the same tuning fork, their message and ministry was marked by unity, and as a result, by great power.

Today's Rooted Principle: Do not allow anything you do or say to bring unnecessary division to your church.

God Wants You to Pray

If a son shall ask bread of any of you that is a father, will he give him a stone? or if he ask a fish, will he for a fish give him a serpent? Or if he shall ask an egg, will he offer him a scorpion? If ye then, being evil, know how to give good gifts unto your children: how much more shall your heavenly Father give the Holy Spirit to them that ask him?
—**Luke 11:11–13**

The great evangelist D. L. Moody once said, "Some people think God does not like to be troubled with our constant coming and asking. The way to trouble God is not to come at all." God cares even about the details we think are small and insignificant. If He knows when each sparrow falls and how many hairs are on our heads, how much more important are our needs and concerns to Him?

Of course God does not need us to inform Him of what our problems are. We never give Him information He does not already have. Why then has God ordained prayer as the means through which our needs can be met and His work can be done? Prayer is meant to build our relationship with God. As we come to Him in faith pouring out our hearts before Him we are giving a visible demonstration of our belief in His promises and His goodness.

Hebrews 11:6 tells us that this is a prerequisite for prayer: "He that cometh to God must believe that he is, and that he is a rewarder of them that diligently seek him." In addition, when we have past answered prayers to look back on and rejoice in, it encourages us to continue to boldly go to the throne of grace to seek help. Nothing shows God's love for His children more than the fact that He is willing to meet our needs. God wants to hear from you today.

Today's Rooted Principle: Don't fail to take advantage of the wonderful opportunity of prayer.

What Your Church Needs

Then the twelve called the multitude of the disciples unto them, and said, It is not reason that we should leave the word of God, and serve tables. Wherefore, brethren, look ye out among you seven men of honest report, full of the Holy Ghost and wisdom, whom we may appoint over this business. But we will give ourselves continually to prayer, and to the ministry of the word.—**Acts 6:2–4**

A uthor E. M. Bounds wrote, "What the Church needs today is not more machinery or better, not new organizations or more novel methods, but men whom the Holy Ghost can use—men of prayer, men mighty in prayer." Our culture has a fascination with new methods to accomplish God's work. The "seeker-sensitive" church movement has abandoned many core truths of the Scripture in their effort to make the church attractive and comfortable to the lost.

Instead of seeking new tools and leaving behind our convictions, we should go back to what the Word of God commands and do things His way. A praying church will be a powerful church. And while there is an important place for corporate prayer, it is also true that a praying church is characterized primarily by having praying members. In our individual time alone with God, we must seek His power and resources for the church to accomplish His work.

Jonathan Edwards said, "There is no way that Christians can do so much to promote the work of God and advance the kingdom of Christ as by prayer." As a pastor, it is a blessing to know that people are praying for me in the work. Your prayers for the work of your church are important. The Bible warns us that the enemy is seeking to devour us, and prayer provides a shield against his attacks. I encourage you today to spend time praying for the power and protection of your pastor and your church.

Today's Rooted Principle: Be a man or woman of mighty prayer today and do your part to build God's work.

No Scars?

For we wrestle not against flesh and blood, but against principalities, against powers, against the rulers of the darkness of this world, against spiritual wickedness in high places. Wherefore take unto you the whole armour of God, that ye may be able to withstand in the evil day, and having done all, to stand.—**Ephesians 6:12–13**

The Christian life is not a picnic but a war. We are called to be part of a great battle. Yet too many times we look for the easy way out and try to avoid the conflict. Dr. John Rice said, "People don't mind being in the army of the Lord as long as they can serve in the quartermaster corps." God is looking for His children to be willing to stand and fight in the spiritual battle.

There is always a place where the battle is raging, and that should be where we choose to take our stand. Scars of battle are tokens of courage and character, not defects. However, we live in a day when many believers have none. Vance Havner said, "Where are the marks of the cross in your life? Are there any points of identification with your Lord? Alas, too many Christians wear medals but carry no scars."

I do not want my life to be characterized by staying in the back of the fight while the battle is raging. Knowing the enormous price that Jesus paid for our salvation, it is a privilege to stand in the battle for Him. When the apostles were threatened and beaten by the Sanhedrin, they refused to quit preaching and returned to the church "rejoicing that they were counted worthy to suffer shame for his name" (Acts 5:41). Let it be true of us.

Today's Rooted Principle: Take your stand for the Lord today, even if that places you in the hottest part of the battle.

Exercise It to Increase It

And the apostles said unto the Lord, Increase our faith. And the Lord said, If ye had faith as a grain of mustard seed, ye might say unto this sycamine tree, Be thou plucked up by the root, and be thou planted in the sea; and it should obey you.—**Luke 17:5–6**

The normal response of Jesus to His disciples when they asked Him for something was to grant their requests. Yet in response to their plea for increased faith, Jesus simply told them that a tiny amount of faith—mustard seeds are very small—was enough to have a tree picked up and planted in the sea. The problem was not that they needed more faith; the problem was that they were not exercising the faith they already had.

We often think of people who see God work in amazing ways as if they had some secret and superior level of faith that allowed them to accomplish so much. Instead, the key is found in their willingness to use their faith. Think of the early church praying for the release of Peter from prison. Herod had already killed James and was planning to kill Peter. As the church met to cry out to God for deliverance, an angel came and freed Peter from the prison.

When he knocked on the door where they were meeting, the young lady named Rhoda who answered the door was so happy to hear Peter's voice that she ran back inside, leaving the delivered prisoner standing in the street. But when she told the church that their prayers had been answered, they did not believe her. "And they said unto her, Thou art mad" (Acts 12:15). When they finally did let Peter in, the Bible says they "were astonished" to see him. Did they have great faith? No. They were surprised when the answer came. But they did have enough faith to pray, and God answered their prayers.

Today's Rooted Principle: The faith you already have is enough if you put it into action.

How Faith Is Lost

And also all that generation were gathered unto their fathers: and there arose another generation after them, which knew not the LORD, nor yet the works which he had done for Israel. And the children of Israel did evil in the sight of the LORD, and served Baalim: And they forsook the LORD God of their fathers, which brought them out of the land of Egypt, and followed other gods, of the gods of the people that were round about them, and bowed themselves unto them, and provoked the LORD to anger.—**Judges 2:10–12**

God's plan for faith to be transferred from one generation to the next is for those who have seen His work for themselves to pass that knowledge on to their children and to those they lead to Him. If we are not faithful to accomplish that task, the results will quickly become catastrophic. Joshua and the leaders of his generation served God faithfully and led the people well. But they failed miserably at transferring their knowledge of God to the next generation.

Former Education Secretary William Bennett wrote: "Today's ordinary citizen is living off the stored up moral capital of another century's experience." That accurate description highlights the true problem facing our country and our churches today. We cannot continue to coast on the faith of the past. We need people who are walking with God now rather than simply reliving the days of the past when others walked with Him and saw Him work.

Our children and grandchildren need to see God as real and at work in our lives so that they too will love, fear, and serve Him rather than following other gods in their heart. The knowledge of the true and living God is a vital inheritance—far more important than money or property or anything else that we could leave to those who follow us.

Today's Rooted Principle: Do your part to pass on your faith to your family and church so that the future will not be without that faith.

Isaiah 59–61   2 Thessalonians 3   329

Unquestioning Obedience

And it came to pass after a while, that the brook dried up, because there had been no rain in the land. And the word of the LORD came unto him, saying, Arise, get thee to Zarephath, which belongeth to Zidon, and dwell there: behold, I have commanded a widow woman there to sustain thee. So he arose and went to Zarephath...—**1 Kings 17:7–10**

God sent Elijah to King Ahab with the message that it would not rain because of the people's worship of Baal. Ahab attempted to kill the prophet because he did not like the message, and God sent Elijah to hide by the brook Cherith where He sent ravens to feed Elijah. When the brook dried up, God sent Elijah to Zarephath.

To our logic and reasoning, the command to go to Zarephath was a crazy instruction. Zarephath was in Zidon—the home country of Jezebel. If there was anyone who wanted Elijah dead more than Ahab, it was his evil wife. Now God was sending His prophet deep into enemy territory.

Furthermore, God sent Elijah to a widow who did not have the resources to take care of him. When he arrived in Zarephath she was preparing one last meal for herself and her son—she was literally scraping the bottom of the barrel. But that was God's place for His prophet, and Elijah obeyed. There is no record in Scripture that he argued with God. God said "Go," and Elijah went. Through his faith and obedience, he was kept safe and provided for until the famine was over.

When we obey God, we honor and please Him. There are people doing things in the name of God which God has not told them to do, and that is not faith no matter what it may be called. God's directives for our lives are found in His Word. Each command of Scripture is to be obeyed, regardless of whether it fits our logic or not.

Today's Rooted Principle: When you do what God says without question, you receive the rewards of obedience.

Isaiah 62–64   1 Timothy 1

The Power of Righteous Prayer

Confess your faults one to another, and pray one for another, that ye may be healed. The effectual fervent prayer of a righteous man availeth much. Elias was a man subject to like passions as we are, and he prayed earnestly that it might not rain: and it rained not on the earth by the space of three years and six months. And he prayed again, and the heaven gave rain, and the earth brought forth her fruit.
—**James 5:16–18**

Hudson Taylor said, "The prayer power has never been tried to its full capacity. If we want to see mighty wonders of divine power and grace wrought in the place of weakness, failure and disappointment, let us answer God's standing challenge, 'Call unto me, and I will answer thee, and show thee great and mighty things which thou knowest not!'"

One of the great tragedies of modern day Christianity is that we simply do not pray as we should. The Lord has placed all of the power and resources of Heaven at our disposal to do His work, yet we "have not, because [we] ask not" (James 4:2). Prayer is not an empty ritual. It is not a religious exercise. It is how a child of God goes to the throne of grace based on the relationship He has freely given us to seek His help which He has promised to give.

Elijah is used as a model for prayer because he "prayed earnestly" and he "prayed again." In these brief statements we see both the importance of intensity in our praying and the importance of continued prayer. Though there are times when a quick prayer is all that is needed—think of Peter sinking beneath the water—in most cases, the serious issues we face will require sustained, fervent and serious prayer. God is waiting to hear from us to work on our behalf.

Today's Rooted Principle: If you are seeking to follow God with your whole heart, you can confidently claim His promise for answered prayer.

October
23

Things Have Changed

Know ye not that the unrighteous shall not inherit the kingdom of God?
Be not deceived: neither fornicators, nor idolaters, nor adulterers, nor
effeminate, nor abusers of themselves with mankind, Nor thieves, nor
covetous, nor drunkards, nor revilers, nor extortioners, shall inherit the
kingdom of God. And such were some of you: but ye are washed, but ye
are sanctified, but ye are justified in the name of the Lord Jesus, and by
the Spirit of our God.—**1 Corinthians 6:9–11**

I read a beautiful story about a young lady who wanted to join a church.
One of the deacons asked, "Were you a sinner before you received
the Lord Jesus into your life?" "Yes, sir," she replied. "Well, are you still a
sinner?" "To tell you the truth, I feel I'm a greater sinner than ever," she
admitted. He asked, "Then what real change have you experienced?" "I
don't quite know how to explain it," she said, "I used to be a sinner
running after sin, but now that I am saved, I'm a sinner running from sin!"

The transformation that the Holy Spirit works in our lives when
we are saved goes far beyond changing our eternal destiny. He also
changes the desires and appetites of our hearts. The sins that once were
so attractive are no longer what we seek. As He sanctifies us, we can leave
the past behind and move forward "to be conformed to the image of his
Son" (Romans 8:29).

Someone once told Charles Spurgeon, "If I believed what you preach
about eternal security, I would sin as much as I wanted." Spurgeon replied,
"I sin more than I want to!" Our flesh will never be fully eradicated in this
life, but we should be growing and maturing in grace and leaving the sins
of the past. The same power that provided our salvation is available to
provide our sanctification as well.

Today's Rooted Principle: Live today in accordance with your new
nature as a child of God.

332   Jeremiah 1–2   1 Timothy 3

God Has Something for You to Do

For by grace are ye saved through faith; and that not of yourselves: it is the gift of God: Not of works, lest any man should boast. For we are his workmanship, created in Christ Jesus unto good works, which God hath before ordained that we should walk in them.—**Ephesians 2:8–10**

For more than forty years, Margaret Stringer faithfully served the Lord as a missionary in Indonesia. She worked among some of the most primitive people, including a number of tribes that still practiced cannibalism when she arrived on the field. She surrendered her life to be a missionary when she was just twelve years old. Later she wrote, "Nobody really expected that I really would do it, but they had not taken God into account."

Not everyone is called to a full-time ministry, but every child of God has a work to do for Him. God did not save us to sit back and enjoy the ride to Heaven; He saved us to serve. Jesus said, "As my Father hath sent me, even so send I you" (John 20:21). There are things that you can do and people you can reach that are part of God's plan and purpose for your life.

Annie Johnston Flint wrote:

> Christ has no hands but our hands to do His work today,
> He has no feet but our feet to lead men in the way,
> He has no tongue but our tongue to tell men how He died,
> He has no help but our help to bring them to His side.

God could have chosen any means for the Gospel to go throughout the world. He could have had angels make the announcement of the Good News or had clouds spell out the message in the sky. Instead, He calls us to be His messengers, walking in the works He has prepared for us to do.

Today's Rooted Principle: Find the work that God has for you to do today and be busy doing what you can for Him.

Faith that Does Not Waver

And being not weak in faith, he considered not his own body now dead, when he was about an hundred years old, neither yet the deadness of Sara's womb: He staggered not at the promise of God through unbelief; but was strong in faith, giving glory to God; And being fully persuaded that, what he had promised, he was able also to perform.
—**Romans 4:19–21**

The Christian life cannot be separated from faith. We are saved "by grace…through faith" (Ephesians 2:8). We "walk by faith" (2 Corinthians 5:7). We "live by faith" (Romans 1:17). Yet despite this truth many people do not really understand what faith is. In its simplest form, faith is believing what God says and then acting on it. It is treating what God says as true even before it happens.

Over and over Scripture tells us that nothing is impossible for God. Yet all too often, Christians live as if they were orphans, with no heavenly Father able and willing to work in their lives and meet their needs. George Müller said, "Faith does not operate in the realm of the possible. There is no glory for God in that which is humanly possible. Faith begins where man's power ends."

Can your life and work for God be fully explained by things that can be seen, or is there something going on that shows God's power? Do you believe the things that God has said in His Word are true? Are you living as if they are true? When God told Abraham to offer Isaac as a sacrifice, no one had ever been resurrected. Yet Abraham believed that would happen. He went to Mt. Moriah "Accounting that God was able to raise him up, even from the dead" (Hebrews 11:19). Let nothing shake your faith today. Every promise of God is certain and true, and you can trust it completely.

Today's Rooted Principle: Trust God today for things that are beyond your ability to accomplish and believe that He will work.

Living Sacrifices

I beseech you therefore, brethren, by the mercies of God, that ye present your bodies a living sacrifice, holy, acceptable unto God, which is your reasonable service. And be not conformed to this world: but be ye transformed by the renewing of your mind, that ye may prove what is that good, and acceptable, and perfect, will of God.—**Romans 12:1–2**

In Old Testament times, bringing a sacrifice to the priest was something every Israelite was familiar with doing. Animals were brought for offerings, not to take away sins but as an expression of faith in the coming Messiah who would provide salvation through His blood. Hebrews 10:12 contrasts the work of the priests whose work never finished, with the completed ministry of Jesus Christ who "offered one sacrifice for sins for ever, sat down on the right hand of God."

Though the sacrifices for sin are finished, there is still a sacrifice we are to make—of ourselves. We are exhorted to place our bodies at the complete disposal of God. There is a beautiful picture of this in the story of Abraham and Isaac. God instructed Abraham to offer his son as a sacrifice. Though Isaac was a strong young man and Abraham was well over one hundred years old, Isaac willingly allowed himself to be placed upon the altar.

Our tendency is to regard making such a sacrifice as something large and out of the ordinary. Yet Paul described it as "reasonable service." In light of all that God has done for us, providing us the free gift of salvation through Jesus Christ, sending the Holy Spirit to dwell within us and promising to hear our prayers and supply our needs, it is not at all unreasonable for us to cheerfully offer ourselves for His service. Those who truly understand the magnitude and wonder of salvation will not hold back from yielding their lives to the King who rescued them.

Today's Rooted Principle: Place everything you have and everything you are at the complete disposal of God today for His service.

Follow the Plan

And at the end of the days I Nebuchadnezzar lifted up mine eyes unto heaven, and mine understanding returned unto me, and I blessed the most High, and I praised and honoured him that liveth for ever, whose dominion is an everlasting dominion, and his kingdom is from generation to generation: And all the inhabitants of the earth are reputed as nothing: and he doeth according to his will in the army of heaven, and among the inhabitants of the earth: and none can stay his hand, or say unto him, What doest thou?—**Daniel 4:34–35**

I once read a story of a sea captain who was out on a dark night. He saw a light far in the distance and immediately instructed his signalman to send a message: "Alter your course ten degrees south."

The reply was prompt: "Alter your course ten degrees north."

The captain ordered another message: "Alter your course ten degrees south. I am a captain!"

The reply came back: "Alter your course ten degrees north. I am a midshipman, second class."

The captain was furious. "Alter your course ten degrees south. I am a battleship!"

The sailor behind the other light replied, "Alter your course ten degrees north. I am a lighthouse."

We are often tempted to think we know better than God what should happen or what we should do. However, we should never forget that like a lighthouse that can see for miles and is there for protection, God sees things we do not and is our protection. His perspective allows Him to always point us in the right direction if we are willing to follow orders. Rather than insisting on having things our way, we should yield in grateful obedience to what He has shown us in His Word and walk according to His will.

Today's Rooted Principle: Follow God's will in your life today rather than walking by your own wisdom.

Jeremiah 12–14 2 Timothy 1

God's Calendar

Truly my soul waiteth upon God: from him cometh my salvation.
My soul, wait thou only upon God; for my expectation is from him.
—Psalm 62:1, 5

One day a visitor came to see Pastor Phillip Brooks and found him pacing the floor and somewhat distracted.

"What's the matter, Pastor?" the visitor asked.

Brooks replied, "I'm in a hurry and God isn't!"

Often when we pray, we have a specific timeframe in mind for the answer. Yet God is operating on a schedule that we cannot see, and it is only in the "fullness of time" (Galatians 4:4–5) that He works according to His plan. George Müller famously prayed for the conversion of two friends for more than fifty years. One was saved just before Müller died and the other not long after. For more than five decades he was faithful, trusting God would answer even when he saw no results.

God has never yet been late. His provision is certain. His promises are secure. However, if we allow our faith to fail, we can miss what God has for us. Galatians 6:9 says, "in due season we shall reap, if we faint not." This is a conditional promise. The reaping requires not fainting.

When we do not think God is working we must remember that we can expect the harvest in what He defines as the "due season." If you pull the potatoes out of the ground every day to see how fast they're growing, you are not going to have healthy produce—and it is the same with our prayers. We must patiently trust God and His timing.

Today's Rooted Principle: Do not allow God's work—though it may seem slow—to shake your faith. Trust His timetable. He never fails.

God Knows

Remember the former things of old: for I am God, and there is none else; I am God, and there is none like me, Declaring the end from the beginning, and from ancient times the things that are not yet done, saying, My counsel shall stand, and I will do all my pleasure: Calling a ravenous bird from the east, the man that executeth my counsel from a far country: yea, I have spoken it, I will also bring it to pass; I have purposed it, I will also do it.—**Isaiah 46:9–11**

In late 1940 and early 1941, as part of the preparation for Hitler's planned invasion of England, the German Luftwaffe air force launched a massive aerial assault on the island nation. Thousands of German planes crossed the English Channel to drop bombs on London and other major cities. Hundreds of thousands of homes were damaged or destroyed, and thousands were killed.

In an effort to protect young people, almost two million children were sent to live with relatives in the countryside or with those who volunteered to take them in. The story is told that one young boy was on the platform waiting for the train that would take him away from home. A passing man asked if he knew where he was going. "No," the young boy replied, "but the king does."

All of us face situations where we are not sure what to do. We make the best plans and decisions we can from the principles of Scripture and wise counsel, but we do not know the end of the path that we will take. God does. Even before the world was created, He knew everything that would happen. He is able to move people around the world or across the street to accomplish His purposes. When we are tempted to doubt, we can take comfort that God knows where we are going.

Today's Rooted Principle: God knows your path today, and you can confidently trust that He will lead you to the destination He has prepared for you.

Obstacle or Opportunity

And when the disciples saw him walking on the sea, they were troubled, saying, It is a spirit; and they cried out for fear. But straightway Jesus spake unto them, saying, Be of good cheer; it is I; be not afraid. And Peter answered him and said, Lord, if it be thou, bid me come unto thee on the water. And he said, Come. And when Peter was come down out of the ship, he walked on the water, to go to Jesus.—**Matthew 14:26–29**

How do you view storms when they come into your life? J. Sidlow Baxter wrote: "What is the difference between an obstacle and an opportunity? Our attitude toward it. Every opportunity has a difficulty, and every difficulty has an opportunity." When the storm arose on the sea of Galilee, it was so strong that even the disciples who had been fishermen, like Peter, feared for their lives. Matthew 14:24 says, "the wind was contrary."

It was then, when their progress was stopped and their future uncertain that they saw Jesus walking on the water toward them. One of the wonderful benefits we receive as children of God is that He is always present with us, even in our storms. In every trial of life, He is there. We are not abandoned, even when we cannot see Him. "…he hath said, I will never leave thee, nor forsake thee" (Hebrews 13:5).

God's presence with us means that every problem we face can become a triumphant overcoming. We may not be delivered from the problem, as Paul was not with his thorn in the flesh, but in those cases we will receive God's sufficient grace to deal with it. What we can know and trust and act on is that with God all things are possible. Rather than being daunted and dismayed by what comes into our lives, we can confidently go forward, walking with God through the storms.

Today's Rooted Principle: Look at the challenges and difficulties you face today as opportunities for God to do something great in your life.

Helping Each Other

And Simon answering said unto him, Master, we have toiled all the night, and have taken nothing: nevertheless at thy word I will let down the net. And when they had this done, they inclosed a great multitude of fishes: and their net brake. And they beckoned unto their partners, which were in the other ship, that they should come and help them. And they came, and filled both the ships, so that they began to sink.—**Luke 5:5–7**

It is very rare in the history of God's work to find great things done by an individual working alone. The pattern that Jesus established when He sent the disciples out in pairs to preach is not a coincidence but rather a recognition of an important truth. We are much stronger when we are together than we are alone. Solomon said, "Two are better than one.... For if they fall, the one will lift up his fellow" (Ecclesiastes 4:9–10).

Each of us has a responsibility to be an encouragement, help, and support to those around us. Some people focus only on their own needs— who is caring for me? But the pattern established by Jesus was to care for others rather than self. At the Last Supper He washed the disciples' feet. That job was considered so demeaning that only a foreign slave could be commanded to perform it—a Hebrew slave had to be asked if he or she was willing to take on the job. Yet the very Lord of Heaven took a towel and performed a task no one else was willing to do.

If we are focused on ways in which we can be a help and encouragement to others, we will find that we always have an effective ministry. There is no shortage of people who are struggling and carrying heavy burdens. As we help lift those burdens, we build up the body of Christ.

Today's Rooted Principle: There is someone today to whom your word of encouragement could make all the difference in the world.

NOVEMBER

Holiness

Depart ye, depart ye, go ye out from thence, touch no unclean thing; go ye out of the midst of her; be ye clean, that bear the vessels of the LORD. For ye shall not go out with haste, nor go by flight: for the LORD will go before you; and the God of Israel will be your reward. Behold, my servant shall deal prudently, he shall be exalted and extolled, and be very high.—**Isaiah 52:11–13**

The Scottish pastor Robert Murray McCheyne wrote to a missionary friend who had just been ordained and said, "In great measure, according to the purity and perfections of the instrument, will be the success. It is not great talents God blesses so much as great likeness to Jesus. A holy minister is an awful weapon in the hand of God."

Though we live in a world that is defiled and filled with sin, we do not have to succumb to the temptations that drag down so many. As Christians, it is possible to live a holy and God-honoring life even when surrounded by great wickedness. Joseph and Daniel illustrate that it is possible to be in the middle of a heathen culture and yet do what is right. Too many in our day have adopted the mindset that we must become more and more like the world to be effective in our witness. And yet, this view is not consistent with Scripture.

The Lord Jesus was called a "friend of publicans and sinners" (Matthew 11:19), but He remained pure and sinless. We do not have to isolate ourselves from the world to ensure our holiness. Rather, we should walk through the world with our eyes fixed on Jesus. Loving Him rightly and realizing His love for us helps ensure that we can be in the world without the world becoming part of us.

Today's Rooted Principle: Your ability and usefulness to God for His work is determined by your holiness far more than it is by your talent.

Unfailing Encouragement

And David was greatly distressed; for the people spake of stoning him,
because the soul of all the people was grieved, every man for his sons
and for his daughters: but David encouraged himself in the LORD
his God. And David said to Abiathar the priest, Ahimelech's son, I
pray thee, bring me hither the ephod. And Abiathar brought thither
the ephod to David. And David enquired at the LORD, saying, Shall I
pursue after this troop? shall I overtake them? And he answered him,
Pursue: for thou shalt surely overtake them, and without fail recover all.
—1 Samuel 30:6–8

All of us have times when we need encouragement, and almost all of us have known the experience of not finding anyone with a good or kind word to say. In that situation where do we turn for help? I've heard about some pretty heated board meetings, but I've never heard of one where they were ready to vote on stoning the leader. Yet David's men were so distraught that they were ready to kill their leader.

At that crucial moment, without the help of friends or encouragers, the Bible tells us that David encouraged himself "in the LORD his God." This is not the humanist notion of telling ourselves that we are good and things will get better, but rather the biblical truth of resting in the faithfulness of God even when we cannot see Him at work. No matter what our circumstances, we can always find strength and encouragement in His nature.

What we believe about God is never really put to the test until we face difficult days. It is easy to proclaim a strong faith when things are going well. It is something else entirely to be encouraged rather than defeated when everything is going wrong and even those who should be friends turn against us. The one source of encouragement that never fails is your loving Father in Heaven.

Today's Rooted Principle: God is working in your life today, and His faithfulness can encourage you even when all others fail.

When Sin Is Finished

Let no man say when he is tempted, I am tempted of God: for God cannot be tempted with evil, neither tempteth he any man: But every man is tempted, when he is drawn away of his own lust, and enticed. Then when lust hath conceived, it bringeth forth sin: and sin, when it is finished, bringeth forth death.—**James 1:13–15**

A 1982 ABC Evening News special reported an unusual invention, with an even more unusual response to it. Someone had attached a chair to a loaded shotgun. People could sit in the chair and look directly down the gun barrel. The only drawback was that the inventor had set the gun on a timer, and it would fire at a predetermined (but unreleased) date sometime within the next one hundred years.

The incredible response to this invention was that people would actually wait in line for their chance to sit in the chair and stare down the loaded gun barrel. Every one of those people knew the risk, but they thought it was worth taking their chance so they could brag on it later.

One of the most common and most tragic mistakes of our day is the belief that the results of sin will be different for us. When we fall prey to the lie of Satan that we are somehow exempt from the consequences of sin, he has us right where he wants us. It is rare for someone to sin with a full understanding and appreciation for the awful results that will follow. Instead, we rationalize and convince ourselves that we will be able to avoid them somehow.

God has written the law of sowing and reaping into the very fabric of the universe. As Moses warned the children of Israel, "be sure your sin will find you out" (Numbers 32:23). When we do what we should not or fail to do what we should, we will suffer the consequences just as God declares in Scripture. How much better to instead resist sin at the point of temptation!

Today's Rooted Principle: Sin always brings painful and devastating consequences, and none of us are an exception to that rule.

What It's All About

For whosoever will save his life shall lose it; but whosoever shall lose his life for my sake and the gospel's, the same shall save it. For what shall it profit a man, if he shall gain the whole world, and lose his own soul? Or what shall a man give in exchange for his soul?—**Mark 8:35–37**

The famous missionary to India, Henry Martyn, was a brilliant man. A Cambridge University student, Martyn's gift for mathematics was early seen when he was honored at only twenty years of age with the highest recognition possible in that field. Yet Martyn still felt empty. He even stated once that instead of finding fulfillment with his accomplishments, he only grasped a shadow.

But while in college, Martyn trusted Christ as his Saviour. Stirred by the testimonies of missionaries William Carey and David Brainerd, Martyn committed his own live to missions. When he arrived in India at twenty-four years of age, he prayed, "Lord, let me burn out for You." Seven years later, he was seized with a fever and died. But he left behind the New Testament translated into three Eastern languages.

The only true success and ultimate fulfillment in life is found in pleasing God rather than pleasing ourselves. This is true whatever our vocation is. Every Christian is to live for the eternal, rather than for the temporal.

God is not negotiating with us for control of our lives. He is the King, high and lifted up; and we either obey Him or disobey—there is no middle ground. He alone has the right to place demands on our lives which cannot be ignored if we wish to follow Him. The meaning of life is not found in anything that we can accumulate or achieve on the earthly level. And none of those things will ever truly satisfy the longing in our hearts that can only be met by God Himself. Live for Him, and you will be eternally thankful you did.

Today's Rooted Principle: It is impossible for us to follow Christ without surrendering our life to Him.

Jeremiah 32–33   Hebrews 1

Forgiving and Forgetting

Then came Peter to him, and said, Lord, how oft shall my brother sin against me, and I forgive him? till seven times? Jesus saith unto him, I say not unto thee, Until seven times: but, Until seventy times seven.
—**Matthew 18:21–22**

Clara Barton, who helped save the lives of many soldiers and bring relief to those suffering from disaster and tragedy as the founder of the American Red Cross, suffered a number of attacks. When someone reminded her of one of them, she acted as though it had never happened. "Don't you remember that?" the friend asked. "No," Barton replied, "I distinctly remember forgetting it."

It is not possible for us to fully forget what has happened, but we do not have to allow it to dominate our thoughts and actions. The key to forgiveness begins when we stop keeping track of wrongs done to us. Peter seemed to think he was going above and beyond the call of duty by forgiving someone who sinned against him seven times. Jesus went far beyond what Peter expected by setting the standard at 490 times. Of course the point of that is not that we count until we get close to 500, but that we keep on forgiving.

God freely forgives us. Ephesians 4:32 says, "And be ye kind one to another, tenderhearted, forgiving one another, even as God for Christ's sake hath forgiven you." God forgave us because of the sacrifice Jesus made for us—and based on His forgiveness He expects us to extend forgiveness to others. We do not forgive others because they deserve it. Instead, we forgive them because it is right. If you are holding tightly to wrongs done against you in the past, you will never experience the freedom and joy that comes with letting go. Each time you are reminded of what happened, remind yourself that you have already forgiven that and let it go.

Today's Rooted Principle: Nothing that has been done to you is beyond forgiving if you trust God enough to obey.

Lights in a Dark World

Ye are the light of the world. A city that is set on an hill cannot be hid. Neither do men light a candle, and put it under a bushel, but on a candlestick; and it giveth light unto all that are in the house. Let your light so shine before men, that they may see your good works, and glorify your Father which is in heaven.—**Matthew 5:14–16**

God does not have in mind His children blending in with their surroundings. We are meant to stand out as a witness to the world. Too many of God's children have, like a chameleon, adapted to their surroundings in such a way that they are no longer visible. This defense mechanism is effective for animals but damaging to believers and to God's work. The desire to fit in and be accepted, the fear of criticism or persecution, and the temptation to avoid conflict, often lead those who should be the brightest testimonies of grace and the Gospel to instead hide their lights from view.

D. L. Moody said, "A holy life will make the deepest impression. Lighthouses blow no horns, they just shine." If the way in which we live reflects the glory and grace of God, we will not need to make loud pronouncements of our faith—it will be evident. The best witness is that which comes when our lives and words match and we are glorifying our heavenly Father.

If we are faithful to follow God's Word, do what is right and good, and share His plan of salvation, we will have an impact on our world. When the darkness is greatest, even small lights shine brightly. We do not have to be the largest or brightest lights that shine—merely faithful. Take your light out of hiding and make sure everyone who sees your life knows from your actions that you are God's child.

Today's Rooted Principle: God placed His light within you so you will hold it high to give hope to a dark and needy world.

Jeremiah 37–39 Hebrews 3

Who Do You Love Most?

*And there went great multitudes with him: and he turned, and said unto
them, If any man come to me, and hate not his father, and mother, and
wife, and children, and brethren, and sisters, yea, and his own life also,
he cannot be my disciple. And whosoever doth not bear his cross, and
come after me, cannot be my disciple.*—**Luke 14:25–27**

We live in a culture that is obsessed with making people feel good
about themselves. We give trophies to every child on the team so
no one feels left out, and we've stopped keeping score in children's games
so no one feels bad about losing. We promote children to the next grade
so that they don't feel embarrassed, even though they have not learned
the material they need to know. This unhealthy focus on self and self-
esteem is one of the worst influences in creating a culture of entitlement
and indifference to the needs of others.

In a study on the scope and impact of narcissism in our society,
Dr. Keith Campbell, co-author of the study, voiced concerns about the
results of this continual focus on self. He said the study shows narcissists
"are more likely to have romantic relationships that are short-lived, be at
risk for infidelity, lack emotional warmth, and to exhibit game-playing,
dishonesty, and over-controlling and violent behaviors."

God's focus is different from ours. Rather than teaching us to love
ourselves and feel good about ourselves, He teaches us to love Him and
give up our own rights and privileges for the sake of others. God deserves
first place in our hearts and lives. Nothing, particularly not our own love
for self, can be allowed to take His place if we want to truly follow Him.
Our love for any person, desire, or thing should pale in comparison to
our love for God.

Today's Rooted Principle: Anything that you love more than God is an
idol, and it needs to be removed from that position in your life.

November
8

Our Greatest Need

But it shall not be so among you: but whosoever will be great among you, let him be your minister; And whosoever will be chief among you, let him be your servant: Even as the Son of man came not to be ministered unto, but to minister, and to give his life a ransom for many.
—Matthew 20:26–28

A missionary was preaching in Philadelphia. At the close of the service a man came and said, "I don't like the way you spoke about the cross. I think that instead of emphasizing the death of Christ, it would be far better to preach Jesus, the teacher and example." The missionary replied, "If I presented Christ in that way, would you be willing to follow Him?" "I certainly would," said the man without hesitation.

"All right then," said the missionary, "let's take the first step. He did no sin. Can you claim that for yourself?" The man looked confused and somewhat surprised. "Why, no," he said. "I acknowledge that I do sin." The missionary replied, "Then your greatest need is to have a Saviour, not an example!"

Jesus was perfect, and He is a wonderful example—but it is an example that we are incapable of following apart from the power of the Spirit of God. Setting an example was not the primary purpose for His coming. Instead, He came to provide salvation for all who believe. This willingness to meet our greatest need is a striking testimony to the deep love God has for us.

Having received His salvation, we have the responsibility to share that Good News with others. Many churches have fallen into thinking that if they provide food or medicine or clothing for the poor, they are doing all Christ called them to do. It is certainly important to meet physical needs, but these are not the greatest needs of those we serve. They need the salvation that can only be found in Jesus Christ.

Today's Rooted Principle: Since God has provided our greatest need—a Saviour—we should be busy telling others about His wonderful provision.

Jeremiah 43–45 Hebrews 5

The Reason for the Cross

Now then we are ambassadors for Christ, as though God did beseech you by us: we pray you in Christ's stead, be ye reconciled to God. For he hath made him to be sin for us, who knew no sin; that we might be made the righteousness of God in him.—**2 Corinthians 5:20–21**

Many years ago, the famed pastor R. G. Lee visited the Holy Land. When he reached the place where Jesus is believed to have been crucified, he wanted to go to the top of the hill. His guide discouraged him from climbing up, but the elderly pastor insisted. When they reached the top the guide asked, "Have you ever been here before?" "Yes," Dr. Lee replied, "I was here some two thousand years ago."

Jesus died on the cross for the sins of the world, but He also died specifically for my sins and for your sins. All that I have done that I should not have done, and all that I have not done that I should have done was placed upon Him while He hung on the cross. Jesus—the perfect and sinless Son of God—became sin because of me so that I could be righteous in the sight of God. What a treasure! What an enormous price!

Though I have been saved since an early age, I never want to lose sight of the fact that my salvation is an unmerited gift of God's grace that transformed my life and my eternal destiny. I never want to forget that Jesus went to the cross because of my sin. I never want to get so accustomed to my salvation that I lose the wonder and gratitude that God loves me so much. The Christian who has forgotten that he stood at Calvary has lost one of his main sources of joy and one of his main motivations for service.

Today's Rooted Principle: God's salvation is a gift beyond price, and we should rejoice and give thanks to Him for it.

Amazing Grace

For I am the least of the apostles, that am not meet to be called an apostle, because I persecuted the church of God. But by the grace of God I am what I am: and his grace which was bestowed upon me was not in vain; but I laboured more abundantly than they all: yet not I, but the grace of God which was with me.—**1 Corinthians 15:9–10**

I've often heard people describe grace as "God's riches at Christ's expense." A. W. Tozer put it this way: "Grace is the good pleasure of God that inclines Him to bestow benefits upon the undeserving. Its use to us sinful men is to save us and make us sit together in heavenly places to demonstrate to the ages the exceeding riches of God's kindness to us in Christ Jesus."

We should not need to be reminded that everything good that we have or do is a direct result of the grace of God. Yet our pride constantly tempts us to take the credit that rightly belongs to God. We would probably never say out loud what Nebuchadnezzar did: "Is not this great Babylon, that I have built for the house of the kingdom by the might of my power, and for the honour of my majesty?" (Daniel 4:30). But too often we look at our accomplishments and achievements as if they were solely the result of our effort and intelligence.

The thing that makes God's grace so amazing is that it is both completely undeserved and completely free. His grace is given to us because of His great love for us. Rather than focusing our attention on ourselves, the grace we receive should cause us to glorify and praise Him. The realization that it is only because of grace that he was anything at all made it possible for Paul to recognize that the great things he accomplished for God were not because of his efforts in his own strength but because of God's grace.

Today's Rooted Principle: Give thanks to God today for all that you do and have, for it is only because of His grace.

Armistice Day

Israel then shall dwell in safety alone: the fountain of Jacob shall be upon a land of corn and wine; also his heavens shall drop down dew. Happy art thou, O Israel: who is like unto thee, O people saved by the LORD, the shield of thy help, and who is the sword of thy excellency! and thine enemies shall be found liars unto thee; and thou shalt tread upon their high places.—**Deuteronomy 33:28–29**

Today we stop to honor the courage and sacrifice of those who have served in the military to protect and defend the freedoms that we enjoy. It was on November 11, 1918, that the First World War—the "war to end all wars"—reached its conclusion. This day was set aside to honor those who fought in what was then the greatest conflict the world had ever seen. As further conflicts have followed, proving that war has not ended, honor for veterans of other wars has been added to the observance of this day.

The failure of the treaties drawn by men to bring about lasting peace and the continued drumbeat of conflict and war highlight the truth for us that God is the only source of peace, and the only true defense for any nation. Though we may have impressive military might, apart from God's hand it can quickly be brought to nothing.

To those who, as our national anthem put it, placed their lives "between their loved homes and the war's desolation," we owe a debt of gratitude. To God who is our hope of peace, we should not only give thanks, but also pray. Though many in our land have turned away from Him and snub His Word and His law, we should thank Him for the thousands of righteous people who love and honor God. We should pray today for His protection and peace.

Today's Rooted Principle: Give thanks for those who have sacrificed so much for our freedom, and pray to God that He will be our sure defense.

Speeding Up and Slowing Down

Wherefore, my beloved brethren, let every man be swift to hear, slow to speak, slow to wrath: For the wrath of man worketh not the righteousness of God. Wherefore lay apart all filthiness and superfluity of naughtiness, and receive with meekness the engrafted word, which is able to save your souls.—**James 1:19–21**

Some of our problems come from the fact that we are slow to do things we should and fast to do things we should not. One of the areas in which this displays itself for many is in our hearing and speaking. Lehman Strauss asked, "Could it be that we are not more 'swift to hear' because we are not 'slow to speak'? God gave us two ears and only one mouth. Should we not be twice as swift to listen and learn?"

Many times conflicts arise in churches, marriages, friendships and work relationships because someone jumps to a conclusion without knowing all of the facts and begins telling everyone they know what they think happened. These people may be quite sincere in what they are doing, but they can be destructive nonetheless. It is impossible to recall words once they have been spoken. Mark Twain said, "A lie can travel halfway around the world while the truth is still putting on its shoes."

Do not be in a hurry to repeat things that are told to you, and be sure to evaluate the facts before you reach a conclusion. Solomon reminds us, "He that answereth a matter before he heareth it, it is folly and shame unto him" (Proverbs 18:13). While there is a time to speak up for what is right, we should never respond in haste or anger. Rather, we should be quick to listen and make sure that we fully understand the situation before we begin to speak.

Today's Rooted Principle: Be faster to listen than you are to speak, and you will find your life much more peaceful.

Childhood Foundations

But continue thou in the things which thou hast learned and hast been assured of, knowing of whom thou hast learned them; And that from a child thou hast known the holy scriptures, which are able to make thee wise unto salvation through faith which is in Christ Jesus.
—2 Timothy 3:14–15

God's primary plan for the spiritual education of young people is the family. Our church works hard to provide sound teaching to children, but nothing can fully take the place of godly parents teaching and living the truths of Scripture for their children. It is in the home where we first learn about God and His Word.

Charles Spurgeon wrote this about the way Puritan parents reared their children. "Not being obliged to worry over some of the recent theories of education, they were accustomed to 'bring up the babies on the body of truth,' so that a child of twelve in a Puritan home could talk with intelligent skill on central New Testament doctrines. These Puritans reared their children in the atmosphere of their own fiery convictions."

One of the reasons that our churches and culture are so saturated with false ideas is that the truth has not been well and fully taught to young people in Christian homes. The foundation that this provides protects them later in life from error. But this teaching does not end when our children start school or even when they leave home. We are to be teachers all the days of the lives of our families.

Young adults need godly examples of faith and commitment from older adults. Young children need grandparents who show them faith in practice, demonstrating that what they are hearing at home and at church is true in the "real world." The time you take to teach and model the truths of the Word of God for your family is precious and incredibly valuable.

Today's Rooted Principle: Take the time today to invest in the future by teaching and showing your children or grandchildren that God's Word is true.

Making a Difference

But the Jews which believed not, moved with envy, took unto them certain lewd fellows of the baser sort, and gathered a company, and set all the city on an uproar, and assaulted the house of Jason, and sought to bring them out to the people. And when they found them not, they drew Jason and certain brethren unto the rulers of the city, crying, These that have turned the world upside down are come hither also; Whom Jason hath received: and these all do contrary to the decrees of Caesar, saying that there is another king, one Jesus.—**Acts 17:5–7**

When the Apostle Paul came to town, it was never a quiet event. The powerful preaching of the Gospel not only saw many converts, but it also stirred up serious opposition. The world did not ignore Paul. Even his enemies declared that he "turned the world upside down." Yet today, many churches and many Christians are having very little impact on their communities at all. In large measure, that is because we have lost the fire and commitment that drove the early church.

Noted historian Thomas C. Reeves, who for many years was a professor at the University of Wisconsin-Parkside, wrote: "Christianity in modern America is, in large part, innocuous. It tends to be easy, upbeat, convenient, and compatible. It does not require self-sacrifice, discipline, humility, an otherworldly outlook, a zeal for souls, a fear as well as love of God."

God did not save us solely so that we could go to Heaven. He calls and commands us to have an impact here on Earth as well. When we trade the shame of the cross of Christ for the plaudits and acceptance of men, we have forfeited the power to shake the world. Far better to be despised and even persecuted than to live a life without making a difference for God.

Today's Rooted Principle: Be willing to take a stand and make a difference today, even if it means not fitting in with a world going the wrong direction.

Lamentations 3–5   Hebrews 10:19–39   355

Freedom or Bondage

*Then said Jesus to those Jews which believed on him, If ye continue in my word, then are ye my disciples indeed; And ye shall know the truth, and the truth shall make you free. They answered him, We be Abraham's seed, and were never in bondage to any man: how sayest thou, Ye shall be made free? Jesus answered them, Verily, verily, I say unto you, Whosoever committeth sin is the servant of sin.—*__John 8:31–34__

We live in a world which places great value on individual liberty but which also is committed to pursuing paths that inevitably lead to bondage. The Devil knows our weaknesses well, so he presents the "fun" of sin in hopes that we will overlook the consequences that are certain to follow. The truth makes us free, but because it requires us to follow God and restricts us from fulfilling our own selfish desires, many look for an alternate and find it in sin.

The deception of the enemy keeps them from even realizing the chains have been placed upon their lives until it is too late. The Jewish people proudly boasted to Jesus that they had never been in bondage. That reveals an amazing disconnect from reality. Throughout Israel's history they had been in bondage, first in Egypt, then to Assyria and Babylon, and even as they spoke Israel was under the rule of Rome.

But far more important and more damaging than political or physical bondage was the spiritual bondage they failed to recognize. They thought that because of their heritage they were guaranteed their freedom. That is not true in any realm—political, financial, religious or spiritual. The only pathway to freedom is found in personal commitment to walking in truth and rejecting sin. Every person serves something. Either we will find freedom in serving God, or we will find slavery in serving sin. There are no other choices.

Today's Rooted Principle: Find your freedom in obedience to God's truth, and you will not have to endure the bondage of Satan.

The Snare of Impatience

And when the people saw that Moses delayed to come down out of the mount, the people gathered themselves together unto Aaron, and said unto him, Up, make us gods, which shall go before us; for as for this Moses, the man that brought us up out of the land of Egypt, we wot not what is become of him. And Aaron said unto them, Break off the golden earrings, which are in the ears of your wives, of your sons, and of your daughters, and bring them unto me.—**Exodus 32:1–2**

When we take matters into our own hands rather than waiting for God to work in His time, disaster follows. The children of Israel worshipped the golden calf that Aaron made because they were not willing to wait for Moses to return from Mt. Sinai where he was receiving the Law from God. Their impatience led to idolatry and immorality.

G. Campbell Morgan wrote, "Waiting for God is not laziness. Waiting for God is not going to sleep. Waiting for God is not the abandonment of effort. Waiting for God means, first, activity under command; second, readiness for any new command that may come; third, the ability to do nothing until the command is given."

We live in an impatient culture that prizes haste and busyness. Certainly we should not use the excuse of waiting on God to avoid doing what we already know He wants us to do. But we must also be careful not to try to provide solutions and choose directions apart from His plan. Think of the tension that still exists in the world today four thousand years after Abraham and Sarah decided to involve Hagar in producing the son God had promised to them. The enmity between the descendants of Ishmael and Isaac would not exist had they been willing to wait for God to do what He said He would do.

Today's Rooted Principle: Do not run ahead of God today—though He is not early, He is never late.

Ezekiel 3–4   Hebrews 11:20–40   357

Being Full

Blessed are the poor in spirit: for theirs is the kingdom of heaven. Blessed are they that mourn: for they shall be comforted. Blessed are the meek: for they shall inherit the earth. Blessed are they which do hunger and thirst after righteousness: for they shall be filled.—**Matthew 5:3–6**

In *Lectures to My Students,* Charles Spurgeon wrote, "When your own emptiness is painfully forced upon your consciousness, chide yourself that you ever dreamed of being full except in the Lord." Each of us has a choice to seek fullness in the things of God or in the things of the world. When we settle for satisfaction in less than God has for us, we are doomed to failure and to disappointment.

The things of the world never truly satisfy. Jesus said, "Woe unto you that are full! for ye shall hunger" (Luke 6:25). Not only do things of the world not satisfy, but they also leave no room for us to be filled with the Spirit of God. His presence is in our lives from the moment we are saved, but that does not mean that we are walking in the fullness of His power. God's plan is for His Holy Spirit to not just influence, but to control, our lives, our thoughts, and our actions.

There is no way to receive the blessings of God in the measure He wants to give them apart from being filled with the Spirit. And there is no way to be filled with Him unless we are hungering and thirsting to be filled. What we want most is revealed in what we choose, rather than in what we say. The things for which we truly hunger are those we think about, talk about, and focus on. The world is filled with distractions and temptations, but if our appetites are focused on the right things, we will find our lives filled with the Spirit of God.

Today's Rooted Principle: The more you are filled with the Spirit of God, the less of the world you will desire.

We Need a Saviour

*For when we were yet without strength, in due time Christ died for the
ungodly. For scarcely for a righteous man will one die: yet peradventure
for a good man some would even dare to die. But God commendeth his
love toward us, in that, while we were yet sinners, Christ died for us.
Much more then, being now justified by his blood, we shall be saved
from wrath through him.*—**Romans 5:6–9**

First published in 1967, the self-help book *I'm OK, You're OK* by Dr.
Thomas A. Harris has sold more than fifteen million copies and has
been translated into more than a dozen languages. It is not surprising
that a message that tells us to feel good about ourselves would prove
popular. However much that view may appeal to our vanity, it does not
match what God says about our condition.

The Bible's picture of man's condition is dire. We are not okay. Not
only that, but we do not have the strength or the ability to save ourselves
or make ourselves okay. Yet there is hope—because God loves us. The
judgment that should rightfully come to us for our sins has been taken
away and replaced with the reward for the perfect righteousness of Jesus
Christ which has been placed on our account.

God's love was great enough to provide the ultimate sacrifice so
we could be reconciled to Him. As we consider things for which we
should be thankful, nothing comes before our salvation. This provision
of God altered our eternal destiny, transformed us with a new nature,
and changes the way we walk through this world. None of this happens
because we deserve it or because we earn it. When Christ died for us, we
were His enemies, yet His love overcame every obstacle so that we could
trust Him for salvation and enjoy fellowship with Him.

Today's Rooted Principle: Give thanks today for the love of God that
sent His Son to die for you and that made you His child.

Ezekiel 8–10   Hebrews 13

Don't Take It for Granted

And it shall be, when the LORD thy God shall have brought thee into the land which he sware unto thy fathers, to Abraham, to Isaac, and to Jacob, to give thee great and goodly cities, which thou buildedst not, And houses full of all good things, which thou filledst not, and wells digged, which thou diggedst not, vineyards and olive trees, which thou plantedst not; when thou shalt have eaten and be full; Then beware lest thou forget the LORD, which brought thee forth out of the land of Egypt, from the house of bondage.—**Deuteronomy 6:10–12**

In the post-World War II era, a church was launching a building campaign. After a service in which the pastor laid out the vision for the project, two families waited in line to meet with him. The first father said, "Pastor, as you know, our son was killed in the war. We would like to give $200 toward the building as a memorial gift." The second father said, "Pastor, we were going to give $200, but our son came home from the war. We will give $5,000!"

It should be true that the good things we receive from God make us more grateful, but in reality often they make us complacent and self-satisfied. We can quickly forget that He is the source of all of our blessings and benefits. In truth, nothing good that we have is the result of our own strength and ingenuity. Though we should be diligent in our work, even the strength to labor comes from God.

Rather than looking at our possessions as tokens of our effort, intellect, and superiority, we should look at them as tokens of God's love and grace. He gives us so much more than we deserve, and giving thanks helps us remain on guard so that we do not forget Him.

Today's Rooted Principle: God does not bless us because of our goodness but because of His goodness. Remembering this helps us remain grateful.

Unfailing Compassion

This I recall to my mind, therefore have I hope. It is of the LORD'S mercies that we are not consumed, because his compassions fail not. They are new every morning: great is thy faithfulness. The LORD is my portion, saith my soul; therefore will I hope in him. The LORD is good unto them that wait for him, to the soul that seeketh him.
—**Lamentations 3:21–25**

I read of a missionary who was visiting a church in India where they were taking a special offering during harvest time. One elderly widow came with a very large offering of rice, far more than would have been normal for someone in her situation to give. The missionary asked if she was making the gift as thanks for something special that had happened in her life. "Yes," replied the woman. "My son was sick, and I promised a large gift to God if he got well." "And your son has recovered?" asked the preacher. The widow paused. "No," she said. "He died last week. But I know that he is in God's care; for that I am especially thankful."

There are times when God does not answer our prayers as we expect, but there is never a time when He does not do what is best for His children. His faithfulness, love, mercy, and compassion are unchanging. Rather than complain that we do not get exactly what we want, we should be grateful that He is constantly guarding and enriching our lives. Every good thing that we have is from God.

Because He has perfect knowledge, perfect power, and perfect love, we can count on Him to know what is best, to be able to do what is best, and to give us what we most need. Our thanksgiving and gratitude should be as consistent as the compassion of our loving Heavenly Father.

Today's Rooted Principle: God's compassion never fails, and even when He chooses to give us something other than what we ask, it is what He knows is for our best.

Ezekiel 14–15   James 2   361

A Grateful Heart

O give thanks unto the LORD; for he is good: for his mercy endureth for ever. O give thanks unto the God of gods: for his mercy endureth for ever. O give thanks to the Lord of lords: for his mercy endureth for ever.—**Psalm 136:1–3**

Ravensbruck was known as one of the worst German concentration camps during World War II. When Corrie ten Boom and her sister Betsie found themselves imprisoned there, they were disgusted to discover that their barracks were infested with fleas.

When Corrie began to complain, Betsie insisted that they instead give thanks, quoting 1 Thessalonians 5:18, "In every thing give thanks: for this is the will of God in Christ Jesus concerning you." With some persuasion, Corrie finally joined her sister in thanking God for the fleas.

Several months later, the two sisters expressed their surprise that the camp guards had never come back to their barracks to disrupt or prevent the evening Bible studies they held for their fellow prisoners. It was then that Corrie realized that the very fleas which she had so despised had actually been a God-sent protection from the cruel guards.

When we think we deserve good things, we find it hard to be thankful, and we often miss the blessings God sends "in disguise." Greed, materialism, and selfishness destroy a grateful heart. God, our society, and our parents don't owe us anything, no matter what others may say or think.

Rather than complaining about what we don't have or don't get, it is important that we are grateful for what we do have. Every one of us will suffer setbacks and experience loss. But there are always things for which we can be grateful—things we can never lose. As believers, our eternal destiny is settled and can never be changed. We always have the promises of God on which we can fully rely.

Today's Rooted Principle: Focusing on what God has done for us is the key to maintaining a grateful heart.

Ezekiel 16–17   James 3

The Sacrifice of Praise

For here have we no continuing city, but we seek one to come. By him therefore let us offer the sacrifice of praise to God continually, that is, the fruit of our lips giving thanks to his name. But to do good and to communicate forget not: for with such sacrifices God is well pleased.
—**Hebrews 13:14–16**

What could you give to God that would express your gratitude and convey honor to Him? Hebrews 13 suggests the "sacrifice of praise." All throughout Scripture we see people offer this sacrifice to God. Job worshipped God when he had nothing (Job 1:20–21). The book of Psalms chronicles David's praise in both the good times and the bad. Mary expressed praise when she learned she was to be the mother of Christ (Luke 1:46–55). And one man from the group of ten lepers Jesus healed offered thanks and praise (Luke 17:15–16). From these testimonies, we see that our sacrifice of praise should be continual—not contingent on our mood or current circumstances.

A. W. Tozer said, "Gratitude is an offering precious in the sight of God, and it is one that the poorest of us can make and be not poorer but richer for having made it." Even in times when we do not have as much as others in the way of material blessings, we still have so much for which to be thankful. And when we purposefully give thanks to God, that sacrifice of our heart is pleasing to Him.

The giving of thanks is a habit which we can develop and cultivate. By focusing on the good things we have and realizing that every one of them came from God, we find that even in times of lack we can be thankful. "Every good gift and every perfect gift is from above, and cometh down from the Father of lights" (James 1:17). Thanksgiving requires that we set aside our pride and our desire to take credit for what we have and that we acknowledge the goodness of God in providing for us.

Today's Rooted Principle: Your praise and thanksgiving for the blessings you have received is pleasing to God.

Ezekiel 18–19 James 4

Rescue the Perishing

So thou, O son of man, I have set thee a watchman unto the house of Israel; therefore thou shalt hear the word at my mouth, and warn them from me. When I say unto the wicked, O wicked man, thou shalt surely die; if thou dost not speak to warn the wicked from his way, that wicked man shall die in his iniquity; but his blood will I require at thine hand. Nevertheless, if thou warn the wicked of his way to turn from it; if he do not turn from his way, he shall die in his iniquity; but thou hast delivered thy soul.—**Ezekiel 33:7–9**

Fanny Crosby loved sharing the Gospel with anyone who would listen. In 1869 she penned the words to "Rescue the Perishing." When asked about the song, she explained, "It was written following a personal experience at the New York City Bowery Mission." She went on to explain that she would go one night a week to talk to "her boys."

One night while speaking to them, she kept having the thought that there was a boy present who had wandered away from his mother and must be rescued that night, or he would be eternally lost. She made a plea to each boy that was there that night. At the end of the service, one of the young men came forward and said, "Did you mean me, Miss Crosby? I promised my mother to meet her in Heaven, but as I am now living that will be impossible." She prayed with him and led him to Christ. As they finished, he said, "Now I am ready to meet my mother in Heaven, for I have found God."

There are many things in life that are important, but the greatest task we have been assigned is to do our part to rescue those who are perishing before it is eternally too late. The sacrifices that we make for the sake of the Gospel, whether they are physical or financial, are worth it. Do not allow anything to deter you from reaching those in danger of spending eternity in Hell.

Today's Rooted Principle: God has chosen you to reach others with the Gospel. Are you faithfully doing that vital work?

A God without Limits

And Jonathan said to the young man that bare his armour, Come, and let us go over unto the garrison of these uncircumcised: it may be that the LORD will work for us: for there is no restraint to the LORD to save by many or by few. And his armourbearer said unto him, Do all that is in thine heart: turn thee; behold, I am with thee according to thy heart.—**1 Samuel 14:6–7**

D r. Tom Malone often said, "When God is going to do something wonderful, He starts with the difficult. When God is going to do something miraculous, He starts with the impossible." We have limits and restraints on our abilities and resources, but God does not. He is able to do things that are completely impossible in the natural order of things. The miraculous power of God is not merely a relic of the past. His nature never changes, and He is still able to do great and mighty things.

Many believers tragically live as if they are orphans. A lack of faith keeps us from claiming God's promises and from relying on God to do the things He has promised in His Word. Certainly, there is much false teaching that leads people to expect things God has not promised, but we should not let anything keep us from claiming the full extent of our birthright as His children.

Psalm 81:10 says, "I am the LORD thy God, which brought thee out of the land of Egypt: open thy mouth wide, and I will fill it." As long as our will is submitted to His will and we are walking in His Spirit, we have every right to make big requests of an Almighty God and expect Him to hear and answer. It was only in unbelief that the children of Israel "limited the Holy One of Israel" (Psalm 78:41). May that never be said of us.

Today's Rooted Principle: Do not let the obstacles you face today keep you from trusting God to do what He has promised.

Finding Contentment

Not that I speak in respect of want: for I have learned, in whatsoever state I am, therewith to be content. I know both how to be abased, and I know how to abound: every where and in all things I am instructed both to be full and to be hungry, both to abound and to suffer need. I can do all things through Christ which strengtheneth me.
—**Philippians 4:11–13**

Many people are searching for contentment, but very few seem to find it. That is largely because most people are seeking contentment in the wrong place. It is never found in possessions or circumstances. It is never based on what is happening outside. Contentment flourishes despite circumstances either good or bad, because it grows in a grateful heart.

F. B. Meyer said, "If we would find content, let us go to homes where women are crippled with rheumatism, or dying of cancer, where comforts are few, where long hours of loneliness are not broken by the intrusion of friendly faces, where the pittance of public charity hardly suffices for necessary need, to say nothing of comfort, it is there that contentment reveals itself like a shy flower. How often in the homes of the wealthy one has missed it, to find it in the homes of the poor! How often it is wanting where health is buoyant, to be discovered where disease is wearing out the strength!"

God did not promise us that things would be easy. Some of the greatest Christians in all of history suffered great persecution, bouts of grave illness, financial lack, and times of despair. What God promised us instead was His presence, and in that presence we can find contentment regardless of what else is happening in our lives. God knows everything about your circumstances today, and nothing comes into your life that does not first pass through His hands.

Today's Rooted Principle: When you learn to accept whatever God has chosen to give you, you are on the pathway to learning true contentment.

Never Alone

*And I will pray the Father, and he shall give you another Comforter, that
he may abide with you for ever; Even the Spirit of truth; whom the world
cannot receive, because it seeth him not, neither knoweth him: but ye
know him; for he dwelleth with you, and shall be in you. I will not leave
you comfortless: I will come to you.*—**John 14:16–18**

Jesus promised that we would not be left alone—that a Comforter, the
Holy Spirit—would come and dwell with us forever. This happens at
the moment that we are saved. Though we are to surrender to God's
leading so that we can be filled with the Spirit, we do not need a second
baptism to get more of Him in our lives. Instead, we need for Him to have
more of us. This is vital to every aspect of our lives and walk with God.

Charles Spurgeon rightly said, "Without the Spirit of God, we can
do nothing. We are as ships without the wind, branches without sap, and
like coals without fire, we are useless." It is impossible to live a victorious
Christian life or do any meaningful and lasting work for God apart from
the power of His Holy Spirit. Our own strength was never meant to be
equal to that task. As the old hymn says, "All is vain unless the Spirit of
the Holy One comes down."

There is no substitute for the Holy Spirit's presence and power. No
plan, no program, no effort will replace what only He can do in and
through us. Jesus did His work on Earth in the power of the Spirit of
God. John 3:34 tells us, "God giveth not the Spirit by measure unto him."
Jesus had unlimited Holy Spirit power, and though we will never reach
that level, we must have His power active in our lives.

Today's Rooted Principle: As you yield to the Holy Spirit who dwells in
your heart, you will find power to do what God calls you to do.

The Rightful Place of Scripture

We have also a more sure word of prophecy; whereunto ye do well that ye take heed, as unto a light that shineth in a dark place, until the day dawn, and the day star arise in your hearts: Knowing this first, that no prophecy of the scripture is of any private interpretation. For the prophecy came not in old time by the will of man: but holy men of God spake as they were moved by the Holy Ghost.—**2 Peter 1:19–21**

Someone said of the Word of God: "This Book is the mind of God, the state of man, the way of salvation, the doom of sinners, and the happiness of believers. Its doctrines are holy, its precepts are binding; its histories are true, and its decisions are immutable. Read it to be wise, believe it to be safe, practice it to be holy."

Although we know what God has told us about His Word, men keep trying to alter and change it and find some way other than God's way to determine what we should do and how we should live. We do not need new translations or new concepts, we need to trust that God's promise to preserve His Word is true and we need to follow what the Bible we have says.

I have learned much from good men and good books, but the only source of infallible truth is the Word of God. It should be the focus of our study and the guide for our lives. The Bible tells us that it is God's plan for our words, thoughts, and actions to be filled with and directed by what He has told us in Scripture. Psalm 119:105 says, "Thy word is a lamp unto my feet, and a light unto my path." It is a tragedy for us to take the great gift of God's Word and not study and heed it.

Make a commitment now to regularly spend time in God's Word. Allow it to saturate your mind and heart so you can know the mind of God and follow His wisdom.

Today's Rooted Principle: Since God has given us His Word, we must be diligent to learn and follow what it says.

Being in Christ

Wherefore remember, that ye being in time past Gentiles in the flesh, who are called Uncircumcision by that which is called the Circumcision in the flesh made by hands; That at that time ye were without Christ, being aliens from the commonwealth of Israel, and strangers from the covenants of promise, having no hope, and without God in the world: But now in Christ Jesus ye who sometimes were far off are made nigh by the blood of Christ.—**Ephesians 2:11–13**

Salvation changes far more than just our eternal destiny. It also changes our current situation. We move from the family of Satan to the family of God. We move from being in the world to being in Christ. Yet too often we fail to fully recognize the changes that have taken place, and thus we do not benefit from them as we should.

R. A. Torrey said, "When Jesus died, He died as my representative, and I died in Him; when He arose, He rose as my representative, and I arose in Him; when He ascended up on high and took His place at the right hand of the Father in the glory, He ascended as my representative and I ascended in Him, and today I am seated in Christ with God in the heavenlies. I look at the cross of Christ, and I know that atonement has been made for my sins; I look at the open sepulcher and the risen and ascended Lord, and I know the atonement has been accepted. There no longer remains a single sin on me, no matter how many or how great my sins may have been."

We have already received these blessings as part of our conversion. The challenge is for us to overcome the snares of the world and the guilt of the past and begin to live as if what God says about our new position in life and in Him is true.

Today's Rooted Principle: Live up to your position and privileges as a child of God today.

Ezekiel 33–34   1 Peter 5   369

Being Faithful

And unto the angel of the church in Smyrna write; These things saith the first and the last, which was dead, and is alive; I know thy works, and tribulation, and poverty, (but thou art rich) and I know the blasphemy of them which say they are Jews, and are not, but are the synagogue of Satan. Fear none of those things which thou shalt suffer: behold, the devil shall cast some of you into prison, that ye may be tried; and ye shall have tribulation ten days: be thou faithful unto death, and I will give thee a crown of life.—**Revelation 2:8–10**

I had the privilege of meeting a missionary who had served God faithfully for fifty years. He labored in Lebanon, starting a Baptist church, until he and his wife were kidnapped and held hostage for a period of time before being released and having to leave the country. Rather than abandoning the ministry, they began a new work with the Lebanese people living in Australia. Why did they serve the Lord so long through so many difficulties and dangers? Because they realized that their lives were not their own.

Vance Havner said, "What our Lord said about cross-bearing and obedience is not in fine type. It is in bold print on the face of the contract." We are not promised that our lives will be easy or that things will go according to our plans. We are promised that God will always be with us and work to make all of the things that happen in our lives produce good.

When we trust Him to do what He has promised, it gives us the strength to endure the challenges and trials we face. The rewards that come from faithfulness are not primarily in this life but in the next. We can be confident that God is in control and that one day He will reward our work for Him.

Today's Rooted Principle: God has every right to expect your faithful service no matter what may come.

A Portrait of Grace

But without faith it is impossible to please him: for he that cometh to God must believe that he is, and that he is a rewarder of them that diligently seek him. By faith Noah, being warned of God of things not seen as yet, moved with fear, prepared an ark to the saving of his house; by the which he condemned the world, and became heir of the righteousness which is by faith.—**Hebrews 11:6–7**

One of the most beautiful pictures of grace in all the Word of God is found in the story of Noah. At a time when the world was filled with great wickedness—much like our day—Noah found grace from the Lord and was saved along with his family from the flood that destroyed the world. Our modern world skeptically laughs at the story of the flood, just as Peter said that they would. He wrote that in the last days men would deny the truth of this particular Bible story.

Peter said these scoffers "willingly are ignorant…that…the world that then was, being overflowed with water, perished" (2 Peter 3:5–6). Why would men deny the flood? The answer is twofold: First, denying the flood is an attempt to deny the fact that we must one day face judgment. Second, denying the flood is an attempt to deny that the only way of escape from the judgment that is to come is found in the grace of God.

As you remember, the ark only had one door—symbolizing that Jesus Christ is the only way to salvation. This message of an exclusive means of salvation is not popular in our day, but it is true. There are not many roads that lead to Heaven; there is only one way. For those of us who have received salvation by grace through faith, there is a responsibility to do as Noah did and invite others to join us in escaping the coming judgment.

Today's Rooted Principle: Find someone today who has not experienced the grace of God in salvation and point them to Christ.

DECEMBER

The Good Tidings

And the angel said unto them, Fear not: for, behold, I bring you good tidings of great joy, which shall be to all people. For unto you is born this day in the city of David a Saviour, which is Christ the Lord. And this shall be a sign unto you; Ye shall find the babe wrapped in swaddling clothes, lying in a manger.—**Luke 2:10–12**

Though Christmas should be a happy and blessed time as we celebrate the gift of God's Son, it often becomes a hectic and frantic time as every minute is filled with shopping, parties, travel, and extra work. The poet and humorist Ogden Nash wrote, "Christmas was once the season of peace and good will; now it's the holiday that there's so many shopping days until."

It is a tragedy if we lose sight of the simple and vital message that is at the heart of this special time of year. The point is not getting the most packages under the tree or impressing the neighbors with our display of Christmas lights. The point is that we are celebrating the coming of the Saviour—the greatest gift that ever has or ever could be given. Christmas is not a commercial invention designed to sell things, but instead a spiritual celebration.

The fact that God loved us enough to give His Son for our salvation should be at the center of our thoughts and activities at Christmas. The meaning of the season cannot be found anywhere but in the message the angels brought to the shepherds that night near Bethlehem. And as we celebrate, we should also do what the shepherds did when they returned from seeing Jesus in the manger—tell others what we have heard and seen. This is a wonderful time of year to share the Gospel with family and friends and remind them that the Saviour has come.

Today's Rooted Principle: Do not allow the hectic pace of the Christmas season make you forget the Gift we are celebrating.

The Gifts of Christmas

But unto every one of us is given grace according to the measure of the gift of Christ. Wherefore he saith, When he ascended up on high, he led captivity captive, and gave gifts unto men.—**Ephesians 4:7–8**

After unwrapping all of her presents, a little girl was asked, "Did you get everything you wanted for Christmas?" She thought for a moment and said, "No. But then, it's not my birthday." There is a lot of attention paid, and rightly so, to the over-commercialization of Christmas. This is not a season for seeing how much stuff we can pile under the tree and how deeply in debt we can go to make sure everybody in the family gets everything they want.

This is a season that celebrates the good gifts that we have received from God. Of course, the gift of Jesus is the "unspeakable gift" (2 Corinthians 9:15)—a gift so precious there are no words that can adequately describe it. Yet that is far from the only gift that we received because of Christ's coming. As David put it, God "daily loadeth us with benefits" (Psalm 68:19). The Hebrew word used here signifies a load that is almost too heavy to carry—that's a lot of benefits!

It is a measure of how much God loves us that He not only gave us His Son but so much more along with Him. We should never forget all that He has graciously bestowed upon us. The gift-giving season of Christmas is a time to share our expressions of love with others, but it is also a time when we should be grateful for all that we have received. If you maintain that focus this Christmas, you will find yourself enjoying a truly merry holiday no matter what is under the tree.

Today's Rooted Principle: All of the blessings we enjoy as children of God can be traced to the gift of God's Son on the first Christmas.

To Know Him

That I may know him, and the power of his resurrection, and the fellowship of his sufferings, being made conformable unto his death; If by any means I might attain unto the resurrection of the dead.
—**Philippians 3:10–11**

I t's too easy for Christmas to simply be *about* Jesus. We do our best to remember to include Him in the holiday, and we genuinely try to focus on Him. But how much better for our lives to be *consumed* with Jesus!

What if instead of trying to make sure that we *include* Jesus, our relationship with Him is so close—during Christmas and all year long—that we are continually focused on Him? This was the desire Paul expressed when he penned the words "That I may know him."

December can be a sparkling month of celebrating Jesus' birth. But our tendency is to reduce our walk with Him to mere head knowledge, rather than the heart relationship that He desires to have with us.

Jesus came as Emmanuel—God with us (Matthew 1:23). He wants us to know Him in an intimate relationship. It starts with salvation, and it carries into our daily experience. Once you begin to know Christ like this, He becomes your passionate pursuit, the true quest of your heart. Nothing but Christ can fully satisfy the person who has closely walked with God.

Even many of those who knew Jesus as He walked on Earth didn't really know Him for who He is. Some disbelieved Him. Some ignored Him. Some mocked Him. And some crucified Him.

Being around Jesus isn't enough to know Him. If we would truly know Him, we must spend time with Him and seek Him through His Word, believing He is who He has declared Himself to be.

Today's Rooted Principle: This Christmas, ask the Lord to help you know Him better—to help you focus on Him and deepen your love for Him.

Think Down

Who, being in the form of God, thought it not robbery to be equal with God: But made himself of no reputation, and took upon him the form of a servant, and was made in the likeness of men: And being found in fashion as a man, he humbled himself, and became obedient unto death, even the death of the cross.—**Philippians 2:6–8**

We aren't accustomed to the downward mobility that brought Christ to the manger and then to the cross. In fact, our thought processes are the very opposite of God's.

We think "up." By our human standards, we want more recognition, more achievements, more praise—more us.

But Jesus thought "down." He chose more humility, more service, more sacrifice.

We tend to think in terms of self-promotion. But Christ thought in terms of self-emptying: "And she brought forth her firstborn son, and wrapped him in swaddling clothes, and laid him in a manger; because there was no room for them in the inn" (Luke 2:7).

We think of how we can have more self-gratification. But Christ thought of how He could serve: "For even the Son of man came not to be ministered unto, but to minister, and to give his life a ransom for many" (Mark 10:45).

We think of our comfort. But Christ thought of the Father's will: "I do always those things that please him" (John 8:29).

Our thinking may bring short-term success, but Christ's sacrifice bought our salvation.

Philippians 2:5 instructs, "Let this mind be in you, which was also in Christ Jesus." This Christmas, ask the Lord to help you think the way that Jesus thinks.

Today's Rooted Principle: Look for ways to humble yourself and serve others. It will change your life—and transform your Christmas.

He Shall Save His People

No man hath seen God at any time. If we love one another, God dwelleth in us, and his love is perfected in us. Hereby know we that we dwell in him, and he in us, because he hath given us of his Spirit. And we have seen and do testify that the Father sent the Son to be the Saviour of the world.—**1 John 4:12–14**

There were many reasons that Jesus came to Earth, but the primary purpose for His coming is found in His name. In Hebrew, the name *Jesus* means "Jehovah saves." This was not a name that Joseph and Mary selected. Instead, it was a name given to them from Heaven. The angel told Joseph, "And she shall bring forth a son, and thou shalt call his name JESUS: for he shall save his people from their sins" (Matthew 1:21).

The ultimate message of Christmas is not a long trip by an expectant woman, the search for a place to stay, a baby in a manger, the angel's message to the shepherds, nor the journey of the wise men to see the newborn king. The ultimate message of Christmas is that there is a Saviour who has come to deliver us from sin. This is the greatest need of a lost and dying world. God loved us enough to provide a way of salvation for us, and that is why there is a Christmas at all.

We hear people talk about "keeping Christ in Christmas," and it is important that the holiday not be overtaken with commercialism and secular pursuits. But Christmas is not just a religious event. Christmas is the story of God's plan to redeem those who have been separated from Him by sin. Christmas is a redemptive story. As we celebrate with family and friends, we should never lose sight of that primary truth.

Today's Rooted Principle: Make sure that God's provision of salvation through His Son is at the very center of your Christmas celebration.

Live the Gospel

Only let your conversation be as it becometh the gospel of Christ: that whether I come and see you, or else be absent, I may hear of your affairs, that ye stand fast in one spirit, with one mind striving together for the faith of the gospel; And in nothing terrified by your adversaries: which is to them an evident token of perdition, but to you of salvation, and that of God.—**Philippians 1:27–28**

Charles Spurgeon said, "A man's life is always more forcible than his speech. When men take stock of him they reckon his deeds as dollars and his words as pennies." There is no substitute for a Gospel witness that is matched by a Gospel life. When we fail to live as we should, we forfeit what is meant to be a mainstay of our witnessing.

Paul instructed the Philippian church to live in a way that was becoming to the Gospel. Our very lifestyle should adorn the Gospel that we share with others. For example, how ridiculous would it have been if, when the shepherds came to visit Christ in the manger, Mary and Joseph were loudly complaining about the raw deal they had been given—having to bring Jesus into the world in a stable? There probably would not have been much worship taking place that night!

Even so, everything about our lives—our speech, our demeanor, our habits, our responses, our relationships—all of it, either gives credence to or discredits our message. If our lives do not reflect that our faith is real to those we meet, it is not likely that they will be interested in listening to any message we give them.

The central message of Christmas is that Jesus came to save us from our sins. And Christ has commissioned us, His people, to actively share this message. Yet if our lives are not what they should be, we will not be effective in winning people to the Lord.

Today's Rooted Principle: Live in such a way that your conduct matches and strengthens your witness to others.

Seeing God

Who being the brightness of his glory, and the express image of his person, and upholding all things by the word of his power, when he had by himself purged our sins, sat down on the right hand of the Majesty on high;—**Hebrews 1:3**

I distinctly remember sneaking around the house as a young boy in search of a highly coveted Christmas gift. I was praying to find a BB gun hidden somewhere in my house, and there was something exciting about the prospect of being able to capture a quick and hopeful glimpse of that highly anticipated Christmas gift!

I am thankful that when it comes to the greatest Gift ever given to man we don't have to hope for rare moments of secrecy to catch a glimpse of Him. He is the "brightness of [the Father's] glory and the express image of his person." Contrary to my childhood experiences of quickly peeking at gifts, Christ calls us to fix our gaze on Him!

It is vitally important that we have a clear picture of who God is. Our society portrays a god who is a joke—a distant, distracted comic figure. But the God of the Bible revealed both His power and His love when He entered our world through a manger.

John 1:14 captures the heart of the Christmas message: "And the Word was made flesh, and dwelt among us, (and we beheld his glory, the glory as of the only begotten of the Father,) full of grace and truth." When Mary and Joseph and the shepherds looked into the face of the infant Christ child, they looked into the face of God. What an awesome and humbling thought!

In the pressures of daily life and the busyness of a holiday season, it is easy for us to take our eyes off the Lord and to begin to focus on ourselves. Resist the pull to become so wrapped up in the intricacies of daily living that you miss taking time each day to seek the face of God.

Today's Rooted Principle: Spend time meditating on how Jesus Christ is the revelation of God to us.

Daniel 5–7   2 John

God Is in Control

And it came to pass in those days, that there went out a decree from Caesar Augustus that all the world should be taxed. And all went to be taxed, every one into his own city. And Joseph also went up from Galilee, out of the city of Nazareth, into Judaea, unto the city of David, which is called Bethlehem; (because he was of the house and lineage of David:) To be taxed with Mary his espoused wife, being great with child.
—**Luke 2:1, 3–5**

The Christmas story has many wonderful aspects. One of the aspects that sometimes goes unremarked is that it is a demonstration of God's sovereignty. God exercised sovereign control over the fulfillment of the Old Testament prophecies regarding the birth of Christ.

The world would have said that Caesar Augustus was the ruler, but God was the one in control. He used the decree from Caesar Augustus to move Mary and Joseph from Nazareth to Bethlehem so that Jesus would be born where the prophet Micah had said. Christmas is the story of God working to fulfill His prophetic promises so that everything happened just as He said it would.

Though it's not usually one of the things we focus on at this time of year, I encourage you to view Christmas as a demonstration of God's power and allow the wonderful story of the birth of Christ to build and to strengthen your faith. The same God who sent the angels to the shepherds and the star to guide the wisemen is in control of your life today. His power and wisdom have not diminished. He is just the same today as He was when Christ was born. Things may happen that we do not understand, but we can trust that God is in control—orchestrating our circumstances for our good and for His glory.

Today's Rooted Principle: As you reflect on the Christmas story, allow the wonderful way God worked to give you confidence in His working in your life.

Fellowship

Then they that gladly received his word were baptized: and the same day there were added unto them about three thousand souls. And they continued stedfastly in the apostles' doctrine and fellowship, and in breaking of bread, and in prayers.—**Acts 2:41–42**

My wife enjoys baking during the Christmas season, but she especially delights in the opportunity it provides for fellowship as loved ones gather together to enjoy the delicious fruit of her labor. One of the precious, although sometimes overlooked, gifts we have through Christ is Christian fellowship. It is impossible to overstate the importance and benefit of Christian fellowship to our walk with God.

One of the keys to the power of the early church was the fact that they spent so much time together. It is a hallmark of genuine believers that they long to be together. Praying and learning the Word of God together strengthens the bonds of unity in the church, but it also strengthens each individual who takes part. The challenges and struggles we face as part of daily life in a fallen world require more strength than any of us has on our own. While we receive strength from God to face these battles ("the inward man is renewed day by day," 2 Corinthians 4:16), He has also ordained that we encourage and minister strength to each other during difficult times.

Christianity is not meant to be lived in isolation but in groups. Regular fellowship with other believers—both as part of church services or activities and on a personal basis—is meant to be a source of strength and encouragement as we face the challenges and struggles of life. Thank God for the fellowship you have with His people and together enjoy the celebration of His birth.

Today's Rooted Principle: Build and strengthen your relationships with God's people. True Christian friendship is a gift from Him.

Peace on Earth

Be careful for nothing; but in every thing by prayer and supplication with thanksgiving let your requests be made known unto God. And the peace of God, which passeth all understanding, shall keep your hearts and minds through Christ Jesus.—**Philippians 4:6–7**

Perhaps the most remembered message of Christmas was spoken by the angels: "Glory to God in the highest, and on earth peace, good will toward men" (Luke 2:14). While Christmas should be a time of peace, it is often the opposite for many. Worry, family problems, and financial stress can rob us of the peace God desires for His children to enjoy.

The Old Testament prophet Daniel provides a perfect illustration of God's peace. Notice the specifics of how Daniel prayed: "Now when Daniel knew that the writing was signed, he went into his house; and his windows being open in his chamber toward Jerusalem, he kneeled upon his knees three times a day, and **prayed**, and **gave thanks** before his God, as he did aforetime. Then these men assembled, and found Daniel praying and **making supplication** before his God" (Daniel 6:10–11).

The prescription for peace that Paul provided in Philippians is exactly the same pattern Daniel followed in his prayers. Although Daniel was thrown into the lions' den, he still had a peace that was beyond human understanding. This peace did not come to Daniel because he was immune to fear, but because of how he prayed and trusted God.

When we take our requests to God while thanking Him for all that He has done for us, we will have His perfect peace. All the worry in the world will never change things for the better. Until we seek God's face in prayer, we will never know His genuine peace.

Do you want to know the reality of the angel's Christmas message? Do you long to experience peace on Earth? Take your needs to the Lord in prayer, and thank God for His never-ending faithfulness in your life.

Today's Rooted Principle: The key to great peace is not found in our resources or in our circumstances but on our knees.

The Presence of God

And it came to pass at that time, when Eli was laid down in his place, and his eyes began to wax dim, that he could not see; and ere the lamp of God went out in the temple of the LORD, where the ark of God was, and Samuel was laid down to sleep; That the LORD called Samuel: and he answered, Here am I.—**1 Samuel 3:2–4**

One of the simple pleasures I cherish during Christmas time is to sit in front of our wood burning stove. Something about the crackling of the wood, the rustic smell, the glowing light, and the enveloping warmth brings comfort after busy days of festive activities. The serenity these moments offer, however, significantly pales in comparison to the warmth of God's presence in my life—during the Christmas holiday and throughout the year.

In the life of Eli, we see how vital it is that we desire God's presence. Though Eli was the high priest over Israel, he was not the faithful servant of God he should have been. In the story of the boy Samuel being called by God, we see a significant indication of Eli's failure. The lamp of God in the tabernacle was supposed "to burn always" (Exodus 27:20). The fire represented God's presence among His people, yet Eli apparently allowed it to go out every night. We need a new sense and appreciation of God's presence in our day.

What a joyous and eventful time of year Christmas brings! If we are not careful, however, it is possible for us to replace the presence of God with busyness in the things of God and not recognize the loss. The things that we do in service to Him and in celebration of Him must not replace the time we spend with Him. Allow the light of His presence to warm your heart this season.

Today's Rooted Principle: Keep the fire of the presence of God burning brightly in your heart this Christmas.

The Prince of Peace

For unto us a child is born, unto us a son is given: and the government shall be upon his shoulder: and his name shall be called Wonderful, Counsellor, The mighty God, The everlasting Father, The Prince of Peace. Of the increase of his government and peace there shall be no end, upon the throne of David, and upon his kingdom, to order it, and to establish it with judgment and with justice from henceforth even for ever. The zeal of the LORD of hosts will perform this.—**Isaiah 9:6–7**

Our world is certainly in need of peace. There are wars and conflicts and battles constantly raging. One of the attributes of Christ and one of the promises He brings is peace. Because He is the Prince of Peace, He provides us with what we have no other means of obtaining.

Jesus offers us "peace from God" (Romans 1:7). This is a peace unlike anything known by the world. Such peace is a gift bestowed upon us through His grace. Jesus offers us "peace with God" (Romans 5:1). This is the peace that comes from having our sins covered in His blood and His wrath and condemnation turned away from our lives forever. Jesus offers us "the peace of God" (Philippians 4:7). This is the peace that calms our fears and allows us to trust and obey even during the storms of life.

Of course, the entire world will never know peace until Jesus returns. But we who are His children and are already part of His Kingdom can enjoy peace in our daily lives. Because of the coming of Jesus into the world, and His promises to us, we can have peace regardless of our circumstances. Is the peace of God ruling your heart today? If not, spend time with your Prince of Peace and allow Him to comfort your heart in a way only He can.

Today's Rooted Principle: Rejoice today in the wonderful peace that only comes when we know and walk with the Prince of Peace.

Don't Be Double Minded

Submit yourselves therefore to God. Resist the devil, and he will flee from you. Draw nigh to God, and he will draw nigh to you. Cleanse your hands, ye sinners; and purify your hearts, ye double minded. Be afflicted, and mourn, and weep: let your laughter be turned to mourning, and your joy to heaviness. Humble yourselves in the sight of the Lord, and he shall lift you up.—**James 4:7–10**

Christmas is a time of feasting! From family meals to church functions to cookie exchanges—the season offers many opportunities to eat! Commentator Andy Rooney once observed that the fastest moving items in bookstores were cookbooks and diet books. "The cookbooks tell you how to prepare the food, and the diet books tell you how not to eat any of it," he wryly remarked. Christmas is not usually a time for dieting because, when we are not fully committed to a course of action, it is highly unlikely that we will achieve success. This principle is just as true in the spiritual realm as it is in the physical.

There will always be things to distract us from the path God wants us to walk. We cannot allow anything—even good things—to draw our attention away from God.

Rather, we must walk with a firmness of purpose and a singleness of heart. One of Aesop's fables tells of a donkey that starved to death because he could never decide which of the two bales of hay that were set before him he should eat first. Once you have determined what God would have you do, fix your mind and focus your efforts toward that end. If you allow yourself to be double minded, your chance of success is small indeed. Instead, be like Jesus and walk with a firm and determined purpose in the path which God lays before you.

Today's Rooted Principle: Do not allow the busyness of the season to distract you from living out God's daily purposes for your life.

Unlikely People in Unlikely Places

Philip findeth Nathanael, and saith unto him, We have found him, of whom Moses in the law, and the prophets, did write, Jesus of Nazareth, the son of Joseph. And Nathanael said unto him, Can there any good thing come out of Nazareth? Philip saith unto him, Come and see.
—**John 1:45–46**

The city of Nazareth was not held in high regard by the Jewish people of Jesus' day. It was considered to be a small village not worthy of notice or attention. No one expected much of anything from that source, as evidenced by the question Nathanael asked Philip when he was told about Jesus.

What Nazareth did have was a young woman who was completely yielded to the will and purpose of God. When she was presented with a plan for her life that was impossible and would expose her to ridicule and possibly even death, she did not protest against it. Instead, she praised God for choosing her to be part of His plan. Mary did not have any financial or social advantages. She was not the person we would have immediately identified as the most likely candidate to be the mother of Jesus, but God saw what was in her heart.

In her song of praise to God, Mary said, "He hath put down the mighty from their seats, and exalted them of low degree" (Luke 1:52). Great works of God rarely start in big places or with big people. Instead, they usually start in small places with little people who have a big commitment and a big faith to be used of God. Good things can come from your Nazareth as you follow Mary's example of dedication and devotion. First Corinthians 1:27 says, "God hath chosen the weak things of the world to confound the things which are mighty." God has a plan for you—embrace your role.

Today's Rooted Principle: God can do great things with your life— beyond what anyone expects—when you are yielded to Him.

Christ Is All We Need

For ye know the grace of our Lord Jesus Christ, that, though he was rich, yet for your sakes he became poor, that ye through his poverty might be rich.—**2 Corinthians 8:9**

If you were to make a list of everything you want or hope to receive this Christmas, how many items on your list would be things you couldn't live without?

In truth, the only One that we cannot live without is the One whose coming we celebrate in this season of gifts. Without Jesus we have no Christmas. Without Jesus, we have no eternal life, no abundant life. In John 10:10, Jesus said, "I am come that they might have life, and that they might have it more abundantly."

Every need of the human heart can be met in Jesus. First Corinthians 1:30–31 tells us, "But of him are ye in Christ Jesus, who of God is made unto us wisdom, and righteousness, and sanctification, and redemption: That, according as it is written, He that glorieth, let him glory in the Lord."

What a miracle of God's power that He—the Creator of the universe—could clothe Himself in flesh and come to us as a tiny, helpless baby, and that in that coming, He could meet every need of our heart and soul. What love of God to desire to give us eternal life—at His expense. And what love of God to give us full, abundant life through *His* life!

As you approach Christmas this year, take a moment to reflect on the riches that we have through Jesus Christ. Christmas was God's most valuable gift delivered to Earth—to you. And in this precious Gift, you have all you need.

Today's Rooted Principle: Jesus humbled Himself to give us His great riches. Thank Him for His grace.

Serenity for the Soul

But Mary kept all these things, and pondered them in her heart.
—Luke 2:19

On Christmas Eve, a frazzled and stressed mother was running from store to store trying to get her last minute gifts. In the middle of her shopping, she realized she'd lost track of her three-year-old son. In a panic, she retraced her steps and found him standing with his little nose pressed flatly against a frosty window. He was gazing at a manger scene.

When he heard his mom call his name, the little boy turned and exclaimed, "Look Mommy! It's Jesus! It's baby Jesus in the hay!"

The frazzled mom took his arm and led him away saying, "We don't have time for all that right now! Can't you see that Mommy's trying to get ready for Christmas?"

How easy it can be to lose sight of the meaning, wonder, and true joy of Christmas! Obligations of the season combined with the normal pressures of life can produce stress, fatigue, and frustration—the opposite of serenity.

Mary could have easily succumbed to this same temptation. With the strain of travel and stress of finding a place to give birth, combined with the emotions of holding her Saviour in her arms and the excitement of the shepherds—she had a lot to take in that first Christmas season.

Yet the Bible says Mary took time to ponder all these things in her heart. In a moment of peaceful contemplation, she found serenity for her soul. She chose not to stress, analyze, fret, or worry.

Yes, there is much about which we can worry and fret—especially during the busy seasons of life. But there is also much for which we can praise and thank God. If your soul lacks that God-given peace, pause for a moment today and spend time with your Saviour. Ponder His goodness in your life and enjoy the serenity He can bring to a frazzled heart.

Today's Rooted Principle: Ponder the goodness and provision of God in your life, and rest in the peace He offers.

Amos 4–6 Revelation 7 389

Obedience to God

But while he thought on these things, behold, the angel of the Lord appeared unto him in a dream, saying, Joseph, thou son of David, fear not to take unto thee Mary thy wife: for that which is conceived in her is of the Holy Ghost. Then Joseph being raised from sleep did as the angel of the Lord had bidden him, and took unto him his wife: And knew her not till she had brought forth her firstborn son: and he called his name JESUS.—**Matthew 1:20, 24–25**

One Christmas when my children were teenagers, our family carpooled home from a Christmas gathering in Southern California. As we drove past Staples Center in Los Angeles, my wife and I made a last minute decision to create a special family memory by watching the Lakers play that night. Knowing how much joy this would bring to my sons who were following in the car behind me, I called and told them to follow me as I took a different route home, but I did not tell them why or where we were going. They obliged my request, and we were able to surprise them because of their quick obedience! As we later discussed what a great night we had together, my sons told me that after I called they almost took the normal route home so they could get to bed sooner. But they were glad they chose to follow dad's leadership!

When Joseph found out that Mary was going to have a baby, he did not know exactly what to do. He did not want to publicly humiliate her, but he was contemplating a private "putting away" because of what appeared to be her unfaithfulness to him. Yet when the angel came to him and explained that what was happening was part of God's plan, Joseph immediately submitted to God's role for him and did as God instructed.

Obedience is not based on understanding or rationalizing but on faith. We don't have to be able to figure out how things will work out. We simply have to choose to obey and follow His plan.

Today's Rooted Principle: As you celebrate the season, remember that you can trust and obey the God who planned Christmas.

Join the Shepherds

And it came to pass, as the angels were gone away from them into heaven, the shepherds said one to another, Let us now go even unto Bethlehem, and see this thing which is come to pass, which the Lord hath made known unto us. And they came with haste, and found Mary, and Joseph, and the babe lying in a manger. And when they had seen it, they made known abroad the saying which was told them concerning this child. And all they that heard it wondered at those things which were told them by the shepherds.—**Luke 2:15–18**

The angelic host returned to Heaven after announcing the birth of Christ to the shepherds. God could have sent these angels across Israel and even around the world to make the same announcement. Yet instead, the *shepherds* were the ones who spread the news that Jesus had come. God's plan for spreading the message of salvation is that those who have heard it will take it to others all around the world.

Writing to the church at Corinth, Paul said that God, "hath given to us the ministry of reconciliation" (2 Corinthians 5:18). We have a calling to proclaim the Gospel. This task falls not just on those in vocational ministry, but on every believer. The shepherds had no training, but they could tell what they had experienced.

Our focus on the shepherds in the Christmas story often begins with the appearance of the angels and ends with them at the manger, but there is more to it than that. They became messengers for God. This is a wonderful time of year to share the Gospel with others. Even people who are not normally interested in spiritual things may be more open because of the season. Be alert for opportunities to share the true meaning of Christmas and God's plan of salvation with everyone you can.

Today's Rooted Principle: One of the best ways to celebrate the meaning and spirit of Christmas is by sharing the Good News with others.

Emptied of All—but Love

And being found in fashion as a man, he humbled himself, and became obedient unto death, even the death of the cross. Wherefore God also hath highly exalted him, and given him a name which is above every name: That at the name of Jesus every knee should bow, of things in heaven, and things in earth, and things under the earth; And that every tongue should confess that Jesus Christ is Lord, to the glory of God the Father.—**Philippians 2:8–11**

O ne of the things that I love about Christmas is that, when we observe it as we should, Jesus is the center and focus of our attention. He deserves all of the praise and glory and worship that we can possibly give Him. Jesus is the Creator of all, yet He left behind the splendor of Heaven and, as Charles Wesley put it in the wonderful old hymn *And Can It Be*, "emptied Himself of all but love."

> He left His Father's throne above
> So free, so infinite His grace—
> Emptied Himself of all but love,
> And bled for Adam's helpless race.

We should worship and give thanks all year long, but at this time of year we focus our attention on the gift of His love in a special way. Salvation is a wonderful gift that we receive only through grace; the gift of Jesus Himself is beyond anything that we could ever imagine.

He had everything, yet He gave it up so that we "through his poverty might be rich" (2 Corinthians 8:9). As you celebrate Christmas this year, take time to praise our wonderful Lord and Saviour who is the gift of Christmas. His high and holy name is above all others, and it is through His grace and sacrifice that we become the children of God.

Today's Rooted Principle: Jesus emptied Himself that we might be made complete in Him and filled with all the fullness of God.

The World's Greatest Prayer

And the angel answered and said unto her, The Holy Ghost shall come upon thee, and the power of the Highest shall overshadow thee: therefore also that holy thing which shall be born of thee shall be called the Son of God. And, behold, thy cousin Elisabeth, she hath also conceived a son in her old age: and this is the sixth month with her, who was called barren. For with God nothing shall be impossible. And Mary said, Behold the handmaid of the Lord; be it unto me according to thy word. And the angel departed from her.—**Luke 1:35–38**

William Barclay once said that the world's most popular prayer is, "Thy will be changed." But the world's greatest prayer is, "Thy will be done." Mary displayed this attitude of submission to the will and plan of God when she received the news that she would be the mother of the Messiah. I'm sure she didn't fully understand everything that was going to happen. What she did understand was that she was willing to do whatever God wanted her to do.

The role that God had for Mary to play involved a great deal of difficulty and sacrifice. There is a popular but false teaching today that if we love God He will make sure only good things happen to us and that we will get everything we want. It's easy to see why people like that message, but it does not match the Word of God. God's plan for us frequently involves things that we would not choose for ourselves, but these are things that He knows are best for us.

Rather than fight against His purpose or have our faith be shaken when things don't go as we think they should, we should be yielded to His will. Let us say with Mary that we want our lives to go according to God's Word.

Today's Rooted Principle: As you yield your will to God's will, you are prepared for usefulness in service to Him.

Micah 1–3   Revelation 11   393

Holidays and Commandments

*As the Father hath loved me, so have I loved you: continue ye in my love.
If ye keep my commandments, ye shall abide in my love; even as I have
kept my Father's commandments, and abide in his love. These things
have I spoken unto you, that my joy might remain in you, and that your
joy might be full.*—**John 15:9–11**

Benjamin Franklin said, "How many observe Christ's birthday! How
few His precepts! O 'tis easier to keep holidays than commandments."
As we celebrate the love of God demonstrated to us at Christmas, we
should also be showing our love for Him through our obedience to His
commandments. God offers salvation freely through His grace, and we
do nothing to earn His favor. He has every right, however, to expect
our obedience.

The proper understanding of grace does not lead to us to live any
way we please. Instead, it leads us to live in a way that is pleasing to God.
Paul wrote to Titus about the role of grace: "Teaching us that, denying
ungodliness and worldly lusts, we should live soberly, righteously, and
godly, in this present world" (Titus 2:12). When people declare that they
can do something wrong because of grace, it is a sign that they really
don't understand what grace is.

The more we love God, the more we want to do what He says—not
out of a desire to earn our place or favor with Him, but from a desire
to please Him. This is the way Jesus lived His life on Earth. Speaking of
His Father in Heaven He said, "I do always those things that please him"
(John 8:29).

How would the next few days of this Christmas season be different
for you if you were as observant of Christ's commandments as you are of
commemorating His birthday?

Today's Rooted Principle: Honor God this Christmas and show your
love for Him by obeying His commandments.

Micah 4–5   Revelation 12

What People Don't Know about Christmas

He was in the world, and the world was made by him, and the world knew him not. He came unto his own, and his own received him not. But as many as received him, to them gave he power to become the sons of God, even to them that believe on his name: Which were born, not of blood, nor of the will of the flesh, nor of the will of man, but of God.
—John 1:10–13

There are points throughout the Christmas season when I don't know what to do—primarily when it comes to gift giving. I don't know what to purchase. I don't know how the gifts will be received. Maybe you can identify with this feeling. Perhaps you don't know which Christmas event to attend. Some people may not even know how much money they are spending! But there is one important truth—one important Person—that people often don't recognize during this season.

Christmas is a tangible expression of God's great love for us—a love so great that it led Him to send His Son to be our Saviour. Yet most of the world does not recognize the love of God or the meaning of Christmas. This is not true just for our day. It was true when Jesus was here as well. When the wise men came to Jerusalem looking for the place where Jesus had been born, the religious leaders knew exactly where to send them—to Bethlehem. Yet though they knew this, they showed no interest in going to see Jesus themselves.

The world did not and does not recognize the gift of God's love. Even worse, the very people to whom Christ came rejected Him. So many people today are repeating that tragic error. Though they may celebrate Christmas, they do not know the Christ of Christmas. Take time this Christmas to introduce someone to Jesus Christ.

Today's Rooted Principle: As you share the Gospel with others, you show them the meaning of Christmas they do not know.

Micah 6–7　　　　　Revelation 13　　　　395

The Ancient of Days

I beheld till the thrones were cast down, and the Ancient of days did sit, whose garment was white as snow, and the hair of his head like the pure wool: his throne was like the fiery flame, and his wheels as burning fire. A fiery stream issued and came forth from before him: thousand thousands ministered unto him, and ten thousand times ten thousand stood before him: the judgment was set, and the books were opened.—**Daniel 7:9–10**

We enjoy the novelty of gifts given at Christmas. Once the gifts are unwrapped, it is fun to learn and experience new gadgets or toys. But our greatest gift at Christmas is not the latest technological gadget. Our greatest Gift has always existed. And even though He is the Ancient of Days, the joy, renewal, and peace He gives far surpasses the happiness found in any temporal Christmas gift ever given.

Jesus did not become God, nor was He created. He always existed, and He always was God. The full divinity of Christ is shown by Daniel who used the term "Ancient of days" to refer to both God the Father and God the Son. The Christ that much of the world pictures when they think of Christmas, if they stop to think of Him at all, is much less than the Christ the Bible describes.

This was not just any baby who was lying in the manger at Bethlehem. This was God Himself, come to Earth to be the Saviour. It is impossible for us to fully comprehend how Jesus could be both completely God and completely human, yet we believe this vital truth because the Bible tells us that He was. Without being fully God, Jesus could not pay for the sins of the world. Without being fully man, Jesus could not die and become the sacrifice that was required. Christmas should be more than just a special time of year. It should be a time when we meditate on and rejoice in the truth of who Christ is and what He has done for us.

Today's Rooted Principle: As you celebrate the birth of Christ, remember that His coming is a powerful declaration of God's love for you.

Make Room

And Joseph also went up from Galilee, out of the city of Nazareth, into Judaea, unto the city of David, which is called Bethlehem; (because he was of the house and lineage of David:) To be taxed with Mary his espoused wife, being great with child. And so it was, that, while they were there, the days were accomplished that she should be delivered. And she brought forth her firstborn son, and wrapped him in swaddling clothes, and laid him in a manger; because there was no room for them in the inn.—**Luke 2:4–7**

Because of the census that had been decreed by Caesar Augustus, when Joseph and Mary reached Bethlehem, after a long and difficult journey of some eighty miles, they could not find anywhere to stay. Travel was quite demanding in Bible times, and there was nothing like the widespread system of accommodations for travelers that we take for granted today. There would have been only a few places for visitors to stay, and there was no room in the inn.

Of course, this initial rejection was symbolic of the reaction of the world to Jesus. They did not receive Him or His message. His brothers did not believe Him until after the resurrection. The people of His hometown tried to kill Him after His first sermon in Nazareth. The Jewish leaders rejected His message and conspired to put Him to death.

But the tragedy of the full inn can easily be repeated in our own lives as well. While we would never knowingly turn Jesus away from staying in our homes, we can allow ourselves to become so busy—often with things that are right and good—that we simply have no room in our thoughts or schedules for spending time with Him. Make time during this Christmas individually and with your family to focus on Jesus and thank Him for coming to save you.

Today's Rooted Principle: Make room in your heart and life for Jesus, not just at Christmas but throughout the year.

Right Here—Right Now

Behold, a virgin shall be with child, and shall bring forth a son, and they shall call his name Emmanuel, which being interpreted is, God with us.—**Matthew 1:23**

Christmas—the first Christmas—was a package of miracles. A virgin birth, God clothing Himself in human flesh, the Father giving His amazing love to an undeserving world, Christ making Himself poor that we might be made rich. It's an unspeakable gift that we can't begin to wrap our minds around.

But we can open the gift. We can receive the truth that it brings to us. Emmanuel—God with us.

Take any word of that phrase, and it is astounding.

God *with us.* The very God of the universe humbled Himself to take on human flesh and enter our world through a manger. Lying there in the straw was God Himself. And He chose to come to our world.

God **with** *us.* Not only has God come to our world, but He is near. His very coming proved that He wants us to know Him, to be reconciled to Him. He is not a distant God, but a God who loves us and has chosen to show His love for us in a phenomenally unthinkable way—by giving Himself for us.

God with **us.** We don't deserve God's love. Yet He came. He chose to be born into a common family and grow up in a common home and learn a common profession. He proved that He can identify with us—with you, with me.

Who would have expected that God would even *want* to come to us? Who would have thought that God *could* come to us? But God did the miraculous. He came.

And because of Christmas, every child of God can know with certainty, God is with me—right here, right now.

Today's Rooted Principle: As you rejoice in the miracle of Christmas, thank the Lord for His immediate and continual presence in your life.

The Precious Word of God

And it shall be, when he sitteth upon the throne of his kingdom, that he shall write him a copy of this law in a book out of that which is before the priests the Levites: And it shall be with him, and he shall read therein all the days of his life: that he may learn to fear the LORD his God, to keep all the words of this law and these statutes, to do them: That his heart be not lifted up above his brethren, and that he turn not aside from the commandment, to the right hand, or to the left: to the end that he may prolong his days in his kingdom, he, and his children, in the midst of Israel.—**Deuteronomy 17:18–20**

Long before Israel foolishly rejected God in search of a king to rule over them, God gave instruction to Moses for what the king should do when he assumed office. One of the critical assignments each king was supposed to follow was to make for himself a handwritten copy of the law of God from the scrolls carefully kept and preserved by the priests. This would be a labor-intense task that would consume a great amount of time in the life of a busy man with many responsibilities. Yet God commanded that the investment of time and effort be made.

This command illustrates the vital priority that the Word of God should have in our lives. It is from the Scriptures that we learn to fear and obey God and keep His commandments. It is from the Scriptures that we learn to be humble and to instruct others to follow God. In our day when copies of the Bible are readily available, it is easy for us to take the Word for granted. Instead, we should treasure and cherish it, and make it part of our daily lives.

Today's Rooted Principle: Treasure the amazing gift you have in the Word of God. Read it and heed it, and you will do well.

Prone to Wander

But he was wounded for our transgressions, he was bruised for our iniquities: the chastisement of our peace was upon him; and with his stripes we are healed. All we like sheep have gone astray; we have turned every one to his own way; and the LORD hath laid on him the iniquity of us all.—**Isaiah 53:5–6**

The well-loved hymn "Come Thou Fount of Every Blessing" is more than 250 years old. It was written by Robert Robinson when he was just twenty-two years of age. Robinson left the Church of England when his study of the Word of God convinced him that infant baptism was not scriptural, and he faithfully served for many years as a Baptist pastor. Even at a young age he was aware of the tendency of our hearts to be drawn away from God.

Solomon warns us of the importance of guarding our hearts. By divine inspiration the wise king wrote, "Keep thy heart with all diligence; for out of it are the issues of life" (Proverbs 4:23). This natural tendency of our hearts to stray from God is not limited to the days when we are young. The Bible contains many examples of those who followed God for years but then later turned away from Him. Tragically, one of those was Solomon himself. Despite his warnings to others, he turned from following God, and the nation of Israel was divided as a result. This set off a civil war that raged for years.

Solomon's testimony highlights the importance of the example we set for others. When we turn from following God to go our own way, it can have a devastating impact on those who are watching. Whether we realize it or not, each of us serves as an example to others. As we guard our hearts and continue to follow God closely, we not only protect ourselves but others also.

Today's Rooted Principle: Because your heart is prone to wander from God, you must guard it with all diligence.

Fiery Trials

Beloved, think it not strange concerning the fiery trial which is to try you, as though some strange thing happened unto you: But rejoice, inasmuch as ye are partakers of Christ's sufferings; that, when his glory shall be revealed, ye may be glad also with exceeding joy.—**1 Peter 4:12–13**

In 1555, as part of her campaign to re-establish the Catholic Church in England, Queen Mary, also known as Bloody Mary, arranged for John Philpot, one of the leading Protestant ministers of the day, to be burned at the stake. When his death sentence was pronounced, Philpot said, "I am ready; God grant me strength and a joyful resurrection." Philpot walked to the place of execution on his own, rather than having to be dragged to it, and when he reached it, he knelt and kissed the stake at which he would be burned.

It is easy for us to focus on our problems and think that they are larger than they really are. Most of us have never endured genuine persecution for our faith. A few times people have gotten upset with me for sharing the Gospel with them, but none of them have tried to kill me. There may come a day when we must make the same life-or-death decision to be loyal to Christ regardless of the consequences. However, even in lesser trials we have a definite choice to make. Will we stand firm for what is right, or will we lower the standard to avoid trouble?

Christ could easily have avoided the cross, yet He chose instead to suffer for our salvation. When we suffer for doing right, we should rejoice because we have the opportunity to follow His example. The joy that is coming when we reach Heaven is so great that we should willingly endure whatever trials come to us in this life. May God give us grace to be faithful to Him.

Today's Rooted Principle: As you prepare for a new year, ask God for the strength and grace to remain faithful no matter what the future holds.

Wasted Years

Wherefore he saith, Awake thou that sleepest, and arise from the dead, and Christ shall give thee light. See then that ye walk circumspectly, not as fools, but as wise, Redeeming the time, because the days are evil. Wherefore be ye not unwise, but understanding what the will of the Lord is. And be not drunk with wine, wherein is excess; but be filled with the Spirit.—**Ephesians 5:14–18**

Someone once observed that a wasted life is really nothing more than a collection of wasted days. As God gives us life, each one of us starts the new year with the same number of opportunities—365—that we can choose to either use and invest in eternal things or allow to drift by without taking advantage of the gift we have been given. The difference between those who succeed and those who fail is not found primarily in talent but in diligence and effort.

Each day is precious, and it represents an opportunity that will never come again. Instead of allowing time to pass without effort and productivity, we are to redeem it—to make the most of it. Benjamin Franklin said, "Dost thou love life? Then do not squander time, for time is the stuff life is made of." The time of the past year cannot be recaptured, but the pages of the coming year are still blank and waiting for us to write on them.

Because we are living in days when evil is growing, it is more important than ever that we be aware and attentive to what is happening around us. The will of God for each of us in this new year is that we be filled with and controlled by His Spirit so that we can accomplish the work which He has prepared for us to do. Commit yourself to using your time wisely, and you will have a productive year.

Today's Rooted Principle: Be alert to the opportunities for service and ministry and growth that cross your path—they may not come again.

Building Project

Therefore watch, and remember, that by the space of three years I ceased not to warn every one night and day with tears. And now, brethren, I commend you to God, and to the word of his grace, which is able to build you up, and to give you an inheritance among all them which are sanctified.—**Acts 20:31–32**

As our church has grown over the years, we have built a number of buildings so we can worship and study the Word together. I have noticed as we have gone through the building process again and again, that while the structures may have different designs and different purposes, every building project has one feature in common. For instance, no building project that I have ever seen or heard of has been quick! They all take time.

It is the same way in the Christian life. We want to see immediate results, but the work that God is doing in our hearts through His Word and His grace takes time. Before any building is constructed, a foundation must be laid that will provide structure and stability so the building will last. As you look toward the new year, remember that the foundation for God's work in your life must be solid before anything great can be done for Him. Don't be discouraged in the preparation process.

It's also important during any building project not to let delays and problems deter you from your purpose. Things aren't always going to go according to plan. There will be days when it seems like nothing is happening. Yet we must not be discouraged "for in due season we shall reap, if we faint not" (Galatians 6:9). Keep on moving forward through the new year. The blueprint God has given us in His Word is tested and proven. Live each day in such a way that at the end of the year you will be closer to God than you were at the beginning. Simply trust Him to build your life!

Today's Rooted Principle: Allow God to do His work in your life on His timetable, and you will be amazed at the results.

Zechariah 13–14   Revelation 21   403

Numbering Our Days

For all our days are passed away in thy wrath: we spend our years as a tale that is told. The days of our years are threescore years and ten; and if by reason of strength they be fourscore years, yet is their strength labour and sorrow; for it is soon cut off, and we fly away. Who knoweth the power of thine anger? even according to thy fear, so is thy wrath. So teach us to number our days, that we may apply our hearts unto wisdom.—**Psalm 90:9–12**

As we prepare to start a new year it is important for us to stop and take into account the brevity of life. When we think about how long we might live, we may take into consideration the lifespan of our parents and grandparents, our health, and where we live. Insurance companies invest heavily in actuarial tables giving statistical information on life expectancy, and they use these tables to establish insurance rates and premiums.

When we consider our lives from God's viewpoint, two things become immediately clear. First, no matter how long we live there will come a day when our lives will end. It may be death or it may be the Rapture, but in either case our lives on this Earth are not going to continue forever. That places a premium on making wise use of the days we do have. The psalmist tells us that carefully numbering our days will lead us toward wisdom.

The second certainty is that we are not in control of the length of our lives—God is. The only day that we know for certain we have is today. James warns those who make their plans for the future without considering God. "Ye know not what shall be on the morrow" (James 4:14). Realizing that you may only have this one day, use it wisely for God.

Today's Rooted Principle: Because the future is unknown, it is important that we make the very most of each day as it comes.

INDEXES

Title Index

May

1 Grace Abounded More
2 Who Can You Trust?
3 The End Result Is Settled
4 The Sign Doesn't Change
5 God's Face Is Toward You
6 God Always Does Right
7 More Than a Promise
8 Make Your Choice
9 Truth in Advertising
10 Love and Sacrifice
11 God Is in Charge
12 It All Belongs to God
13 The Only Way
14 The World Hates the Word
15 Be Real
16 A Generous Heart
17 No Condemnation
18 God Has Plans for Your Life
19 Understanding Who God Is
20 Character Counts
21 Swim Upstream
22 The Purpose of Trouble
23 A God Who Is Faithful
24 Every Promise Stands
25 You Are Being Followed
26 A Testimony of Fruitfulness
27 Keep Looking Up
28 God's Transforming Power
29 Understanding Grace
30 One Way
31 God's Grace Is Enough

June

1 If We Faint Not
2 Faithful Promises
3 Sacrifice
4 The Crowns Are Yet to Come
5 Through the Fire
6 The Process of Bearing Fruit
7 God Wants People to Be Saved
8 How God Treats Those Who Repent
9 The Precious Name of Jesus
10 Citizenship in Heaven
11 Pray, Then Pray Again
12 The Hinges of Opposition
13 You Don't Have to Stand Alone
14 Saved for a Purpose
15 Follow
16 Wasted Correction
17 Invest in Your Children
18 Courage
19 Waiting on God
20 Grow Up
21 Don't Lose Your Freedom
22 When We Sin
23 Good Forgetters
24 Open Your Mail
25 Under Pressure
26 Someone Cares
27 The God Who Does the Impossible
28 Standing in the Face of Hardship
29 Spend Time on What Matters
30 What You Can Count On

November

December

Scripture Index

Proverbs

Ecclesiastes

Isaiah

Jeremiah

Lamentations

Ezekiel

Daniel

About the Author

Dr. Paul Chappell is the senior pastor of Lancaster Baptist Church and the president of West Coast Baptist College in Lancaster, California. He is a powerful communicator of God's Word and a passionate servant to God's people. He has been married to his wife, Terrie, for thirty-two years, and he has four married children who are all serving in Christian ministry. He enjoys spending time with his family, and he loves serving the Lord shoulder to shoulder with a wonderful church family.

Dr. Chappell's preaching is heard on *Daily in the Word*, a radio program that is broadcast across America. You can find a station listing at: dailyintheword.org.

You can also connect with Dr. Chappell here:

Blog: paulchappell.com
Twitter: twitter.com/paulchappell
Facebook: facebook.com/pastor.paul.chappell

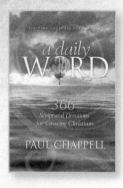

A Daily Word

Designed to compliment your daily walk with the Lord, this book from Dr. Paul Chappell features 366 daily devotional thoughts to strengthen and encourage your spiritual life. Each devotion features a one-year Bible reading selection. Also included are helpful reference resources as well as Scripture and title indexes. (424 pages, hardback)

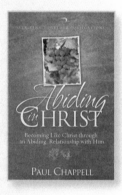

Abiding in Christ

In these pages, Dr. Paul Chappell will lead you on an exciting and encouraging journey to discover the authentic Christian life. You will learn how an intimate relationship with Christ produces a genuine heart and life change. You will find the source of true love, abundant joy, lasting fruit, spiritual maturity, emotional stability, and purpose in life. (168 pages, paperback)

Stewarding Life

God has given you one life and filled it with resources—time, health, finances, relationships, influence, and more. How you steward these resources will determine whether you successfully fulfill God's eternal purpose for your life. This book will challenge and equip you to strategically invest your most valuable resources for God's eternal purposes. (280 pages, hardcover)